The AMERICAN JEW

Voices from an American Jewish Community

Dan Cohn-Sherbok
and
Lavinia Cohn-Sherbok

WILLIAM B. EERDMANS PUBLISHING COMPANY
GRAND RAPIDS, MICHIGAN

For the Jewish Community of Metropolis
in gratitude and admiration

First published 1994 in Great Britain by
Fount Paperbacks, an imprint of HarperCollinsReligious
Part of HarperCollins*Publishers*
77-85 Fulham Palace Road, London W6 8JB

This edition published 1995
through special arrangement with HarperCollins by
Wm. B. Eerdmans Publishing Co.
255 Jefferson Ave. S.E., Grand Rapids, Michigan 49503

Printed in the United States of America

00 99 98 97 96 95 7 6 5 4 3 2 1

ISBN 0-8028-4138-4

CONTENTS

PREFACE

Who are the Jews of America? What are the values, beliefs and hopes of the Jewish community in the late twentieth century? This volume attempts to answer these questions by focusing on a single community. It is composed of a series of interviews with religious and community leaders; the young, the middle-aged and the old; business people and professionals; those who serve the community, those who have chosen to join it, and those who have left.

The Jewish community which serves as the basis for this book is composed of approximately 40,000 individuals and is located in a large metropolitan conurbation of about two million people. We have deliberately chosen not to identify this American city; instead it is simply called 'Metropolis'. Further, we have changed the names of all those we interviewed as well as those of the institutions mentioned so as to provide a degree of anonymity. As will be seen, the Jewish population of Metropolis is made up of a wide variety of sub-groups representing the major divisions of contemporary American Jewry: the Jewish institutions of Metropolis are typical of those in other cities, and the voices of the Metropolitan Jewish community could be heard throughout the United States.

The aim of this study is to provide a snapshot of American Jewry in the 1990s. The book begins with a tour of Jewish Metropolis supplemented by a map of the Jewish community. This is followed by the interviews. Over a hundred voices are recorded to give a multi-dimensional view of American Jewish life on the threshold of the twenty-first century.

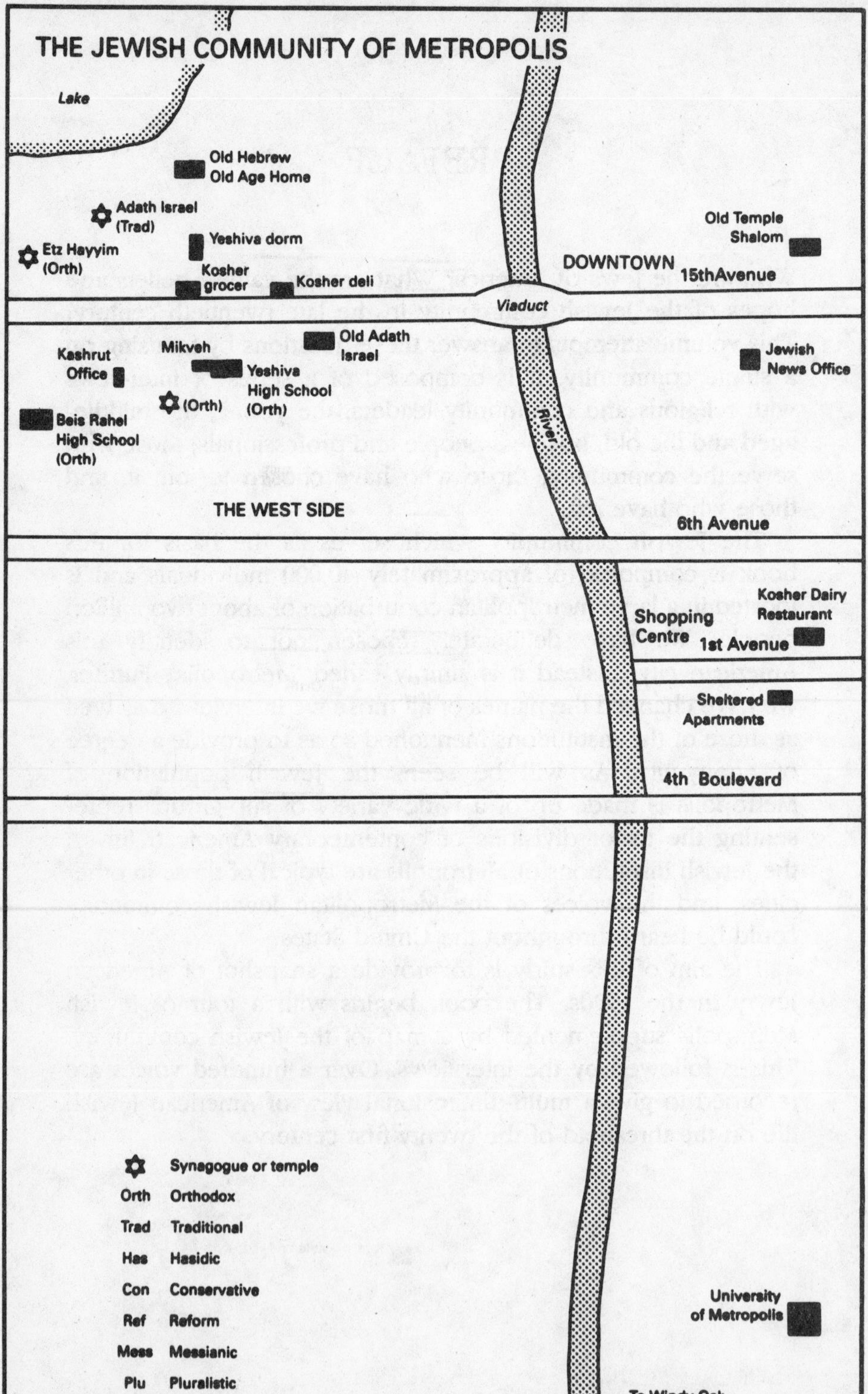
THE JEWISH COMMUNITY OF METROPOLIS
Lake
Old Hebrew
Old Age Home
Adath Israel
(Trad)
Yeshiva dorm
Etz Hayyim
(Orth)
Kosher
grocer
Kosher deli
Old Temple
Shalom
DOWNTOWN
15thAvenue
Viaduct
Old Adath
Israel
Kashrut
Office
Mikveh
Yeshiva
High School
(Orth)
(Orth)
Jewish
News Office
Beis Rahel
High School
(Orth)
River
THE WEST SIDE
6th Avenue
Kosher Dairy
Restaurant
Shopping
Centre
1st Avenue
Sheltered
Apartments
4th Boulevard
Synagogue or temple
Orth Orthodox
Trad Traditional
Has Hasidic
Con Conservative
Ref Reform
Mess Messianic
Plu Pluralistic
University
of Metropolis
Map not to scale
To Windy Oak
Country Club

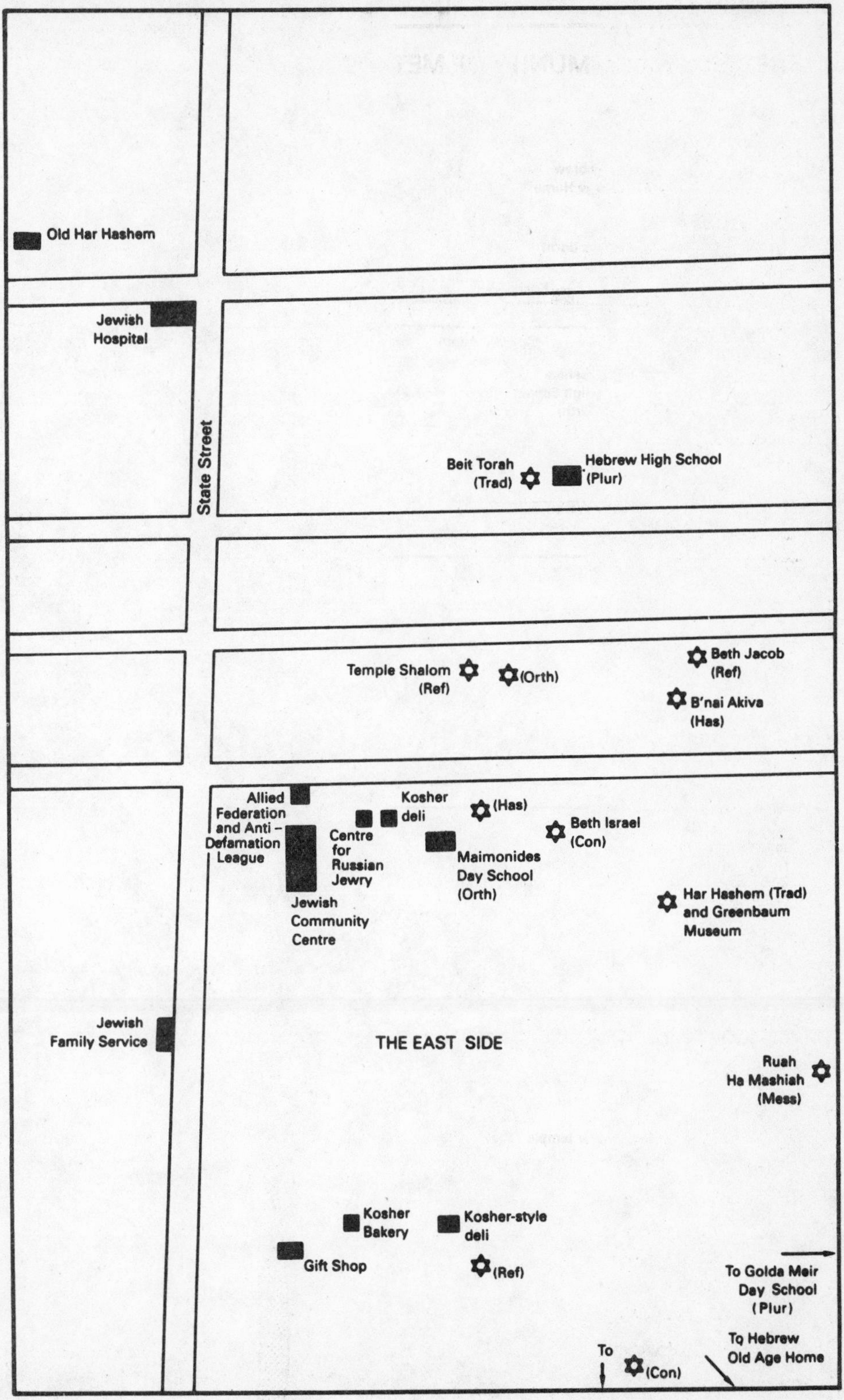

Old Har Hashem
Jewish Hospital
State Street
Beit Torah (Trad)
Hebrew High School (Plur)
Temple Shalom (Ref)
(Orth)
Beth Jacob (Ref)
B'nai Akiva (Has)
Allied Federation and Anti-Defamation League
Kosher deli
Centre for Russian Jewry
(Has)
Beth Israel (Con)
Maimonides Day School (Orth)
Jewish Community Centre
Har Hashem (Trad) and Greenbaum Museum
Jewish Family Service
THE EAST SIDE
Ruah Ha Mashiah (Mess)
Kosher Bakery
Kosher-style deli
Gift Shop
(Ref)
To Golda Meir Day School (Plur)
To Hebrew Old Age Home
To
(Con)

One

A TOUR OF JEWISH METROPOLIS

On our second day in Metropolis we were given a tour of the Jewish community. We had been introduced to Leah Silver on an earlier visit. She was the Editor of the city's Jewish newspaper; she had lived in Metropolis all her life and was a real power in the community. We agreed to meet her at 11 o'clock on a Sunday morning in the newspaper offices downtown in the city. Leah came out to meet us. She was a small, dynamic grey-haired woman dressed in a blue and white trouser suit. She sat in the back of the car and directed us west down 15th Avenue. We drove through the deserted downtown until we reached a viaduct which divided the West Side from the rest of the city. Here Leah officially began our tour.

Under the viaduct were two coal-yards run by two very dedicated Jewish citizens. One was my father. They used to give tons of coal away as needed. My father was president of Central Jewish Aid which has become the Allied Federation, and he was very involved in the community.

We reached the other side and found ourselves in a largely Spanish-American neighbourhood. Off 15th Avenue on both sides was a series of little streets. This had been the Jewish area before the First World War.

My husband was born in this neighbourhood . . . we just passed his street. Near it there used to be a Yiddish theatre many years ago. On our left is the former old *Adath Israel* synagogue building. It looks very much the same. The congregation moved out about thirty years ago and built a new building because this one is too small. Turn right here just before the *kosher* deli. That deli has always been very famous for its pickles. Now these streets north of 15th facing the lake were where the richer citizens lived. Some very prominent Jews still live here.

This is the former building of the Hebrew Old Age Home. It's now been moved to South-East Metropolis. My mother lived here for the last few years of her life. It was very well run. The manager spoke to everyone every day, moving from table to table. They had a synagogue here and a beauty shop, where they could get their hair done and manicures. It had a *kosher* kitchen. Every evening they had clean white table-cloths. It was very good. My mother liked it, and she had high standards. Now you should turn back and go towards 15th Avenue. In the old days all these houses were occupied by Jewish families.

We're passing an apartment block which is now used by the boys of the *Yeshiva* High School. Long ago it was considered a classy place to live. Then just next door is the *kosher* grocer. We don't have a *kosher* butcher in Metropolis any more. The last one closed down a few years back, and meat is now flown in from elsewhere. Go back on 15th and then right again and towards the lake.

We reached the lake and drove west along it. Overlooking the water were some beautiful modern houses.

Adath Israel, the synagogue, thought so much of their last rabbi – he was so well-beloved that the congregation purchased one of these homes for him and his widow. She still lives there – I think this one belongs to her. In fact I believe this road is still almost entirely populated by Jewish families. Now if you turn left here . . . This is *Adath Israel*. Yes, Rabbi Oppenheim's (*The Traditional Rabbi*) synagogue. They have magnificent *Torah* scrolls here, and the Ark is really beautiful. It's a Traditional synagogue – in other words it's basically Orthodox, but the men and women are no longer separated in the congregation. Families sit together. There's still a section in the front which is separate seating. They are thinking of leaving this area altogether and moving to the East Side. Only a very small proportion of their members live in this part of town now, so they have to travel quite a long distance to services and, as you know, you're not meant to drive on the Sabbath . . . yes, of course, many of them do!

Go straight across over 15th Avenue a couple of blocks and turn right . . . Here we are. This is *Beis Rahel* Girls' High School. It's strictly Orthodox. My granddaughters went there, and I was very impressed by the education they received. I thought at first they would be so laden with Jewish education they couldn't do anything else, but they're well versed in the American political scene as well. The boys of the same age go to the *Yeshiva* High School down the road. The girls from Metropolis live at home, but there's a dormitory for the girls who come from out of town. One of the advantages of being in an Orthodox neighbourhood is that these girls are all invited to Sabbath dinner at various homes. It's a very close community. If a woman has a baby, immediately the neighbours bring in food and look after the other kids. Everyone helps each other.

If you turn the car round, we're just passing Rabbi Berkovski's (*The Hasidic Rabbi*) old house. He's from an old *Hasidic* family from Europe. His father was the rabbi of *Etz Hayyim*, the strictly Orthodox synagogue, and when he died, the son, our present Rabbi Berkovski, returned to Metropolis. He stayed in his father's house a little while, but now he's moved and has a congregation over on the East Side. Why did he move? I think it was complicated . . . You must ask him.

On the street we're just passing is the *Kashrut* office. That's where Rabbi Vardin (*The Kashrut Supervisor*) looks after the food supervision for the community. There is a problem with *kashrut* in this town. Rabbi Berkovski is an alternative authority. I'm not sure how far they tread on each other's toes; you know how it is. On your right is a small Orthodox synagogue and on your left – that big square building across the street – is the *Yeshiva* High School. That's where boys of high school age and older receive their education. And that little building next door is the ritual bath, the *mikveh*; it's the only one in the city at present . . . Oh we've forgotten *Etz Hayyim*! That's the largest strictly Orthodox synagogue. We'll have to cross 15th Avenue again . . .

I like this part of town. There's no show and blow round here! They're really down to earth. People manage. They're not big houses for the number of children some of them have. This is *Etz Hayyim*. They have services every day. Why is it so successful? Well definitely Rabbi Marmorstein (*The Orthodox Rabbi*) is a factor. The synagogue is built round the centre so they can have weddings as if it were outdoors. There's certainly no mixed seating here!

We drove back across the viaduct and turned south to an upmarket shopping area. We stopped at a tiny basement café. It was a kosher dairy restaurant. There was a certificate of kashrut issued by Rabbi Vardin and signed by Rabbi Marmorstein. The food was delicious – Middle Eastern, vegetarian and freshly cooked. Leah was well-known to the proprietor, who was also the chef. It was made clear to us that eating the newly-cooked cinnamon buns was not merely a pleasure – it was a duty. All through lunch we were interrupted by people coming to greet Leah. She was recognized by everyone. At the end of the meal, she flatly refused to let us pay the bill.

We returned to the car and headed to the prosperous East Side of the town. After about fifteen minutes we drew up at an enormous modern edifice.

This is Temple *Shalom*. It's the largest Reform Temple and the oldest congregation in the city. Robert Reinhardt (*The Reform Rabbi*) is the rabbi. The old building which is now a designated historic landmark was near downtown. Don Samuelson's (*Havurah Leader*) daddy was one of the early men to find this site and refound the Temple. There are classrooms here, and a library. This is the sanctuary of course. Right here on the left is Danny Mizel's (*The Bar Mitzvah Teacher*) house; he's the best-known *Bar Mitzvah* teacher in town. It's so nice and handy for Temple. The Temple was a very expensive building; the glass was Italian and was shipped in – it's very impressive from the inside. Yes, I think it's still the largest congregation . . .

There are many, many Jewish families living in this area, but increasingly Jews are living all over the city. They're particularly moving to the South-East suburbs. On your right is a small Orthodox synagogue. People can comfortably walk over here on the Sabbath from all over the East Side. If you turn left here we'll go to see the Metropolis Hebrew High School. It's just a couple of blocks north of 6th Avenue. As you see this is also a very nice residential area. It's still got a sizeable number of Jewish families – maybe not door-to-door any more. I know which are the heavy Jewish neighbourhoods because of the newspaper. We consistently have more subscriptions from around here than from anywhere else in the city.

Ah, here's the Hebrew High School. It's for twelve to eighteen-year-olds and it's what is called Pluralist. It's not just for Orthodox kids; it's also for Traditional, Conservative and Reform. And it's boys and girls together which you'd never get in an Orthodox high school. Actually the Principal's a gentile (*The Principal of the Pluralist High School*). It's just next door to one of the Traditional synagogues, *Beit Torah*. Rabbi Oppenheim (*The Traditional Rabbi*) used to be here before he went to *Adath Israel*. It's like *Adath Israel* – they don't have separate seating, but they do have a *kosher* kitchen. It has a magnificent sanctuary. The interior is very, very nice. The old cantor (*The Traditional Cantor*) was Orthodox by persuasion and practice and had a wonderful voice. He lived quite far away, but he walked to services.

If you go back south again we'll take a look at *B'nai Akiva*, Rabbi Berkovski's (*The Hasidic Rabbi*) new synagogue. As I told you, he moved from the West Side. There – we're passing on our left *Beth Jacob*. That's another Reform Temple. It broke away from Temple *Shalom* in the 1950s. Something to do with Zionism, I think. Yes – it's an interesting looking building. The congregation's not large – they only have a part-time rabbi nowadays (*The Woman Rabbi*). Rabbi Berkovski's synagogue is just a couple of blocks away. Here we are, *B'nai Akiva* was orginally built as a church. They did some alterations and they now have separate seating and a balcony on the first floor. Round the other side are the state offices for Concern for Soviet Jewry. There's talk of building a *mikveh* (ritual bath) on the property here. It was going to be attached to the Jewish Community Centre, but that was rejected. The synagogue has many members who are devoted. They're here day in and day out.

You want to see *Beth Israel*? It's Conservative, and there's another Conservative synagogue down in the South-East. Max Goldstein (*The Conservative Rabbi*) is the only Conservative rabbi in town at the moment. Just go straight across 4th Boulevard and turn right. Here we are. Do look at those beautiful windows; they were done by a local artist. She did the cutting of the lead glass, and she physically put them together. Each one represents Sabbath or a holiday. Now turn left and let's go and see *Har HaShem*. That's the big Traditional synagogue. You'll meet Rabbi Kornfeld (*The University Professor of Judaica*). It's two long blocks over, and down and turn right.

There . . . it's right there across the street. This is the social hall. This is the entrance for the synagogue and the Greenbaum Museum. Yes – it's a Jewish museum; they have changing exhibits. Inside the courtyard is the *sukkah* (ritual tabernacle) – it's quite a large one – and here are the administrative offices. It's truly a big operation. You can see Rabbi Kornfeld's name by the entrance. Big letters. He's also head of the Department of Judaic Studies at the University of Metropolis in the south of the city. His Chair was financed by one of the big benefactors of the community (*The Holocaust Survivor*).

Right, we'll go on to the Maimonides Academy Day School. After this block, turn right here please, and turn left at the top of the hill. This is the building and the playground is on the left. It's Orthodox – there are kids from both the West and East but they bus the kids in from the West Side. This was the city's first elementary Jewish day school. They take boys and girls, but even little kids can't be in the same class. There's a Holocaust memorial in the front, and they have Holocaust memorial services here every April. The survivors gather here. When they first came to Metropolis, this was the place of education for their children. The school has athletic programmes, and it has a good reputation. They have kids here from kindergarten until fourteen. They then either go to the Pluralist Hebrew High School, or the *Yeshiva* or *Beis Rahel* on the West Side. A few go to public high schools. Many go away from Metropolis – parents feel they'll have a better education in the East. There's also a Pluralistic elementary school in the South-East. It's called the Golda Meir Jewish Day School. It's been very successful. You should talk to some people from there.

Just nearby is the *Lubavicher Habad Hasidic* synagogue. And just round the corner is the East Side *Kosher* Deli with the Centre for Russian Jewry next door. That's an agency that looks after the Russian refugees who have recently arrived in Metropolis. Tony Fishman (*The President of the Centre for Russian Jewry*) is president of the organization. I think there are about 3,000 Russians. Most of them live fairly near here. Of course the Jewish Family Service also does a lot . . .

Now go straight. This big complex is the Jewish Community Centre. Turn right. This building facing us is the tennis facility which is a large part of the Centre. This is the theatre, given by one of the big philanthropic families of the community. They do a good job culturally. They have a very high-level pre-school here, with a very nice reputation. The whole Centre is going to be enlarged and rebuilt. They have a new Director and I sure hope she's going to be able to turn it around. They would have encompassed more of the community if they had gone through with building the *mikveh* here. I don't know why they didn't. I wasn't on the committee. Haven't you ever heard of Jewish anti-Semitism? It would have made a whole additional group welcome. I mean, you don't have to participate. Those who want *mikveh* – fine! And those who want tennis – also fine! After all, not everyone plays tennis or goes to the theatre . . .

Just next door are the offices of the Allied Jewish Federation. They administer all the community funds. The offices of the Anti-Defamation League are also in that building as well as several other agencies. The Jewish Family Service has moved and is now further south on State Street.

And really that's about it. The cemeteries are further to the east, the new Hebrew Old Age Home and the Golda Meir Day School – that's the Pluralistic one – are sort of south-east. That's the direction in which the community is expanding . . .

We delivered Leah back to the offices of the Metropolis Jewish News. *We made her promise to be interviewed later during our stay and we thanked her for a marvellous tour.*

Oh I loved being with you . . . I think I did all the talking!

Two

CONGREGATIONAL RABBIS

The Orthodox Rabbi

RABBI AVRAHAM MARMORSTEIN

Orthodox Jews believe they should keep every detail of the Jewish Law. We interviewed Rabbi Marmorstein in his synagogue Congregation Etz Hayyim on the West Side of Metropolis. He was an energetic, bearded man in his forties.

I was brought up in Cleveland, Ohio, and I went to the Jewish day school there. Then, at the age of thirteen, my parents sent me to a *yeshiva* (talmudic academy) in Brooklyn, New York. I went with two other friends from Cleveland. My parents chose that particular *yeshiva* because many of the teachers were *Hasidim.* My father came from a *Hasidic* family in Poland; he was a survivor of the war, and he himself had been to a very famous *yeshiva* in Poland. He wanted me to go to a *yeshiva* with a real sympathy for *Hasidism.*

I had my high school education in Brooklyn and spent three further years there just learning *Torah* (Jewish Law). In order to get *semihah* (rabbinic ordination), they will either test you on a little bit every month, or test you three times on everything. The comprehensive testing was considered to be the better standard of *semihah*, and that is what I did. It's actually put on the document how you got the *semihah* and smart people do ask to see the document. I never planned on becoming a congregational rabbi. At that point in my life I wanted to be a teacher at high school or even elementary level. I wanted to teach Jewish Law to the next generation. Of course it's more than just teaching. A teacher must set an example. Theory and practice go hand in hand.

Then I went to *yeshiva* in Israel. In America, *semihah* is bestowed by an institution but in Israel it's given by individual rabbis. I wanted to get *semihah* from a number of rabbis. I went to them and said there was a possibility that I might want to become an authority to answer questions. I went to a lot of people and in every case there was an oral examination. Did I prepare? Oh boy did I prepare! I must have gone over the text a hundred times! They can ask you anything. Where do you look in the text for the problem of a chicken with a broken neck? Anywhere! I was in Israel for a year. It was a real challenge. I remember waiting with another fellow to get *semihah* – and did he know it! He could speak the language! He could quote it verbatim! It was a big *yeshiva* in Israel. There were 500 or 600 students; the competition was huge, and some of those people were brilliant.

I suppose I could have settled in Israel. In fact, I'm thinking right now of eventually settling in Israel. The question is – where can I accomplish most for G–d? What does G–d want me to do? If I were just for myself, I could go into business and make a lot of money, but that's not the point. I was created for a purpose. So I asked myself, 'Would I be doing G–d's work in Israel? Maybe there are plenty of other people there who could do it better? Maybe I could be of more use in America?' One of the responsibilities of rabbis is to extend the knowledge of Jewish Law to the next generation. When the Messiah comes, there must be a future generation. Between 1900 and 1950 so many people were lost through Reform, assimilation, intermarriage . . . I stand for Orthodox Judaism. We are dedicated to the transfer of the tradition from generation to generation. And thank G–d, this has been happening for the last thirty-five years through the day schools, the *yeshivot* and the higher education movement. Children are the future. I wanted to be a teacher, and I am still tremendously involved with the children of my congregation.

After Israel, I went back to my old Alma Mater in Brooklyn for a further two years. I went to the *kollel* (talmudic college), and we studied in small groups. Everyone had to give lectures every week or every two weeks, and we had to publish original work. That was how the testing was done. You are tested by your peers.

I met my wife in New York. She's from Metropolis. She went

to *Beis Rahel* High School, and then to seminary in New York. *Beis Rahel* was created because of my wife. She was in the first graduating class. My mother-in-law refused to move to Metropolis unless there was a Jewish school for her daughters so my father-in-law (*The Community Patriarch*) founded *Beis Rahel*. I didn't move to Metropolis straight away; I was busy in New York, publishing and editing a *Torah* magazine. We published the work of some of our great leaders. Do remember that our leaders are the most scholarly and the most righteous of our people – they are not necessarily the best fundraisers, or the best speakers! The journal was considered the major publication of the *yeshiva* world. I loved it! It was my niche. I was doing that, and at the same time I was the dean of five different *kollels*. I was beginning to specialize in particular areas of Jewish Law, and I was busy.

Then the rabbi of *Etz Hayyim* synagogue here in Metropolis said he was going to quit. This was six years ago. I moved here for personal reasons. I had four children by this stage, and I saw how much easier it was for my wife to be near her parents. My parents-in-law are wonderful people. My mother-in-law helps my wife in every way. Anyway, when I came, everything in Metropolis was very depressed economically. The city was not just going through a financial recession; it was a depression. It was a real challenge! The congregation is not big here, but thirty-five families left. Everyone was asking everyone, 'When are you going to move out?' Everything was shrinking – the East Side as well as the West Side. I'm a man who likes a challenge. I'm not interested in taking a congregation of 1,500 people and slowly burying them and watching them disappear over fifteen years! Things got better. My father-in-law has helped us enormously. Over the last six years, we've added forty families and we have a tremendous number of children in the congregation. I'm very proud of that!

The West Side is like one family. The *Yeshiva* also has a synagogue but the teachers come and pray here. We sink or swim together. I make it clear to the people over here that the *Yeshiva* is our school, and we have the responsibility to support it. The younger ones go to the Maimonides Academy on the East Side. They go over there on a bus. They have separate classes, but it is a school for both boys and girls. Once they finish the eighth grade (at fourteen), the boys go to the *Yeshiva* and the girls to *Beis Rahel*. The *Yeshiva* is a complete lifestyle – they all live in the dorm. I teach a class on practical Jewish Law. I have a special group, and I test them and give prizes. I told you – I'm a teacher.

Then there's a class every evening in the synagogue; it's mainly for retired people, and they study between the afternoon and evening services. Then I'm head of the *talmudic* college. The students study here in the morning and in the evening, but I send them over to the *Yeshiva* High School in the afternoon. There are four in their thirties and most of them have *semihah* (rabbinic ordination). One of our college student's wives is in charge of the women's classes. They study as and when they want. Rabbi Klein (*The Yeshiva Official*) also gives a class in the synagogue to the women but they mainly study in small groups.

I work very compatibly with the Traditional rabbis. I get along nicely with them. We all agree on the importance and necessity of a *kosher* divorce, and I'm in charge of the divorces in the city. I also bring in someone who's very experienced. He's done it for forty years. We don't have a formal permanent Rabbinic Court. There's no need for it. When I need a Rabbinic Court, for a conversion say, I ask two other rabbis like Rabbi Klein or Rabbi Vardin (*The Kashrut Supervisor*). It all goes back to what G–d wants from me. Is it more important to have a permanent Court or to have peace and harmony?

It's hard for me to answer any questions on my fears for Judaism. I'm Orthodox. My view is that there are those who are religious, and those who are not yet as religious as we would like them to be. We ourselves are trying to grow and we believe that growth is achieved by studying the *Torah*. When you study *Torah* and really work at it, *Torah* penetrates the whole person. I believe that the continuity and continuation of Judaism is the most important thing. It's not easy to be a committed Jew, and if the Jewish people are to survive, adults must provide role models for their children. Children are smart. They see inconsistency, insincerity or hypocrisy. My job as a rabbi is to encourage a deep commitment in people. You can believe in G–d in a thousand ways. What is special about Judaism is that it is passed down from grandfather, to father, to son, to son's son. You have to be sincere in your desire to pass down your grandfather's religion. It is terribly important. I do believe that when someone dies, their soul will go before the Heavenly Tribunal. They will be judged on their commitment.

I don't want it to be like the early 1900s when people were careful for themselves, but not for their children. You have to spend a lot of time and a lot of money transmitting the tradition to your children and your children's children. Thank G–d, there is a lot of *Torah* Judaism being learnt. But we will never give up on the non-religious Jew – the non-religious Jew is my brother or sister, and I will do anything within my power to bring him back. Many people see *Torah* Judaism as just a bunch of restrictions. Of course there are restrictions! When you walk into a store you don't take what doesn't belong to you: that is a restriction. The *Torah* was given by G–d, and for those who follow it, it gives such comfort, such joy. We're an active, dynamic community. We should be extroverts and concerned for every Jew however far he has fallen away. He is my brother, and we belong to one family. Of course we don't accept the legitimacy of Pluralism, but that doesn't stop us being concerned, worrying, caring and feeling that we are one . . .

The Hasidic Rabbi

RABBI YITZHAK BERKOVSKI

Hasids are immediately recognizable by their clothing (black hats, dark suits, dark ties, fringes, beards, side-curls). Hasidism as a movement emphasizes spirituality, joy and devotion to one's particular rebbe or religious leader. The rebbe is not elected; he is the son of the previous rebbe.

We interviewed Rabbi Yitzhak Berkovski in his small office in B'nai Akiva synagogue on the East Side. When we arrived, he was in the middle of a frantic negotiation on the telephone with lawyers and other rabbis, trying to organize a Jewish divorce. The office was cramped and untidy. There were family snapshots on the wall and among the papers cascading over the desk was a book entitled Enlightened Leadership. *On a small noticeboard there was a dog-eared sheet enunciating: 'Seven Habits of Highly*

Effective Families' and another asking, 'Are a few dull moments too much to ask?'

Rabbi Berkovski was a direct descendant of a famous family of Hasidic rabbis. A tall, handsome, charismatic man, he was dressed in the Hasidic fashion which was a notable contrast to his hearty colloquial American speech.

I was born and raised here in Metropolis in a rabbi's house and I have been watching the transitions of the community from childhood. My father was the rabbi of *Etz Hayyim* synagogue on the West Side. Things haven't changed since then. The organizations are pretty much set in their ways – their philosophy has always been 'This is the way things are gonna be; this is what we're gonna do, and if we're unhappy, we'll fire somebody!' That's supposed to be the remedy! They think the way to solve the problems of the community is to hire somebody new! But it doesn't change anything! And the basic reason I believe it doesn't change anything goes back to the core of my experience of watching it all. I had the benefit of sitting, like a fly on the wall, in the rabbi's home, listening to a cross-section of the community. And I had the opportunity to talk to my father both as a child and as an adult.

What was it like to grow up as a Berkovski? I haven't stopped growing up as a Berkovski! I'm still growing up! My father was an impossible act to follow. He was larger than life in everybody else's eyes, and obviously in the eyes of a child. His brilliance, his oratorical skills, were legendary. He was also a very understanding father. He understood; he tried to encourage and to motivate his children to rise to their excellence. I was the only son! I had five sisters! Okay? I was number three, so on the one hand the expectations were probably enormous; on the other, my father did try to make me grow up as an average American with a baseball bat and a bicycle. Except for that every time he bought me a bicycle, the people in the synagogue would say, 'Aha the rabbi's been buying bicycles for his son! Aha he's got a new bicycle!' So that didn't quite work. My father was also a very sensitive man and had absolutely no defences against people's criticism. Every criticism struck home straight to the depth of his personality, and we felt it all very intensely. We grew up often very angry at the community for having hurt him. He took it, and he internalized it, and it ate away at his stomach, and he ended up with a whole series of operations for gastro-intestinal problems.

I went to school at Maimonides Day School. Then after day school I went off to *yeshiva* in Cleveland, and then New York. As a teenager I imagined I would follow this dynasty of rabbis, and when I became an adult, I decided it was the one thing I didn't want to do. So I told my wife after we got married, 'I'm going to school. I'm going to become an accountant. I will never be a rabbi.' Why didn't I want to? It was too painful! I knew exactly what it meant to be a rabbi, and I said, 'I can't do it!' I imagine my father was probably disappointed, but he said, 'Do what you have to do!' When I was about seven years old, I asked how many generations of rabbis there had been in the family. He said, twenty-six generations. I was the only son out of six kids. Imagine! It was quite a set up, wasn't it? Anyway, I went to college and got my degree in Business Management in a year and I left Metropolis and became an accountant.

Then, when my sisters called me and said my father had been diagnosed with cancer – which was two years before he passed away – my world turned upside down. I was running away from something I could not run away from. A number of other things happened. My parents got divorced five years before my father passed away. At that point I was already married and had my own children. And I had to learn to see him as one adult sees another. Our relationship changed drastically – and it became much closer. I became able to see him as another man who struggled with what I could identify with. Then he remarried – he was married for two, maybe three years. That whole segment of his life gave me new insights into him. I was being successful in business, but it gave me none of the spiritual satisfactions. I knew I was not happy. I kept on blaming G–d for not making me happy. I was in agony and in turmoil, so I made the decision in the last year of my father's life that I would make time and come and study with him. So I came for the Day of Atonement with plans to stay for six months. Then he passed away ten days later.

Then I had to look, and the community had to look,

drastically to decide if his work was going to continue or to dissipate. Would all the work that he had done simply dissipate? None of my sisters or their husbands wanted to come back. None of them wanted to do it. Then the question was, What do I want? So they said, 'What do you want?' And I said, 'I don't know what I want!' We went through several months of indecision, and I resolved there was no way for me to avoid accepting the challenge. I tried to be very business-like about it. So we said, 'Look, we'll give it a year or so – see if it works.'

At that point *B'nai Akiva* was in my father's basement. He had left *Etz Hayyim* in 1970 and had started *B'nai Akiva.* He believed it would be the answer for a new generation searching for Judaism. How did I finally decide to return? I'm still trying to decide! I took over on the West Side. I had got my doctorate of Divinity from the *yeshiva* and was ready to roll! So I started rolling! When he was alive my father had been talking about moving over to the East Side. We started doing quite a number of Outreach programmes, and I was being invited to run programmes over here at *Har HaSh'em* synagogue and speak to different groups. I was spending most of my time on the East Side and coming back late at night to my home on the West Side. It was impossibly hard. I'm sure you've heard the joke that the longest bridge in the world is the West Side viaduct! I know Rabbi Klein (*The Yeshiva Official*) is now trying to do Outreach programmes for the West Side, but he has the benefit of the *Yeshiva* and other things . . .

We are trying in *B'nai Akiva* to provide a healthy *Torah* involvement for Jews and to give them a *Hasidic* perspective. When somebody comes and tells me they're searching for something, my first reaction is probably, 'Me too! But if you want to join me as I search, maybe we'll find some answers that'll work for you.' I can tell them the things I have found; I can tell them the experiences that led to my search. If it's something they can use, then what I've shared will be relevant. If it doesn't work, that's also okay! I design my classes to offer a wide variety of approaches. People will say, 'I want something really deep and spiritual . . .' Others will say, 'I don't know how to open the Prayer Book.' Then people will say, 'I wanna participate in class . . .' I recognize that the variety of desires and needs are multi-faceted. I also study one-to-one with people because that's what they need. Every morning we also have a class of three-quarters of an hour on a page of *Talmud* (Oral Law). Being multi-faceted is the only answer . . . It's very challenging. At times it's overwhelming! Sometimes I wish I was a normal person in a normal position . . . But I did make the choice to do this and at the end of the day I am both exhausted, and my need for challenge is amply satisfied!

I also do *kashrut* inspection. There's a mutual respect with Rabbi Vardin (*The Kashrut Supervisor*) . . . and a distance. One of the things I learnt firsthand from my father is this: that the amount of innovativeness needed to encompass all the technological changes that are happening in our society is so great that you have to be open. The processes of food production are always shifting, and you must be ready to respond and be inquisitive and curious without compromising Jewish Law. In fact my standards are every bit as high as the West Side's. I do know the West Side party line is not to use some of the products that are produced under my inspection. Most individuals have no problems. But if you want to know their policy line, their policy line is . . . 'Mmm, we're not so sure!'

I think of the Jewish community as a dysfunctional family and a dysfunctional family needs healing. The first step in healing a family is getting the family members to acknowledge that they are a family and that they're reacting in patterns that are fairly predictable. Even if the family doesn't talk to each other, they're still a family. Even if one child is no longer at the table, the empty chair will speak as loud as the chairs that are filled. The unaffiliated, the assimilated, and the intermarried are telling the rest of the family, 'It's not safe to be in the same room as you! It's too painful! I would rather marry someone that doesn't even resemble my mother, or my father! I don't want that kind of family!' And the family says to that child, 'We don't want to talk to you! Stay out of our house!' Maybe there's one member of the family – let's say in this instance the Reform – who takes on the rôle of the kindly sister who feels for her brother whom the family rejects. 'Come on, I'll talk to you,' she says, 'they won't talk to you, but I'll talk to you.' Now it is true that I personally can't run an 'Every Day, the Jewish Way' programme like Rabbi

Reinhardt (*The Reform Rabbi*). I can't do an Outreach programme that talks to intermarried couples, because of my own position within the family. The rest of the family would get too angry at me. But I do have this little sister over there . . . she's really nice . . . she'll talk to the outcast when nobody else is listening . . .

The reason I haven't written up my views on the community is that you can't come to your family and say, 'Okay, you guys. This is how you do it!' What you can do is say, 'Would you like to talk a little bit? Maybe we can get together . . .' What is my own position in the community family? I am a rabbi, and therefore a parent, but I am also a child of the West Side – a very naughty child! I'm also still trying very hard to be a family hero! I try to help them, but they don't appreciate me! I have learnt to acknowledge that . . . I hope I have learnt not to fight them . . .

You want to ask a last question? You want to know how many children I have? I have seven children . . . Yes! Only one son? Yes! He is number three!

The Traditional Rabbi

RABBI DAVID OPPENHEIM

Traditional Judaism is a modified form of Orthodoxy. Metropolis is unusual in having only two Conservative synagogues. The three Traditional synagogues must be seen as akin to Conservative congregations in most cities.

Rabbi David Oppenheim spoke to us in his small study in Adath Israel synagogue. There were two exquisite antique Torah pointers in a glass case on his wall. He spoke quietly and shrewdly; he was in his sixties, he had been a congregational rabbi for most of his adult life first at Beit Torah and then at Adath Israel.

I grew up in a small town in Pennsylvania and went through high school there. My father was an Orthodox rabbi, but not old-style Orthodox – modern Orthodox. We were Sabbath observers and dietary observers. My grandfather and great-grandfather had also been rabbis in the Lower East Side of New

York in the early 1900s. My family originally came from Hungary.

I went to the University of Chicago, and at the same time I went to the Hebrew Theological College in Chicago. I was there from 1942 to 1951. My intention was to be a rabbi, mainly because of my family background – but no, there was no direct family pressure. In those years it was not uncommon for *yeshiva* boys also to go to college. Remember the big right-wing Orthodox swing occurred after the Second World War – this was earlier. America at that time needed so-called 'modern Orthodox' rabbis: it was defined like that because they didn't make a fuss about their graduates taking mixed-seating congregations. That was the major differentiation. In the 1940s and 1950s 'modern Orthodox' meant you accepted men and women sitting together in the synagogue.

After the *yeshiva* I came straight to Metropolis. This was 1951, and in those days *Beit Torah* was the only synagogue east of State Street. They needed a rabbi, and they picked me. In those days the community was still mainly on the West Side; the old buildings of Temple *Shalom* and *Har HaShem* were both on the East Side, but west of State Street. They still hadn't moved to where they are now. The community was different in those days. There was less institutional activity. There weren't so many things going on. There was no *Yeshiva*, no Maimonides Academy. There was a small Rabbinical Council. I was at *Beit Torah* synagogue from 1951 to 1971. As I say, we were the first congregation east of State Street so we had an explosion in membership. We grew from twenty-five families to 700 in just a few years. The Allied Jewish Federation became more active, and all the institutions began to flourish and to grow. Then the Maimonides Academy began – and that's where all our children went to school, and that became a feeder for the *Yeshiva* and *Beis Rahel* High School. Then Golda Meir Day School came along and did a wonderful job supporting the Hebrew High School. There was a lot of good activity.

The orientation of *Beit Torah* synagogue echoed *Adath Israel*, except that *Adath Israel* still had separate seating. The men sat at the front and the women at the back with a very low railing between. It wasn't acceptable to the Orthodox because the division was too low. I myself had considerable contact with *Etz Hayyim* – the Orthodox synagogue on the West Side – because I was a close personal friend of Rabbi Berkovski's (*The Hasidic Rabbi*) father, may he rest in peace. We went to the University of Chicago together between 1942 and 1944, and we remained very close over the years. There wasn't much contact with the other rabbis except at meetings of the Rabbinical Council and at social occasions.

How observant were my congregants in those years? In the three traditional congregations of Metropolis (*Adath Israel*, *Har HaShem* and *Beit Torah*) to this day, very few of the members are strictly observant. Many years ago we had a number of Orthodox people, but over the years that number has steadily decreased. Quite a few keep *kosher*, but there are very few complete Sabbath observers and almost none who go to the ritual bath on a monthly basis. None the less they expected the rabbi to be Orthodox – that was the pattern in those years throughout the country.

Between 1971 and 1979, I changed gear and had a marvellous, wonderful seven years as a family counsellor. It saved my life spiritually, physically, mentally, emotionally. I had my adolescent rebellion and mid-life crisis at the age of forty-five! My dear wife stuck it through with me. Then in 1979 the long-serving rabbi of *Adath Israel* retired, and the gentlemen of the synagogue came and made me a very attractive offer. I was missing the people; I had enjoyed the rabbinate; but I had just overdone it. Anyway, I made the decision and I moved to the West Side. But do remember, the West Side community has got smaller. Of the 500 families of *Adath Israel* today, only twenty-five live on this side. They all travel. That's why the congregation is thinking of moving to the East Side when I retire. Yes, it will mean that there will only be strictly Orthodox synagogues on the West Side.

It was different at *Adath Israel* because I was different. I had learnt how to say 'No'; I was no longer so obsessive about my work; I took more time off. Also, with the extra training, I was more helpful to people. There's another important point. I came to a very well-established, grounded congregation. They had had the same rabbi for forty-seven years; they were very loyal and devoted to the synagogue. So I came to a very fine situation.

How has the community changed over the years? I've been asked that question before. I'm called the 'middler' in Metropolis – cars going down the middle of the street get hit by other cars going in both directions! I'm a moderate politically and religiously . . . So I'm not extremely gloomy about the community, and I'm not extremely happy. In general I lean to optimism! The present picture shows a lot of enthusiasm for Jewish life. The younger generation seems to want to know more and understand more. At the same time there's a lot of apathy and a lot of indifference while simultaneously there's a lot of potential enthusiasm.

The cause is Americanization. We Jews fought for Americanization, and we got it up to a great point, and now we're realizing the consequences . . . mixed marriages and a lack of observance. We live in a society that emphasizes autonomy and individual choice. It's not too hot on nationalism or ethnic identity or religious beliefs. People start to marry late, to have alternative lifestyles, to live together before marriage, to be homosexual, bisexual, to adopt and have children as single people. Anything goes in America. This whole smorgasbord is bound to affect the Jewish people. Those of us in the middle are caught in a bind. We have sympathies for choice and for rights, but religiously, it's very difficult. So we're hit by both sides. While Americanization is taking place, there are still residual feelings of guilt, puzzlement and bewilderment. We're carrying around a lot of unresolved Jewish baggage. We want to retain our identity, but at the same time we live in a culture which says you must participate in the mainstream. Yes, it's difficult.

What am I going to do when I retire? I'll tell you what I'm not going to do. I am not going to be tied to the telephone, or to my appointment book, or to a synagogue membership list. I'm going to stop, travel more with my wife, see my children and grandchildren more, catch up with some reading and study, do athletics, and be generally released from my schedule. Then I hope to find a worthwhile project with the Jewish community. But before that I've got to clear out my books, articles, pictures, papers, everything: I get quite queasy thinking about it . . .

The Conservative Rabbi

RABBI MAX GOLDSTEIN

Conservative Judaism is more traditional than Reform Judaism, but unlike Orthodoxy does not expect its adherents to keep every detail of the Jewish Law.

Rabbi Goldstein was tall and bespectacled. He sat in his book-lined study with a paper cup of iced water in front of him. Apart from books, the room was littered with piles of paper, old magazines, and letters. He spoke gently, giving every question his full attention.

I grew up in a fairly non-religious household in California, but we were members of this congregation, and I was just this kid who got involved. I participated in the youth group, worked in summer camp, led junior congregational services, and then moved up into being a teacher in the religion school. So it was very much an evolution. I planned to be a doctor, but was very unhappy in my pre-med programme at the University of California in Los Angeles.

I loved teaching in religion school in the congregation in which I'd grown up. It dawned on me as an epiphany from on high that I didn't have to be a doctor. I could be a rabbi. It all fitted together in one moment. I was sitting in an organic chemistry class in fact. And that gave me a way of getting out of Los Angeles and going to a different campus. So I went to Santa Cruz and majored in Philosophy, and then went to the Hebrew Union College (the Reform rabbinical seminary).

My parents never said very much about the change. My mother died a year later while I was still a junior (third year) at Santa Cruz, so she never knew I was going to be a rabbi. My father to this day sees it as rather odd that someone from his household should end up being so active in the Jewish community because he is not. In that respect I'm something of a black sheep in the family: I returned to something that our parents had rejected.

My first congregation was as a student rabbi in Carefree, Arizona. I was the first rabbi they'd ever had, and it was kind of awesome. I was twenty-four, and I was conducting services for people who were at a minimum of fifty-five and often-times sixty-five to ninety. As part of the Vietnam generation, I remember preaching about how the older generation mistreats the younger generation, based on the story of Abraham's willingness to sacrifice Isaac in the Bible. I fully expected that I'd get them very angry, but at the end of my sermon, everyone came up and said it was a wonderful sermon. They loved it. I was trying to figure out what I had done wrong. What I had done actually was to confirm their suspicion that their children were doing a rotten job raising their grandchildren!

I serve in a small synagogue here in Metropolis (*Beth Israel*), and I also do some university teaching. It's a Conservative congregation which was founded twenty-five or thirty years ago; the people who founded it were very much traditional Jews. They liked to think of themselves as Orthodox. They liked an Orthodox style, but that's not really how they lived their lives. As the city grew, younger people started moving into the area and several of them infiltrated *Beth Israel*. By the time I came, the younger element was beginning to take over. This more traditional element called itself Conservative. I don't think if you look at the congregation now you would see anything in the people's lives that was identifiably Conservative. The members are typical of what you'd find in a Reform congregation. A huge number of mixed marriages (Jew married to a gentile), a low amount of ritual in their homes – so my being trained as a Reform rabbi has not been much of a problem. I'm certainly more traditional than any of them. I do recall having a conversation about mixed marriage, and asking them hypothetically what they want their rabbi to do, and they all felt there was nothing wrong in a rabbi officiating in a mixed marriage in a church on Saturday (the Sabbath) with a priest. So I was outnumbered by everybody!

To the best of my knowledge there is no rabbi in Metropolis who will officiate at a mixed marriage, though there is one who is widely rumoured to do it if it's done very quietly. My general philosophy is that the wedding ceremony ought to reflect the marriage. It ought to belong to both members of the couple, and since religion in a mixed marriage is obviously something they have chosen not to share, then it shouldn't be part of the ceremony. At *Beth Israel* I always open the door for conversion if that's something that is likely to be down the road. In every congregation there are large numbers of hangers-on. People who are not officially Jewish, but don't conceive of themselves as much of anything else, and just come and are very quiet. Unless somebody asks flat out, 'Are you Jewish?' these people sort of blend into the community, as I suspect has happened throughout our history.

Non-Jewish spouses can be members of *Beth Israel.* We allow them to come; we allow them to join. I do not call them to the *Torah* or anything like that, I try in a *Bar Mitzvah* (coming-of-age ceremony) to help the non-Jewish parent find an appropriate place in the service. It might be reading a prayer for peace, something like that. But sometimes there are problems. When people have a *Bar Mitzvah* they're supposed to call me a year in advance. So I get this call from a family that have this boy in our religion school. The Principal of the school mentioned that the youngster only showed up one day a week. However the *Bar Mitzvah* programme is two days a week. He came on Tuesdays, but not on Sundays. And it finally came out that on Sunday the kid was at church! This was a couple who had decided that Christianity was the fulfilment of Judaism. They thought of themselves as Jews as well as Christians, and were quite shocked when I suggested that perhaps a *Bar Mitzvah* was not quite the right thing for this particular youngster.

I always encourage conversion. I say, 'Why not go through a little bit of ritual?' Then the non-Jewish partner can participate fully in his son's *Bar Mitzvah.* I mean most of these people are living as Jewish a life as the rest of the congregation. It wouldn't be done on the spot. We'd have a little trip over to the ritual bath. I always hope they're circumcised already. I've wrestled with circumcision. I insist on the ritual bath. The problem with circumcision, as I understand it, is if a male is not circumcised as a child, you're talking about major surgery on an adult. I don't know how I feel about that . . . I'd want to talk to a doctor. If the risk is serious, I'd want him to make the decision and not me . . .

In general my congregation doesn't look over my shoulder. They respect me. I can do as I think best. Just telling them what they want to hear is a waste of their time and mine. I'm protected by being in a small synagogue like *Beth Israel*, and I'm always reasonably careful of what I say and do. I'm also President of the Hebrew High School – that's the Pluralist Jewish high school and that's quite a public role. Jews are very uncomfortable saying or thinking anything negative about their community. It's a lack of security. They feel as if they're being disloyal. They believe they're playing into the hands of some real or imagined enemy. I'll give you an example. I was invited to speak to the Sisterhood of another congregation, yeah, Temple *Shalom*, on the topic of women in Judaism. There we were in this large chapel in this affluent Temple with probably fifty or sixty wealthy Jewish women, very nicely dressed. I tried to be entertaining and non-frightening. Things go better if you can get them to laugh. So I was trying to point out in a subtle way that women have a secondary role in the Jewish community. I said they ought to be more assertive. One of the women said, 'Don't you think what you're saying is dangerous? That it helps our enemies?' And I looked at her and thought, 'I am in the chapel of the richest synagogue in Metropolis with a bunch of Jewish women. Yassir Arafat can't hear us. What are they worried about?'

The Reform Rabbi

RABBI ROBERT REINHARDT

Reform is the least traditional branch of Judaism. Temple Shalom is the oldest synagogue in Metropolis. Situated in the middle of the affluent East Side, it is housed in an expensive modern building and there are small children everywhere. The pre-school is important; it provides an annual income of $100,000 for the Temple.

Rabbi Reinhardt sat behind his kidney-shaped desk in his large grey-carpeted study. There was a litter of books and papers round the room, and on the walls were hung photographs of three attractive teenage children. He was a dapper man in his late forties. He wore a blue blazer, grey flannel trousers and an immaculate white shirt. He had a Hebrew wedding ring on his manicured hands, and sported a jazzy silk tie. He was freshly shaved and his dark greying hair was expertly barbered.

I was born in Milwaukee, Wisconsin. My father's family was from Russia, and my mother's family was from Germany. My father's father, the grandfather whom I was closest to, was from Eastern Europe. He was a communist, but later in his life he returned to Judaism. My parents came from different socio-economic backgrounds. My mother's family were very, very wealthy, and my father's family were very poor. My dad's father thought of my mother as the *shiksa* (gentile girl) because she came from a Reform background. My parents were very active in the Reform synagogue so I was raised in a Reform background. When I graduated from the eighth grade, I wanted to be the senior rabbi of the Temple of Milwaukee. That was my goal in life. I always wanted to be a rabbi.

I went to the University of Wisconsin in Milwaukee. I started with Hebrew Studies, and then I had a huge fight with one of the professors and I just dropped out of the programme. So I picked up Philosophy in my senior year. Then I went to the Hebrew Union College in Cincinnati. I wasn't unhappy at the College – I thought it was hard. As I look back on it, I think the College ought to be more of a professional school, and less of a school which imitates what a *yeshiva* is supposed to be. I think they could package the curriculum differently. What I would have liked was an understanding of how to make a sacred text speak to the people who are sitting in the pews, who haven't the foggiest notion of what that text is all about. That wasn't how it was done in the College, but if you wanted to be a rabbi that was the hurdle you had to get over.

I loved my student congregation. It was in a little town in Tennessee, and I stayed there for three years. I loved it! I loved the people; I loved the opportunities. I trained the choir there; it wasn't great, but for them it was wonderful. I did Sunday school; I trained some teachers down there; and I had some people with whom I became very close and looked forward to going there. They were wonderful! They loved me! That's what I find exciting – to take a project and to think about it and to move it through the process.

After I was ordained I came to Metropolis as an assistant – yeah, as an assistant. Do I have to talk about this? It's going to be difficult. You know I've been in this congregation for twenty-three years. By and large this has been a wonderful experience, but the hard part was my time as an assistant. I had all sorts of ideas that I wanted to try, but Rabbi Green's chief statement to me was, 'What do you need it for?' He never wanted to do anything, and that was disappointing to me. Let me tell you what the synagogue was about when I came here. It was about Friday night services, High Holy Day services, *Bar Mitzvah*, Sunday school, and life-cycle ceremonies which were all things he wanted to do. Nothing else happened here! It was very frustrating.

I loved the man – this is why this is difficult – I loved the man, but he was lazy. Frankly he didn't do anything. He wouldn't see it that way, but by the time I came on the scene, he was fifty-six years old. Rabbi Green was never a controversial figure. He walked the narrow rope, and I understood that. He perceived himself as a peacemaker. The congregation was building this building when he came in the 1950s. They were committed to it. Temple *Beth Jacob* had just broken away as an anti-Temple *Shalom* presence, for the people who didn't want to pay the bill here – yeah, that's Yael Fox's (*The Woman Rabbi*) group. She used to be my assistant. That made him angry. He wanted to make sure things went well here, and his way of doing that was to keep a lid on everything, keep it smooth.

Here's what happened: Rabbi Green only kept his assistants for two or three years. The guys had to turnover. When I came he was fifty-six, and when I was interviewed halfway through Rabbi Green got up and left. The president of the congregation then said it wasn't a two-year-and-out deal. They weren't offering a permanent position. They were only saying that they would like to have someone come and stabilize the situation. Rabbi Green was going to retire – this is the key – he was going to retire at sixty-five. They were saying that if I got to like the congregation and the congregation grew to like me, there was a possibility that this might be a permanent thing.

This is where young guys get screwed every time. I always assumed Rabbi Green agreed to all this. So after five years, I kept trying to do things. I'm building and building. But everything was a fight. We started the pre-school. After five years, I said, 'Look, I don't know what the future is. I'd like to be a little more secure.' And Rabbi Green said, 'I don't know what you're talking about. I'm not going to retire. I never said I would retire at sixty-five.' After two more years, I said to the congregation, 'Either you make a commitment to me or I leave.' So they tried to make a commitment, but by that time Rabbi Green made it clear he wasn't retiring. Either he reneged or the congregation was duped. I don't know. I was the guy in the middle.

Then a group of people got together to try to change the by-laws to force a retirement at sixty-five. That didn't go through, and it led to a terrible, terrible situation here. There were calls for me to be fired and all. Mrs Green wouldn't speak to me. But Rabbi Green didn't want me to leave because he knew I would start my own congregation here. By that time I had a group of guys come to me; they put $50,000 on the desk. This is 1977. They put the money on the desk and said, 'We want a new congregation.' Rabbi Green knew this. We patched it up. We made a public apology from the pulpit for anything we had done to create this problem in the community, and we vowed that we would work together. More than that you can't do!

After I was here for nine years, he had a minor heart attack, and of course Mrs Green blamed me for it. But do you know, till the day he retired, he insisted that I could only preach once a month. He was so insecure. I'm a good speaker. People didn't like listening to him; they do like listening to me. I'm not trying to boast, but that is the truth. After his heart attack, about six months later, he had bypass surgery. Then he was feeling great, but he said, 'I'm going to retire.' And he retired at age sixty-seven. I had now been here eleven years.

Then came the question, Who was going to be the new rabbi? There were some people who wanted to interview a lot of people, and I said to them, 'Look, I've been here eleven years. You are free to go and interview whoever you want, but I want you to know that if you decide to interview, I'm not going to be an interviewee. Why not? Not because I'm afraid of my skills. That's not the point. The point is either you have confidence enough in me to allow me to be the rabbi or you don't. You vote on me now or . . .' Some of the Board did not like that at all. I said, 'Either you decide to hire me as the Senior

Rabbi or you don't. That's okay. I'll be happy. I'll go someplace. I'll be fine.' Well, that's what they decided to do. Things have worked out . . .

There were thirty things I wanted to do, mostly programmatic things. We've got a very active social action programme. The thing that this congregation has become known for is the Outreach work we've done. We do a lot of stuff here with Outreach. We developed some programmes for people who already had converted to Judaism – how to integrate them into the congregation. We did some groups for parents whose kids had converted – I'm talking about the Jewish parent in a mixed marriage. Then we did a group for non-Jewish parents. Then we decided the one missing piece was for kids whose parents had intermarried, and we created another programme called 'Every Day, the Jewish Way'. It's run by Naomi Marks (*The Director of an Outreach Programme*). You should talk to her. Intermarriage is not on the horizon. It already is . . . maybe a third of the congregation is intermarried, I really don't know.

Nobody's a member of the synagogue who's not Jewish. I don't want non-Jewish people determining who the rabbi of the synagogue's going to be; I don't want non-Jews determining what the Jewish ritual of the synagogue is going to be; I don't want non-Jews voting about the future of the synagogue. Don't misunderstand me. We do everything we can to bring non-Jews into the synagogue, to have an influence over them so maybe they will convert. I do everything I can to allow a non-Jewish parent to be a participant in a *Bar Mitzvah* . . . They can't bless the *Torah* scrolls, but they can stand there while the *Torah* is being read like any other parent. I want to include them, not exclude them because I think ultimately we gain by including them appropriately.

I'll do everything I can to help an intermarrying couple, but I will not do that which my tradition says is impossible for me to do. Whether I accept the bindingness of Jewish Law or not, it's still my tradition . . . I'm not telling couples not to be married . . . I'm just saying to them, 'Please don't ask me to do that which I find impossible to do.' Intermarriage is not authentic Jewishly. If they're married by a judge, I will always go to a wedding in a hotel or a club, and I will do more than a blessing. I will meet with them, and I'll give them a charge, and I'll bless them. I'm happy to do that. There used to be a rabbi here. He was a marrying Sam! He used to charge $500 for a wedding and stuff. He was doing it for a living. At least if you're going to do it, don't be a whore! That's what I keep saying to these guys. They're just whores, that's all . . .

This congregation has the resources to do the things that need to be done. Don't misunderstand me. But if I ever had the opportunity to join a large synagogue or a small synagogue, I would choose a large synagogue any day. I'll tell you the reason. Everybody doesn't like me. There's no question about that! But if the issue is liking the rabbi, there are three rabbis here; there's an Educational Director here; there's an Educational Director Emeritus here, and there's a wonderful administrator. A big congregation has a staff that can help nurture people and bring them under the wings of the Almighty, so to speak. A small congregation just has the rabbi. And if you don't like the rabbi, you're stuck . . .

The Russian Rabbi

RABBI MOSHE LUBETKIN

The Metropolis Centre for Russian Jewry was located in a square prefabricated building. It was situated along a major highway among fast-food joints and secondhand car dealers. Inside were prayerbooks in Russian and English, an old piano, and several stacking chairs. The rest of the furniture was clearly secondhand. Next door was the kosher deli of the East Side. Rabbi Lubetkin was the only paid employee of the Centre. He was a Hasid. Outside, the thermometer stood at over 90 degrees, but he wore a heavy dark suit. His shirt was coffee stained, but his tie was silk. His skull cap was heavy black velvet and his fringes were visible outside his trousers. He was in his forties, with a thick beard, and his English was heavily accented.

I was born in Soviet Union, in the suburbs of Moscow. I consider myself a bit different than the main majority of Russian Jews because I received Jewish education and upbringing in Moscow. It was underground which means nobody knew about it. In some way I can say I was leading two lives; like outside. in school and on street I was like everybody else, and at home we observed all the holidays and traditions. After the public school I went to learn Bible and *Talmud*. When we had the chance to leave Russia, we was one of the first ones to apply, and we was denied the visa for three years, and then we was able to leave Russia to Israel.

In Russia, I study *Talmud* with three or four boys in Yiddish. Yiddish was alive among older generations. After the Revolution they start to close down everything. Jewish books could be kept in the house. You said, 'This belong to my grandfather.' They didn't care when old person was reading Hebrew. They care that nobody teach Hebrew to young people – this was dangerous. We was coming in one by one; we was going out one by one. It was, I would say, a community of 150 families. I would say a hundred people was *Hasidic* and fifty wasn't, but they was religious. My father was *Hasidic*. There was no official circle. I mean Moscow had an official *yeshiva*. It had three students there. But this *yeshiva*, the KGB was creating. Until we get an exit visa, I never stepped into the official synagogue because my parents was afraid there would be a question right away about how a young person knows how to read and knows what it is about. All the Hebrew underground classes started in the early 1970s. We worshipped in underground congregation. In one home for two times, and then we move to another home.

In Israel I decided to receive full Jewish education. I just wanted to have the full knowledge, so I went to a *yeshiva*. During the course of being in *yeshiva*, I was sent to New York. After receiving my ordination, they said it was appropriate for me to give back to my peoples what I had received because I was one of the lucky ones to get an education. This is how I end up being rabbi specially working with Russian Jews. My parents are still in Israel. I consider myself a *Hasid* follower, but the organization I am running is a community organization for the Russian Jews.

After I married my wife, I had offers to go to Australia, California, Canada and Metropolis. I chose Metropolis. I first came in 1981. There was approximately 250 Russian families in Metropolis. There was perhaps about five last names. They all relatives. Usually they didn't speak English. The Jewish Family Service was helping them for four months. They found them an apartment, and they had English classes for them. There was all kinds of people – engineers, factory workers . . . Somehow everyone was able to get, not the job they had in Russia, but some job.

At those times everyone was leaving Russia with Israeli visa. Then what happened is they was coming to Vienna, they would say: 'We don't want to go to Israel. We want to go to America.' Then they was taken from Vienna to Italy. Italy was the base for all immigrants who wanted to come to the United States. I would say, they didn't want to go to Israel mainly due to war. Russian Jews suffered in Second World War and they had many relatives who was killed. They was afraid their children would have to go in military. You must understand, in the 1970s people who was close to Zionist idea was going to Israel. People who was going for economical reasons, they wanted to go to America. Basically I would say therefore they came to Metropolis for political and economical reasons.

I would meet with families; we got to know each other; I would speak Russian. Then later I started to invite them for Jewish holidays which they didn't know nothing about. They didn't know nothing about Judaism. Some of them had never saw a Hebrew letter. They saw themselves as Jews, and liked to come to the holidays. I was renting big halls. Basically it wasn't worship but celebrations for the holidays. The difficulty was in Russia the propaganda put Judaism on such a negative level. So in their mentality Judaism is something to be ashamed of. One of my goals was to show them how wrong was the propaganda which made them feel guilty about their nationality. Also religion in general in Russia is very negative. I couldn't push religion because this was something that was negative. Some of them believed always, but they was mixed up by the propaganda. Being in America, in a free country, they observe other people; seeing successful Americans and finding out they are a religious people – is a big lesson for them. I always say to them, the first contact the Russian immigrant has with America is the dollar. It is on the dollar written – 'In God we trust'.

They was interested in the Jewish history and the Jewish

traditions. They wanted to know why they was hated. Not knowing what is a Jew, you don't understand why they hate you. I would say peoples who is more intellectual became more religious. They think; they ask questions; they want to know. It is a little bit different people who are coming now from Russia than the people who came fifteen years ago. People who are coming out now are, I would say, more open to religion because the freedom that now goes on in Russia. People then came out for materialism. It was a gradual increase. Then an explosion. Say from 1989 to 1991, the population doubled. The ones who are coming now are more educated about America. Now most are coming out of fear – what will happen in Russia – but take two years ago, they was coming purely because it was better here.

This Centre was founded in 1991. I left Metropolis in 1989 to work in New York, but I came back when Centre was founded. The purpose of this Centre is mainly to bridge the Russian Jewish community with the American Jewish community. It was Tony Fishman and Bernard Black's idea (*The President of the Centre for Russian Jewry* and *The Community Patriarch*). The problems that we have here is to educate people; to make them closer to our roots. Then when you look on the statistics, in 1975 the intermarriage and assimilation in Russia was approximately 35 to 45 per cent. When we take the statistics of the Russian Jews in America, the assimilation is 70 per cent. The point is, if they was in Russia, there would be less assimilation. The reason was in Russia it was not easy to change in your passport you are a Jew. In a way the government kept these Jews from assimilation! Here, because it is a free country, the assimilation is much faster. Also different missionary groups are preying on them – like the Messianic Jews and even the cults. So it is very important to educate these people. I read in New York by year 2000, every fifth Jew in New York will be a Russian immigrant. Imagine! If we do not educate them, then they will be lost for American Jewry. Intermarriage is a big threat because they didn't have no connection with Jewish roots.

Is there anything more? You ask me, 'Am I Russian or American?' A good question! I am Jewish . . .

The Woman Rabbi

RABBI YAEL FOX

The Reform movement has ordained women as rabbis since 1972. Both the Conservative and Reconstructionist movements have recently agreed to ordain them, but the Orthodox do not even consider doing so.

Rabbi Yael Fox sat in her pleasant modern living room. On the floor, leaning against the wall, were framed prints of Hebrew calligraphy. Children's clay models sat on the glass coffee-table. A tiny baby slept next door in a rocker and a three-year-old small boy ran in and out of the room as we talked. He was wearing his mother's apron around his neck as a cape and was pretending to be Superman.

Becoming a rabbi had very little to do with my parents, that's for sure. I grew up in a Conservative congregation in Phoenix, Arizona. My family is entirely secular and for my parents any form of religious observance is a waste of time. My father thinks the best thing a rabbi can do is to get a proper job. But there was something about the Jewish environment when I was growing up that just touched me. All through grade school, all through high school, I was really involved in a Jewish youth group, and I loved going to religious school – I was one of those weird kids who liked it.

I studied Biblical Hebrew in college, and really loved it. I liked learning how to analyze texts and finding I could understand what they said when they read *Torah*. One of the reasons why I wanted to become a rabbi was I would be able to read the *Torah*. When I was growing up in the Conservative movement, girls weren't allowed to do that. When I became *Bat Mitzvah* (female coming-of-age ceremony), I had to read the *Haftarah* (prophets) at Friday night even though I knew just as much Hebrew as any of the boys. The tradition was that whoever was *Bar Mitzvah* the next day not only got to read the *Torah* but also sang the prayer over wine on Friday night. I had a better voice, and this boy got to sing. It was horrendous, and I just didn't think that that was quite right.

I went off to Los Angeles to the Hebrew Union College (the Reform rabbinical seminary) not knowing anything about

Reform Judaism because when I was growing up the Reform kids were like Christians to us. We used to call them 'Reefers' partly as an abbreviation of Reform, and partly because they smoked a lot of dope in those days. That's what the Reform kids did on their youth events! We Conservative kids studied and prayed and were really serious Jews while they went off partying all the time . . . But I found the programme at the seminary really comfortable and appealing.

In my class there were eighteen rabbinical students, five of them women. The women of course were much cleverer – much smarter. I'm not making that up – our teachers used to say that to us . . . in the College everyone was treated the same. I had no idea there was any issue being a woman rabbi until I left. There were no role models. I only ever met one woman rabbi before I went to the College, and there weren't any ordained women around the College. I never made the connection between the fact that there were only men as role models. I just looked up what rabbis were doing and I figured I would like to do that too. As far as jobs go, once you are a rabbi, it's not necessarily that congregations won't hire women, but that the differential in pay between women and men in rabbinical positions is as much as 20 per cent. You see, we keep getting pregnant, and they don't like that too much. On the one hand that's understandable, but on the other it's kind of aggravating.

I got married when I was a student. My husband is also a rabbi, and we've been very lucky and always got positions near each other. I haven't taken his name. He questioned that, and my father questioned that. But I wanted to keep my own identity, and I like my name. And sometimes it's advantageous that people don't always know that I'm married to Harold. In fact it's funny sometimes when they discover it. I want to be my own person, and Fox is the name I've always had and the one I want to keep.

We came to Metropolis ten years ago, when I was hired as the Educational Director of Temple *Shalom*. They'd never had a rabbi in that position before, and because of the nature of Temple *Shalom* and the nature of the Senior Rabbi, Robert Reinhardt (*The Reform Rabbi*), I had the opportunity to do things that are not traditionally associated with the Director of Education. I thought it would be good for the Temple school. In supplementary Jewish education there's so much negativity that I felt that if parents and kids saw me on the pulpit it would give the school authenticity and weight.

I was at Temple *Shalom* for five years. Why did I leave? Well the position I had: I was working six days a week and anything from three to five nights a week after work. I was never home, and I had two children. I was really tired. I had no time for myself. I felt very overwhelmed all the time. I didn't really enjoy the administrative part of what I was doing. I was number three among the rabbis even though I'd been there longer than the assistant rabbi. As an educator, I was never seen as a real rabbi. The assistant rabbi was named associate before it was even thought to make me associate. I always felt I had to be proving myself and that was tiring. I always had to be better, to speak better, be more creative. I had to come up with new things all the time whereas the associate male colleague could do the same thing year after year. That's wrong! A lot of women rabbis are taking non-traditional rabbinic positions. The reason for that is you don't have to fight these battles all the time. You don't have to be in competition. I always felt that I was competing, and it's only so long that you can go on doing that. When I decided to leave, I felt I was giving up and that was really hard.

Then I went off to teach second-graders (six and seven-year-olds) at the Golda Meir Jewish Day School. It was an enormous drop in salary and prestige. I had no authority and I wasn't in charge of anything except this group of forty-six children who thought I was wonderful. I loved it, but I didn't stay there. I got bored.

I've got three kids now. It's a very interesting question about my husband. When I was at Temple *Shalom*, things were more equal than they are now. The more I do things for him like his mother, the happier he becomes, and the lazier he gets. I don't know. It's very interesting. Even when I was working full-time, and he was working full-time, I was the one who had the kids with me. Now I've got a job as the rabbi of Temple *Beth Jacob*, but I'm not full-time. It's a tiny Temple and I'm the only rabbi. In fact it's defined as a quarter-time position. I do services twice a month. People pay separately for things like life-cycle events. What they pay me is a joke. But the situation is good for them; it's good for me; and we live with it right now.

The really difficult issue is that I'm married to a male rabbi. At present he's an associate, but he is a man who has this image of himself as being at the head of a medium-size congregation. That's his ideal. That's what he wants to do. Probably we're going to have to move someplace else. What I say to him – and I feel very strongly about this – we have to look at the overall picture. For us to be happy, we need to consider three aspects – quality of life, job satisfaction, and financial situation. If these three things fit in some other place, then I'd be willing to go there, but until he finds something at least as good as what we have here, I'm not willing to go. It must be a better life for both of us.

I think men and women see things differently. And I think it starts with the way small girls and boys are treated. When I was in college, I wanted to go to Israel. I was eighteen years old, but my parents wouldn't let me go. My brother was fourteen, and they let him go on a European tennis tour to play tennis. It had nothing of educational value whatsoever, but he was getting good at tennis. Here was his opportunity, and so off he went to Europe. But I wasn't allowed to go to Israel! From very early on that kind of stuff happens, and it affects you. I'm the result of a male chauvinistic father, and a mother who let him do whatever he wanted. When I decided to leave Temple *Shalom* my father celebrated. He thought it was the best thing I could do. I should be home with my children . . .

The Former Rabbi

RABBI DR SAUL BLEEFELD

Rabbi Dr Saul Bleefeld was tall, thin and jolly-looking. He talked of his rabbinical experiences ruefully and with humour.

I was born in Las Vegas, Nevada, and grew up in Washington State. My father was a rabbi who had studied in the rabbinical school in Berlin. He had become the rabbi in Heidelberg, and through some family connections, he had gotten to England just before the war started in 1939. Then through some other connections he got to the United States and served in Ohio, Nevada and Washington. I grew up in Seattle in a liberal Conservative congregation. I went to religion school in my father's congregation; I attended public schools in Seattle and then I went to the State University of Washington, where I studied Social Science.

I thought by being a rabbi, I could do serious Jewish study, have a position in the community, exercise leadership, and do something to help people – the rabbinate seemed to combine all those goals. I think my father was immensely pleased. It was a real reaffirmation of who he was. I was accepted at the Hebrew Union College and spent three years in Los Angeles and three years in Cincinnati. I was ordained in 1970.

My great seminary tale took place in my penultimate year. I was leading a service in the College, and I was wearing my *yarmulke* (skull cap) and *tallit* (prayer shawl). I was about a quarter of the way through the service when the Dean of Students came up and whispered in my ear that I should not be wearing a *tallit.* I whispered back to him that I appreciated his concern, but I was going to wear my *tallit* and perhaps we could talk about it afterwards. In any case, someone else finished the service. That lunchtime there was a protest meeting by the students, and I'm told there was a faculty meeting. The faculty decided not to make an issue of it and not to throw me out of rabbinical school, but expulsion was mooted – I think it was a serious threat. The sequel to this is that when it came to ordination, I wore my *tallit.* When I sat with my classmates, I couldn't be seem, but when I walked up to receive my ordination wearing the offending article, apparently there was an audible gasp in the congregation! Times have changed? They sure have! Anyway, that was my great rebellious moment at the College!

My last summer before ordination, I had three goals: the first one was to finish my rabbinical thesis; the second one was to work part-time; and the third goal was to find a wife – and I achieved all three. It was a wonderful, wonderful summer. I got a job as a part-time army chaplain; I worked assiduously at my thesis; and I dated like crazy – in other words, I interviewed; I went to any and all Jewish social functions. One Saturday night I went to a volleyball game and barbeque and within minutes sat down next to Mimi. We ended up on the same volleyball side, and the net result was I asked her out for the next day. Literally ten days after we first met, we were engaged, and literally three months later we married!

I knew I needed to get married. I had come to the conclusion that a single rabbi in the congregational rabbinate was a walking disaster! We looked into the possibility of my taking a pulpit in England, and after ordination we went off to Durham, England, for two years. That was a very mixed review. I made the mistake of thinking I was the rabbi, whereas in fact the old members of the German élite were the rabbi! I made my series of *faux pas*, and I offended people right and left with my American brashness.

So after two years we were going to go back to the United States, but I was interviewed by a congregation in Manchester, England. We loved them; they loved us, and within a week or so we had signed the contract. We had seven wonderful years in Manchester, but in England the non-Orthodox movements are second if not third class, and we thought the grass would be greener. I wasn't making a great salary; America is the centre of Reform Judaism, and there are reasonable-sized congregations. Oh, by the by, while I was in Manchester, I earned my Doctorate. It was a happy time and I can say that for those years I went to work with a smile and came back with a smile.

Then when we moved to America, the rot set in. Quite coincidentally I came back as Senior Rabbi at another Manchester – Manchester, Louisiana. It was one of the prestigious congregations of the South, and it was a large Temple with about 700 families. I fell in love with the idea of being the Senior Rabbi, and I thought I had made it. We moved to a large house in the Jewish area, but what I hadn't figured on was that Manchester, Louisiana, had an Emeritus Rabbi. He had retired three years previously, and he had wanted his assistant rabbi to succeed him. The Emeritus was a very nasty piece of work, but a good fundraiser and very politic. The assistant had been too young to succeed him, but was waiting in the wings in a nearby city.

In all fairness, I am sure I made some mistakes but the Emeritus was standing by undermining me at every point. He had an office in the building, and to say he hung around was an understatement. In 1982 the invasion of Lebanon took place. I had to look at myself in the mirror and in my High Holy Day services I criticized Israel – it was my death warrant. They tried to get rid of me. There was a very, very ugly congregational meeting, and I just squeaked through. Then it was suggested that maybe the right thing would be for me to resign, but I said, 'No thanks!' Then I was given a two-year contract, but less than a year later it was made clear that it would not be renewed. So I had a year to find another position. I was succeeded, by the way, by the former assistant.

I applied for various positions and at that stage I still had the illusion that careers move up! I was offered an associateship to a Senior Rabbi in a large congregation, but that wasn't what I wanted. I ended up accepting a pulpit in a small congregation of a hundred families in Lawrence, Kansas. The great appeal was that it also involved college teaching at the State University. I loved it; it was wonderful. Unfortunately there were some synagogue Board members who were also college faculty, and they felt that my combined salary was more than their salary – this was a source of tension. In time, in the classic words of the Book of Exodus, 'There arose a new Pharaoh who knew not Joseph.' We came to Lawrence under one administration, and by the end of three years a new administration came in who decided for whatever reason that I was not the right rabbi for them. One of the criticisms was that I was supposedly condescending to women. Again I had over a year to look around for a new position.

After several interviews that led nowhere, Robert Reinhardt (*The Reform Rabbi*), who was a classmate of mine in rabbinical school, directed me to a small new congregation in Evanstown, fifty miles outside Metropolis. I sold myself on the basis that I could build a congregation – which I had done in Manchester, England – and I was taken on board. I hoped I could build it into something truly viable, but due to the difficult economic problems of the time, that proved impossible. As a result we also parted ways after about two years.

So here I was without a job. Again Robert Reinhardt was very, very good. He insisted I had a year's free membership at Temple *Shalom.* I have to say, it was tough seeing Robert at *Shalom.* We were classmates; he was less academic than I, and here he was a successful rabbi. It was hard. But he's been a good friend. A real *mensch* (good person). We now belong to Temple *Shalom.* I teach an adult education class there, and our children happily attend the religion school. Robert did try to put me in contact to be Executive Director of this or that, but nothing came of it.

Then Sam Kornfeld (*The University Professor of Judaica*) called me and asked me to teach a course for the Centre for Judaic Studies. One thing leads to another. Some time later I received a phone call asking me to teach religious studies at the Japanese University in Metropolis. I was interviewed; I was hired full-time; and that is what I am doing now. I teach various courses on world religions and ethics. I am absolutely as happy as can be. At this point in my life I am delighted to be in academia full-time. I've been able to do research when writing articles, and I'm having a book published at long last. It'll be coming out next year . . .

Three

CONGREGATIONAL LEADERS

The Traditional Cantor

CANTOR AARON SHEER

A cantor is a synagogue official who chants the liturgy. We met Cantor Aaron Sheer in his wife's Judaica gift shop. He was a clean-shaven man in his sixties with a short, trim moustache. He wore a black skull cap and a diamond little-finger ring.

I was raised in a very, very Orthodox home – ultra-Orthodox I might say – in the Williamsburg section of Brooklyn. When I was a child, I went to the same *yeshiva* as Rabbi Marmorstein (*The Orthodox Rabbi*), but I loved singing. I always sang in the choirs of great cantors so I was raised to appreciate cantorial music. My parents knew I sang well, but they didn't want me to be a cantor. They felt it wasn't a good livelihood for a Jewish boy – not a job for a nice Jewish boy! But at the age of fourteen I got my first cantorial position just for the weekends, so I could continue my studies.

After I got my rabbinical ordination at the age of about eighteen, I got my first yearly position which was at an ultra-Orthodox synagogue in New York. The rabbi there didn't want me to take the position because he claimed that in order to chant the services on the High Holy Days, you had to be a married man. But he was outvoted by the Committee. I was there as guest cantor for a year, and it was a great experience for me. In those days we used to have 1,500 people for the High Holy Days, and on Sabbaths we used to have a thousand people coming. The synagogues were full in those days.

After leaving New York, I went to Philadelphia. I was nineteen, and I was there for eight years. While I was there, I studied at the Curtis Music Institute, and I got a secular degree from there. Then I came to Metropolis where I was at the *Beit*

Torah synagogue. Why did I come to Metropolis? I fell in love with the congregation. I thought it was a terrific opportunity. When I came there were 380 families, and when I left there were close to 800. Now it's down again. Rabbi Oppenheim (*The Traditional Rabbi*) who's now at *Adath Israel* was the rabbi there then. I worked with him for sixteen years.

The duties of a cantor vary. Some cantors are part-time – they just come in for services on the Sabbath and festivals. My duties were what they call a '*Kol bo*' (everything!) – Friday night and Saturday services; all Jewish holidays; I taught in the religion school; I taught *Bar* and *Bat Mitzvah*; I trained choirs (junior choirs, adults' choirs, women's choirs); you name it. Every day we had services, but they were conducted by the people themselves. The cantor's role was to chant all the liturgy. I had nothing to do with speaking, sermonizing, and readings – these were the rabbi's duties. Anything to do with chanting was my job. My main duties were to chant the morning and afternoon services. If there was a *Bar Mitzvah*, the boy would chant one or other of the services. I did all the *Bar Mitzvah* training.

I didn't do anything rabbinic. Not really. When I came to *Beit Torah*, I mentioned to Rabbi Oppenheim that I also had this ordination. He said, 'Don't ever mention it.' He wanted strictly the role of a rabbi, and he wanted me to have strictly the role of cantor. I said, 'That's fine!' I didn't want to have anything to do with rabbinical duties. I didn't like the idea of sermonizing. It just wasn't for me. My main forte was singing. This was the agreement we made when I accepted the position. I was the only full-time cantor in Metropolis. It's very important that the rabbi and cantor work as a team. You bet! Although we each have our own positions, it's a co-ordination thing.

Beit Torah was always a Traditional synagogue. It couldn't be Orthodox because they had men and women sitting together. I accepted this, but my parents didn't like it, coming from an Orthodox background. At home I still keep *kosher*, I still lead a completely Orthodox life. You bet! I will not eat in restaurants; I never ride on the Sabbath; I am Sabbath observant. You bet! The congregation wanted that. I was at *Beit Torah* for twenty-two years. I always lived near the synagogue so as I could walk.

The congregation changed a lot. There's more English

readings. They allow women to ascend to the pulpit a lot more. The cantorial world has also definitely changed. There are a lot of women cantors now. There's one in the South Metropolis Reform synagogue, Shulamith Saloman (*The Reform Cantor*). She's my student. She's a lovely, lovely, very talented, very pretty young lady with a beautiful voice. She's not Orthodox, but she wanted to know the traditional liturgy, how it sounds. She was anxious to learn, and why not?

The main thing I want to bring out is that the role of cantor has changed. People do not appreciate the cantor as they did years ago. No. Because today it's a 'one, two, three' time schedule in a synagogue. The service must be done in a certain amount of time, and the attendance has fallen down. People don't understand the way it used to be. The old-timers used to come and appreciate the cantor. They loved the music. Today they really don't know what prayer means. They say it takes up too much time. They want to be out by 12 o'clock. They don't appreciate it.

After I retired, I had a liquor store. As they say, I went from a cantor to a decanter! During the year I still conduct weddings, funerals, and I do private tutoring for *Bar* or *Bat Mitzvah*. Then I sold the liquor store and now I help out the girls at the gift shop . . .

The Synagogue Lay Leader

MRS DAPHNE AMOS

Synagogues and temples are governed by an elected Board. Mrs Daphne Amos was the first woman President of Har HaShem synagogue, the largest Traditional synagogue on the East Side. She was a pretty woman in her forties whom we interviewed in her large modern house in South Metropolis.

I'm from Bangor, Maine. My father's parents were born in the United States, one in Maine and one in Massachusetts. There are their photographs. Originally the family came from Russia in about 1880. Bangor in the 1880s was a seat of Jewish learning. My family were in the cattle business and the clothing business. I grew up in an Orthodox synagogue. We kept a ***kosher*** home as I still do now and, growing up, we were Sabbath observant. I went to Hebrew school three times a week; we didn't have a day school. I went to Jewish summer camps every year and that was really important to me. The Orthodox didn't have *Bat Mitzvahs*, but we had a formal graduation with cap and gown from Hebrew school at the end of the eighth grade. There were eight of us in my class. It was a small community, but there was a *kosher* butcher. You could get Jewish *kosher* meat there which is more than you can get in Metropolis today!

I went to ordinary public school, and then I went to Syracuse to college. I wasn't allowed to go to the University of Maine because there weren't enough Jews there. I was never allowed to date anyone who wasn't Jewish, and I never really cared to: that was the parental commandment! Most of my best girlfriends were non-Jewish. I had gentile boyfriends, but I didn't date them. At college I studied Sociology. I was a seventeen-year-old, raw, small-town girl mixed in with a lot of outgoing New Yorkers. I came home from my freshman (first) year and my parents thought I had turned into an anti-Semite! The other students were louder and pushier while I was very quiet. But I joined a Jewish sorority and the girls there became my friends, and I dated boys from the Jewish fraternities. I was always real clear I was going to date Jewish people.

I graduated and I went to Boston and worked there for a year, and then I went to graduate school at Boston University. I have an MBA in Marketing and International Business. Then I went to work and met my husband. He was working for the same company – but in Houston. All the managers from all over the country came to Boston, and I was supposed to have a meeting with them to have them put my sales programme into their branches. My husband, who likes to think he is a real chauvinist – he really isn't – said, 'No woman's going to tell me how to run my business . . .' so I married him three months later! I moved to Houston, and we lived there for three years. Then we came to Metropolis in 1975 for his business. We have two daughters.

When we came here, I interviewed rabbis. It was my decision which synagogue we joined. I went to *Beit Torah* and then I went to *Har HaShem*. Rabbi Kornfeld (*The University Professor of Judaica*) really was the perfect rabbi for a new family in town because he said, 'This is what is going on. We have this activity, this activity, and this activity. We'd love to have you join. Why don't you come and try?' And we joined. We didn't really think of a Jewish day school for the girls. Maimonides was too religious and Golda Meir had just begun, so they went to Metropolis public schools and afternoon religious schools. They both had *Bat Mitzvahs*, and they were both confirmed, and they both went on the youth Israel trip.

After we joined *Har HaShem*, I decided they really weren't doing enough for young people, and was angry about what they weren't doing. I wrote a scathing letter to Rabbi Kornfeld. The average age of the congregation was probably sixty-five, and they just catered to the older people. I guess Rabbi Kornfeld read my letter to the Board, and the next thing I knew I was on the Family and Youth Committee. He's excellent at channelling people's energy in a constructive direction! Then I ended up chairing the Family and Youth Committee for years and years, which gave me a seat on the Board. It evolved. I came up through the ranks, and I was asked to be Secretary of the Board. My initial feeling was – oh, the token woman! You make her Secretary, and that's as far as it would get! Then after a short period of time, I got to be Vice-President and then was First Vice-President and next in line. I think most of the people accepted it. Some of the older members may have had a little trouble with it.

Was there any difference in being a woman President? I did not sit up on the *bimah* (dais) during services which the President normally does. I also did not go off to synagogue when it started at 9 o'clock! I felt what's fair is fair! I went up on the *bimah* only to do announcements every Sabbath. So the only real difference was not sitting on the *bimah* and on *Yom Kippur* (the Day of Atonement) not carrying the *Torah* scrolls around. It is mixed seating at *Har HaSham*. I didn't arrive early because after all I didn't count in the *minyan* (the quota of ten men necessary to hold a service). I could do an English reading from the *bimah*. Rabbi Kornfeld has little by little become a little more liberal in some ways, and women now do English readings. No, I don't mean a translation of the *Torah*. Something like a prayer for peace? You've got it! The *Bat Mitzvah* girls are allowed to read the *Haftarah* (prophetic reading) in Hebrew, but they don't do it on the Sabbath. I don't think they resent it. I think they're just as happy not to have to get up in front of the whole congregation on a Saturday morning!

I don't really know enough about it – if it would be a travesty for a woman to sit up on the *bimah*. Probably if the Ark were open. A woman can read from the *Torah* in a woman's *minyan*, but not to a mixed congregation. The woman is supposed to defer to the man! As the President, of course, I was certainly not deferring! But it didn't bother me if I were up there or not. It didn't make any difference.

When I was President of *Har HaShem* there were seven women Presidents of various synagogues in Metropolis over the period of my term. *Beit Torah* and *Adath Israel* both had women Presidents. They are both Traditional synagogues. Then Temple *Shalom* and the South Metropolis Reform Temple and two others in the state also had women. We had our own support group, though we never met! The Reform movement had done it before and the time was definitely right. At *Beit Torah* they had had a woman Vice-President earlier, but they wouldn't allow her to be President. I enjoyed being the first woman President. I was glad I did it. I spent a lot of time there. I really knew what was going on.

I think I governed by dictatorship. I'm not the kind of person who cares how people react. There were certain things I wanted to see done. Rabbi Kornfeld was willing to work with me, and there were a lot of things I got pushed through. I really had a lot of goals in mind for the youth and the family and young people, and I set out to accomplish those. I've always been involved with everything. I've been on the Boards of the Allied Federation and on the Anti-Defamation League. I was on the Synagogue Council; I was on the Board of the Traditional Synagogues' Joint Religion School – I chaired those for a number of years. There are a number of women who are very involved in the Jewish organizations. Sure. We all know each other. We've all worked together. It doesn't necessarily mean we're socially friendly . . .

Havurah Leaders

DON AND SARAH SAMUELSON

A havurah is a Jewish prayer and study group. The Samuelsons sat side by side on a large cream-coloured sofa. A handsome couple in their forties, they were surrounded by all the paraphernalia of a successful family life. There was a large piano covered with photographs of their four children, oriental rugs on the floor, books, a small collection of African sculpture, an open fireplace and antique furniture that was both comfortable and beautiful. They were the founders of the independent Ecclesiastes havurah.

Sarah: Our *havurah* consists of about thirty-five families. We have no rabbi, cantor, or officers. Although we don't own a synagogue building, we recently bought a residential house which has been converted for our needs. Our group began in an unusual way: it originated on top of a mountain in one of the frontier provinces of Pakistan.

Don: That's right. You see, when I was at law school at Yale, I met a Pakistani judge who was on sabbatical. We had many conversations – and I was fascinated by the stories he told which were drawn from the Muslim tradition. After hanging around so much that he would have to chase me away from his house, he said, 'Look Don, if you're really interested in these things, you should go to Pakistan to see my uncle who is an expert on Islam.' So that's what I did. I took a year off from law school and travelled to Pakistan. And then, several years later after I got married, I went back with Sarah to see him again.

Sarah: In the gap between the two visits, Don read Islamic literature and studied Muslim meditation.

Don: During this second visit I asked him how we could make this Muslim wisdom relevant to our own lives. After all, we were due to go back to live in the US. He told us that such traditions can only be transmitted orally. And he went on to say that, in his opinion, of all the cultures that have passed on such a religious heritage, there is only one that has used writing to transmit an oral tradition: in Judaism the *Talmud* is a written repository of oral spiritual truths.

Sarah: What he suggested was that Don and I start studying the *Talmud* with friends back in the States. So that's just what we did. When we got back home, we phoned some of our closest friends who we thought might be interested and we asked Rabbi Berkovski (*The Hasidic Rabbi*) for a bit of help. That was the genesis of our *havurah*, which we called Ecclesiastes.

Don: You're right to ask about my earlier disenchantment with institutionalized Judaism. I remember one *Yom Kippur* (Day of Atonement) – it was many years ago when I was living in my parents' house in Metropolis – they were founder members of Temple *Shalom*, but I walked from one synagogue to another trying to find a place where I felt comfortable. But I couldn't. Each service was so formal. There was no spiritual excitement anywhere. On another occasion I went to services at the Temple and I had the same sensation. When the rabbi gave his sermon it was so foreign to anything that felt religiously meaningful that I walked out. It was basically a political speech.

Sarah: Over the years Don and I have become increasingly observant. But it's always by taking little steps. We've glided into the tradition. We've never taken a leap.

Don: To some extent we've been led into Jewish observance by our children. One of the interesting things that has happened is that our children have witnessed our fascination with Judaism. This has made a big impression on them, and to our surprise and pleasure they've introduced us to a higher degree of practice.

Sarah: Let me give you an example. When our eldest child first started going to a Jewish camp, she came back knowing the entire *Birkhat ha-Mazon* (grace after meals). Previously we always said a little *Birkhat ha-Mazon*. But because she had learned it all, she could lead the whole thing.

Don: Another instance occurred when our daughter came back from six months in Israel where she kept strictly *kosher*. She set an example for all of us, and now bit by bit we've all reached her level.

Sarah: Similarly when our kids said they objected to eating meat that hadn't been *kosherly* slaughtered, we went along with them. The same applies to mixing milk with meat. In all this the kids have led us. We still don't have separate dishes though.

We're *kosher*-style. We don't eat milk and meat at the same meal, and we certainly don't eat foods like shrimp or ham. It's been a matter of gliding upwards as time passed. But we've glided at different rates. Just like when we go running together, Don is always a few steps ahead of me. As we've become more traditional, he's always a few paces in front.

Don: But in all this you've got to know about the Jewish heritage. For this reason I started buying books a long time ago. I was initially particularly interested in medieval ethics. To begin with, I used to buy one book a year. Then it got to be ten. Now there are hundreds I want to buy.

Sarah: You ask about the organization of Ecclesiastes. A co-ed *Talmud* group meets every Thursday noon. And on Friday morning a smaller group meets to talk about the *Torah* portion and holds a short service. Only men are involved in that.

Don: That service is really wonderful because it's done with all the set Psalms in the liturgy. We go through the entire service with traditional melodies as well. We even dance a bit.

Sarah: And then on Friday, we've decided to observe Friday night as a home celebration. Initially we held Friday night services, but we discovered that they disrupted the Sabbath atmosphere. It's paradoxical that there's nothing more disruptive to a real *Shabbat* than having to attend formal worship: we had to get our children ready and drive from all over the city.

Don: But on Saturday mornings we have regular services.

Sarah: We've only just started that. Previously we only held services twice a month since people were used to spending Saturdays on sport or doing errands or whatever. The idea of committing two *Shabbats* a month sounded enormous at first. Then eventually we took a big step, and made it three. Shortly afterwards we said, 'Hey, we want to do it all the time.'

Don: One principle of our group is that you can't transmit Jewishness to your children just by telling them to do something. The parents have to lead by example. The kids learn that this is what's actually done. The hope with all our children is that as they get older, they'll form their own Jewish homes.

Sarah: Something happened recently in this connection that makes me cry . . . . our eldest daughter just called us and told us that she's in love: she and the boy she's met are talking about marriage. She said that the first thing she wanted to do was to go to synagogue services.

Don: I'll give you another example: When we went skiing in December last year, we were on top of the mountain and our younger daughter said, 'I think we should say the New Season prayer before we do the first run.'

Sarah: It all takes time to establish a *havurah*. It takes time to build an organization; it takes time to visit members when they're sick; it takes time to organize the kids on Sunday morning. But I know it's all worthwhile. It's our small way of making the world a better place.

Don: You want to know about our parents' reaction to all this. Well, my family have always been members of Temple *Shalom*. They find our return to Traditional Judaism difficult to understand. At first my father told people that I had become interested in the philosophy of Judaism. But then, after he saw how we've incorporated Jewish observances into our lives, he realized we were serious. Judaism has become a way of life, and the people in Ecclesiastes are like our family. An astounding kind of intimacy takes place. This is partially because of the kind of talking and sharing that occurs. And it's also because we're doing things which the outside world sees as a little bit ridiculous . . .

The Reconstructionist Leader

MR PERRY WATERS

Reconstructionism is a relatively new movement within Judaism. It is traditional in observance but non-theistic in orientation. The Reconstructionists were between rabbis when we visited Metropolis. Instead we interviewed the President of the city's Reconstructionist Federation.

He was a partner in a downtown law firm. His office was in an elegant skyscraper and from his windows there was a wonderful view of the suburbs and surrounding countryside. The carpet was pale mauve. A Burberry raincoat hung on the back of the door and the abstract pictures toned perfectly with the colour scheme. Perry Waters sat at a large desk. He had brown eyes, a hooked nose, and greying curly hair. Among the many files on his desk were a bottle of Canada Dry seltzer and a massive tome entitled Bankruptcy Law Digest.

I was born in Denver, Colorado, and I moved to Metropolis after I was through with law school. I did not belong to a synagogue here though my sister, who also had moved, was a member of Temple *Shalom*. Prior to having kids, my wife and I looked round the various synagogues but didn't find any that met our needs. When we had our first child, like many people, we felt the need to affiliate, and we found the Reconstructionists to be a very warm and inviting environment. The Reconstructionist Federation was not entirely a rabbi-centred group, and it appeared to be very participatory. The other groups in town were more traditional. It was particularly the warmth of the community and their involvement that attracted us.

At that time, about nine years ago, there were about 130 family units involved. They did not have a building. The services were held at the Jewish Community Centre in their social hall. They did, however, sustain a full-time rabbi. At this point we have approximately 200 households divided into about sixteen *havurahs*. We have group events as well as High Holy Day services. We also have a religious school which has about sixty-five kids. That happens every Sunday plus there is a Wednesday programme for Hebrew school. Typically we have Friday night services once a month and one *havurah* organizes the programming. Last time we had about 150 people show up.

These *havurahs* range from four or five families up to, in some instances, fourteen and fifteen families. They meet in each other's homes. What do they do? They all do a variety of different things, from scholarly discussions to life-cycle events, to Sabbath dinners, to picnics. They choose their own programmes. Our *havurah* does a Sabbath dinner once a month at someone's house. This is my particular *havurah*. Others, it's up to them. With a new rabbi, things may become somewhat more formalized but I don't think there'll be Friday night services every Friday night. I don't think there's been an expression of interest for that. I think people tend to like to be with their families on Friday night.

The organization is a federation of *havurahs*. The Federation

Council meets once a month to discuss issues of mutual concern and the governance and operation of the organization. Then we have committees that function for the school, for High Holy Days, for facilities, for the budget, etc. So that's how the organization runs. We have a full-time secretary/administrator, a part-time book-keeper, and soon we'll have a rabbi again. We also have a part-time head of the religion school. I am President and I was elected by the Council.

People who want to join, first go to an orientation session, which is typically about three or four meetings conducted by our members, where you would get a general idea about what Reconstructionism is. We try to give people information about the various *havurahs*. What has often-times happened, and what happened with my *havurah*, is that members of the orientation group find they have some affinity for one another and form into their own *havurah*. They tell their story and some sort of synergism carries them on. Other times people visit existing *havurahs* and find something that they're looking for. After a time there's truly a commitment to people in your *havurah* and they become your extended family and have all the wonderful parts of family as well as the hard parts of family.

Observance is across the board. Some people are extraordinarily knowledgeable, and there are others who are less knowledgeable . . . I think there is an acceptance of all those. We all have the common desire to express our Judaism and to do it in a small community. There is a disagreement over how large this group should go. I don't know what the optimum number is. It is a wonderful community of people, and has a style of participation and deep commitment. A lot of the people are like me – not native to Metropolis. They were looking for an extended family that they have found. It is not only couples. We have single people, some gay individuals, all kinds . . . In my *havurah* we have done births and weddings and divorces and deaths . . . it's a way of making connections. There are many intermarried couples. I don't think we have any policy *per se*. Some of the non-Jewish spouses participate and some don't. Intermarriage is a fact of life and you have to deal with it.

If you're going to get into religious areas I may not be able to comment. I think in the orientation group, a book is mentioned that quotes quite a lot of the Reconstructionist teaching. I don't think I can adequately comment on people's beliefs. I know in Metropolis there is no homogeneity – which I think is typical of Judaism. It's the old saying, 'If you get three Jews together, you get five opinions.' It's a very democratic organization and oftentimes the process and the democracy involved is more important than what the outcome of a decision is . . .

Gay Congregation Leaders

TIM AND GERALD

Tim and Gerald sat together on the sofa. They were both of medium height with beards.

Tim: I was born in Brooklyn. I took a two-year degree in Hotel and Restaurant Management at the New York Community College. Then I came to the University of Metropolis, and after a year I transferred to Business Education. When I graduated, I was hired by the Federal Correctional Institution to teach a business programme. I was there for eighteen years. I retired in 1986 because of my blindness. I have an eye disease. At that point, I wasn't willing to sit home and watch TV, and that's when I decided to design and market memorials – and that's why I'm called Tombstone Tim.

Gerald: I also was born in Brooklyn. I taught math in Connecticut at a liberal arts college. I'd done it for ten years, and I was tired. I had a friend who was living in Metropolis, and I came in 1977 to visit him. I fell in love with the city, and the following year I moved here. I found a job in computer programming. And that's what I do. One of the first things I saw when I came here was a notice in the gay newspaper that a Jewish gay congregation was meeting. I attended, and that's where we met and I got involved.

Tim: Initially it was a social group rather than a congregation. We did Jewish things. We ate – which is a very Jewish thing! We had the best brunches in town! I'm telling you! Immediately when the group was formed, we couldn't believe it, it was like the closet's just opened! We jumped – wham – into sixty, sixty-five members!

Gerald: It went up and it went down.

Tim: You bet! When you try to be everything to everybody it doesn't work, as we found out. But we didn't know how to change it either. There were four separate, distinct groups. There were the Metropolis natives who did not need our religious activities – they attended their own congregations with their families. Then you had the group who wanted some religious activity because they didn't feel comfortable mainstreaming in congregations. Then you had the group such as Gerald and I who did not need the gay congregation – I was already very, very active in a Temple. And then there was the problem of the women. We had initially a large group of women, but no matter what we did, most of them did not want to be around men. As a result, with just a few exceptions, they left even though we made sure that the services were non-sexist. We bent over backwards . . . it was indeed a great hurt.

Gerald: Basically it was the women's movement. They'd had enough of men in their everyday life.

Tim: Instead of sharing the commonality, they broke the diversity into additional diversity. It was very, very disappointing. We're talking about the early 1980s now. I was President of the group for about eight years. All I can say is – at least I held it together. We did not disband, and I give myself a lot of credit for that. Attendance was fairly low. Ten?

Gerald: Yeah, ten or fifteen.

Tim: After I resigned as President, things picked up. Why? Well, I'm me. I'm very much 'What you see is what you get', and some people don't like me. I think it was a matter of being such a small group, and I put so much effort into it, it was looked upon as 'Tim's group'. When I was in the process of stepping down, the membership went up because of new blood and new activities.

Gerald: Membership is now getting up to sixty. And we have more women now again. There was a need for cultural identity. I mean, coming from the East there's Judaism all around you. Here it's really not. You have to make an active attempt to be part of the Jewish community. The group allowed me to do that.

Tim: There are a lot of gay Jews out there who don't belong. They know we're here, but the Metropolis gay community is extremely cliquish. For myself, I'm very active in the Jewish community, but apart from the group, I'm not active at all in the gay community. In retrospect it was a mistake to become a congregation. We were a very successful social group, but as a congregation we had problems. When we initially became a congregation, we held Sabbath services once a month in different people's homes. We wrote our own prayerbook.

Gerald: It was based on the prayerbooks of other gay congregations.

Tim: Then we rented space at a church and held services twice a month. The problem was it was such a limited group and severe burnout set in. Then it really got to be difficult, and we couldn't afford the rent. People didn't understand that a Temple is a business. I did a lot of personal funding for the group – a lot of money – but that's the way it is. Now we have High Holy Day services, a Passover meal, *Hanukkah* . . . That's why I no longer feel comfortable referring to it as a congregation. You can't have a congregation without Sabbath services. Then there are other problems . . .

Gerald: Metropolis is not an open society. There are a lot of conservative elements. It is not easy to be an open gay person.

Tim: When we decided to be a gay congregation, I was well-known in the Jewish community. I'd been on the Board of almost every Jewish institution through the years. Individuals knew I was gay, but it wasn't generally known. When we decided to be a congregation, I just came out of the closet all over town. Some response was negative; some positive. In my own Temple for example, they were very accepting.

Gerald: At that time the Reform movement was coming to terms with homosexuality, and that made a difference. I'd been a member of the Reconstructionists since 1984, and they also were very accepting. Now they even allow gays to be rabbis.

Tim: So does the Reform movement. The rabbi of Temple *Shalom* has been the most active supporter of the gay congregations. To give credit where credit is due, he has been very supportive. Then I deal with a lot of Traditional rabbis. In fairness to Rabbi Kornfeld (*The University Professor of Judaica*), he has put up with me. But all the Traditional congregations look at us as if we have illnesses. I mean Rabbi Oppenheim

(*The Traditional Rabbi*) and I have a very strong mutual respect. On my job he is very helpful. He has been honoured several times, and I always attend the dinners, but officially he cannot change his attitude. And this is a very big hurt. We respect each other so much, but he knows I won't change, and I know he won't change because of the Orthodox position, the *Torah* and so on.

Gerald: The official position is that we're supposed to abstain from sexual activity.

Tim: What do I expect from them? Five years ago I would have said, 'You change your attitude!' Today I understand it's not going to happen.

Gerald: We have had a problem with the *Metropolis Jewish News*.

Tim: Yeah. It went like this: in 1985 Tim comes out all over town. I'm sitting on Leah Silver's back porch one evening, and I came out because I wanted our congregation listed. We were just like any other new congregation and right at the beginning we did have a few listings. Then we were dropped. They argued it was a privately owned newspaper, and they could decide what would be put in it.

Gerald: Shimon Silver (*Editor of the Jewish Newspaper*) held the Traditional line. You know, Leviticus . . .

Tim: It came to a head in 1986/87. I was Vice-President of the Synagogue Council. Yeah, with Ben Samuel (*The Director of the Synagogue Council*). We had our annual Rabbis' and Presidents' Meeting, and the issue of the *Metropolis Jewish News* and the gay congregation came up. I was advised to leave the room because like many gay people, I sometimes get very emotional. It's better that I went. I understand it was not a pretty picture. But do you know, the issue died?

Gerald: They did sometimes list the activities, but they refused to say we are lesbian and gay.

Tim: All we ask from the Traditional rabbis is that if a congregant comes to them and is in need of our services, at least let them know we exist.

Gerald: The Reform Temples have fliers on their boards. Yael Fox (*The Woman Rabbi*) even did a wonderful High Holy Day sermon.

Tim: Her husband's very first sermon to his congregation was on the issue. That took guts as well as other parts of the anatomy! He got some good out of it, and some negative. I know that in all the mainstream congregations there are many, many gays, and many of them won't have anything to do with us. It's sad . . . but I have to tell you that it was not in my best interest to come out all over town. I feel it has hurt me business-wise. There are a lot of people who look down upon me now that didn't when they didn't know.

Gerald: There are also a lot of people who respect you for it. I think overall as a human being you have benefited from coming out. If you had stayed in the closet you wouldn't have had your self-respect . . .

The Reform Cantor

CANTOR SHULAMITH SALOMAN

A beautiful small-boned woman in her thirties, Cantor Shulamith Saloman spoke rapidly and with great animation.

I'm from Chicago. I was raised in a traditional family. My great-grandfather was a *Hasidic rebbe* in the Pale of Settlement. His eldest son, my grandfather, was sent as apprentice to a tailor. He received no Jewish education and was embittered by it. At age fifteen he came to America, and he decided to be an American. My grandmother was the daughter of a samovar cleaner and also had no education as a Jew. My grandfather sold newspapers on the corner of the street in Chicago for fifty years, but he was a bookie on the side and he wrote Yiddish poetry.

My father was raised very strongly Jewish culturally, and spoke Yiddish at home, but the family didn't know much about the religion. My mother and her brother were raised in an Orthodox family; the brother received the best possible education, but my mother received nothing whatsoever. So when my father and mother got together they were negative about the whole Jewish experience. My father was an entrepreneur in business in Chicago. They were going to raise their children just to be free and to be ethically and culturally Jewish, but not to be restricted by all the tenets of Judaism. We lived next door to an Italian family, and one day my sister came home and said, 'Mommy, Jesus loves me! Maria from next door told me so.' And my mother said, 'He may love Maria, but he doesn't like you at all!' The next day we were enrolled in the synagogue religion school!

We belonged to a Conservative Reconstructionist synagogue, and I was *Bat Mitzvah* there. I dropped out after that, but I went to Jewish summer camp which I loved. I never dated non-Jewish boys. That was my own decision, though my parents were very strict about it. My brother brought home a non-Jewish girl once, and my mother wouldn't even speak to her, though in the end he married an Episcopalian girl who converted to Judaism. My parents were always very clear that they wanted me to have a career, but I was expected to get married as well. I knew I was eventually going to do something with music, and my mother thought the ideal would be for me to teach piano while my baby napped in the next room!

After I graduated from high school, I received a scholarship to study piano at the Conservatoire in Chicago. I was very unhappy. I was living at home and everyone had left, and I didn't have friends. So after a year I went to Indiana University, and then after a year I realized I didn't want to be a pianist. I loved playing, but I didn't like performing. By then it was the end of my sophomore (second) year and too late to switch instruments. So I took on psychology as another major besides music; I thought maybe I would go into music therapy, but one summer I did an internship with mentally retarded children and realized it wasn't for me. One has to come to terms with what one is best at . . .

Then at some point I took a pivotal course. It was an honours class in anthropology, and it was taught by a woman who had been a dancer and had been dropped by a partner on her back and couldn't dance. She went on to study the anthropology of dance. This class was so fascinating. So then I had this new idea to go on and study ethno-musicology and Jewish music and what really interested me. Then the University chaplaincy asked me to sing the High Holy Day Services. I had never even thought of being a cantor. I said, 'How can I possibly do that?' and they said, 'We'll teach you all you need to know.' So I was taught by a gentleman who found it hard to teach a woman. Those were early years before there were women cantors. Actually I'd been singing in a synagogue choir for many years, and I had learnt more at summer camp so I knew quite a lot of the services.

I finished college with my Piano and Psychology degree and I applied to the Jewish Theological Seminary in New York to do a Doctorate in Ethno-Musicology. But the programme was cancelled and I had already met my first husband who was doing a doctorate in Boston. So I went to Boston, got married, and I found a position as a cantor in a Reform Temple. At that time I really wasn't connected to the liturgy of Reform congregations, and the few times I'd been in Reform Temples, I'd been significantly unimpressed with the choir and the music – it seemed to be either Protestant hymns or camp songs. Anyway I was with the congregation for five or six years, and I was very unhappy. I stuck it out because my husband was in graduate school. Then I went back to school and got a Masters degree in voice and had a wonderful time. I didn't like the congregation because it was so *goyish* (gentile). We didn't have a loving relationship.

Then my husband accepted a position at the State University here, and we went to live in a small town fifty miles outside Metropolis. We had our first child. It was such an unpleasant community. They were bitter and divisive, crotchety and complaining. Right away I was singing at services in Summertown, a neighbouring community, and I did that for four or five years. Then the rabbi at the South Metropolis Temple heard about me. He invited me to sing in Metropolis, and I loved the Temple. I started off part-time, and now I sing there every week. I have lessons with Cantor Sheer (*The Traditional Cantor*). He's a cantor's cantor, and he's the only one in the whole state who has music in his blood. He has such a love of it.

My job at the Temple is now part-time/full-time. There's about a hundred women cantors in the country now, but it has not been the tradition. I've been so blessed. The Temple was a most saving part of my life. My husband walked out, and I was left alone with two babies. The rabbi and the congregation were like a family. I was being taken out to lunch by people I didn't know from the congregation; they were inviting me to their home with the kids to try to tell me how much I meant to them so that I wouldn't leave. I felt so loved and so much a part of this community. And the rabbi was like a father to me.

I was fixed up with dates by everybody, everybody. My new husband is director of the urban renewal project downtown. He's also from Chicago, and we were introduced by his brother who works for the *Metropolis Times.* He came out from Chicago, and within weeks we had met. It took me a long time to get engaged! He comes from an assimilated family, and he was looking for some form of spirituality. Of the six children in his family, five have married non-Jews. His brother's wife, my new sister-in-law, is training to be an Episcopalian priest. I love her and we are so similar in our approach to religion and, as a woman in the priesthood, she suffers the same kinds of things I do. People come up to her and comment on her appearance, and tell her she's looking thin. They don't do that to male ministers!

Are my mom and dad proud of me? Well it's certainly different from teaching piano while the baby naps, but I think they're very proud. It is bittersweet. They'd be a lot prouder if it was in Chicago! I love Metropolis, but we're not ruling out Chicago. Put that in your book for my parents' sake!

The Temple Lay Leader

MR MERV ISENBERG

Synagogues and temples are governed by Boards of Trustees elected by the membership. A small, slim man in his seventies, Merv Isenberg sat in an upright chair in his immaculate sitting room. It was 90 degrees outside, but the room was cool with air conditioning. There were fragile glass ornaments on the coffee-tables, and oil paintings of French street scenes on the dove-grey walls.

I'm a Metropolis native. In the old days, our father didn't bother much about Temple. After World War One, our mother got quite ill with rheumatoid arthritis. She couldn't hold anything or do anything, and for seven years she lay in the Presbyterian Hospital. I don't know. I guess that turned everybody off. Then when Esther and I got married, we wanted our daughter to learn about Judaism, so we joined Temple *Shalom.*

In those days the Temple was in another building downtown. There were many things going on, but our Temple Brotherhood was nothing. A few of us got together and decided we were going to make it an active Brotherhood. Which we did. We involved people. We got a great many activities going along with our Jewish educational programmes. I was very much involved in the building of our children's summer camp up in Iowa Hills because I was in the construction business. I guess I was outspoken in what our needs were, and when we decided to erect our present Temple building, I worked on that and had many arguments.

You see we had an architect from New York. A very renowned architect, and I complained about certain things. He didn't take into account our climate. He wanted dead level roofs where everything accumulates and evaporates. Then he had drainage into the interior of the building through piping. I said, 'Here it won't work very well. In the East where it's damp and all, and the roofing felt doesn't wear out, that's good. Here we must consider something different.' Well, the members of the committee said that this man was renowned; he was a fine architect. Fortunately I persuaded the Board to purchase a twenty-year bond so the roof would be taken care of. Thank God!

I was on the Temple Building Committee for many years. I was also on the Membership Committee. I set up the ushering, but the Building Committee was the big thing. After leaving the old building, we only erected a portion of our present structure, and then after we accumulated additional funds we erected the sanctuary. Fortunately for us, and unfortunately for him, one of the older members passed away, and we received a bequest of $13,000 which was a lot of money in those days. We needed landscaping round the sanctuary and a parking lot, a drainage system, a sprinkler system, outside lighting, additional walkways, many things. The Board wanted me to get it all paid for with the bequest. Which I did. I returned with $1,800 left over. After that our President of the time said, 'Merv, you're going to take care of things in the future.'

I've served on the Building Committee forever. I'm still on it. At the present time we're installing a new roof on the sanctuary. There was water penetration in the old roof which ended up with our Legal Committee notifying the architect – 'Rectify it or we will sue you!' That was a first for our congregation, a notification of an intention to sue. But that's the way it goes. In our business when you drive the first nail, you start repairing so there's always something to do. Always.

I became a Life Trustee because of my many many activities, the things I've done and the funds I contributed. But basically it isn't the dollar item. It's what you do that counts. For example, I wrote the rules and regulations for people using the building. Then I set up rules for the Ushering Committee, and on the pulpit. Such as: you shouldn't cross your legs when you're sitting on the pulpit. And there's a dress code for everyone involved in the service. Everyone was advised of this prior to their going up to the pulpit. It's gradually broken down over the past twenty years, but they're still not up there in jeans and a sweatshirt!

There's been a lot of change particularly since Rabbi Reinhardt (*The Reform Rabbi*) came. The last rabbi, Rabbi Green, was a very close friend. I was pall-bearer at his funeral. In the past we followed a pattern in the services. Decorum was the thing. We were truly reformed. Now there's more Hebrew; wearing a skull cap and prayer shawl has become more and more apparent. I don't particularly regret the change. I do object to a young man playing the guitar in services. To me this is street-corner religion – like the Salvation Army. In general my personal feeling is as long as people retain their identities as Jews, it's all right by me . . .

Leaders of Humanistic Judaism

JAY AND EDIE PARKIN

Humanistic Jews maintain their Jewish identity while rejecting belief in the existence of God.

We spoke to Jay and Edie Parkin in their family room. It was

a comfortable place with a rustic feel. There were needlepoint cushions and pictures, an old-fashioned typewriter was placed on a desk, a full set of the Encyclopaedia Britannica *was displayed beside the open fireplace, and an American flag was stuck into a vase of pussy-willow. The Parkins were in their early fifties. She was bespectacled with brown curly hair, and he sat beside her, bronzed and relaxed. Among the many pictures was a sepia photograph of Jay's grandfather, dressed for his Bar Mitzvah in knickerbockers and a prayer shawl.*

Edie: I was born in Metropolis, as were both my parents, and had a very Reform liberal upbringing. I would probably classify my father as a non-theist. He was dragged to Temple *Shalom* by my mother, where I was confirmed. I don't remember ever having a Sabbath at home. I remember not having a good time at Temple. The biggest topic of discussion with me and my friends was how to ditch services and go over to a local café for lunch! We did that every Saturday! Confirmation had to be gone through. I don't think I thought much about religion – it was just rote. I remember I had a cousin who said she didn't believe in God, and I remember my mother being outraged. She said that this child was disturbed, but maybe when she grew up, she would grow out of it. Little did she know that her own child would grow into it!

After high school I went to Texas University for a year and decided to major in Psychology. I met Jay the year before I went to Texas so the whole year at Texas I spent writing letters to Jay. We met at Windy Oak Country Club. I saw him from across the pool. The lights went on. The sparks started to fly. It was love at first sight for both of us.

Jay: I saw her across the pool. She had curlers in her hair! I was twenty, and she was seventeen!

Edie: So after a year in Texas, I transferred to the University of Metropolis . . .

Jay: To be with me . . .

Edie: And to study psychology. We got married right after his graduation. I quit school as you were supposed to after the wedding. I was twenty. We had so much fun.

Jay: I was brought up Conservative in Brooklyn, New York.

My dad went to services with me and my grandfather. I remember sitting through *Yom Kippur* services dreading it because it seemed like it took forever. I went to Hebrew school and was *Bar Mitzvahed*, but never got into the heart of Jewishness. I was proud of being Jewish and all that, but I never got into it as far as a belief in a God. I do remember as a younger child having this Jewish star round my neck. Every night – and I remember this vividly – I would recite the *Shema* (a prayer) and ask for whatever I wanted and kiss the little star. That was very strong for a while.

Edie: We got married, and the three babies came as soon as they could. We joined the Reform Temple in South Metropolis for the kids. There was a lot of glitz and show at Temple *Shalom*. The display that went on there with the jewellery and the clothing! It was like a fashion show. It was a younger thing to do to join the other Reform Temple. When the children were little, we had no home celebrations. On Friday nights we let them have pop for dinner instead of milk! So there was something there! Then in the 1970s we pulled them out of Temple.

Jay: We weren't there very long.

Edie: You see, I had gone back to school. When my youngest started school, I got a part-time job and went back to school to finish my degree. For ten years, I took one or two courses a year, and I studied psychology and philosophy. I was looking for the truth – the absolute total answer. The One Truth. My first class was Philosophy of Religion. I remember driving back home from class, and I realized there was no proof for the existence of God. I was absolutely overwhelmed by that and terribly excited. It was like being set free from something. I was giddy with it. All those questions: if God was omnipotent and omniscient, how could the Holocaust happen? Then I felt anger, and that was the beginning of my atheism. Since you can't know anything, I suppose I have to call myself an agnostic. So my philosophy class completely changed me. I went to see the rabbi at Temple, and I said, 'We're out of here.'

Jay: I wasn't the searcher she was. Belief for me was no big deal, but I never had a real strong feeling of God. I wasn't bothered about taking the kids out of Temple.

Edie: I didn't want to say that I didn't believe in services. So I went to see the rabbi and said, 'There is no God.' And he said, 'The expression "The God of Abraham, Isaac, and Jacob" meant that they each kind of believed in their own special God.'

I didn't know how to respond to that. I was shaking in my boots. He said – and this was the hard part – 'How about the children's heritage? You're denying them their birthright.' So I went through many, many years of guilt, but I truly believed in what I was doing. How could you be a non-theist and be Jewish? There was a contradiction there.

Jay: So we tried the Reconstructionists.

Edie: No – we went to the Unitarians first. We went there for three Sundays, but it just didn't fit. What they said was okay, but I just felt I didn't belong.

Jay: It really wasn't comfortable.

Edie: Then I thought that the philosophy of humanism means you shouldn't belong to a little group. You belong to the world. We're all humans. I really believed that, but no one else in the world felt that way. I felt I was giving up something to be this universalist – and I was totally alone. Well that didn't feel too great!

Jay: Then we went to the Reconstructionists!

Edie: And that seemed to be it! They said that God is the human being's ability to actualize himself and become all that it is possible to become. That was the Reconstructionist definition of God.

Jay: At that time, it felt very comfortable . . .

Edie: Then we started going to Reconstructionist study groups – and boy were they observant! They said all the traditional prayers. I kept asking the rabbi why we kept using this God-talk if it didn't refer to God. I felt I was doing mental gymnastics all the time. In services, every time we got to the word 'God', I kept saying, 'My ability to actualize myself and become all that it is possible to become' . . . and it didn't fit! I kept saying this to the rabbi and he got annoyed. So after a bit we quit going and then we dropped out.

Jay: So we started putting together our own services for Passover and *Hanukkah* . . . just for the immediate family.

Edie: I called the Humanistic Jews' headquarters, and I got their prayerbook, and I was doing mini-versions of their services. We would have our friends over to Passover and whenever we got to a certain point they would say, 'This isn't right!'

Jay: They would ridicule us and make jokes.

Edie: We had a beautiful liturgy, but they would demand the traditional service about killing first-born babies. Humanists don't kill babies! I would get so mad.

Jay: We're vegetarians and our friends would say they were going over to the Parkins for a meatless, godless Passover!

Edie: Yet we knew they didn't themselves believe in an all-powerful, all-loving God. I would feel really confused about it all. We were so on our own. Then in 1991, I got a phone call from someone who was trying to get a humanistic group formed and it worked out. Right now we are a bona fide affiliated group accepted by the national body, with ten households. We've had two Passovers without our friends for the first time in years and years and we have it with our humanistic group instead. It's wonderful.

Jay: It's fabulous.

Edie: You're with like-minded people.

Jay: They've all had the same battles and frustrations and it was like everyone found a home finally.

Four

COMMUNITY LEADERS

The President of the Allied Jewish Federation

MRS LAURIE PAINE

The Allied Jewish Federation is the umbrella organization that administers and raises funds for all the Jewish charities. Laurie Paine lived in a luxurious house on a modern development. The upholstery was leather, and we were surrounded by paintings and lithographs on Jewish subjects. Laurie Paine was a pretty, petite woman in her mid-forties. Her curly hair was beautifully cut; her toes and fingernails were painted exactly to match; her skin was sun-tanned; and she wore a large marquise diamond ring.

I grew up in this city and am a fourth-generation Metropolis native. I am the middle of three sisters. My great-uncle was the first rabbi of *Har HaShem* synagogue – so, yes, I'm related to Marion Schwartz's (*The Museum Curator*) husband. We grew up in the synagogue, but my mother was sick for a long period and going to Hebrew school became a big burden to my father. So we ended up moving from *Har HaShem* to Temple *Shalom*. I was confirmed there, but I had a weak Jewish background. I had a very strong Jewish identity always, but my knowledge was weak. I did not have Jewish girlfriends growing up. I did have Jewish boyfriends – in fact I was the official Sweetheart of a Jewish fraternity!

I only started to have good Jewish girlfriends when I went to college at the State University. Before that I didn't really like Jewish girls very much. I thought many of them were snobbish. My family didn't belong to Windy Oak Country Club. It was out of our price range, and I felt if you weren't part of that set, you were excluded. I didn't hate them, but I can't say I was comfortable with them. At college, I studied education. I am not a college graduate. We literally ran out of money so I thought I would work and then go back. So I went to work for a brokerage firm in the back office. I didn't leave for twenty-one years. I worked my way up to Chief Cashier – then I got my stockbroker's license, and I eventually became a partner. I sold out my business and retired five years ago.

I've been married twice. I first married at twenty and was married seventeen years. And then I've been married to my second husband six and a half years. When I was first married, we joined *Beit Torah* synagogue – my husband came from an observant family. They used to have Sabbath dinner, and I loved that. That was my first really positive Jewish religious experience. Then in 1973 I took a course on the Holocaust, and it was cathartic for me. I came home and I said, 'I want to go to Israel.' So in 1975 we went to Israel, and we had an unbelievable time. It was when the United Nations voted that all Zionism was racism. That really was my Jewish awakening. I think I've gone back to Israel every single year since that first trip.

After studying the Holocaust and going to Israel, I felt very responsible for my fellow Jews. I felt like that was my role. I'm a real activist, and I absolutely fell in love with the country. I didn't want to leave. I came back, and my present husband – who I knew very slightly in those days – was the President of the Allied Federation. I went in and said, 'Do you have a business and professional women's group?' And he said they had a women's group with luncheons during the day. That was no good for me. I worked during the day, so I started a very successful professional women's group, and later I began groups all round the country to raise money for Israel. Then I and another woman started a group called 'Women of Distinction', and this was for the top hundred entrepreneurial Jewish women in the country. We spent five years researching these women, and we went to them and said, 'We want you to be part of this group to raise money for Israel.' Many of them make big money, and you would think they would give large sums away, but it's been a struggle to get them to Israel, and a struggle to get them to give. It's been a very eye-opening experience.

Being a top leader was sort of an accident. I have been involved with the Federation for twenty years now. My husband has been everything in this community. He's quite a bit older than me. He is the Life President of the Federation, and he was the National Chairman of the United Jewish Appeal raising money for Israel, and he was Head of the Jewish Community Centre twelve years ago. He's Head of the Jewish Community Centre now again because they are doing a major renovation. Have you met Joanna Miller (*The Director of the Jewish Community Centre*)? She's dynamite! Both my husband and I really love the Jewish community and we really care what happens here.

The Federation is the umbrella organization in the Jewish community. Its purpose is to fundraise for Israel and to take care of Jews in distressed lands outside Israel. Then we have ninety different groups that we give to locally such as Rendez-Vous Singles, the Jewish day schools, the Hebrew Old Age Home, the Jewish Community Centre, the Jewish Family Service, and the Anti-Defamation League. Our primary focus is to raise money. The best way to do this is face-to-face: we have a lot of events; we have doctors' divisions and attorneys' divisions; we have a business and industry section.

Compared with other communities, we do not have the big givers. We have to do it much more broad-based. A lot of our big givers have died or moved away. At one time 70 per cent of our campaign was the bigger givers – now it's less than 50 per cent. We have 6,000 contributors. I've been Campaign Chairman for the past two years, and I worked at it full-time. It's much harder work than being in brokerage. I saw a hundred prospects a year. We have a $1 million overhead, and the irony is our professionals are organizers while our fundraisers are volunteers. Our biggest campaign raised $8 million; then we went through a terrible recession here, and last year we raised $5.3 million, and this year we're down to $5.2 million. With 6,000 contributors we have a bare-bone staff. We can't get our overheads down. You just can't get a Chief Executive who's any good at under $100,000.

We're completely non-denominational. We help all Jewish institutions across the board. So we give to Rabbi Reinhardt's

(*The Reform Rabbi*) programme 'Every Day, the Jewish Way' which works with the children of the intermarried. The Orthodox were very unhappy that we did that, but we also give to the Maimonides Day School and to Rabbi Berkovski's (*The Hasidic Rabbi*) Outreach programme. Isn't he terrific? There's very little money on the West Side outside Bernard Black's (*The Community Patriarch*) hands, and they only really support their own institutions.

I'll be the President for two years. Being Chairman of Fundraising is actually a much harder job. I work with all the agencies, both local and national, and try to deal with all the problems that arise such as difficulties with *kashrut*. *Kashrut* is a mess here. The West Side won't accept Rabbi Berkovski's certification – his philosophy is not their philosophy. None of the Orthodox are on the Rabbinical Council. Rabbi Oppenheim (*The Traditional Rabbi*) and Rabbi Kornfeld (*The University Professor of Judaica*) are on, but they're modern Orthodox. We have a lot of work to do on unity in this community. The West Side and the East Side are very polarized and *kashrut* is one of the focuses of the division.

The Federation works very hard to do the right thing, but we are terribly criticized. We really are. When anything goes wrong it's the Federation's fault. We're told we don't fund enough. Sometimes I speak to groups, and I feel I should have worn a helmet! I do get discouraged sometimes. But what you don't see is the real sense of an extended family. Through the negatives, there are lots and lots of positives. We do a lot of really wonderful things here, and there are real wonderful, loving, interesting Jewish people in the community. There really are . . .

The Director of the Jewish Family Service

DR BRAD MUSSMAN

The Jewish Family Service provides counselling and material help to families and individuals. Dr Mussman saw us in their offices on State Street. In the reception area was a letter signed by President George Bush, awarding a 'thousand points of light' medal for the agency's work. Dr Mussman himself was an alert, bearded man of about forty.

I was raised in New York City, in Queens, in the Conservative tradition. I went to religion school and was *Bar Mitzvah*. That was really my background. After high school I went to the State University of New York at Buffalo. I had a scholarship, and I majored in Sociology. Why did I choose that? Gosh, I don't know. Why does anyone choose anything? After I graduated, I got my Masters degree in Social Work. I did my internship in the children's mental hygiene clinics in the Baltimore Department of Public Health. Then I took a job doing juvenile court order evaluations. That lasted a couple of years, and then I returned to school to do a Doctorate in Human Development and meanwhile worked as a family therapist. Once I got my doctorate, I took a job in Ohio as the Associate Director for the Family Service Association of Cincinnati. I became an administrator.

I was already married and had children by this stage. Anyway, we decided to move back East so I became the Executive Director of the Jewish Family Service in Hartford, Connecticut. At that point I began to realize that everything I was doing in my job bore no relation to my social work training, and that's when I got an MBA. I needed to know about strategic planning, marketing, double-entry accounts – all of that! It was very helpful. I did it part-time, two nights a week for what felt like thirty years but was really three. It then became clear that Hartford was too small a community.

The Metropolis position came open in 1989. So I applied for the job and they hired me. Actually I must tell you I will be leaving this community in December to become the Director of the Chicago Jewish Family Service. My people here don't know that yet, so please keep it quiet. We're just finishing up negotiating the contract. It's a much bigger community; the agency's much larger and, I guess what's important to me, it's a much more cohesive community.

We belong to Temple *Shalom*. We liked the fact that Rabbi Reinhardt (*The Reform Rabbi*) was interested in social action and was prepared to be controversial. Yeah! His wife has worked with the Family Service for years. When I came, the Service had decent programmes and an annual budget of about $2 million, but it had no systems. It had grown like topsy. There was no internal organization; no management information system, and no financial systems. It was just a hotch-potch. So what I did the first couple of years was put all that stuff in place. Then we began to look at productivity. The staff began to appreciate that by doing that, I could get them more money. We may be the Jewish Family Service, but we're non-sectarian. We serve anybody. So I got federal money, city grants and foundation money, and I could give the staff raises every year.

Right now there are about seventy-five staff and about a thousand volunteers. Our mission is to meet all of the social service needs of the Jewish community. Remember, we provide the same services as many other agencies, but Jews need an agency to call their own. The community's not big enough to offer these services exclusively to Jews. For example, our sheltered workshop. You couldn't economically run a sheltered workshop for twenty Jews, but you can for a hundred people – so twenty people are Jewish and eighty are non-Jewish. It means that if you as a Jewish couple have a disabled kid, there's somewhere where that kid can go which understands his particular needs. We also offer a particularly Jewish angle. If you come in and say you are thinking of getting a divorce and need counselling, we will explain the procedure for getting a Jewish *get* (certificate of divorce). You may say you don't care about a *get*, but at least you will have had the opportunity to find out about it and can discuss the implications of your decision.

Infertility tends to be higher in the Jewish community than the non-Jewish community. Let me give you two statistics. Nationally Jews make up about 1 per cent of the US population, but 3 per cent of adoptive homes are Jewish. The second one, which is astounding, 13 per cent of the Jewish couples who are planning on having children in the next three years are going to have to adopt because they're infertile. Why? Because they wait too long to have kids. You're less fertile in your thirties than twenties. If we're seriously concerned about Jewish continuity, without kids there will be no Jewish community in the future. So our adoption agency is very important. Almost all our birth mothers are not Jewish. Why? I don't know. I suppose Jewish women tend to be better educated about contraception and abortion.

The community is more willing to face up to sexual abuse than they were ten years ago. We have a counselling programme here. Two-thirds of the Jewish families who come to us for counselling have experienced some form of child abuse, sexual abuse or domestic violence. We helped initiate the community's domestic violence task force, and we run an information 'warmline' – not hotline – a warmline about family abuse.

Our job is to give people choices. Obviously the opinion of say Rabbi Reinhardt (*The Reform Rabbi*) is very different from Rabbi Marmorstein (*The Orthodox Rabbi*) on many social issues. If a girl comes in and tells us she's pregnant, we present her with the alternatives. She can raise the child; she can put it up for adoption; or she can have an abortion, and we explain the implications of each choice. It's not our job to say, 'As a good Jewish girl you should . . .' The rabbi can say, 'You should . . .' Her mother can say, 'You should . . .' That is not for us to say. Our job is to lay out the choices.

The Allied Jewish Federation's function is to be the umbrella for the entire community. Our job, to take a sociological perspective, is to do the things families used to do, but don't do any more. We get about $300,000 of our budget – about 10 per cent – from the Federation. The rest comes from other agencies, fees for services, and our fundraisers. People on our Board are perhaps more interested in directly helping people than those who are on the Board of the Federation. Often people get involved in our Board as a stepping-stone to being a big *macher* (important person) on the Federation or in the community generally. Our Board is not as prestigious as being on the Board of the Federation. One of the reasons I want to move to Chicago is there's a different level of Board involvement: they're much more high-powered people, if you will; they're clearer that their role is governance and not running the organization; and it's a much stronger Jewish community. Chicago's community is perhaps twice as big as Metropolis', but they raise more than four times as much for their Federation. It's a less fragmented community.

How much do we charge for our service? It's all on a sliding scale. For those who can afford it, there's a set fee. For those who can't, there's almost no fee. It's all income related. Nobody is denied any service because of a legitimate inability to pay. But it's God's honest truth, I've had people say, 'I can't afford $25 a session for counselling because we've just put an addition on the house, and the base payments on the BMW are killing us!' But if people have just been laid off their jobs and need counselling – well, that's another matter.

Yes, the Russian Jews are a major preoccupation. No, we don't abandon them. That's not true. Tatiana Petuchovski (*The Russian Leader*) runs our programme. We get them an apartment; we help them financially for four months; we teach them English; and we get them a job. Less than 1 per cent of our families go on welfare. Nationally the figure is 50 per cent, so we've done a very good job. The truth is most of them are very resourceful and we provide ongoing counselling. The American dream is you pull yourself up by your own bootstraps, and frankly most of them are doing very well at it!

Has the job changed my perception of being a Jew? Ten to fifteen years ago I thought of being a Jew as going to synagogue and celebrating the holidays. Now I think of it as a communal thing. It's making what you do in every moment of your life reflect Jewish values. Fifteen years ago I would never have expected to be a Director of a Jewish Family Agency. When you look at my résumé, it fits together very well, but that's all in retrospect. Maybe it's divine providence? Something like that . . .

The Director of the Synagogue Council

MR BEN SAMUEL

The Synagogue Council is a Jewish agency which initiates charitable projects. Ben Samuel was bearded and in his late fifties. He took off his glasses when he spoke to us. We sat in the den of his comfortable modern house. A New Yorker *magazine was lying on the sofa.*

I'm a Metropolis native. My grandparents came over from Russia or Poland, depending upon who had won the last war, somewhere in that area. I was raised in an Orthodox home; and kept *kosher*. Mom and Dad walked to services. As far as my sister and myself were concerned, no demands were made on us. I got a sense from my parents that they inherited their Orthodoxy more than they necessarily accepted it. When my wife and I got married – we were very young – I always say, 'I robbed the cradle and filled it right back up again.' We had three kids very quickly. We had to make a decision about keeping *kosher*. It turned out to be a monetary one. The decision not to keep *kosher* was based on cost. We were very young; we were both students, my wife dropped out of school to have our first child. She couldn't fit under the lecture desk any longer! We decided we wouldn't keep *kosher*, but we wouldn't have any pork in our home. My parents were quite happy to eat in our house. They had never kept *kosher* out. They had a *kosher* home, but not always *kosher* stomachs!

We belonged to a Traditional synagogue, but it gave us an uncomfortable feeling. At about the time of my boys' *Bar Mitzvahs*, a famous Reconstructionist rabbi came to town. I listened to him and I thought, 'The man says what I've been thinking.' So we became involved in a Reconstructionist study group, and we have become very involved in the Reconstructionist Federation. I chaired the group three times in twenty years. Yes, before Perry Waters (*The Reconstructionist Leader*). So we've gone that spectrum.

In 1976 the Rabbinical Council asked that the Synagogue Council be formed, the Synagogue Council being lay leaders as opposed to the Rabbinical Council which is all the rabbis. It didn't last very long – maybe eighteen months. They couldn't find a project to sink their teeth into to justify in their own minds the reason for their existence. In 1985 the rabbis came back and said, 'We think we still need a Synagogue Council – a place to direct requests for certain kinds of programmes that don't belong with the rabbis.' So we started it up again. I was one of the people who was actively involved in putting it back together. I was the Reconstructionist representative and I was the President of the Council for two and a half years.

We started out with a silent protest for Soviet Jewry down on the shopping mall. We just carried placards and passed out information. Then we started to get involved with a whole series of programmes. Basically what we have become is the charity agency – it's the place to do good deeds. Now we administer the Christmas *Mitzvah* Project. On Christmas Eve and Christmas Day we find volunteers to work in the hospitals for Christmas so the Christians who work there can spend that time with their families. We run Project Ezra, which is a clothing and food drive. We discovered that Jews find a certain comfort level in donating to a Jewish organization even if it doesn't necessarily go to Jews. We distribute the food and clothing whenever appropriate around the city. Initially people think it must be going to the Russian Jews, but I explain that it is for anyone who's destitute – and that's not the situation of most of the Russian Jews. Almost never has anyone said, 'If it's not going to Jewish people, I'm certainly not giving it to you!' Far and away the majority of people say, 'Well, it's nice that there's a Jewish agency that's doing this.'

The Council members are appointed by the synagogue rabbis and presidents. Eleven synagogues are members of the Synagogue Council, and they run the full spectrum from *Adath Israel*, *Har HaShem*, *Beth Israel* and Temple *Shalom*. No, the gay congregation's not a member though we did try to support them against the *Metropolis Jewish News*. Have you met Tim (*Gay Congregation Leader*)? The ultra-Orthodox also do not participate, and they wouldn't be part of this no matter what. I've never gone deeply into a conversation with them about why they don't want to be. They're just non-participants in the community almost in general – as long as their own little world is functioning the way they want it to function. Interestingly enough, one of their congregations will contribute a cheque to our Passover project. We raise the money to buy the food for needy families so they can have an observant *kosher* Passover. That's one time when it's hard not to be *kosher* to a certain degree. The East Side Orthodox congregation provides us with some funding for that. We don't hear anything from the West Side.

The Council members report back to their synagogues about our activities and we also send our minutes to the rabbis. We do other bits of networking. For example, recently we had Paul Karlin (*The Director of an Anti-Cult Organization*) from the Anti-Cult Organization speak to our meeting to let us know what they can offer; they have a speakers' bureau who will come out and talk to synagogue members. We thought at one time we'd alert the schools on the significance of the Jewish holidays, but we realized that should come from a higher level – maybe the Rabbinical Council. We have no problem of reconciliation with the Jewish Family Service. Someone calls the Jewish Family Service and says, 'I have a load of old clothes I want to donate.' They say, 'Call the Synagogue Council. They'll take care of it!'

Recently I came on board as Executive Director. I'm not full-time. We had three Executive Directors over the years. I'm the third. I'd stayed active in the organization for two and a half years after I'd been President, but then I felt someone else should be active for the Reconstructionists. Everybody was beginning to say, 'We don't need to worry about the Synagogue Council. Ben will take care of it!' I was wanting the Reconstructionists to think of the Synagogue Council as something that is theirs – not mine. So I suggested someone else take over.

Anyway I was asked to take over as Executive Director. We function on less than $10,000 a year. My office is down in the basement. There's a small dues structure, and we get a small – a very small – grant from the Allied Federation. I was told it would take thirty or forty hours a month. Well, I'm putting in a lot more than that, but that's all right. I believe in the organization. The wonderful thing about the Synagogue Council is that it brings together all these people from a wide variety of belief systems, and you find there are an awful lot of places where you can work together. How you practise your Judaism specifically within your house, or how your rabbi expects you to practise your Judaism based on his background, doesn't have anything at all to do with your ability to work together to accomplish something good in the community.

The Russian Leader

MRS TATIANA PETUCHOVSKI

In recent years many Russian Jews have settled in Metropolis. Mrs Tatiana Petuchovski ran the Jewish Family Service Programme for new Russian immigrants to the city. She was a chic woman in a royal blue trouser suit and chunky silver jewellery. We interviewed her in her office on State Street; she spoke with a barely perceptible Russian accent.

I have immigrated here about fifteen years ago. I come from Odessa, and I was born in 1946. My dad was a criminal attorney who was, more than anybody else, in touch with the Russian reality. All the time while I was growing up, he was preparing for me to leave the country though I didn't know anything about it. He hired tutors to teach me languages: French, English and Italian for a time. My father was a very educated man. He pushed and pushed and pushed. My parents did identify as Jews though I myself never stepped my foot into the synagogue. I started fasting at the age of thirteen for *Yom Kippur* (Day of Atonement) and we celebrated *Pesah* (Passover). I never know of *Rosh Ha-Shannah* (Jewish New Year) at all. We had no prayerbooks. I remember my grandfather lighting candles, but I had no idea why – I lost my other grandfather in the Holocaust at Babi Yar before I was born. My father was never a member of the Communist Party, but he could have lost his job if it was known that he practised his religion. So we kept it all a secret. We very clearly had two lives – one at home and one in public – and very early we learnt how not to say the truth.

It said in our passports we were Jewish. I can't really tell you I felt any sense of pride in being Jewish – if anything I felt a sense of secretiveness and fear about it. I was not a typical-looking Jew, and in Odessa at least I had a very protected life because my dad was very well-known. He had connections, but I didn't know what I wanted to be when I left school. He wanted me to get an education, and of course get married and get children. You bet! I could not get into law school which was my father's dream – because I was a Jew. In my father's generation there were some Jewish lawyers, but none in the later years. I was a very good student, so I went to the Mechanical Institute of Refrigeration and Air Conditioning, and I became an engineer. I went for five years. After college, I used my languages and did technical translation.

In 1971 I went on a business trip to Leningrad where I met

my husband. He proposed to me on the second date; he was either desperate or it was very flattering! I can't quite figure out which! At that time I was twenty-five which was very late to get married in Russia, so I said 'Yes' almost jokingly. It was a great shock to my family. He was Jewish, but very different Jewish from my family. I don't think they had done anything in their lives to maintain the Jewish culture. My husband's family had no idea. His father was a member of the Communist Party – a big shot at that time. We were both from educated families – we were both intelligentsia. My grandmother had a fit because he wasn't handsome enough, but in fact I married a very nice man, a very nice man.

We lived with my parents-in-law in their apartment in Leningrad. This is where I first came across anti-Semitism. I couldn't find a job. I went for the first year knocking at every door. They always had to see my passport, and once they know I was Jewish, there was no job. I didn't have connections in Leningrad and nothing happened even though I had pretty good credentials. Eventually after a year a very nice non-Jewish man who was just starting a new institute said he would hire me even though he knew my handicap. I worked there for about four years. I was about thirty and we applied to leave the country in 1977.

Why did I apply to leave? I don't know. It was primarily my father. The 1967 war in Israel was instrumental. It made everyone feel different; they felt proud of being Jewish; they felt not as scared. My own father was always anti-political and he was basically talking about us leaving for a long time. My husband's father stopped talking to us when we talked about leaving, and even threatened to kill himself. Then something fascinating happened. My father-in-law was a very prominent director of an institute, and he was sent to Japan on a business trip. This was unheard of for a Jew to be sent abroad. Something happened. He couldn't hide his excitement at seeing Japan; he talked about it, and he was fired from being the director. Then, when he was fired, things changed. So I said, 'Let's go!' In 1975 my husband's uncle went to Metropolis, and we were getting letters and pictures. I did not want to go to Israel but at that time we got our invitation from Israel – I had no idea who it was from. You had at that time to apply to Israel, and we received the permission very quickly. I have no idea how we got it so fast. It beats me. We had twenty-one days to leave the country. That was it.

I couldn't take anything with me. We were allowed to take $150 per person, clothes, pillows, blanket and a wedding band. It was 21 September 1977; we went to Vienna – my husband, me and our little son. We decided we were going to Metropolis because the uncle was here. In Vienna, we said we were going to the United States, and we were helped by the Hebrew Immigrant Aid Society. Then we stayed in Italy for four months to get all the papers processed, and we went to Metropolis from Italy. Our uncle met us at the airport and he found us an apartment.

My apartment in Leningrad was much nicer. Remember, my father-in-law had good connections. I really didn't know what to expect. I was the one who spoke English; I had a little boy and a husband who was totally dependent on me. I arrived on Friday, 3 February 1978, and I can't remember exactly how, but I found myself in Temple *Shalom* my first night. I was totally overwhelmed. I'd never seen a synagogue. It's very difficult for me to tell you what I thought. Looking back I think I was in a state of shock. For the first few months my husband was very depressed. Within two months, I was offered a job here at the Jewish Family Service because I spoke English, and I was the first Russian Jew in Metropolis who did speak English. Debbie Reinhardt, Rabbi Reinhardt's (*The Reform Rabbi*) wife, worked for the Family Service. She is a wonderful-hearted human being, and she pushed the Director to hire me.

Quite soon my husband got a job in a factory operating some machinery. He earned $4.25 an hour. I was making $600 a month and we were ecstatic. At that time, there were maybe ten Russian families in Metropolis. Working for the Family Service, though I did not know it at the time, it put me in a very difficult position. I was in charge of the Family Service Russian Programme. The Russians displaced all their frustration and anger on me. I was the giving hand, and the people are very ambivalent about the giving hand – you hate it and you want it. I tried to do my best, but I was pretty beaten up. I had to learn to be tougher about my own vulnerability.

While I was working, I went to the State University to get a Bachelors degree in Social Work and then I got a Masters degree in Clinical Psychology from Smith College. It was a wonderful programme. During this period of time, I also had to bring my whole family to America. Altogether I brought about seventeen people, and I was the core. They were all in crisis, but I couldn't have the luxury of falling apart. It was only at Smith that I could finally establish a new identity. I had to write, which I found very difficult and my ambivalences surfaced. But I got through and really it was the best thing that ever happened to me. I now have a private psychotherapy practice as well as working for the Family Service.

I got divorced. My husband went through a lot of difficulties here; he did various things and was very depressed. Eventually he moved to Rochester, New York, to form a company with his father. My son went to the Golda Meir Day School – I was very, very clear that whatever happened to me, I wanted him to be *Bar Mitzvah*. He's now at Northwestern University studying economics and maths, and he is a National Merit Scholar. He's a very bright kid – a wonderful, wonderful young man. Then I married again. I married an American. I would never marry a Russian – too narrow, too chauvinistic, though I hate generalizations. I married a non-Jewish man, who converted to Judaism. It was his decision – I wouldn't have minded . . .

Immigration is very, very traumatic, and if there is not a strong loving family, it is very easy to be destroyed. I have seen lots of tragedies. I find that men survive immigration less well than women, because men's identity is very much based on their job. The women have other roles in life. When a man loses his job, he is totally lost. So men suffer more and I find them less flexible than women. Women are more susceptible to growth and there is a large amount of divorce. I work with lots of women, and I am a strong believer in growth. I don't want to break the families, but I believe the growth has to happen no matter what. If the loss of the marriage is the result, well so be it . . .

I sometimes think what my life would have been like if I had not come. There is someone in Metropolis who used to work for me in Leningrad. She says to me she does not observe significant changes, but I do . . . I think I almost lived two totally different lives.

Editors of the Jewish Newspaper

Metropolis has one Jewish newspaper, which has been established for more than eighty years. The offices of the Metropolis Jewish News *were in downtown Metropolis. They were in a squat, ugly building surrounded by car parks and cheap apartment blocks. Inside everything was lively. The front desk was manned by a young man of American Indian origin. The young receptionist who brought us our coffee was blonde and perky. The offices were divided into several separate rooms, but everywhere there were framed copies of previous front covers. The newspaper was the only Jewish periodical in Metropolis and it reported the activities of all the different sectors of the community.*

MRS LEAH SILVER

Mrs Leah Silver had been the Editor-in-Chief of the Metropolis Jewish News *for many years. She had taken over from her late husband when he died. We had already met her when she gave us a tour of the city.*

I'm the Editor and Publisher of the *Metropolis Jewish News* and, in the expression of Harry S. Truman: 'The buck stops here!' But here at the *Metropolis Jewish News* we may have fancy titles but we all do many things. When I say 'I', I also mean 'we'. In the paper we take it very seriously if we make an error. We'll follow up even on the want ads – anything that displeases people we make an effort to satisfy, to correct, and, as is proper in a newspaper, we print a correction. Even if a name is spelt wrong – an 'i' before an 'e', or something like that. It's important that we reach out into the community.

I have a very, very talented staff. We make every effort to meet with people who are here – personalities, whether they're on a national or local level. When someone important comes to Metropolis like Eli Wiesel, we're there. We transcribe his speech as his words to the community, and on the local level we communicate with the community. For example when the Greenbaum Museum honoured Rabbi Oppenheim (*The Traditional Rabbi*), we not only had the information first and the promotion as they wanted it, we also did a follow-on and a thank you, and the synagogue later used it as a hand-out to promote the synagogue.

This newspaper has been in existence since 1913. Many people have come and gone. When Don, my husband, took over, his predecessor was a very, very skilled writer, but he was no businessman – and the paper was about to close. At that time Don had an ad agency, and he was just starting to write for the *Metropolis Herald.* Don took over the paper with very great enthusiasm, and six months later it was more than a one-man job. He got in some marvellous journalists and he also did the advertising. I came aboard in 1965. (Do you want this personal stuff? You can always use blue pencil, put me out on the cutting-room floor.) My background for this business was ad agency for the business side, and on the news side, I had done news production for local television. That's what I brought to the paper.

The paper reaches 50,000 readers every week on a 14,000 print-run. People say, 'I just love your paper and I pass it on to my daughter on Friday night and she gives it to her neighbour.' We do many things to promote. New subscribers get fourteen months for the price of twelve. When people have a baby, if they're not subscribers, we send them an extra paper. Then every boy or girl who is *Bar* or *Bat Mitzvah*, we send them a paper with the announcement. We send people extra papers if there's a death in the family, and, if the deceased was a subscriber, we redirect the paper to the family in the months left.

The only thing in the paper which is our thinking is the editorial page. This may sound smart alec, but we don't make the news. We only report it. I don't say I'm not frustrated every week. I am. But being independent, we are responsible economically for the paper. Not all the news comes in at the same time, and we just make a conscientious effort to cover everything that comes in. If we can, on the front page we have local, national and international stories, but sometimes things happen that are only local. And that's the way it is. We like to feel we have a balance . . .

DR SHIMON SILVER

Dr Shimon Silver was Leah Silver's son. His official title on the Metropolis Jewish News *was Executive Editor. On the wall of his shabby office were several awards for excellence in Jewish journalism, and his bookcases were full of books of Jewish theology. Old newspapers were piled up on the old leather sofa. On the large desk sat a word processor and a modern fax as well as commentaries on the* Torah *and an introduction to Maimonides'* Mishneh Torah *(Code of Jewish Law).*

Some people grow up breathing. Being involved in newspapers was the equivalent. I published a newspaper in the city in 1963 when I was only seventeen, and a magazine in the city when I was eighteen. It's just in the blood. I've never taken a journalism course any place. Maybe I would've been the better for it. It was just part of living. Dad would always be taking out the dictionary at the dinner table. Words, going through words, here, there, and everywhere. In my case, writing and communicating and articulation are just part of the way I grew up. I also learnt that if you're going to publish a high school publication – one of the first things you find is that no one is waving a dollar bill in front of your face to pay for it. The printers aren't going to give it to you for free just because you're a nice little high school kid. So I've been involved with the commercial side since the beginning.

What do I do here? Let me give you a little metaphor. For years the Metropolis Mooses (the football team) had a coach who had a system which was very spontaneous and very free. Lots of football teams have set moves, which they practise over and over again and hope that they'll get to use them in the real game. He was just the opposite. Everyone was moving and running and it was all very fast – not that I understand very much about football. Anyway, he was a very successful coach. The Mooses have never done so well since he left! That's what we do here. We have very capable people who we make very certain not to plug into narrow, confined responsibilities. I do a whole variety of things here. In that I am typical, not atypical. My mother is involved with editorial and with advertising. I am involved with editorial and advertising. There are only two people here who are involved exclusively in advertising work and there's no one involved exclusively in editorial work.

Editorial policy? For many editors balance is a kind of Holy Grail. We definitely don't believe that. If you think about it carefully, if everything is balanced it's controlled. When I hear the word 'balance', the word 'Pravda' comes to mind. You see, the news itself isn't balanced. Sometimes for a whole stretch of time, what's happening in Israel is more important than what's happening in anyplace else. Sometimes what's happening locally is more important. Sometimes that which is happening to one segment of the community as opposed to another is dominant. Now if you're going to balance the news all the time, your readers are going to take that which is important and downplace it. We let the news dictate what's happening. That's what makes us vital. We're following the news. We're not trying to pre-programme into some 'balance'.

In particular, we deal with the Middle East stories in more depth than the secular newspapers. Just look at the length. You'll get 100 words, 200 words maybe 500 words for some critical event in one of the local dailies. I'm not criticizing the local dailies. They have a lot of things to cover. That's their job. What for us is the dominant story in the Middle East may be one of ten stories for them. We will cover things much more extensively, in much more detail. We also have specialized contacts there. So we have contacts; we have detail; we have background; we have history. We don't see ourselves in competition with the dailies over this.

I do read the other Jewish newspapers. I enjoy seeing what they do. It's fascinating. But I'm never looking over my shoulder at them, never. Newspapers and newspaper people are extremely independent folk, and what somebody else does do or doesn't do is not important. We may respect it, we may be fascinated by it; but it's not something one imitates. That's not journalism. We're independent folk. That's the nature of the First Amendment . . .

I think the role of a Jewish newspaper increasingly is to

educate. The conventional wisdom is that newspapers are there to report and other Jewish organizations are there to do whatever they're supposed to do. And that's the way it goes. My view is different. I think that the Jewish community in the United States is in deep crisis. For newspapers to believe that their primary duty is to report is to be living in a dream world because that belief presumes that the community will always be there to be reported on. But that is not so. The picture is not rosy. I think therefore newspapers really have to be educational instruments. You see, for most people, the only Jewish contact they get is from the *Metropolis Jewish News.* They won't get it from the synagogues because they don't go. Maybe they'll go twice a year. Or they'll go for a *Bar Mitzvah.* Most people are not stepping into the synagogues once a week, not to mention once a day. The Jewish information that is coming into the home is coming not from the rabbis, or from books, but from the *Metropolis Jewish News.* So we're very conscious of making that information as educational as possible. It's not always appreciated, but that's what we try to do . . .

The President of the Centre for Russian Jewry

MR TONY FISHMAN

The Metropolis Centre for Russian Jewry is a charity set up to help new Russian immigrants living in Metropolis. Tony Fishman was a big bear of a man in his late forties. He sat on a cream couch in a cream-tiled sunroom. On the wall were examples of Aztec art, and there was a magnificent American-Indian pot on the coffee-table. In the corner was a small wood-burning stove with a matching kettle on the hob. Outside his pretty wife sat reading under a sun umbrella while their small, blonde daughter played with her white terrier puppy on the grass.

I was born and raised in Brooklyn, New York, but I've been in Metropolis for the last fourteen years. I was raised pretty much a holiday Jew: went to synagogue on the festivals, things like that. At *Bar Mitzvah* time my parents joined a synagogue; I studied Hebrew for one year for my *Bar Mitzvah* and never saw the inside of a Temple again, until I got to Metropolis. In the

1960s I had gotten involved with Eastern philosophy which I studied for ten to twelve years. I continued to study it here in Metropolis.

Then I got a call from a Rabbi Lubetkin (*The Russian Rabbi*). He needed a roof on his house, and I'm a general contractor. The next thing I knew I was starting to get involved with Judaism, especially on a mystical level and especially with Rabbi Lubetkin's organization. Moving away from your hometown you lose your family tremendously. These people are all Russians and I'm a Russki too. I missed my family. I now feel a family adherence to what's been going on with the Russian community here in Metropolis.

I can only surmise that most of our Russian immigrants heard about Metropolis from their own grapevine in Russia – family, friends, relative . They have been coming for six or seven or eight years. At the beginning there was a surgency of Russian Jewry to Metropolis. How many, I don't know. Then it stopped for quite a while. I don't know if the Curtain had something to do with it during those days. Then when the walls came tumbling down, I mean all doors were open – no holds barred. The Russians hit this town literally by the thousands. I would guess there are now in the neighbourhood of 35,000.

These people arrived like our great-grandparents arrived in America. Our grandparents came with basically the clothes on their back, same as these people did. They spoke no English, the way these people don't. The jobs were difficult to get – the jobs are difficult to get today. But back in the old days it was easier for an immigrant in the United States because the United States was still labour intensive. There were plenty of jobs around – manual, laborious-type jobs. What we call in my business 'grunt jobs'. There are no such things today. There are no ditch-diggers any more. Everybody today is intelligentsia. These people hit the country: they can't speak the language; they can't get from point A to B; they can't get a job; they can't get help; they can't get anything.

You get the Jewish Family Agency putting them up in an apartment, giving them a little bit of food, giving them a little bit of clothing, and then walking away. They set 'em up and then – gone – that's it! They walk away! The Centre for Russian

Jewry, our organization, tries to get them jobs, tries to get them clothing, sets up a food store, helps them mentally – which is probably more important than anything else. To walk into a home where a father and his wife and their three or four children are in an apartment – Father is literally crying because he can't get a job, and he can't support his family – it's devastating . . .

I've gone on a few of these deals. A year ago at Thanksgiving, I delivered over twenty turkeys – the American turkey and gravy and stuffing and so on – when we got done with the twenty turkeys, these people were so thankful, so incredibly hospitable, that I couldn't do it any more. I had to stop. It was just too much for me. You get to the point where you just want to give them everything you have on you.

The Agency is funded by two people. One is a great benefactor, a very, very big philanthropist (*The Community Patriarch*). The money that he gives to the Jewish community every year runs into the millions. The other is myself – I'm no comparison. We have one employee (*The Russian Rabbi*) and there's a limit to what we can give him. We give him a salary, and the rest is basically what he can raise himself from the community. But what he has done with these people on levels of morality, psychology, has been – I mean, I get emotional thinking about it – this guy has saved lives. These people were going over the deep end, and this guy has pulled them out.

The Russians are assimilating to such a degree, it's incredible. The Jewish schools are opening their doors to these kids to a degree that is absolutely amazing. They're assimilating into the mainstream secular schools. Any kid put into a school – in six months he is speaking English as well as you are. His parents are a different story. The parents will pay the price the same way our grandparents paid the price. But now they're going to pay the price more! These people got it tough.

Some are intelligentsia. Most of them were labourers in Russia, against popular belief. They were not doctors and lawyers and biochemists and physicians. There are a few. But by and large 80 to 90 per cent are just labourers, carpenters and people like that. They came because of anti-Semitism. They say that anti-Semitism in Russia now is worse than it's ever been.

Here is a group of people who are coming from a country which literally hated their guts. They may not know much about Judaism, but they know in the sweetest, loveliest way that you could ever know that they're Jews . . . Cut it any way you want, they're Jews.

On a personal level, I'm not that friendly with these people. At this point in time these people are not culturally adapted to deal on our socio-economic level. People do not want to involve that situation in their lifestyle. They're too complacent. I'll be very honest with you, to a great degree I don't want to either. It sounds very callous and rude. Some of us have been fortunate enough in our life to build up a business and become somewhat affluent. You bring these people into your home, and these people are totally in awe of what you have. These people are devastated to the degree that you feel very uncomfortable. They cannot believe that people can have this kind of opulence. So what you do is push them away. Because it's embarrassing . . . So you go to their house, and then they're so overwhelmed with having the President of the Metropolis Centre for Russian Jewry there – who's just a *schlep* (ordinary guy) making a living – they think he's a prince. Everything in the house comes out. You know they don't have anything. And you don't want to eat what they don't have . . . but I still have an empathy for these people. They're my people . . .

The Hadassah Leader

MRS ANNE GINSBERG

Hadassah is a women's Zionist organization. Its chief function is to raise money for particular projects in Israel.

Anne Ginsberg's house was impeccable. It stood in the middle of the best Jewish residential area. There was thick white carpeting on the floor and heavy, European-style furniture. A large, round, marble coffee-table on a gold roccoco base stood in the middle of the conversation area. Dotted around the room were pieces of German glass and Czech porcelain. On a side table was a small gilded chandelier with crystal drops and on another table stood a small brass tree which held oval family photographs. Anne Ginsberg was a slender, grey-haired woman.

She sat on one of three lime-gold velvet sofas, and as she talked a small, beige poodle bounced up and down beside her.

My parents were from Poland, from a little town. Right after World War One, my father decided he wanted to leave the area because he didn't see a future in Europe any more. My mother and he were married and then immediately after the wedding he went to Germany. After he made some money he went to the United States. My mother stayed home waiting for him to be able to bring her over. When he got the papers to allow my mother to come, he sent for her. They hadn't seen each other for eight years. That's how long it took from the time my father left home. So when this boat load of immigrants were waiting to get off the boat, my father recognized my mother but she didn't recognize him. He hollered and called her name, and she said, 'You're not my husband.' When my father had left, he was a thin man and he had put on a lot of weight in the eight years. So she said, 'Take off your coat.' She thought maybe his clothes were bulky. But she still didn't recognize him. Then she said, 'Take off your hat,' because he had a beautiful head of red hair when he left. Well, he'd lost all his hair. When he took his hat off, he was almost bald. So she said to him, 'Take off your glasses.' He had not worn glasses when he left, and he had these big, black horn-rimmed glasses on. He took his glasses off and she still didn't recognize him. All the people standing by were getting hysterical. Everyone was laughing and one of the group yelled out, 'Tell him to take off his pants!'

My parents had three girls. I was the oldest. My father established a men's clothing business in a small town in this state. My parents didn't believe in too much schooling. They belonged to the Orthodox synagogue, but really weren't into educating girls religiously like they do nowadays. We kept a *kosher* home, and when I was graduating high school, my parents gave up their business and moved to Metropolis because there were so few Jewish boys. They wanted us to marry Jewish.

My dad was always a Zionist. He was already terribly interested in the politics of Zionism. It was always his dream to go to Israel someday but he never did, though we have some cousins there. When he was a young man, he was in a Zionist club in Poland. When I was young, I became a Young Judea leader which was the earliest exposure you get to Hadassah. I was the leader, and worked with some of the kids there. We used to get a lot of material from National Hadassah about Israel and about Zionism. Many years ago the focus of Young Judea was to get people to make *aliyah* (immigrate) to Israel, but that wasn't always received too well. A lot of parents don't want their kids to be pressured to live in Israel, and they had to modify the programme. Now it's just educational. They're told about life in Israel, the *kibbutzes* . . . and that was my first experience.

Then when I moved to Metropolis I was too busy with my own family. I didn't have too much time for organizations until my children were pretty well in school, though we were always members of a synagogue. Yes, *Beit Torah*. Then my sister-in-law was a member of a study group here in Metropolis. So she said, 'Why don't you join the study group?' So I did. I joined the study group of about ten women, and I'm still in that study group. It was a Hadassah study group. In those days there were many Hadassah study groups in the city. We used to do book reviews; we studied quite a bit about Israel and about Judaism because a lot of us didn't have a lot of background in Judaism. At the present time we're all kind of studied out. We've been doing lunch and current events. We discuss what is going on in the community and in the world.

We have fundraising; we do education; we always have a really well-rounded programme. We have one education day; we have an education seminar where we go out of town for two days; we have meetings to raise money because Hadassah is a fundraising organization. Primarily we support the Hadassah hospital, and we have a vocational school in Israel. We have a big luncheon once a year where you have a minimum amount you donate to. It's like $100. We have a programme and a lot of times we have a speaker come from National. Then we have a fundraising dinner one time a year which is for a little bit higher giving. It starts at $250 on up. We also sell cards and certificates. If you have a happy occasion or a sad occasion you donate to Hadassah, and we send a lovely card. We've had raffles; we've had rummage (jumble) sales; you name it. We have to raise about $135,000 a year here in Metropolis for our quota. It takes a lot of work. It is quite a lot of money. Year before last we made our quota. Last year we didn't quite make it, but you don't get drummed out if you don't make your quota!

When I was in it, they asked me if I would do a position. A position in Hadassah generally. Now in Hadassah we're down to under 1,500, but at one time we were 1,800/1,900 members. I started, let's say, at the bottom. I started sending out cards. If people needed cards they would call up, and I would send them. Then they wanted me to be Financial Secretary, so I started doing dues. Then I worked up to Treasurer. I've done fundraising; I've done Education Co-ordinator, and just about every job there is in Hadassah. And then I was President. Yes!

There are a few Orthodox that belong. It's predominantly Conservative, Traditional and Reformed. A certain segment of Orthodoxy doesn't even believe in Israel. They don't believe we should be supporting Israel. There's another segment that believes we have to be *glatt* (ultra) *kosher* in everything we do. The Hadassah guidelines are that all meals must be *kosher*, but that isn't enough for them. They use all these excuses not to belong and not to give. There's not too much we can do about it! A few of the fairly modern Orthodox belong. They give donations, but they don't really participate all that much. They do buy Israel bonds.

I'd never want myself to live in Israel. I admire anyone who will go and who does go and I think it's a wonderful thing to do. I myself don't feel that that's where I would be at home. It's just such a different way of life. I'm just a spoilt American, I guess – I'm not a pioneer-type person. I have cousins in Israel who have been here to visit and they live on the West Bank. They carry a gun. They're in the most dangerous place and we've begged them to come and live here. They loved it here, but they wouldn't dream of leaving their country. That's their country, and this is my country. Much as I want Israel to exist and to help the people there all I can, I just don't have the pioneer spirit I guess . . .

I think Israel is the only thing that affects a lot of Jews, that reminds them that they are Jews. It's quite discouraging the way the trend is towards not being observant and not being involved in Jewish life. There are so many Jewish people in Metropolis who are just sort of in the background. They don't identify as Jews, and they don't live as Jews, and they don't support Jewish causes. It's just at crisis times, or when they run into anti-Semitism, that people really get thinking about what they should be doing. Other times they're very complacent.

Of course we stick up for Israel every chance we get. In private, sometimes you wonder about the leadership just as you do here. I'm sure they make mistakes, but they always have that answer that we don't live there. Their lives are at stake and Israel is at stake. I see myself as a Jew, but not so much religiously as culturally. Then I see myself as an American, and next to that comes my feelings about Israel. Israel is important because of the anti-Semitism everywhere else in the world and it certainly seems to be rising here again. It makes us feel safer to know that there is somewhere, maybe in the future sometime, for our children. If they need to have a safe place, we know that if there isn't an Israel, someday the Jews may disappear in some of the countries they now flourish. For years we thought the United States was the safest place in the world, but I don't think anybody feels that way any more . . .

The President of the Hebrew Old Age Home

MR HARRY TROPE

For many years the Jewish community supported an Old Age Home on the West Side. Recently this has been sold and a new Old Age Home has been built in South-East Metropolis.

Mr Harry Trope was a property developer. His firm, Harry Trope Inc., was housed in a magnificent office suite downtown. We talked to him in an elegant conference room, sitting on leather chairs and surrounded by architectural plans. A slightly frail-looking man in his fifties, he wore a jazzy tie, a grey suit, and a large jade ring on one hand and a diamond on the other.

I'm native to Metropolis. I was born on the West Side, and I went to the old *Adath Israel* for my religious upbringing. I have remained a member of *Adath Israel*, but since I moved to the

East Side, I also belonged to *Har HaShem*. Yes, I have contributed to quite a few of Rabbi Kornfeld's (*The University Professor of Judaica*) projects over the years! My father came to this country at the age of fifteen by himself. His father sent him here to work to bring his family over. He came to New York, and he sold fish in the apartments; then he became a bricklayer there. Then he heard about a gold rush in California, and he left by train and came as far as Metropolis. He stopped here and never really got to California.

My parents raised three girls and a boy. I was the youngest. We came from a *kosher* home. My father became a general contractor; he built supermarkets, things like that. I was brought up in the construction business, working every summer for my father. My children have been in that too. On the West Side of town 99 per cent of my friends were Jewish, and we were very close. We still are. Metropolis is very unique in that regard. After I left high school, I had an athletic scholarship to Metropolis University. I played football. I played halfback. I went there for one year, and I found out I was too small to play in a college team. I quit college and joined the Coastguard. It was during the Korean War. I spent two and a half years, I think, and I was stationed mainly on the mainland. I got a discharge through illness, and I went into the construction business with one of my cousins. Later we focused more on development.

I've been on the Board of the Allied Jewish Federation, and of the Hebrew Hospital. I'm on the Board of the University of Metropolis, though I'm not a graduate! I've been involved with the Jewish community quite a bit. I've been on the Board of *Adath Israel*. I'm not on the Board of *Har HaShem*, my son is. My family remodelled the Ark of *Adath Israel* in honour of my father and mother.

Why did we decide to move the Hebrew Old Age Home from the West Side? Well Morrie Paine (husband of *The President of the Allied Jewish Federation*) was the President of the Federation at that time. He felt they were having difficulty: the building was old; it was beginning to lose money; and it would be a burden on the community. He knew I was interested in the elderly. I've always been. My father was always interested in that and Israel, and I had taken that from him. He was a good donor, and I was taught that way. So I looked into it, and that was twelve years ago.

The problem was you had a Federation who had a Board; the Hebrew Old Age Home had a separate Board, and none of them were playing together! I had been a part of all of them and was able to talk to all of them. We went ahead and looked for a location, and we knew that it had to be down in the South-East because that's the way the Jewish community is moving. We wanted to be ahead of the game. I formed a new little Board, and I was able to entice some very influential people to come on it. A small group. Until we got a location, they didn't know we were for real. Once we got a location, we were able to talk to the Hebrew Old Age Home. They agreed to sell their facility which was very good, so we merged the two Boards and brought the Federation into it. From the inception of the idea to fruition was about eleven years.

You must go see it. I don't think you'll see another facility like it in the country . . . or in the world. It is a 'continuum of care' campus which means that from the beginning of ageing, they take you through to death. We started with a nursing home. We were given the money from the old building, and we raised $13 million. It has 135 beds. We also built a kitchen large enough to service the entire campus. They can even do meals-on-wheels to keep people in their homes. It's a *kosher* kitchen. Oh yes, Vardin (*The Kashrut Supervisor*) is in charge of it. He's been flexible enough to allow it to work. He's worked with us pretty well. Generally raising money would have been done through the Federation, but I was able to get people to give money to this who don't generally give money to the Federation. I could pull on their heartstrings a little bit! I led the way with my family, and then a lot of other people gave substantial amounts of money. We also have a synagogue or chapel in there, a community room that will sit 250 people, and a clinic. Then there'll be three or four further phases of development.

I would not have been involved unless it was also for the indigent out there. Sixty per cent of the places must be maintained for the indigent. And it couldn't be a burden on the Jewish community either, so 40 per cent are private patients. They pay $112 a day while the government pays $84 for the indigent. It's true! We're not allowed by law to discriminate in favour of Jewish patients. The facility is a *kosher* facility; the facility has a synagogue; and most people who want to go there are Jews. Right now the population is 80 per cent Jewish, and 20 per cent non-Jewish. Still anybody who does not want to go there has to have their head examined! Really! I mean compared with the other nursing homes, it is so far ahead!

We do have problems. We have a ward for Alzheimers, and that only has fourteen rooms. We have a person who has donated big money and has a parent who wants to go in there, who is violent. They have to be in the locked Alzheimer's wing, and we're full. We couldn't fit them in. The person doesn't want to hear why, so that is a problem we have to cope with. Those who can pay, have to pay. It's about $40/$45,000 a year, something like that. But when they've worked their way through their money, we don't put them out. We've only been in operation a year, but already we've had eight who've gone from private to indigent. Don't forget, the kids, before they go in, take their money and you have that kind of difficulty. It happens occasionally. We have to sort through that.

Eventually we'll be able to house 800 people out there. We've been open only a year. In fact, we're going to celebrate our first year tonight. If you'd like to come out tonight, you're welcome. We're going to celebrate some of the Board. You should come out. I'm inviting you . . .

We did go. The nursing home was every bit as impressive as he had described.

Five

TEACHERS

The University Professor of Judaica

RABBI PROFESSOR SAM KORNFELD

The University of Metropolis has a flourishing Department of Jewish Studies. Rabbi Professor Sam Kornfeld was not only the rabbi of the largest Traditional synagogue on the prosperous East Side (Har HaShem), he was the first Anna and Thomas Fried Professor of Judaic Studies at the University of Metropolis (see The Holocaust Survivor). *We interviewed him in his large, well-appointed study. On his desk was a fax machine, a telephone and a penholder decorated with an American flag. One wall was completely covered with certificates of advanced degrees and awards from a grateful Jewish community. Opposite was a huge studio photograph of himself and his attractive wife, and another of himself surrounded by his children and grandchildren. He ordered his secretary to stop all calls and leaned back in his chair.*

In 1952 I won an Israeli government scholarship to spend a half year in Israel, and it was then that I knew I wanted to serve my people. I still wasn't clear whether I wanted to do it as a scholar on the campus or as a rabbi in the pulpit. I had both inclinations, and in the end I decided I was going to do both, even though I knew it would compromise my scholarship and compromise my effectiveness as a rabbi. From the first moment I entered a pulpit, I had a corresponding position with a university. The talents and the visions that I had for the wider horizons grew with me as I began to develop my rabbinate and my academic career.

I discovered a long time ago that there are many Jews who are not prepared to be connected to the Jewish community through religion. So I became active in the wider community in the hope that if I built a relationship with people on some other basis, they could then feel more connected to what I really represented to them – which is Traditional Judaism. It was that that led me to create entities in this community, with which people could identify, even if they weren't religious institutions. Hence all of that background, all of my philosophy and feeling merged when I came to Metropolis in 1972. Whatever talents I had in fundraising and dealing with people of all persuasions blossomed here. So I created the Centre for Judaic Studies with a very broad vision to provide a major academic centre, with a full complement of academic programmes at the University and a full complement of institutes and societies that would serve the wider community off the campus. We created the Jewish Historical Society, the Institute for Interfaith Studies and Social Concerns, the Greenbaum Museum of Judaica, the Institute for Israeli Culture, and a Holocaust Awareness Institute, which are flourishing under the umbrella of the Centre for Judaic Studies.

How did I raise the funds? Well my friends say that I can persuade people without teeth to buy chewing gum! My fundraising skills were acquired in my position back in South Carolina. I wanted to create a nursery school in my synagogue, so I got a teacher and she put together what we had to do and what equipment we needed. I then put a package together. It was going to cost $2,000 at that time to get the thing started. At the very first meeting of the Board of Trustees, I proudly presented my plan to them. They said, 'Rabbi, where are you going to get the money?' So I said, 'What do you mean, where am I going to get the money? That's your job. You're the Board of Trustees.' And they laughed at me. The laughter is still ringing in my ears, and that's thirty-seven years ago. They said, 'That's not our responsibility. If you want to build the school, you have to raise the $2,000.' So sure enough, I did raise $2,000, but I said to myself, 'That's the name of the game. Anything that I want to do, I have to raise the money. I'd better be good at it.' So I became a fundraiser within the community; in my next position I did the same, and here we are.

How did I do it? If you could bottle something like that and sell it, you'd make a fortune. The first thing to do, in my estimation, is to have a vision. When I created the Centre for

Judaic Studies, I produced a brochure before I raised a nickel, projecting what I wanted the Centre to be. Then I got a person who I felt could connect to that vision and who had a good name in the community. I said, 'I'm going to need twenty people to give me $5,000 a year for three years to get this thing started. I want you to be the first, and I want you to go with me to get the other funds.' I convinced him that that was what the community needed, and we got thirteen people in the first year to do that. That's the way it started. You have to have a clarity of vision, and you have to find people who have imagination. Most of all, these people must trust you that what you say you're going to do will get done. You want to make people feel a sense of partnership in what you're doing, and you've got to keep stroking them.

Let me give you an example. I got someone to give me $30,000 to build a *sukkah* (ritual tabernacle). It's a nice *sukkah*. You can see it out there. I said to him: 'Look, these are the things that we can do in the *sukkah*. It's only for eight days every year, but for those eight days I can give talks, have dinners, hold *kiddush* (blessing over wine), demonstrate the festival, teach kids. And for every person who goes into that *sukkah*, and who performs the biblical commandment of dwelling in the *sukkah*, you will get credit for that because you made it happen.' Every year, for the last fifteen years, after *Sukkot* (the Festival of the Tabernacles), I provide him with a list of groups that came into that *sukkah*, and I say, 'This is what your gift has done.' I stroke him.

The Centre for Judaic Studies has $1.9 million in endowments now so it is not only raising money for the operating budget, which is now $500,000 a year, it is also raising money to endow the enterprise so it is assured for the future. We started the whole thing with a series of lectures from distinguished scholars. This got the community so excited that I used that as a proof that this community can take a higher level of Jewish culture. But all the institutes need money, and I have that burden because people forget I have a Doctorate in Jewish History. They think of Sam Kornfeld and they think, 'the greatest fundraiser'. It's complimentary in one way, but not in another. The fact that I've authored books – that doesn't stick in their minds. I'm an institution builder; I raise money. That's all they remember. But that's a fact. Every institution you create costs money . . .

People like Avraham, my son-in-law (*The Yeshiva Official*), say to me that if only I could have taken my talents and focused them on Orthodox institutions, I could have built something that would last. All of these things I've created will disappear when I'm gone. He thinks I'm serving people who in one or two generations are going to be gone, lost to Judaism. I sort of agree with him, and I'm concerned about the future of Judaism. The institutions are not the guarantors, and I do believe that real Orthodoxy is the only hope for the Jewish people. Nevertheless, I feel a compulsion to minister to the wider community because they're here now and they need my gifts. Even terminal cancer patients need help . . .

The Yeshiva Official

RABBI AVRAHAM KLEIN

A yeshiva is an Orthodox academy for young men between the ages of fourteen and twenty-one. It also provides adult education for the community. The Metropolis yeshiva, a four-square undistinguished building, stood in a largely Spanish-American area on the West Side of town. The Jews had settled in this area when they first arrived in Metropolis. Most had now fled to the prosperous eastern suburbs, leaving a small, intensely Orthodox community.

The Kleins' house was part of this tiny Orthodox community on the West Side. Just inside the front door on a hat stand was a large black homburg hat. Rabbi Avraham Klein rocked back and forth in an armchair in his small living-room. He was a round young man in his thirties wearing a white short-sleeved shirt, black trousers, ritual fringes under his shirt, bedroom slippers and a black skull cap. The room was not large; it was decorated with Jewish pictures and littered with the toys and the paraphernalia of five children. In the fireplace was a small baseball bat and mitt, a plastic crate full of picture books and some toys. There were folding prams, high chairs, feeding bottles, baby wipes and photographs.

While we talked three enchanting dark-haired little girls aged eight, five and three pored over a photograph album on the sofa. The elder boy, aged seven, was staying overnight with a friend, and a baby was asleep next door. Mrs Klein sat quietly with her daughters. A beautiful, slim woman, she was the daughter of Rabbi Professor Sam Kornfeld (The University Professor of Judaica). *Although tired, she looked absurdly young to be the mother of five children.*

I was born in the city of New York, in downtown Manhattan. The family moved to Brooklyn when I was fifteen where I went to a Jewish high school. Then I studied in a *yeshiva* in southern Israel intensively for three years, and came back to the United States. I continued studying and in late 1983 I married this wonderful young lady, Miss Rivka Kornfeld, whom I had met that summer in Israel. In 1983 I got my rabbinical ordination. When I came to Metropolis in 1984, I studied here at the *Yeshiva* at the advanced institute, and I also took a part-time job in the adult education division. This became full-time. Since we married in 1983 we've had five lovely children, thank G–d!

The *Yeshiva* in Metropolis was opened in 1967 with the support of many people in the community. The building was originally a synagogue, but when it was founded, long ago, they had visions of some day there being a *yeshiva* in Metropolis. So when the *Yeshiva* was founded, they gave the synagogue building. Today there are ten faculty members – two deans who both teach – they teach *Talmud* and ethics. Then aside from that there are four high school teachers, a high school administrator, and two teachers who teach the post-high school students. Then there's myself and an Executive Director.

We have an enrolment of about a hundred students, seventy in the high school and thirty in the post-high school. A hundred is a nice number. Every few years they hit a hundred. Usually they get about ninety. Right now we have quite a few Metropolis students, 25 or 30 per cent. The student body often become extended members of the teachers' families. The *Yeshiva* specializes in giving tremendous individual attention. The majority of the students are not from Metropolis. They live in New York, Baltimore . . . The make-up comes from the entire United States. Now we also have five students from the former Soviet Union. The *Yeshiva* here also raised a generation of Iranian students who fled at the beginning of the Ayatollah's reign, and we did wonderfully with them. Today they are all professionals, paediatricians, surgeons, accountants . . . We've had many students from Mexico, and believe it or not, occasionally a student from Israel.

The students live in an apartment building next to the *kosher* grocery. You saw it when you drove by. That's the *Yeshiva* dormitory. All the students live there including those from Metropolis. They can go home if they live close by at lunchtime. Every few weeks they get off and can go home for the Sabbath. But otherwise we like the students to share everything together, to grow together, and share the same schedules and so on. There certainly is tuition to be paid. The *Yeshiva* tries to secure as much of its budget as it can from the parents. But as in all *yeshivas* in the world, nobody is turned away because they can't pay. Therefore, a substantial part of the *Yeshiva* budget needs to be raised elsewhere.

Many of the students come from very weak Jewish backgrounds. We have special teachers, whether you call them remedial teachers or tutors, who work with them. In the secular studies, the gamut of subjects is taught for three and a half hours a day. The *Yeshiva* has the status of a nationally accredited private high school. This is a test of the quality of education they get. At 7:30 in the morning, they have to be in the main study hall for Morning Prayer. The high school starts classes at 9:00, and they go through to 12:30 with a break of fifteen minutes. Most of that time is spent learning *Talmud* and Jewish Law. Lunch is 12:30–1:00. From 1:00–2:00 they're back in class, learning ethics, the prophets, and Bible and Jewish history. From 2 o'clock they're off till 3:00. They have secular studies from 3 o'clock until 6:00. From 6–7:30 they have dinner and at 7:30 they're back in study hall, but they study with a study partner. As they progress they spend more and more time studying with partners. They need to be weaned off being spoon-fed. The last twenty-five minutes of each day, before they have the Afternoon Service, they study ethics.

The older students have a similar schedule, but they spend

more time working with study partners. The *Yeshiva* has given out rabbinic ordination in the past, but there is no specific programme. That's not the goal of the students as a whole. What is the goal of the *Yeshiva*? American society teaches people how to make a living, but not necessarily how to live. The goal of the *Yeshiva* is to teach people how to live the *Torah* way of life. We have a very high number of graduates from the high school who, in a very significant way, contribute to the communities in which they live, a very high percentage of our graduates.

Many of the students come from non-observant families – by their own definition, not by mine. Some of their parents didn't want them to continue with their Jewish education, but the children were motivated themselves. Some work the other way round. The child doesn't want to come, but the parent says, 'I think you should continue.' When that happens, unless something significant happens here during the process of the student's education, it is difficult to see success in that type of situation. When the student doesn't want to be here, there's not a lot you can do to really make them happy . . . you can't force-feed . . .

There's no question, temptations exist; and it's a good age for it too. That is one of the reasons that the philosophy of the *Yeshiva* is all students should dorm, share the same experiences; but you can't really be sheltered in today's world. Having them dorm together allows them to struggle with their friends, and allows them to try to come through with flying colours. It's difficult, there's no question. If a student is motivated, however, to be a very dedicated and committed Jew and to lead a *Torah* lifestyle, then despite the hormones raging and despite outside society, he will allow the teaching to imbue him.

They never get to see girls? I would say that's 100 per cent incorrect! Officially and formally they don't get to socialize with girls. No! But you walk on the street, you see the girls! Everywhere you see girls! I understand the rules very well having been a *Yeshiva* student myself. I understand it's difficult. I knew that as a *Yeshiva* student trying to be serious in my studies, I wanted to focus on them. I really said to myself, 'This is a time of my life when I can really benefit from not having outside distraction, interruptions, or things that would take away my mind from my studies.' There's no question at this age – at any age, but certainly at this age – one of the greatest distractions is members of the opposite sex. Occasionally there might be a slip-up, but that's what they want to do at this point. There's a time and place for everything. Just because the hormones rage, there's still a time and a place.

Are marriages arranged? I'll tell you how I met my wife and that, I believe, is how many marriages are. I was in Israel in the summer of 1983. Rivka was in Israel in the same summer. She was tutoring in a school. We had a mutual friend. He said to me – he knew that I was at the point of life when I was seeking my mate – and he said, 'I'm teaching this summer with a fine young lady. Are you interested?' I said, 'Sure, why not?' He went to her and said the same thing in reverse. So he set us up. Occasionally it'll happen that you'll meet somebody, but these occasions for *Yeshiva* students don't present themselves very often. So in that sense they are arranged; through family, through friends, through somebody in the synagogue . . .

The *Yeshiva* adult education programme is directed towards any Jewish person or their spouse who really has very limited or no Jewish background. As people get older, they start to ask themselves, 'What is life all about?' My job, I truly believe, is not to convert anybody to Orthodox Judaism or a *Torah* way of life. My objective is to educate people and let people make their own decisions. Judaism smacks in the face a lot of the philosophies and living and beliefs of American society. To that I say, 'If Abraham had caved in to the beliefs of his time, we would all now be pagans. Judaism did not give in to the times . . . that's how it remained Judaism!' The world has become bankrupt of any real important values that people instinctively know to be important – family, friendships. Although people will pursue money to no end, I don't believe they are more happy. They feel instinctively that that's not where happiness lies. Other people feel cut off from their roots. In recent years the *Torah* way of life has gained respect because people see that it's meaningful.

I think the return to *Torah* Judaism is part of G–d's plan. There's a very beautiful song and when I got married I marched down to the marriage canopy to its tune: 'Behold the days are coming, promises G–d, and I will send a hunger in the land, not a hunger for bread, not a thirst for water, but to hear the word of G–d.' Today every community in the United States has 100, 200, 500 people who have returned to Orthodox ways. It's not just by accident. Logic can tell you that.

The Governor of the Orthodox Girls' High School

MRS CHANA VARDIN

The Beis Rahel is the Orthodox high school for girls between the ages of fourteen and eighteen. Mrs Chana Vardin lived on the West Side of Metropolis. She was the wife of Rabbi Vardin (The Kashrut Supervisor), *and the mother of five daughters and two sons. She was the Chairman of the Ladies' Committee of the Beis Rahel Girls' High School.*

I was born in Israel, and I lived there until I was about ten years old. Then my parents, who were both survivors of the Holocaust, moved out to the United States. We lived in New York where I went to a Jewish high school in the Brooklyn area. I graduated, and by then I had met my husband. I was working for a day camp, and my husband also took on a job there – he happened to be doing a favour for a friend of his. So there he was . . . I was eighteen, and my husband was twenty-three going on twenty-four. I was one of the younger ones. Girls today in the Orthodox community seem to be getting married about twenty.

I'm now President of the Ladies' Committee of *Beis Rahel.* There is a Financial Board, with a President and so on. That is all men. Then the Headmaster decides on the curriculum. We are a separate organization which is basically a support group to the school. We have luncheons once a year; the girls in the school will also make a programme and perform at the luncheons. They do a play with dramatics, singing. It's a very professional job. I always feel bad that not enough of the community see them, though we do get about 120 women. I have one daughter who is very dramatic, and she always gets a leading part. But everyone does something. Some of the girls are involved in art, some in costumes or in helping produce things.

There are about twenty to twenty-five women involved in the committee, and a nucleus who participate. As well as the annual luncheon, we have these things called the restaurant night. There's not too many *kosher* restaurants in this city, so we have a regular dinner about seven or eight times a year. The women come in, prepare the food, serve it out, charge a fee and whatever money we get, we give it to the school. Last year we pledged $10,000, and we were able to fulfil our pledge. That's our fundraiser for the school. Anyone can come, and generally there are between 150 to 200 people. All the cooking is done in the school, and many times the girls will help us. Then at graduation the women give a gift – some sort of nice Jewish book. We give each girl a gift from the Ladies. These books cost anything from $25 to $50 each, and there are between fifteen to twenty graduates each year. Altogether there are about sixty girls in the school.

The school gives a very good secular education – they have won national awards. I would say the secular education is on a higher calibre than the boys'. Why is that? The boys are into learning a lot more – the *Torah*, the *Talmud* (Oral Law) – and they do that for a much longer period. That is our way. Our world survives on three things, and one of them is learning the *Torah*. It's also important that the girls learn – they have an excellent religious programme – but it is not so intense. They don't actually learn the *Talmud*. In secular studies they do science; they do math; and next year there's a choice between journalism and calculus. I told my daughter I want her to take journalism. The math she can take later in college if she so chooses. Many of the girls are more brilliant than the boys, and they can learn a lot. There's an awful lot to learn in the *Torah* itself. I don't think any woman feels deprived that she hasn't learned *Talmud*. They do have home economics: they can learn about keeping *kosher*, everything in today's life, having babies, human psychology, every aspect . . .

The girls do not socialize with the boys of the *Yeshiva* High School. I mean, if they have a brother there and they see each other on the street, there's nothing wrong in saying, 'Hello'. I don't think they're losing anything in that. In the public school system, in the lower grades, they hate the opposite sex. They don't like to play with each other. Because it's a religious school, everyone says they're missing something. They really don't care, and if they're starting to take notice, they're better off apart! In Judaism, in our way of life, the woman has the greater part. The men show the outer side with the prayer shawl and the fringes and so on, but the woman is the controller of the Jewish way of life. Definitely. For example in marriage, the woman tells the husband whether she's permissible to him or not. She has the control. She tells the husband when or what. She puts the food on the table. She raises the children. They see the mother so much more than the father – that's why the father comes first in 'Honour your father and your mother.' Children have to be reminded to honour the father; they honour the mother anyway because they see her doing all the work. It's not because he's superior to the mother. I never felt rebellion or anything as a woman – I always felt very honoured and lucky.

The girls in the *Beis Rahel* will go on and either study in Israel or go on to a seminary. Living here in Metropolis, they have to leave. I sent my girls to New York, and they stay a year or two years. They can usually get a teacher's certificate from the seminary. My third girl tells me she wants to be an obstetrician. I say 'Fine'. She will either be that or she will be a very good teacher. She's very good with children; she leads a Sabbath group and I could see her being a very good teacher. There's no social life for them here, because if they want to get married there are many more opportunities back East. Here is a beautiful place to raise a family; it's a neat, close-knit community. But for young people there is really not too much for them. They must go East.

With my eldest daughter, she was in seminary. A friend of a friend said, 'I know a real nice boy for you.' This girl had lived in this boy's parents' house, and she thought they would be a real good match. As it turned out, it was! She's now married and has two babies of her own. We try to check out the boy to see if things match each other. You always know somebody who knows somebody who knows somebody. So basically we called up and checked up on the school and the synagogue and the rabbi and so on. Sometimes you check up and it's a wonderful person, but it's not for your child. You want somebody suitable for them. There were times that I called, and I didn't like what I heard. There's no point for her to go out with somebody if you know it is not going to work out. Usually a girl will go out of her parents' home. The boy will pick her up from the home. The parents will be there. Usually you don't bombard the poor guy with the whole family! They will go out to a hotel to sit and talk. They'll pay $20 for a 7-Up, and they talk to see if they enjoy each other's company. Of course as my daughter is in New York, I don't see the boy first so I have to depend on my daughter and on who I can check with. If I was not satisified, I would not let her go out. For example, a boy called for my daughter and he checked out fantastically. The only trouble was he was twenty-seven and she was nineteen. She's a little too young. I think he's a little too settled for her, so I said 'No', and she herself did not want to go with this one.

I've never had a problem with this. If I say, 'I do not care for this person', I do not think she would go against me. It's very scary for her. She goes out . . . and it's scary. Most children are happy when their parents lead them . . .

The Bar Mitzvah Teacher

MR DANNY MIZEL

Bar/Bat Mitzvah is the Jewish coming-of-age ceremony. The boy or girl at the age of thirteen or twelve reads before the congregation some of the sacred texts of Judaism.

Bearded, with greying hair, Danny Mizel leaned back in his chair in the impersonal lounge of Temple Shalom, the largest Reform synagogue of Metropolis. He wore a sports shirt, khaki trousers, and an expensive wristwatch which had been the gift of one of his students. Although he had been President of Beit Torah (Traditional) synagogue, he was well-known as a Bar Mitzvah teacher throughout the community. He fitted us in at lunchtime – 'Nowadays,' he said, 'I have to fit in my sessions around the kids' tennis.'

I was born in Metropolis. I grew up in the city and I've never left it. It's my home, the place that I love. I came from a Traditional home; we observed the Sabbath and kept *kosher*. It was a routine to go to synagogue on the Sabbath, but it was not an Orthodox home. *Beit Torah* was my congregation. When I was eighteen years old, I was approached by the rabbi to teach at the synagogue on a full-time basis at the *Talmud-Torah* (the after-school Hebrew school). I was there Monday through Thursday, 3:30–6:00. I was at the youth services for young people on the Sabbath, and eventually I became Youth Director of the congregation.

I started teaching in 1960, and now more than thirty years later I'm still at it. I actually have another job. I'm a printing salesman; I work on commission, and I've worked at it for about twenty-seven years. That's basically my job. I sell about six to eight hours a day. Then I go and teach during the school year round 3:30 in the afternoon. In the summer my hours are a little more open. I do anything between twenty to twenty-five kids a week. Each session is forty-five minutes. I teach almost all the *Bar Mitzvahs* at Temple *Shalom*, and I have for a long time; a large percentage at Temple *Beth Jacob*; I do some for Rabbi Goldstein (*The Conservative Rabbi*) at *Beth Israel*; some at *Adath Israel*; some at *Har HaShem*; and some for the Reconstructionists.

The first thing is learning how to read Hebrew. Kids from Traditional backgrounds are supposed to know more, but I'm not sure that's what ends up happening. I think it's pretty equal, particularly as all the congregations are attempting to emphasize Hebrew skills. Because of the time constraints, they have nothing really in depth unless they're going to a Jewish day school. A lot of those young people come in with a much stronger Hebrew background. Hebrew skills are very important to me. Once they have that, the *Bar* and *Bat Mitzvah* programme goes very smoothly. Once the Hebrew skills are strong, the *Bar* and *Bat Mitzvah* is very easy. Then we can concentrate on singing and chanting and things like that.

If they don't have the skills, it's much harder; the whole process is not so much fun. The most important thing is for them to enjoy their Jewishness and Hebrew accomplishment. We're talking about reading. We're not talking about comprehension at this point. They're gaining some understanding of various words, some understanding of the prayers, what they're all about, but they're not speaking Hebrew. Not unless they're coming out of day school. I can teach somebody to read in about six to eight weeks. That's strong reading skills. They can pick up a prayerbook and read very slowly. This depends on the student. We're talking about the ability to sit down and find the time and energy to do what it takes in terms of drilling. Using the skill and learning to become proficient at it. Speed only comes through practice, practice, practice . . . and drilling.

I always do it as a family. I meet with the parents and with the youngster. We sit and we talk about the reading portion, the background to the portion, and then we try to relate it to them and to today. We talk about being Jewish and the importance of being Jewish. As a teacher, I talk not only about being *Bar Mitzvah*, but also my hopes and dreams for them in the future in terms of their commitment to Jewish life. I want to see a commitment morally and ethically. I want them to come to synagogue. I want them to become part of the congregation, and I want them to keep that commitment eventually down the road. I don't want synagogues to become museums. I want them to keep Jewish traditions of their own – holidays such as Passover, *Shavuot* (Festival of Weeks), *Sukkot*. We do a lot of talking about that.

I find some people do begin to do little things that we've talked about, whether it's making *kiddush* (blessing over wine) or coming to synagogue once a month. One of the best students I ever taught was a student who came to me and said, 'You know, I really don't want to do this.' A very nice, bright, good-looking young man. Then he proceeded to say to me, 'But I'm willing to do it because my parents want me to do it, and they do so many wonderful things for me.' I was taken aback by that. When he made that statement, I really felt very strongly about working with him. The end result was he became one of the better students. It's surprising. Some of the kids who are most unwilling become the kids who are most willing. I think the most important thing is to have the chance to build a relationship with them. That can make a difference to their feelings about being Jewish.

The more Traditional synagogues let the girls read from the

prophets or they read the *Torah* to a women's congregation. The Conservative and Reform synagogues are egalitarian. Most girls don't resent it, as long as they can have the ceremony and do their reading. Even that kind of service has come a long way. Originally in the community *Bat Mitzvahs* were done as a group. That's all changed. The girls have an hour to an hour-and-a-half service. It's really very lovely. The only thing they can't do is read the *Torah*.

They have just as many presents, just as big a party . . . The party is a very private thing. Most of the parties are in keeping with the tradition. Some of them are a little more extravagant than others. We've had everything from a blessing over wine after the Sabbath morning service to extravagant parties, large social events like all over the country, perhaps a couple of bands, performers, decorations . . . The real extravagant ones tend to be in a hotel . . . That's a whole very difficult area for me . . . I can't tell somebody how to spend their money!

The kids do the service. The rabbi really plays a small role. He just gives the charge. If the young person is capable of doing the whole service, he does. We encourage them to do as much as humanly possible. Confidence is all part of the training. I really feel very good about that. That's not really a problem. They really look forward to their day. I try to emphasize the privilege of the Sabbath, and the privilege of being able to lead a congregation in prayer. I find it changes their whole attitude. I point out that the *Bar Mitzvah* kid is probably the only person in the whole congregation who can lead the service on a given Sabbath. I think that relaxes them. Most of the kids are very relaxed, and very confident and very poised. It's a lot of fun. It's a wonderful feeling . . .

The Teacher in the Pluralist Day School

MRS AUDREY KAYE

A Pluralist school recognizes that there are different denominations within Judaism. We met Mrs Kaye in her pleasant modern house in a South-East suburb of Metropolis. She taught the sixth grade at Golda Meir Day School, and we had been encouraged to talk to her by both Rabbi Reinhardt and by Sophie

Ginsberg (The Reform Rabbi *and* The Convinced Convert). *She was a small, dark woman in her fifties, and she spoke with animation and humour.*

I was born and raised in Brooklyn, New York. My parents were both Orthodox and as with most girls in my generation, I really did not receive a Hebrew education. I learned to speak Yiddish fluently at my grandparents' home. I went to the public schools. My father went to synagogue, and my parents kept *kosher* and were fully observant. I have a younger brother, and my father always wanted him to be a doctor and me to be a teacher. In defiance, the son couldn't handle mathematics and he became a very successful attorney. The daughter decided to do anything at the time *but* pursue teaching! I went to Brooklyn College and majored in English. But it was only after my children were born that I decided education was a vital part of the future and this was where I wanted to be.

The expectation in my generation was that I would get married and have children. I got married at the very normal age of twenty-two. I met my husband, who is a native of the Bronx, on a vacation in Nantucket, Massachusetts. Our first date was a bike ride. He is an atmospheric physicist. He had just gotten his Masters degree from the University of Chicago and had a job in Massachusetts. We lived there for sixteen years, minus two years when he went back to Chicago for his Doctorate degree. We had four children, and I was a homemaker.

I would take courses which interested me, because I was going out of my mind just being a housewife. I took Great Books courses and volunteered in my children's school and led discussion groups, which further stimulated my interest in education. When my youngest son entered kindergarten, I began a Masters programme. I did my Masters degree on a part-time basis from 1969 to 1974 and it was in Education and Curriculum Development. I was one of those parents who would look into every single educational toy and game available, and education became a real passion of mine. I sent my own kids to neighbourhood public schools. They were fine, and I wasn't so aware then of differences in the quality of schools.

In 1975 we moved to Metropolis – my husband had a job opportunity here. We joined a Reform Temple in South Metropolis. I had turned away from Orthodox Judaism, and we belonged to a Reform Temple in Massachusetts. How did I get involved with the Golda Meir? We moved here in mid-1975 and I had already gotten my Masters degree the year before. Shortly after that, I began looking for a teaching job. A friend of mine mentioned that there was this new day school, only two years old, so I interviewed for it and I was hired. At the beginning, it was very small and there were only a handful of teachers. By last year we had more than 300 children. When I first started in 1977, I had a combined fifth and sixth grade class of seven kids, and now I have classes of twenty and twenty-one.

Each grade has up to forty-six kids and there are two secular teachers, a Judaic teacher, and a Hebrew teacher. The children are almost all Jewish, and we have a two-hour-a-day Judaic Studies programme. The education is really good: maybe I'm partial. Over the past few years, there has been an increase in children from more Traditional families, but not ultra-Orthodox. The Orthodox do not send their children to Golda Meir. I don't know the Maimonides Academy at all, but that's where the Orthodox go. The philosophy of Golda Meir is a Pluralistic philosophy which believes there is more than one way to approach religion. The school respects and honours the child's background, whether it be Orthodox, Conservative, Reform, Reconstructionist, or secular. We do have a *kashrut* policy; children bring in their own dairy lunches and if we provide any food, it must have the *kosher* label.

In my opinion, the secular education is considerably better than what is offered in the public schools. Are you asking about any areas that might be censored or off-limits? There are none whatever! I teach sex education and mythology, and boys and girls are taught together. I have hundreds of books in my classroom library, and we don't believe in censorship. We encourage kids to think! When they graduate after the sixth grade, some children go on to their neighbourhood public schools; a very small number of families send them to Sussex, which is a posh private school; and more and more – a good 50 to 60 per cent – go on to the Hebrew High School. Many only stay for two years there. For some, it's a holding pattern because the public junior high schools are having problems. Then most go on to public high school. Unlike the Maimonides Academy, we don't have a seventh and eighth grade, and the main reason is an ethical one . . . it would hurt the Hebrew High School too much.

Of the secular teachers, I'd say about half are not Jewish, but all the Judaic teachers are Jewish. The aim of the school is to provide the kids with a well-rounded academic programme; give them a background in their culture and religion so they will feel comfortable in any synagogue, and have them grow up to be good people. I would say the vast majority of the parents who send their children to Golda Meir send them there not only for the Jewish education – they send them there because it is a good school. The Judaism they get is a bonus.

Of course you get the occasional frantic phone call from people who don't agree with everything we do, but the policy of the school on Judaic matters is clearly established in a fat handbook that every parent receives. Things like wearing of *kippot* (skull caps), the observance of the holidays, the celebration of *Hanukkah* (the Festival of Lights), and the building of the *sukkah* (ritual tabernacle) are part of what the school is. People accept that. Do I think children who go through the school are more likely to marry somebody Jewish? What a wonderful question! I can probably count on the fingers of one hand the marriages we have had, since our oldest alumni are still in their twenties. They have not always been Jewish marriages, but the school is still new and the sample is very small. I suppose the tendency for mixed marriages in the future might be less, especially for those who have some Jewish identification at home. Only time will tell.

I love the school. The administration is very supportive. I can virtually teach what I want; I am trusted as a professional to do what I feel is best for my students. It is a pleasant environment with small classes. I would be paid a bit more in a public school, but think what I would be giving up! When I first accepted the job, I was looking for a teaching position. I was not necessarily looking for a Jewish day school job. As a result of working at the Golda Meir for sixteen years, I have become more in tune with myself as a Jew and much more aware of my own Judaism. If I were raising young children all over again, this is where I would be sending them.

The Teacher in the Orthodox Day School

MRS SUSAN LEVINE

We interviewed Mrs Susan Levine in a small house on the West Side. She was the first grade (five to six-year-olds) teacher at the Maimonides Academy and had been recommended as a favourite teacher by Rabbi Klein's (The Yeshiva Official) *eldest daughter. She was a pretty, plump woman wearing a long, print dress and, like all the Orthodox women, a wig. Her blond six-year-old son played quietly beside us. He was dressed in jeans, T-shirt, and track shoes as well as a skull cap and ritual fringes.*

I grew up in Phoenix, Arizona, in a non-religious background – very non-religious. We belonged to a Reform Temple, and I suppose I did go to religion school. When I went to college at the University of Arizona I spent one year in Israel, for which I got college credits, and for the other three years I studied Elementary Education. After university I started to teach, although I did some religion school teaching while I was still in college. I started off in a Reform Temple, but as I was progressing at that part of my life, I then taught in a Conservative synagogue pre-school. After I graduated I worked in the Phoenix Orthodox Hebrew Academy teaching first grade, by which time I was married.

I met my husband at the rabbi's table in Phoenix. He is native to Metropolis, but he stopped off in Phoenix on the way to Los Angeles. He grew up here on the West Side: he went to Maimonides Day School; to the *Yeshiva* High School; and actually he went to Rabbi Berkovski's synagogue (father of *The Hasidic Rabbi*). Rabbi Berkovski's family has known my husband's family for five generations. The grandmothers played together in some little town in Russia! It's a big family connection. When I was in college, for about two years I stayed at the Phoenix rabbi's house every Sabbath. By the time I met my husband, I had become Orthodox. It just felt right for me.

Little by little I took things on. It just felt good.

My husband called up the rabbi because he needed a place for the Sabbath. He was at the table. We met each other – and he never left Phoenix. I was twenty-three and he was twenty-four. What did my parents think? I think they still to this day are not comfortable with my religious lifestyle. I'm sort of the black sheep of the family! My sister married someone who is not Jewish, and my brother married someone who converted to Reform. I think my family thought it distanced me from them. It was hard when I went to visit. I couldn't eat the food and my mother first thought her house wasn't clean enough. My parents are very upper-middle-class and socially prominent, and my lifestyle is different. My son's birth has helped. We waited six years for him. He's very special, and he's close to his grandparents.

After we were married, we lived in Arizona for four years. We knew we couldn't stay there. It's not a growing, vibrant Jewish community. There's nothing like the West Side there. It's more Orthodox-style than Orthodox. We were visiting Metropolis, and I thought I would just call up the rabbi to see if there was a job in the Maimonides Academy. He said he didn't have any vacancies, but to come in just to talk. When I went in three days later, an hour before I arrived the first grade teacher had called and quit. So I talked to him and a week or two later he called me and said I could have the job. Yes, we came here for my job. My husband's health isn't very good. He works part-time for Rabbi Vardin (*The Kashrut Supervisor*).

I would say I have more freedom in the school than the teachers who are not Jewish or not religious. They come to me and say, 'What candy can I buy for treats?' They give me their money, and I go to Woolworths to buy the candy. Many of the teachers are not Jewish. There are buses that drive the kids over to the East Side. The buses hold seventy-seven, and I think they are quite full. The school has grown: when I started there were about 200 children, and last year there were nearly 400. The children are taught separately – boys and girls from first grade – though they used to be taught together up to the sixth grade. Last year I had twenty-five students in each class. I have two classes, and I share them with a Hebrew teacher. Each grade has one English and one Hebrew teacher. It was a lot of kids, but I did have a teaching aide. I have had as little as twenty-five children in two classes.

I teach reading, writing, spelling, science, social studies, phonetics, art, math. They do have gym and they do have library. I do a lot of work with them on the computer also. The children are not all from an Orthodox background. Maimonides is very much a community school. There are Russian kids, Israeli kids, and kids of varying religious backgrounds. Last year probably about twelve children in my class did not have English as their first language. We do have special education for those who can't keep up. That's unusual in a Jewish school outside New York, and it's one of the things that is kind of neat about Maimonides.

I'm very close to the Hebrew teacher. We try to integrate a lot of things together and support each other. So, for example, when she was teaching about Hebrew blessings, I made a grocery store. We hung up signs indicating which blessing was for which thing and the kids went shopping. She teaches them Hebrew language and religious education. They learn to read and write Hebrew – they can't understand it at that stage. Then I teach them to read English, and by the end of the first grade they'd better be able to read and write English well!

Now that I've been here eight years, I've had lots of brothers and sisters through my class and everyone knows me. Why do less observant parents send their children to Maimonides? A lot of them want their kids to be around other Jewish kids. A lot of parents do it to please the grandparents. Some want their children to have the information to make their own choices. Sometimes the kids do help the parents to be more observant, but sometimes the next year we find the kids are just not in the school. It's like too much of a pressure for the parents. The school does not put any restrictions on the parents, and sometimes you find kids with very little religious background reaching the highest level in Hebrew subjects.

Each class prays separately, but grades six to eight (twelve to fourteen-year-olds) meet together before school begins. In the morning it depends on the grade level. It gets more as they get older. By the sixth grade, they go through the whole morning service. Then of course we have all the blessings before and after meals. The Principal is a rabbi.

When they leave Maimonides, some boys go to the *Yeshiva* High School and some girls to *Beis Rahel.* A few – but not very many – go to the Pluralist Hebrew High School, and some go to public high school. Sure, that's a big transition! The school costs somewhere around $5,000 a year, but not everyone pays full fees. The school does get some outside finance. Needy families fill in an application form for scholarships, and they have to go before a committee. They really don't turn anyone away though there are people who say, 'We don't want to pay this much because we want a new house,' and the committee says, 'We need you to do your part.' I think they have got tougher recently.

The fees don't pay for food. You have to bring a dairy lunch every day, and once a week the mothers make a hot lunch. It costs $2.25 and you can buy it if you choose to. Money is tight even though people give donations. The school spends a lot of money on English as a second language for the Russian students. They have a social worker available, and they have remedial English and Hebrew. The building is a very nice facility for a Jewish school. It's very modern and up-to-date, and it all costs money.

The purpose of the school is to give the kids knowledge and information to become observant Jews. Not all go on to Hebrew schools, and not all stay the full course at Maimonides. It's a tough school, and a kid really has to work hard to be successful in both English and Hebrew at the same time. You have to be willing to work hard. The policy on homework is fifteen minutes times the grade. So, for example, first grade gets fifteen minutes' homework, and in eighth grade they have a couple of hours. I certainly don't remember doing a couple of hours' homework when I was at elementary school! But most kids seem to thrive on it. By the end you should be able to read and understand the Prayer Book and the Bible. The boys start on *Talmud*, and the girls learn the prophets and other areas. Yes they have a different religious curriculum for boys and girls in the higher grades. They also have to do well in secular subjects. I taught in public schools in Arizona and the standard in English subjects is much, much higher in Maimonides. It's an excellent education, and that's why people choose it . . .

The Religion School Teacher

MRS SYLVIA GOODMAN

All temples and synagogues have religion schools attached to them. Students attend in addition to their normal secular schools.

We sat in the living room of Sylvia Goodman's ranch-style house. It had a high sloping ceiling like a barn, an open fireplace, and modern prints and lithographs on the walls. Near the fireplace were open shelves with an extensive array of Jewish objects. On the large, glass coffee-table was a clay model of a rabbi reading. The sofas were deep and comfortable; the carpet thick; and oatmeal linen covered the walls.

Mrs Goodman herself was a short, jolly woman in black trousers and a black T-shirt. She must have been in her early sixties, but her hair was still dark and her speech lively.

In 1966 my father died and the rabbi came round to social work me. He asked me to take over a religion school class because one of the teachers had left. And I said: 'How can you ask me this? I have no Jewish background; I didn't even graduate from College,' you know, this kind of thing. And he said, 'I just know you'll be good. You're a good Girl Scout leader and you'll read the books I give you to read, and I know you'll do a good job. It's only for a short while. You can do this for me.' He was my friend so I did it for him.

When I got into the classroom I started lecturing, which was the way I imagined people taught, and it didn't work. So I started to read about education. It was the 1960s and I came across some wonderful techniques like debates and psychodramas. I tried them out and the kids loved it. After that short time I knew that somewhere in education was the place for me.

The next year the rabbi asked me if I would originate a new junior high school programme with him. It was going to be different from anything anyone was doing at that time. It was going to be strictly a weekend programme. We were going to take thirteen to fifteen-year-olds, put them together from 9–4:00 Saturday and 9–4:00 Sunday, but only once a month. The idea behind it was we were having a lot of attendance problems because of sport, and also we felt there was so much more we could do with a large block of time. We had a lot of difficulty selling it to the parents, but we succeeded in doing that and the programme was extremely successful. The kids loved it. They could go off and play their sports the other three weekends, and we had them for the full fifteen hours. We brought in top-notch speakers and showed films and did all kinds of involving, interactive things. It was subsequently copied in about fifty congregations in the country at one time. Then it sort of fell out of favour because there were things wrong with it . . . There are still a few congregations doing it, which gives me a thrill!

The kids from those days, whom I run into now and then, tell me it was a positive experience. Several of them later became Directors of Education themselves, and Marion Schwartz (*The Museum Curator*) is the Director of the Greenbaum Museum here. She was one of my students. The parents were very supportive. Once it got going the parents loved it and saw its benefits. They saw the change in attitude in their children. It served its purpose.

Then I became Director of the Temple education. I was flying by the seat of my pants in those days. I really didn't have the know-how. But a few years later I went back to school, and I did finish my course. Then I went off to the Hebrew Union College (Reform rabbinical college) in Los Angeles, and I got my Masters degree in Jewish Education. My official title now is Curriculum Consultant at the Temple. This will be my third year doing this, and it's about ten hours a week.

There has always been a problem with Jewish religious education in the past. It was taught by dreary people who were roped into doing it and weren't very enthusiastic about it. Generally they were much older, quite often very Orthodox, and they didn't relate well to kids. The textbooks were often very drab and boring. I've talked to many parents about their own religion school experience and they were so turned off by things like that. They just couldn't wait to get to the *Bar* or *Bat Mitzvah*, and get it done, get it over with and out. It didn't fit with the modern life they were leading. They thought their parents big hypocrites because they were supposed to keep the Sabbath, but they all kept their stores open on Saturday. They had shrimp when they went out, but wouldn't have it in the house. There seemed to be a lot of conflict.

Now in the religion schools I've had to do with, you get a different type of teacher. For a start the community has a wonderful *Bar Mitzvah* teacher in Danny Mizel (*The Bar Mitzvah Teacher*). Mostly the teachers are much younger; they're very committed; they're very enthusiastic; they know how to sing Jewish songs; they've grown up in Jewish camp; and they've also had different experiences from the teachers in the 1950s and 1960s. It's jazzed our schools up in a lot of ways. But even now I'm not sure every kid finds religion school a very pleasant and positive experience. Many still don't. I think part of that is parental attitudes. It's still the laundry bag metaphor: they drop the kids off at religion school like they would drop off the laundry, and pick them up when they're done.

Education is essential: without it Judaism will not continue. The only hope is the educated Jew. Otherwise, it's going to drift off and every generation will become less knowledgeable than the last. And then it's going to get lost. It's going to get watered down into nothing. I think observance and education go hand in hand. Few of them light Sabbath candles at home. I'd say less than half, which is horrific – very, very upsetting. We started something new this year. We designed a Sabbath basket and into the basket we put a wine cup, candlesticks, candles, a little plaited loaf, a little bread cover, and a tape with all the blessings. This goes into our kindergarten classes and every week a different child takes this basket home. The parents are sent a letter encouraging them to have a Friday night blessing over wine and bread. The feedback has been terrific. The kids fight to take it home, and every child gets to take it home once during the year.

Jewish continuity for me is the whole thing really. Why? That's a good question. Why? There's always the argument that says you give Hitler the posthumous victory, but I'm not one that says we have to survive because Hitler said we shouldn't. I think there's inherent value in what Judaism has to offer to ourselves and the world. I think we have a very rich tradition which would be a shame to abandon. I think we have a great set of values, wonderful celebrations, great ethics. It can be a very joyous experience; it isn't always, but it can be. There's a wonderful tradition of study and I think it can enrich anyone's life who really digs into it in any meaningful way . . . . I know it has done so for me personally.

The Museum Curator

MRS MARION SCHWARTZ

The Greenbaum Museum is situated in the building of Har HaShem synagogue, on the affluent East Side. It is composed of a large exhibition room and a small office which was shared between three women, one of whom was The Jewish Feminist. *Marion Schwartz, the Curator, spoke to us in the exhibition room. Around the walls were photographs of Russian Jews emigrating to Israel: there were some people boarding airplanes; others were waiting in line; and still more, clutching all their possessions, were bidding goodbye to weeping relatives. She was a dark, bespectacled woman in her mid-forties, wearing a black and white check dress. She sat with her hands folded in her lap and spoke fluently and rapidly.*

I'm a Metropolis native. I was born in 1949. My grandparents had emigrated to the United States from Europe – one grandfather was a peddlar, and the other was a *kosher* butcher. My parents had a wholesale tobacco business which still exists. I was raised at Temple *Shalom*, and was very involved with the Temple youth group which was a large part of my growing up. My husband is the grandson of the first rabbi of *Har HaShem* synagogue. He was engaged here in 1901. He was here either as a rabbi or as Emeritus until 1972. Even though I grew up in Metropolis, I never knew him because my family were Reform and were members of Temple *Shalom*. Since my marriage, we have affiliated with *Har HaShem* but, to be honest, we pray more frequently in Rabbi Berkovski's (*The Hasidic Rabbi*) congregation. For me, because I work here five days a week, I like a change of scenery on the Sabbath. Also I prefer the scale at *B'nai Akiva*. It's very intimate. I find this is too big – it has the same problem as Temple *Shalom*.

I didn't get married until I was thirty. Before that I went to Wellesley College to do Art History. Then I went to New York to study at the Cooper Union School of Art, and subsequently returned to Wellesley for a fifth year. After graduation I worked for various art organizations as an administrator, and when the Greenbaum Museum was founded in 1982 I was invited to sit on the Board. Professor Kornfeld (*The University Professor of Judaica*) was, and still is, the Director. Then in 1986 they asked me if I wanted to become the Museum Co-ordinator. Prior to that I served as manager to two commercial galleries so the background I came to the job with was an administrative one, as a Programme Director and a hands-on one at commercial galleries.

The Museum has mounted an average of five exhibits a year. The types of exhibits run the gamut, dealing with different aspects of Jewish history and Jewish culture all over the world. We've had shows on the Jews of Yemen, Kurdistan . . . I'm trying to think what else . . . We have had shows of ceremonial objects such as *Torah* ornaments . . . We have had exhibits on the festivals, on the Yiddish theatre, on Sephardic customs, on pioneer Jews of Colorado, and on maps of the Holy Land. We get our exhibits from various places. For example, we had a show on Jewish ritual lights, and that show went to Jerusalem, Amsterdam, New York, San Francisco, and our little museum here in Metropolis – we were delighted to be on that circuit. Then, we ran a very successful exhibition of local Jewish artists. The response we got was one of terrific appreciation because so often attention goes to artists with larger national reputations. There's a certain condescension towards regional artists, purely because they're local. It's a kind of snobbishness and we were filling a gap.

We have a definite commitment to an interfaith connection. For example, we did an exhibition on headwear symbolism in Judaism, Christianity and Islam. So we showed black broad-rimmed hats from the Mennonites and the *Hasidic* Jews. We had skull caps from Muslim countries, from Jews, and of course what the Pope wears! We had a fez wrapped with a turban, which was a rabbinical hat in Turkey. It was a fascinating show! We want to reach both Jews and non-Jews.

Within the Jewish community we definitely see ourselves as an educational institution, and that's how we justify whatever community funding we get. This is not just an outlet of this synagogue, though the connection is there. Professor Kornfeld is Director of the Museum and initially we occupied the space rent-free. Three years ago we became independent corporately of the synagogue, but it's always been a challenge to overcome the association with the synagogue.

Our primary benefactor is Henry Greenbaum, but he is no longer the largest source of our funds. We also have 1,200 members who pay dues – membership of $15 up for individuals. We instituted a community-wide fundraising dinner four years ago. The first year we had 325 people. This past year we had 900 people here. It was held in the sanctuary, which has moveable seating, combined with the social hall. It was wonderful! Every year we honour someone who has contributed to the cultural enrichment of the community. Last year it was Leah Silver (*Editor of the Jewish Newspaper*). This year it was Rabbi Oppenheim of *Adath Israel* (*The Traditional Rabbi*). A lot of people came to that. The theme of the dinner was the world of our fathers and mothers. The food was Eastern European. The entertainment was a *shtetl* band. We had dancers doing Ashkenazi dancing. It was a fun evening. The cost of a single ticket was $125. Most of the Jewish institutions charge from $300 a couple and so our charging $250 is still somewhat low. That's not where we make the money. We make the money on the corporate tables, and the higher levels which go up to a $5,000 table for a party of ten. No, no . . . Rabbi Oppenheim was a guest – he didn't have to pay!

This has been the most wonderful professional experience for me, professionally and personally. I have three children: my two daughters are at the Golda Meir Day School, and my two-year-old is in Jewish pre-school here. Having a job that combines my background in the visual arts, art history and arts administration, and having it in synchronicity with something Jewish is fabulous . . .

Six

INSIDERS SERVING THE COMMUNITY

The Mobel

RABBI AMOS FEIGELBAUM

A mobel performs ritual circumcisions. As well as being a community mobel, Amos Feigelbaum kept a jewellery store in downtown Metropolis. It was a modern showroom on the third floor of an old building decorated in a tasteful eau-de-nil. He was a young-looking man in his early forties who wore a black skull cap. We sat around a small table among the showcases. He was drinking a clear malt drink and eating yoghurt-covered raisins.

I'm native to Metropolis. I was born here forty-three years ago, and my mother, may she rest in peace, was also native to Metropolis. My father was a native Lower East Side of New York boy! He came over to Metropolis on a visit and, as they say, the rest is history! I lived in the ghetto on the West Side, and I still live in the ghetto! I now live right across the street from where I grew up. I went to Maimonides Academy in this city, and then I went to *yeshiva* in Chicago. I spent two years there, and then I finished my *yeshiva* high school education in Manhattan. Shimon Silver (*Editor of the Jewish Newspaper*) and I used to sit next to each other. That was 1969, and a lot of exciting things were going on in the world. At that point my parents allowed me to continue my studies in Jerusalem, and I was in Israel for three years.

I got *semihah* (rabbinic ordination) in Israel. Unlike Rabbi Marmorstein (*The Orthodox Rabbi*) I only got three. At that point I wanted to go into Outreach teaching. I was young and idealistic. It was before children came on the scene, and I had to make a living for them! I remember going to a circumcision one December. Something told me to go and ask the *mobel* if he was training people.

I thought it was something important to learn, practically speaking. I always knew there were some problems in Metropolis about *mohelim*. The training was fairly intense. First of all the *mohel* really checked me out thoroughly. He made some calls to the States. He wanted to know who he was training. He saw it as a holy vocation, and it wasn't for anyone. Then he took me through the basic commandments. Then I spent four months *shlepping* around with this *mohel*. He was doing an average of six of them daily. This was all over Jerusalem. I probably witnessed 400 procedures prior to being on my own. We saw quite a bit of abnormality during that time, and it was immensely interesting. Then the next step was for him to give me a licence which is now at home displayed on my wall.

I came back to the United States aged twenty-one with my nice certificate, ready to roll. There didn't seem an opening for a *mohel* in Metropolis so I went to Seattle and taught in the Jewish day school for two years. It was marvellous. I was single, footloose and fancy free. It was a very wonderful time, and I did a fair number of circumcisions. It's important to do a certain amount or you get rusty – and you don't want your *mohel* to be rusty, unless he knows how to do tetanus shots! My jokes get worse by the way!

Then one summer in Metropolis I met a young lady who was going to the *Beis Rahel* High School. She was a kid. I tell people I did not rob the cradle; I got right in with her! When we got married she was nineteen. After we got married we went back to Israel to study for a year. Then we didn't know where we wanted to go so we ended up in a little town in upstate New York, and we were there for a year. Our first daughter was born there. I get a little teary-eyed over this. She just graduated from *Beis Rahel*, and she is the first second-generation student to graduate!

Anyway to make a long story short, which is what a *mohel* does, we stayed in Los Angeles for two years. We had two children by then. My wife wasn't working, and things were a little tight. I was offered a position in a jewellery institute and got out of teaching. At that point I wanted to come home to Metropolis, and that is what we did. I set up in this store. You've seen my card? It says, 'Amos Feigelbaum, Mohel', and in small letters, 'Now let me handle the rest of your family jewels.' So I came back, and now we have five children. I have two girls as bookends, and three boys in the middle.

The *mohel* in Metropolis was tapering back. I put up my shingle independently and it's now a good seven or eight years since he's done a circumcision. Right now I have no rivals in Metropolis. Except for the surgeons, I have a monopoly. Do remember, I do one procedure. This is the age of specialization. A diaper rash is below my territory, and the umbilical cord is above my territory. I go right down the centre, and if I can't do this procedure effectively by this time, something is wrong. I do it for everyone in the community, from the Reform and Reconstructionists to the *Hasidim* and super-Orthodox.

What do I do if the mother isn't Jewish? Provided they are intending to raise the child as Jewish, I do a circumcision with the presumption of a conversion. So I get calls from Mrs Lisa O'Brien, and I say to myself, 'Good! That's a Jewish mother and a non-Jewish father, and I know what I'm dealing with! The kid is Jewish.' The problem comes when the father's name is Goldberg and the mother is called Christina; then I know I've got to bring a Rabbinical Court along. We hope in that case that the child will continue and, when he gets to *Bar Mitzvah* age, he will go to a ritual bath for conversion. The two who make up the Court with me just sit on the sidelines. I normally use boys from the *Yeshiva* High School. I don't make a big deal out of it. The blessings are a little bit different but no one notices that . . . and I have to say the Reform rabbis are very understanding about it all. I would say 50 per cent of people who call me, one parent is not Jewish. So in 25 per cent of cases the mother is not Jewish and some sort of conversion of the child is needed. I feel that if I do this right, and I don't cause more conflict between the religions, we have a chance maybe later of the non-Jewish parent being comfortable in raising her child as a Jew.

How much do I charge? Good question! I don't give a one-word answer to this by any stretch of the imagination. What I basically say is I dedicate these fees to my kids' tuition. I have five kids in Jewish schools. It comes to about $35,000 a year.

I've also got to pay my malpractice insurance. So, the standard is round about $300, but if people can only afford $100, that's fine. I say this extremely sincerely; I have a responsibility in the community. There is no such thing as a Jewish child who will not have a circumcision, no matter what. If you can't afford a dime, I'll be there, no matter what. It's my pleasure. That doesn't mean I'll do it for nothing if people can afford to pay. People have to understand, there's a value for keeping a commandment. Unfortunately in America people value things according to what it costs. They shouldn't, but that's the way it is!

Yeah – paediatric opinion goes back and forth on circumcision. At present the pendulum is swinging back a little in favour. I do get calls from people saying, 'I don't know about this . . . persuade me.' I really find it not too difficult today with Jewish parents. I can cite a bit of medical evidence that seems to be positive. Then I always say, 'If your child in later life is going to identify as a Jew, then talk to people who have been circumcised later in life.' It is just incredibly painful! There's also negative talk about nerve endings and less sensitivity, but then I've heard the opposite from people who have been circumcised later in life. I had one guy who converted in his forties and he said that he was so much more sensitive after the operation . . . Anyway most people are never in a position to make the comparison!

Yeah – I have thought of writing a book about it all. I thought I could call it *Short Cuts to Circumcision.*

The Director of the Jewish Community Centre

MS JOANNA MILLER

The Jewish Community Centre was built thirty years ago in a modern style in the centre of the East Side Jewish suburbs. It had been in constant use since then and was looking a little shabby. On the day of our visit, a group of pre-school children were making models in one social hall; a group of teenagers were rehearsing Fiddler on the Roof *in the theatre; a swimming lesson was being conducted in the pool; the tennis courts were fully booked; there was an exhibition of photographs in the upper gallery; a group of middle-aged ladies were being initiated into the mysteries of the potter's wheel; there was an energetic aerobics class and several jaded businessmen were walking brisk miles on the electronic treadmill in the gym.*

Joanna Miller, the Director, met us in her cool modern office. She was a vivacious, brown-eyed woman in her mid-forties. As she talked, she gesticulated with her hands towards a large architect's plan that leaned against one wall of the room.

From the time I was about nine, I guess, I lived in El Paso, Texas. I grew up there. My father was chief astro-physicist at White Sands Missile Range. I got my Bachelors and Masters degree in Public Administration and Political Science at the University of Texas, and then came to the big, wicked city. What do I mean? I grew up in El Paso: for me Metropolis is the big, wicked city!

My religious background is a little unusual. I didn't know I was Jewish until I was about twenty-five years old. I had been raised in a largely non-religious way. We were, I suppose, raised as Methodists. I'd always understood that my mother's family were Methodist and my father's family was German Catholic. Purely by accident I met a cousin here in Metropolis. He was passing through town. He came over and he kept talking about Jews. So I said, 'Are you Jewish?' and he said, 'Aren't you?' And he told me that my father's brothers and his sister and his parents and his everybody are all Jewish! And sure enough, when I met them, they all were! So I asked my father about it. He clearly did not want to talk about it. Then I had the opportunity to go to Israel on a Ford Foundation grant. When I came back, I decided that even though I considered myself a Jew, probably nobody else would. So I did a formal conversion so there wouldn't be any question. I was thrilled to death to find out I was Jewish. I had always hated being a regular, old boring WASP (White Anglo-Saxon Protestant), and I was thrilled to death to find out that I was something better than that – at least better to me – and that there was a rich culture to cotton on to. So I have lived my life as a Jew since I was twenty-five. I belong to *Adath Israel* on the West Side. The rabbi there, Rabbi Oppenheim (*The Traditional Rabbi*), is a long-time friend and he's the main reason I'm there. I feel very comfortable there. I love his *Torah* lessons: they're intellectual, funny, spiritual, wonderful . . .

I don't think of myself as a convert at all, and I'm resentful when I'm labelled as such. Frankly it's something that shocks me about the Jewish community here. Until I came here, I was never closely involved in the community even though I went to synagogue regularly. I had a stereotype of what a Jew is – that is liberal and tolerant of everyone and everything. We're intolerant of everyone and everything. We're intolerant of the very religious; we're intolerant of the Reform – they're not Jewish enough; the very religious are embarrassing; the *Hasids* are even more embarrassing; the West Side are the poor Jews that no one really wants to associate with; the East Side are the hotshots with the jewels and the minks; everybody hates the Russians; nothing is more despicable than a convert. The things that I have heard come out of people's mouths! People say things that absolutely blow my mind!

Our mission here in the Centre is to reach out to the unaffiliated, the intermarried, and to bring people back into contact with something Jewish. I think as far as my Jewish background is concerned, I may be a perfect choice for this position because I'm who we're looking for. I was unaffiliated; I am the product of a mixed marriage; I feel very lucky to have found this part of my life. It has been a very enriching, wonderful thing, although this last year has been a real eye-opener!

I have a Board of Directors here who are quite remarkable. Laurie Paine's (*The President of the Allied Jewish Federation*) husband is Chairman. They were looking for someone with strong management and financial skills, and I guess they thought that if my background was going to be an issue with the community, there were trade-offs. This is a place where the Director needs to be Jewish; the entire Board is Jewish, even though 40 per cent of the people who use this place are not Jewish or are intermarried.

We are not a religious institution. We are not a synagogue; we do not have services. We are a recreational and cultural institution. We are a place where people can come to be in a

Jewish environment to play and to recreate and to experience Jewish culture with other Jews. But we are not a religious institution. We are not competing with the synagogues – our agendas are very different. Here we have everything ranging from indoor and outdoor tennis courts and an athletic facility with indoor and outdoor swimming pools. Because it has been allowed to run down, it is not as active as it was in its heyday, but we are about to rebuild the whole athletic facility. We encourage singles' activities. We have an excellent pre-school which is successful substantively and financially. We have a superb established children's summer camp; we have a very successful day camp here – in fact on any given day in the summer, we have about 400 children here at this facility; and we have a 300-seat theatre.

We have Rabbi Berkovski (*The Hasidic Rabbi*) supervise *kashrut* here for us. He's magical. He's loved by the very religious and the heathens alike. The guy is brilliant; he is charming; he makes it all come to life. What's there not to love? He's quite wonderful. This facility is completely *kosher*. Nothing is served here that is not *kosher*. Anything that you bring in for yourself, like the kids' lunches, has to be dairy. We're in the process of putting together at the moment a handbook explaining what constitutes a dairy luncheon – that kind of thing. Whether it's cookies and punch at an art opening or lunch every day for the seniors, everything we serve is *kosher*. We have a meat kitchen and a dairy kitchen. For a child's birthday, we either do the baking here or buy pre-done *kosher* stuff. I've done all this since I've got here. I certainly don't keep *kosher* myself at home, but I believe that a community centre needs to be accessible to everyone. We used to have a schizophrenic policy on *kashrut*. Everything was supposed to be *kosher*, but nothing was. Even in the vending machines, you could have anything – there were pork rinds in one of those machines when I first came here! When we did a celebration of Israel this year, I noticed there were a lot of Orthodox people here – I felt very good about that.

Our art programmes also have a heavy Judaic content. We do a Judaic art show every year; we do a *Purim* (Feast of Esther) mask show that is absolutely brilliant; we do a local juried art show which is wonderfully successful for the whole community – we had thousands of people through it this year. We have a proud tradition in art here. We have really a pretty wonderful permanent collection that has not been highlighted, and has really been mistreated in this facility. In our renovation, there will be a whole new cultural arts building – a big chunk of that will be a gallery. Some of our most popular classes here are the pottery classes, and we do pottery shows as well.

Eighty per cent of our revenue comes from programming fees, about 11 per cent comes from the Allied Jewish Federation, and the rest comes from here and there. Increasingly we're moving this institution in the direction of being financially self-supporting. It must stand on its own feet. As long as the quality of programming is there, we believe we will be able to support ourselves. Some of the programmes such as the pre-school and the summer camp already contribute to the bottom line – they both draw off a net of six figures. At present we have about 1,200 members, and then another 3,000 users who pay as they go. What we want is for as many people as possible to belong to the Centre, so they are on our mailing list, so they see what is going on . . .

It has been a turn-around situation. The Centre has been operated as a charity, a do-good. It was not run as a business, as something that should be self-supporting. There has been a lot of criticism of the changes that I've been making. People have had to be laid off. We've had to modify our programmes. I've laid off many of the physical education faculty; I've laid off many of the design and publicity staff; I've laid off many of the art staff temporarily while the new building takes place. It's a very painful, wrenching thing. There's a lot of anger. I am sure you will hear a lot about the Wicked Witch of the West who runs the Jewish Community Centre just now. It's very hard, but we have to be responsible . . .

Before I came here I owned a cable television company which I operated for eight years, and then sold about three years ago. I wasn't going to work again. I had retired. I was going to travel and putter about and sit on boards and stuff, but I got bored. Since I didn't have to worry about paying the mortgage, I was looking for something where I could give back to the community which has given a great deal to me. One of the reasons I can be effective in this job is because I don't need this job, and I'm going to stay here as long as it takes to get it done . . .

The Kashrut Supervisor

RABBI YAAKOV VARDIN

A kashrut supervisor is engaged in checking that food which advertises itself as kosher conforms to the Jewish dietary law.

Rabbi Yaakov Vardin lived in a house on the West Side of Metropolis. A patriarchal figure with a long beard, he sat in a rocking chair in his shirt-sleeves with a black yarmulke on his head. Around the room were an array of family photographs of himself, his wife (The Governor of the Orthodox Girls' High School), *and their seven children. The children ranged in age from twenty-three to one, and the eldest girl was married with two babies of her own. While we talked a small girl tripped around, and Mrs Vardin sat quietly nearby on a comfortable old sofa.*

I was born in England. My parents had fled there from Germany, escaping the Nazis. Then they moved to New York when I was five years old so I lost my Brummie accent! I went to high school and rabbinical college back East. Then I had a position as a rabbi in Pennsylvania. Then I spent a couple of years in the service as a military chaplain. Uncle Sam said, 'You will come here', and I said, 'Yes sir!', and we wound up on a base near Metropolis. In fact my eldest children were born in a military hospital nearby.

I became a rabbi accidentally. I was faced with the situation that I had proposed to my wife, and the trouble was she said 'Yes!' So I said to myself, 'What am I going to do now?' And this opportunity in Pennsylvania knocked on my door, so to speak, and I thought I would give it a try. Then after military service, I thought I would start my own business. I started selling Italian porcelain round the state. But in order to make a good living, I had to do a lot of travelling. It turned out I was away nine months of every year. I mean we had a happy marriage but . . .

Then I found out that in Metropolis there were really no *kosher* breads, and in fact very little *kosher* food. Most of the people here were doing their own baking. At that time I saw a little grocery store open and I said to myself, 'Maybe this guy would like to become *kosher*.' Anyway he was convinced, and I did such a good job helping him become *kosher* that the rabbi of *Etz Hayyim* came to me and stared at me and said, 'Now we have found someone to take care of *kashrut*.'

I have to look at the ingredients to make sure they are *kosher*, check the cleaning, the food processing and see that everything is in accord with the dietary laws. From the grocery it snowballed, and now we have about thirty-four accounts in the region. I act as a consultant to companies that want to become *kosher*. Once this company becomes *kosher*, my next step is to keep it *kosher*. I inspect. They don't know when I'm going to come in. In most cases I have 24-hour accessibility to all the plants. They can't put me off; they have to let me in.

We do everything except actual meats. We do dairies, cottage cheese, sour cream, bakeries, snack foods, pasta . . . Some companies are very small, mom-and-pop sort of stores, and some are large corporations. We work with everyone who is willing to meet the standard and our organization is nationally recognized. You see, the problem is that according to government standards you can call something a vegetable oil and still have between 2 and 7 per cent animal product. Then it won't be *kosher*. But if we say something is animal free, then it *is* animal free and that is very important not only for Jews but also for vegetarians and people with allergies. There are millions, and I'm not exaggerating, of Seventh Day Adventists, Moslems, vegetarians and health people who are looking for the *kosher* symbol.

I must make it clear. Gentiles who eat non-*kosher*, there's absolutely nothing wrong with that. We don't look down upon that. But we Jews were commanded to eat *kosher*. In the past people started to move away from *kosher* for whatever reason, but now they're coming back to it. There's an old expression – what you eat is what you are – and for us to keep *kosher*, it helps us elevate between the physical and metaphysical and brings us closer to G–d.

It doesn't sound like much, but I help *kosher* between three and four homes a month. People who've made the decision to keep *kosher*: I speak to people; I go through their kitchen; I tell them what to expect; and also I try not to force my standards upon people. I try to make it as easy for them as I can. I don't want you to think there are different standards of *kosher* because there aren't, according to the *Code of Jewish Law.* When we *kosher* a pot, there's no hocus-pocus: we put it into a big pot of boiling water and then cold water. Everything has to be done: pots, stoves, sinks, silverware. There's no blessing. But before you use your pot, you should take it and dip it in the ritual bath – you make a blessing there. I explain to them about the ritual bath, but I leave it up to them. Most of them want to. It just takes two seconds.

There are a few *kosher* restaurants in Metropolis like the deli on the East Side and the dairy restaurant in the shopping centre. We also go into clubs and hotels and transform them from a non-*kosher* status to a *kosher* status for a particular function. We've done it in as little as an hour and a half. It depends on the standard of cleanliness in the hotel. If it's not clean, we can't *kosher.* If we can't *kosher,* the party can't happen and nobody wants that. Chefs love us because it's the one time they get the kitchen really clean. Yeah, we've done Windy Oak Country Club. We then go through the menu and generally 90 per cent of the purchasing can be done through their own channels. Once it's really clean, then we start *koshering* with the high temperature blow-torch, burning off all the old stuff. So far in fourteen years we've never done any damage. Someone once dropped a glass bowl! They have to get in new dishes. Yeah, they could use paper plates, but places like the Windy Oak want that sophisticated look so paper won't fly. But every hotel is always breaking dishes, and they're happy to add new ones to their stock. Or they can rent new dishes.

I'm the only full-time employee. The office is about three feet beneath where you're sitting now – underneath your feet! I have two people working for me part-time, and I hire extra as I need them. Yes, Susan Levine's (*The Teacher in the Orthodox Day School*) husband is one of my people. We're totally independent though we are connected to Rabbi Marmorstein (*The Orthodox*

Rabbi) of *Etz Hayyim*, who's our rabbinical administrator. As a family we're part of the West Side community, but we also work with Orthodox and Traditional communities on the East Side. The *Yeshiva* High School students are interested in *kashrut*. I speak to them occasionally, and I'm told they had one of their biggest turn-outs then. They like it because it's to do with what they do every day! They eat candy; they eat cakes; they eat potato chips; and they want to know what makes them *kosher* and what's not *kosher* . . .

The Administrator of a Singles' Agency

MS SANDY SIEGEL

We interviewed Sandy Siegel in the offices of the Metropolis Allied Jewish Federation, just next door to the Jewish Community Centre. She was dark, slim and athletic-looking. Her ears were pierced, and she had a pair of stud earrings as well as a dangling moon on her left ear and a crystal drop on her right. She wore spectacles and her face was not made up, but her fingernails were painted pink. There was a Hebrew charm around her neck, but she wore no rings on her fingers.

I was born and raised here in Metropolis. I was active in the Conservative movement and grew up in *Beth Israel* synagogue. I've got two older sisters. I went through the Metropolis public schools and went to the State University. After I finished there, I went to Israel and stayed there for four years. Then I came back to Metropolis in 1988. My father was very ill, and after he passed away I stuck around as I was still trying to figure out what I wanted to do. So I ended up in England doing a MBA degree in Bath, where I got very friendly with many of the Jewish community – I loved it there. Then I went back to Israel looking for work, but I couldn't find anything I was really happy with. So I came back to the States and I ended up getting the job here.

Rendez-Vous is a Jewish singles' resource agency. Metropolis has a very high intermarriage rate. No one knows the full statistics, but they're not good. In recent years we think we've been doing a bit better, but we don't know why. The Agency is funded by the Allied Jewish Federation and is connected with the Jewish Community Centre – oh, you've talked to Joanna Miller (*The Director of the Jewish Community Centre*). We have different groups for the various age ranges and, except for the very Orthodox, all sections of the community are involved. In general the West Side is not very involved in Federation activities – that's just a fact. We're the umbrella organization that helps to facilitate the activities of all the groups. Some groups are not age specific; some encompass ages twenty-one to thirty-five; we had a group that was thirty to forty-five but that recently stopped functioning; and now there's the new group for forty-five and over – they call themselves Prime Time Movers! We also serve as a resource for individuals, for newcomers to the community, and for the newly-single. People call us up, and we send them notices of all the singles' activities in Metropolis.

Let me give you an example of a singles' group. Temple *Shalom*, the Reform Temple, runs a programme which is open to everyone in the community. It's run by Rabbi Acker (*The Administrator of a Dating File*). They have an introductory service; it's basically a dating agency. You fill out a form which talks about yourself – who you are, what your background is, where you work, etc. Then your form is put in a book which anyone can look in. If they feel like contacting you they send you a card, and either you meet or, when you've looked at their details, you send back a card saying, 'No thanks!' It's all on computer. You can go in and say, 'I want to see the details of all the men between twenty-one and twenty-eight, who don't smoke and have never been married before.' And the computer prints it out.

There's no question there's dysfunction about marriage in the Jewish community. I think it's a problem in American society as well, not just in the Jewish community. I think in the United States things are changing, things are shifting. People are not following the same course that their parents followed. My mother, for example, met my father when she was at college and married before she graduated. I think she was twenty. Two years later she started having children, and she had her three kids before she was thirty. And that was the end of it. That's something you don't see a whole lot any more. People are making other choices. Let me give you another example: My father worked for the same company for thirty years and was very proud of that fact. People don't do that any more; they move on. I think these shifts are affecting when people decide to get married. In the 1980s people didn't seem to get married. So besides the twenty-five-year-olds who are coming up, there are a whole lump of thirty-five-year-olds who have never got married.

Then you have to add on to all that the fact that Judaism is a family-based religion. There's always been an emphasis on marriage and starting a family, and a lot of people get very anxious. They look around and they say, 'Goodness, I'm thirty! In the secular world that's not so old not to be married, but everything in my Jewish upbringing says I should be married by now!' So I think you get a lot of anxiety from that. I don't know why all this singles' activity doesn't generate more marriages. The introductory service at Temple *Shalom* has been in existence for two years, and it has sixteen marriages to its credit. They're quite proud of that. I don't know why people aren't finding who they're looking for. If we could figure that out, we'd solve a lot of problems.

You can't generalize. There was a rather infamous article in the *Metropolis Jewish News* several months ago. A single man (*The Accountant*) wrote about what was the matter with Jewish single women. He had six or seven points and they were all very stereotypical. He said all Jewish women have pets and are more devoted to their cats and dogs than to any individual in their life. He also claimed Jewish women were too interested in continuing their education. He complained that women aren't interested in material things as much as they should be. Again this was one individual and his opinion, and there was a lot of furore in the singles' community . . . He was a bit embarrassed by it, and rightly so!

I think that people go into a dating situation with a list in their head. A lot of people want particular physical characteristics; like someone who's thin or in-shape, or dark hair or blonde, or petite or no one under 5 feet 6. They want a particular education and income level. This comes from both parties. Involvement in the Jewish community is very important to many people. They want a good cook – I've seen that one!

The mere fact that you have a list in your head is where a lot of the problems come from. If you've got certain minimum acceptable requirements, and you meet someone who is close on everything except for one, then they're out and you don't establish that relationship. I think sometimes the lists are completely unrealistic. I'll give you an example taken from the Temple *Shalom* books. There's a form filled out by a man who is in his sixties. He wants to go out with a petite, attractive woman in her thirties. Maybe this is realistic, maybe it is not. It probably isn't. His picture does not show him as sleek and young – but that is his image of who he wants to go out with. After all, this is America. Every boy believes he can grow up to be President!

I don't know if men are more willing to intermarry than women. Traditionally there are supposed to be more men with gentile wives than women with gentile husbands. I don't know. But of course not everyone who participates in singles' activities is committed to marrying someone Jewish. I read an article that said Jewish men are put under such pressure from their Jewish mothers that they look outside the Jewish community for a partner because they don't want to marry someone like their mother. I don't know if that's true. You must ask a Jewish single man – or one who has married out. I really don't know. Why people marry out goes back to the whole situation of the Jewish community in America. In the Reform movement in particular, there is much more acceptance of intermarriage – not just tolerance, but real acceptance. When you've got that, you don't have the same societal pressure to marry Jewish . . .

Everybody comes at it from their own angles. If you talk to people who run the Jewish day schools, they say the whole problem is lack of Jewish education; or they will say they got a good Jewish education, but it is not being reflected in the home. Parents will say they did everything they could in their homes, but the schools just really dropped the ball. The synagogues say there's nothing for them at university; and the university chaplains will tell you that the kids come to them with no Jewish education or synagogue background. So everyone is blaming someone else. I think the reality is that it's a much bigger problem than anyone realizes . . .

The Administrator of a Dating File

RABBI HARVEY ACKER

Rabbi Harvey Acker was the Associate Rabbi of Temple Shalom. He was a tall young man who looked as if he had played American football in college. In his office there were several photographs of his wife and three daughters.

I grew up in Seattle, Washington, and we were members of the large Reform Temple there. I went to religion school, which I hated, but two things happened in high school that really turned me on to the Judaism experience. I went to summer camp and I also went to Israel for six weeks. I just loved both experiences and they led me to think about working in the Jewish realm. The young rabbi of my congregation advised me to look at the University of Wisconsin, which had a wonderful Judaic Studies programme. It's where Robert Reinhardt (*The Reform Rabbi*) went. So that's where I ended up, and I got a BA in Hebrew Studies and Sociology.

I decided I wanted to be a rabbi and applied to the Hebrew Union College in Los Angeles. I spent two years there, and in the middle of my second year I met my wife. She was working in the museum that is housed in the College; she was the Director of Membership. She was divorced and had a child. I saw her in one of the lounges, and one of my classmates said, 'Oh you're not interested in her. She has a kid. She's divorced.' But I was interested in her. We became friends and we started to date, and by the end of that second year I was madly in love with her. She was learning to love me, but she was a little cautious. She'd just been divorced and here I was, a younger man, still studying in school. She wasn't about to jump into any relationship, but I was going to spend an extra year doing an Education degree in LA, which gave our relationship time to grow. A week after classes ended we got married, and I had a built-in family because she had a daughter. She was six when we got married and now she's fourteen. I had to woo both of them at the same time, and she started calling me 'Dad' the day we got married. And then we have two more daughters from our marriage.

Temple *Shalom* is my first pulpit since being ordained. Robert

Reinhardt came out to the College and interviewed me, and I started here three years ago. Why did I start the Dating File? It was really a couple of things. One of the things is that we regularly get complaints from Jewish singles that the synagogue does not meet their needs. Our services are sometimes called Family Services, and they feel excluded. It's an uncomfortable feeling – like going to the movies or eating out alone. The other issue is that at least once a week I am called up by an interfaith couple who want me to marry them. I don't do interfaith marriages, but I always see them. Often they are very disappointed and that is frustrating for me. Because of these two things, I sat down and said, 'We need to do something for the Jewish singles.'

Have you met Sandy Siegel (*The Administrator of a Singles' Agency*)? Rendez-Vous, the Jewish singles' agency, was created about a year ago. I was on the committee that founded it, but that happened after the Dating File came into existence. What happened was about three years ago I developed this idea of a Jewish introduction service. I wanted it to be self-selective. I didn't want to tell people who they should be going out with; I just wanted to create some kind of programme which would facilitate Jewish singles meeting one another. I envisioned a video service with people making little videos of themselves. I sat down with ten singles – both genders, ages ranging from twenties to sixties – and I bounced ideas off them. The outcome was the Dating File. There would be no videos, but there would be forms people would fill in.

One side has information about the person; the other side gives information about the kind of person they hope to meet. There's no address, last name or phone number on the form. They remain anonymous, and that way it's safe. A photograph is optional, but not required. Then it's self-selecting: they go through the forms and pick those they'd like to meet. We want to keep it inexpensive. We charge $50 for the first year and $25 for each additional year you're on the books. That way anyone can afford it. The final page of the form is a release. If you have had a bad dating experience, you can't sue the Temple. This was required by the Temple *Shalom* Board because they were concerned about the possibility of date rape and sexually transmitted diseases. These are concerns. They were persuaded to do it partly because creating Jewish marriages is a tremendous *mitzvah* (good deed), and also because it might bring a lot of people into the congregation. In fact we've had many people join the Temple because of the Dating File.

We now have 710 members in the File itself. We don't do any screening, but everyone in the programme has to meet at least one person who goes through the form with them. To date, we have had sixteen marriages between people who met through the File. Why haven't there been more marriages? It's a great question. There is a reason why some of these people are single. I don't want to put any of them down, but the reality is some of them are looking for the perfect match; that person is also looking for the perfect match, and they aren't it! People are looking for the perfect partner, and the perfect partner has to have all the qualities that they want. But no one is the perfect partner in every respect. Some of those who have been divorced are being extra-cautious the second time around. Some have never been married because they are afraid of making the commitment. They'd like to, but they're afraid and they're not sure how. Some of them simply don't know how to develop the relationship because they've been single for so long, and they don't know how to share with another person.

I think it's both a problem in American society and a problem in the Jewish community. Some of these people have so much baggage with them. There's some gender stereotyping going on in the Jewish realm. Some people look at all Jewish women as being 'The Princess'. They never get beyond it. I know two individuals in the File: they are both outdoors people, both active in the Jewish community, of a similar age. I encouraged one to send a card to the other. It didn't work out because the person was balding on top! Talk about shallowness! I've seen provisos like 'No facial hair' or 'full head of hair' or 'must be between this height and that height'. We also get the comments from the men, 'This woman is overweight'. You look at them, and they're not underweight themselves. They're looking for a model, and they don't realize that they're not model material themselves!

I have a standing rule, that if I get more than one complaint about an individual I will consider asking them to leave the File. I've expelled a couple of people when they've been really inappropriate. One of them, when he was turned down by a woman, called her in the middle of the night. Then there was another complaint about him so I gave him back his money and his form. The Dating File does build up hope which can lead to a lot of disappointment. We have more women than men – about 58 per cent to 42 per cent. About 50 per cent of the people over thirty have been married before, and the vast majority of people under thirty have never been married. A lot of the divorced women are the custodial parents of children, but the vast majority of those who are willing to date divorced people say they will date people with children.

Why is there so much intermarriage? I think because there are such a small number of Jews percentage-wise. If we make up 3 per cent of the population or whatever, the chances of running up against someone who is Jewish and single are not great. Whenever you go anywhere, 97 per cent of the people you run into are non-Jewish. So there's a pretty good chance that the Jewish individual will meet someone who meets their categories in every single way except for religion. It's nothing more or less than the function of an open society. We send our kids to college to learn; they learn, but they also meet non-Jewish kids. It's the numbers game!

In any event, in our society today it's more acceptable to be single. Women earn their own living and don't need to get married. I live with four women: I have three daughters. If I wasn't pro-equality and pro-choice, I'd be in serious trouble. None the less in my mind, feminism has made it harder for a woman and a man to get together. I think many men are intimidated by these very qualified women. They have a hard time handling it. Men are going to have to get used to the change, but they haven't got there yet.

The Owner of a Jewish Gift Shop

MRS RUTH FRIEDMAN

The Jewish gift shop was in a modern shopping complex in South Metropolis. It was full of Passover plates, candlesticks, wine cups *and jewellery charms. There were cards for every Jewish holiday, and a book corner. There were T-shirts bearing the legend of 'Kosher Kid' or 'Little Mensch'; a large selection of prayer shawls; and innumerable statuettes of fiddlers on the roof. Israeli music played constantly in the background. The shop was owned and run by two ladies – Mrs Marcia Sheer, the wife of Cantor Sheer (*The Traditional Cantor*), and Mrs Ruth Friedman, who spoke to us. She was an elegant, slim woman with grey hair, a sage green trouser suit, and two beautiful diamond rings.*

I came from a Conservative religious upbringing in Denver, Colorado, and I moved to Metropolis some forty years ago. I went to public high school in Denver. We kept a *kosher* home, but we were not Sabbath observant. We rode on the Sabbath, but we rode to the synagogue. That's where we went on Saturday morning. After high school, I went to college at the University of Denver and studied Home Economics and Education. I really was more interested in getting married, because in those years if you did get married, you didn't have to graduate college. I did graduate college, and that's why I came to Metropolis: I didn't have a husband. It was 1953. I was the only person among my friends who wasn't married, and at twenty-two, a Jewish girl of twenty-two – well that was very bad! So I left Denver. I was afraid I was going to get married for the sake of getting married.

I came out here to be a counsellor at the Jewish Community Centre summer camp, and I was offered a lot of good jobs. I taught first and second grades at one of the Metropolis public schools, and I taught a religion school at *Beit Torah* synagogue. I'm still a member of *Beit Torah* after all these years. Then I met my husband and got married. I accomplished my search – I was twenty-five.

After I got married I taught school. Then I got pregnant; then I got pregnant; and then I got pregnant. After I had my three children in 1960, for economic reasons, I went back to teaching. I taught for three years and then my husband said, 'That's it! You should stay at home. I don't like you working.' And as a dutiful wife I said, 'Okay'. He's very traditional. He felt my going to work was a blot against his manhood. But I'm not a person who looks back; I keep right on going. Then I got involved in volunteer work. My husband and I were very active in the Jewish community: he was President of the Allied Jewish Federation, President of the synagogue, President of the Maimonides Academy – that kind of thing. I sent my children to Maimonides, but my grandchildren go to the Golda Meir Day School. The Maimonides Academy is not what it was when my children went to school, unfortunately. I'm very strongly into Jewish education. I always say I was born too soon because I would have become a woman rabbi. Yup! Absolutely! I have deep feelings that women can't possibly do a worse job than many of the male rabbis have done!

I did a lot of volunteer work. Then my husband called up and I was crying. Why was I crying? Because it seemed all I could do was bake chocolate chip cookies. I had nothing in my life. So in 1977 Marcia and I were having breakfast with our husbands and we decided we were going to open up a gift shop, because we knew there was such gorgeous Judaica available and people in Metropolis didn't know about it. So we started our business. Our husbands gave us six months, and that was sixteen years ago!

Our shop is like home to a lot of people. They come and they tell us their problems, and we try to help them. We are a Jewish resource centre in the community. I have to tell you that the bane of our existence is that we are not utilized by the rabbis. Maybe we threaten their synagogue gift shops, I don't know. They don't even come here to find out what is going on. We're not looking for them to send us their people, but it would be nice if they asked us what we're hearing. When a new Messianic congregation started, we called Shimon Silver (*Editor of the Jewish Newspaper*); we called Professor Kornfeld (*The University Professor of Judaica*); we called everybody but no one was very interested. And then six months later they woke up to all the problems. Anyway, we tried . . . We do our best to promote anything that's going on in the community, but it's difficult . . . We're here when a couple get engaged, maybe an intermarried couple. They're very nervous; we try to help them. We're here to try to encourage the observance of Judaism on any level. We tell people what the resources are here in Metropolis.

Right now, after sixteen years, we're a household word. It's amazing the number of people who find us when they're just moving into the community. We're natural people to ask! We have a complete cross-section of the community, but we do not hit many of the West Side Orthodox. The *Yeshiva* has a bookshop over there, and most of the West Side do not come in here. There's a big schism between the East Side and West Side, and let me tell you, anyone who tells you there isn't, is not telling you the truth. It's too bad! We're very interested in the Jewish community, and we don't like to see it fragmented.

In our shop we try to bring people together. People call us from all over. Lots of non-Jews come to us. They feel it's a very deep emotional experience to wrap themselves in a prayer shawl. They don't buy the least expensive either – they buy the one they like! We also get the Messianic Jews – yes, I know Jake Stern (*The Pastor of the Messianic Jews*). It's very sad. One of the reasons we started business was so that people could give Jewish gifts for Jewish occasions. We get the kind of books that can be bought for *Bar* or *Bat Mitzvah*. Non-Jewish people come in to buy a Jewish gift for a Jewish occasion more readily than a Jewish person will. We try to explain to people that their home should not only smell Jewish but it should look Jewish, and that Judaism is a way of life. That's it! We have a marriage gift registry. We are selling a lot more Jewish marriage documents, and people are coming in wanting to spend money on something that is one of a kind. A marriage document is an integral part of a Jewish home. Absolutely. A lot of intermarried couples want a document, but they can't get one for an intermarriage. It says 'according to the laws of Moses and Israel' so you can't get one. Now different documents are being produced for the intermarried, and Marcia and I have got to decide if we are going to carry them. We're not sure. Marcia is Orthodox and I am Traditional, and we haven't yet decided. We do carry some cards which are both Christmas and *Hanukkah*, but very few. They're produced by a company called Mixed Blessings!

I think in Metropolis there is a concerted effort to be more traditional. For example, we've just sold a $600 Passover plate. A few years ago no one was making a $600 Passover plate except perhaps in silver. In Metropolis, people are more interested in pottery and craftsmanship. It is wonderful that so many Jewish people are making beautiful Judaica that it is worth their while to market. For many of them it is not an avocation; they do it to make money. And people are buying it. People will now spend more money on a prayer shawl. We have more women buying prayer shawls than we used to. One of the problems is that children should be *Bar* and *Bat Mitzvah* at a much later age, because so many of them stop their Jewish education. It's not their fault. Mom and Dad don't really care. That's why we have this shop. To advocate Judaism in the home is far more important than in synagogue. In the home a child sees that Judaism is something you live every day, and if he sees that, with just a little luck, you have a better chance to keep him as a Jew . . .

The Manager of a Kosher Bakery

MR ASHER GRODZINSKI

The kosher bakery was in South-East Metropolis. Its kashrut certificate was given by Rabbi Berkovski (The Hasidic Rabbi). *Asher Grodzinski, the manager, was a stout, jolly, dark-haired young man in his late twenties. The shop smelt deliciously of fresh bagels.*

I was born in the Bronx, and then in 1971 we moved to Metropolis. My did moved to open a bakery in Metropolis: we liked the area so we stayed. My grandparents were Orthodox, but my parents had problems with it so we weren't raised Orthodox at all. We don't belong to a synagogue, and I didn't have a *Bar Mitzvah*. None of that. My sister is religious, and she has the Jewish holidays at her house. I've got seven sisters and two brothers. I was the youngest for sixteen years, and then my parents started again, and there are three after that. Yeah! My parents enjoyed us all. They really did.

I graduated from high school. Religion never came up with my friends. I don't care what people are. They can be black, German, chocolate: they're my friends! As long as you're a person, I don't care. So I don't know if my friends were Jewish, and I didn't go to church to find out! I started work at the bakery with Dad when I was about ten years old. I used to work graveyard with Dad, and then I went to school. Graveyard is when you come in at night at 10 o'clock and work until 6:00 in the morning. Then I went to school, and then I went home and passed out! I've worked a long time! I need a vacation!

After graduation, I went to culinary arts school for a year, and went into restaurant management. I worked my way up from catering manager, assistant manager, and then general manager. I liked it because it was a very quick pace. You have to do 1,500 lunches within a certain amount of time. In the *kosher* bakery, you have to sell the 400 dozen bagels, but you have all day. I like the pace better in a restaurant. But my dad wanted me back in the bakery.

We've always been *kosher*. Rabbi Berkovski is our Supervisor. He has someone come in and check everything out every week. He'll come in at 10 o'clock at night and look around. You never know when he's coming. Why don't we use Rabbi Vardin (*The Kashrut Supervisor*)? To tell you the truth, rabbis seem to conflict with each other. They don't seem to want to get it together. Right now we're having problems. We sent something over to one of the functions that Vardin was doing, and he said we weren't *kosher*. So they refused 120 dinner rolls. Now there's a big conflict, and there's no way to resolve it. Vardin won't accept our supervision. There's another bagel store that he supervises, but we're very busy. We are *kosher*, but we have lots of gentile as well as lots of Jewish customers. We do very well. We have a real good product. People come from all over to buy from us. It gives us a good feeling because we know we have the best product we can.

My dad used to own it, but he sold it and still works there. It's less stress on him, and the same amount of money. We start baking at 4:00 in the morning. It makes for a long day, and we bake anything between 250 and 350 boards per day. Each board takes three dozen bagels. We do three bakes a day. My dad's been baking bagels for forty-five years; he really knows what he's doing. We also make pastries, *hallah* (plaited loaves), rye bread, and Jewish rye. I'm manager; my dad's the baker; my sister is the one who makes the bagels; and my brother also bakes at night. The whole family's involved!

All our bagels are big sellers. We make sesame seed, pumpernickel, blueberry, salt, poppy seed, onion, and chocolate chip bagels. I'm a traditionalist, but I'll try anything once. I can't understand people who eat chocolate chip bagels with *lox* (smoked salmon) and cream cheese! We supply hotels and restaurants as well as individuals. We have a standing list for bagels and we have a standing list for *hallah*. They come in every Friday and they come in before sundown! We sell about 300 for the Sabbath blessing. I know a lot of our customers. I try to make most people smile before they leave the bakery. It's good for PR, and I enjoy people. I know their name, and they know mine. For example, there's a Mr Comb, and I always call him Mr Brush because he's losing his hair and all! We have real regulars. One very nice blonde lady comes in every day to buy two plain bagels. Another comes in seven days a week to buy four sesame seed bagels. Another buys six – two plain, two onion and two sesame seed. We don't ask – we have it ready for them as they get out of their car. If I don't serve the best product, I get real upset.

What's my ambition? Me and my friend are looking into buying a pizza parlour, a bakery, and a delicatessen all in one shop. It'll be Italian, and you can't really be *kosher* if you're Italian. *Kosher* has got a little bit carried away. To buy *kosher* meat, it's going to cost you 50 per cent more than buying ordinary meat. All it means is that the rabbi says, 'This is *kosher*'. We know that, but the rabbi has to be paid, and his people have to be paid, and they have to pay the synagogues. It's basically a bunch of nonsense.

We do a nice business. Come here on Friday morning, and you'll see a line of people outside the front door. We are open on Saturday morning. The only way we can do that is if the owner doesn't come in on *Shabbos* (the Sabbath). I'm in, because, like I said, I don't follow any religion. My own view is people wouldn't be killing people if God was out there protecting them . . .

The Funeral Director

MR MARTIN NATHAN

Nathan's mortuary does almost all the funerals for the Jewish community of Metropolis. The business was situated in an old part of the city near the old Har HaShem building. The offices themselves were spotless. We interviewed Martin Nathan in a pale grey room, tastefully furnished with reproduction antiques. There was a large painting of a resigned-looking Hasid clutching a book in front of the Wailing Wall, and on another wall were a couple of certificates from the State Board of Funeral Directors and Embalmers. On the mantle were displayed samples of funeral stationery and memorial candles.

Martin Nathan himself looked younger than his fifty-three years. A handsome man with hazel eyes, he wore a blue blazer, grey flannel trousers and a silk tie. His shirt was monogrammed on the sleeves, and he wore gold-rimmed spectacles for reading.

I was born in Metropolis and my religious upbringing was probably Conservative. My family belonged to *Har HaShem* synagogue, but a transition was made to Temple *Shalom* when I was about fifteen. Since I have come back to Metropolis in 1980, I have become a very involved member of Temple; I served on the Board and became Treasurer of the congregation – so that is pretty much my religious background. I feel very comfortable there.

My grandfather started this business in 1936. He was a very big man; he was well-known in the community and somewhat robust and outspoken. He had a limousine service as I understand it, and was used by a funeral home which was not Jewish but was doing most of the Jewish business. The funeral home told him they were going to purchase their own livery, and they wouldn't be using him so much. Perhaps I shouldn't say what he is supposed to have said – basically, 'To hell with you, and I'll start my own business.' And his following was such that many people went with him. He unfortunately died a year later of a stroke, and my father – who had no experience whatsoever in the funeral industry – decided to give it a try. It was a job, and he felt that if he worked hard and persevered, as he always did, and treated people with respect, courtesy and sensitivity, he could do it. He worked this business from 1937 to 1981 when he retired for physical reasons.

At the beginning he did everything literally himself. He had one employee who worked for him for twenty-five years. To me it was a dynamic duo, and they did everything day and night. As a matter of fact, the man was a very religious Irish Catholic. He went to mass every day before he went to work. They dealt with both the West Side and the East Side. The opportunity was there. By word of mouth and the Metropolis grapevine, people began to realize that there was a need for an exclusively Jewish mortuary. Being the only Jewish funeral home, we wear a number of hats – literally as well as figuratively. You learn the dialogue for the Orthodox and for the Reform. You must speak to everyone in the language they feel comfortable with. The Orthodox observe the full *halakhic* (Jewish legal) requirement – seven full days mourning, burial in a shroud only, and a wooden casket with no metal whatsoever. Then we go to the other extreme which is cremation for the most part. Cremation is not part of Jewish Law, but people need choices and if people make that choice, then we deal with that.

As a boy, for a long time, there was embarrassment. There were a lot of jokes about funeral directors – it was not the kind of occupation people talked about in a bright light. I was uncomfortable with that. In fact, when I was going to high school, my father would take me to school. At that point in time, we didn't have a personal car; we had two limousines. I would make him drop me off around the corner where no one would see me! We did live with the business. It was very paramount in his mind, and when I moved away from Metropolis, he was very upset.

After I graduated from the State University, I worked for my father for three years, and he was difficult. He expected close to perfection from me. Other people could mess things, but if you were part of the family, you did it his way. His way was: 'There's a right way and a wrong way to do everything and my way is the right way!' So when I was twenty-five years of age, I moved to St Louis. My wife was from that city so I had an opportunity in a furniture manufacturing plant to have some sort of position.

I had a vision from my college degree of being in charge of personnel. It was a factory of about a hundred people and what I found out very quickly was that my father-in-law didn't run that business much differently from the way my father ran this business with four employees. A sort of seat-of-your-pants operation, with his fingers in all pies at all times. I maintained that job for fifteen years. I was relatively happy, but when my father got sick the timing was right, and I sensed that I should move back.

Dad was at a point when he really wanted to retire, and he helped me for a period of six months and then said, 'You're on your own!' It was always a joke within the family: my father had three children, and we always said the business was the fourth child! My mother was also involved. She still keeps some records at home. In fact, for years it was a real family situation. Cousins and aunts used to answer the phone which kept costs down, that kind of thing. My mother has a mind like a real computer: she knows how everyone in the community is related to everyone else. It's a tremendous help, and I still consult her when I'm not absolutely sure about this or that. She tells me who married whose brother-in-law, and how they were related through a second marriage! The Metropolis grapevine is tremendous. You can have a call Friday morning, and they want to have the service by Friday afternoon because of the Sabbath. You'd be amazed at the number of people at the service who heard of it by word of mouth. One tells two, and two tells four, and four tells eight . . . and the next thing you know, you have 200 people there. It is good.

Because it's a Jewish funeral home, we need to get everything done as quickly as possible. If someone passes away at night, there's a good chance that the funeral will take place the next day. So we have to find the doctor to sign the death certificate; get the necessary papers from the city for a burial permit; have newspaper notices ready for insertion; contact rabbis and check their schedules; and the cemetery has to be co-ordinated with. The grave has to be dug in time and, if it's an Orthodox case, we have to make sure the ritual washers are on hand. You have to connect with all those people very quickly. Other mortuaries might have three or four days to coordinate, but we pretty much have to have everything in hand on the first call. The sense of urgency has to be there. It has to be done well, and it has to be done professionally. You're always dangling on the end of a string, and not knowing what the next day will be like. I used to play golf with my father at Windy Oak Country Club, and they used to send someone out in a golf cart to tell him that a death had occurred. With a little arm-twisting I finally persuaded him to get a pager and eventually the pager became part of his life.

It helps that I have some idea of family connections – the rapport is there as soon as they walk in. I always express my condolences. It's important to get to that personal level. There are times I have found that they walk in, and you try every little thing you know to build this rapport, this comfort level for the family, and maybe they have resisted it to a point where they don't want to talk much about it. That happens. And then sometimes when the dust has settled, occasionally these people will write a glorious note and say 'thank you'. I keep a special file on complimentary letters. In this occupation, there's a lot of abuse. The abuse comes from anger not at me or the mortuary, but anger because a death has occurred. We seem to be the ones up front who get the brunt of it.

I feel strongly we should try to serve someone, and make them realize that we're not trying to take advantage of them, to sell them more than they need to be sold. Prices are regulated by the government, and I'm comfortable with that. Often-times when you go to a doctor or a lawyer, you don't know how much something is going to cost, and there's a nervousness. But we're regulated, and I like that. We absolutely give them a price list. Some people want to go through it itemized, item by item; others trust you to send them an account after. In this community 99 to 98 per cent pay up with no trouble, and that's a pretty good percentage.

I tell you who per capita spend the most – the middle-class. People who have worked a lifetime for what they have. They do not have a great deal of money, but they have put enough money away to lead a conservative-type life. Dollar for dollar they will spend a lot more because, number 1, they believe in it and, number 2, they have prepared for it. They are the people who will always pay on time or before time. The more educated don't look at it the same. That's fine too; that's another choice. The super-rich can go two ways. More times than not, they don't spend much proportionally. They say, 'We are simple people!' – that means, 'I do not want to spend much for the funeral!' We also have welfare cases. Everybody is treated nicely, but it is a very poorly administered part of our system. People take advantage of it.

Funny things do happen. A little old lady came in here to choose a casket for her husband. She didn't have much money, but she wanted the best. She chose the cherry wood. Then she turned to her son and said, 'Your father would die if he knew how much I was spending!'

We really only do Jewish funerals. As long as the rabbis will do it, we're comfortable. But we live in an age – and I will be honest with you – that there are so many suits for discrimination that if someone calls, we try to screen it and say we don't really have the expertise. We refer them to other funeral houses, and ultimately they're far more comfortable. But you have to be careful. Christian funerals are very different. The Jewish way of funerals is hopefully to do it within 24-hours. I think that's good. The anxiety of waiting is pretty overwhelming . . . I've had Christian people say to me, 'The Jewish way is better'.

I remember people used to beat on the door of the hearse and call out to the deceased and fall down. Some I think was play acting, and some was real, depending on the individuals. I don't see it as much as I used to. For the most part, there's more composure now. It's not fashionable so much any more. In the past, hysteria was almost expected. I'm told the Italians and Hispanics have very emotional-type services. Most funerals now are pretty much orderly. We have very little viewing and the percentage of embalming is significantly less. I would say we have 25 to 30 per cent embalming. Viewing is pretty much relegated to immediate family only, and we have to work around religious requirements. In general it is done here in the chapel, before we go to the cemetery. We set features. I tell people, 'I don't want you to have a memory which will be bad for the rest of your life.' Often-times, if people were at the bedside when the death occurred, they said their goodbyes then, and they don't need to view. That makes sense to me.

Saying goodbye is very, very, difficult and letting go for the last time is something you don't want to do. But you know you have to. I realize that I'm providing a service for people, and it's really helping them. Certainly I do it for financial reasons – we all work to make a living – but the real reward is to help people. I feel very good – especially when someone leaves and says that we've made it easy for them. People appreciate that you're part of their grieving and you care enough to get yourself involved. Yeah – I cry sometimes with families . . .

Seven

THE YOUNG

The Student from the Orthodox Day School

MISS ALISON SILVER

Alison was the daughter of Shimon and the granddaughter of Leah Silver (Editors of the Jewish Newspaper). *Although Leah was Traditional, Shimon had become Orthodox as a young man and Alison grew up in an Orthodox home. The family lived on the East Side near the Orthodox elementary school (Maimonides Academy) and they worshipped at Rabbi Berkovski's* (The Hasidic Rabbi) *synagogue and the East Side Orthodox synagogue. Alison was nine and a half years old.*

My eldest sister is twenty-one; my second oldest sister is twenty; my brother is eighteen; my other sister is fifteen; and then there's me. I'm nine and a half. They all went to Maimonides Academy. My brother went to *yeshiva* in Chicago, and my sisters went to *Beis Rahel* High School. My eldest sister is in Israel now.

I went to Maimonides when I was four. Then I went into Mrs Levine's (*The Teacher in the Orthodox Day School*) class. I learned to read in kindergarten. This summer I just finished the fourth grade. There were eighteen kids in my class. There was just one fourth-grade girls' class. I don't know how many boys there were. We learn reading, English, social studies, science and maths. The last thing we did was the history of the state. We went to a kind of outdoor museum. They have a school from the olden days, a blacksmith shop and tepees and stuff. In science we were doing weather. We do Hebrew reading. I can read *Siddur* (Prayer Book) and *Humash* (Bible). Sometimes we do stories from the Bible. We don't do music. We only went out of class for computers and library. Yeah, we do gym. All kinds of sport: soccer, kickball, gymnastics, and I don't remember what else.

My mother drives me to school. Maybe once in a while we

take someone else. The bell rings at 8:30, but sometimes we don't begin right away. First we *daven* (pray). Then if it's Hebrew, we do *Humash*. Every day we learn a new reading. Usually the teacher gives us the paper that says the words in Hebrew and you write it in English next to it. Then after he reads it, he gets people to read it after him. Then we work on posters on what we've learnt. I don't really remember what we did. We have recess at 10:30. I bring potato chips, and they have a drinking fountain. If we're in Hebrew, we might go back to *Humash* if we haven't finished. If we're in English, we do all different subjects. Sometimes we read out loud from a reading book. You get lunch at 11:45. My mom packs me a lunch, but usually every Wednesday they have a hot lunch with meat. Then we can play. After lunch we *bensh* (say grace) in classrooms. School ends at 3:40.

I sometimes have homework. A lot. Sometimes I do it right away. I only do it after dinner if I have a lot. I go to bed at 8:30 to 9:00. We don't have a television. I like to read or ride my bike after school. I read some books from the family and some from the library. I usually read *The Three Valley Twins* books or *Babysitters' Club* books. They're my favourites. Three of my friends live in my neighbourhood. I sometimes see them after school though one lives across the main road. Lots of kids in my class live on the West Side. They come over on a bus. It's the biggest bus they ever had! They have to be ready at 7:30 in the morning and they're there by 8:00.

On Friday in winter we get out at 2 o'clock, because *Shabbos* starts earlier. But in the spring and fall we get out at 3:30. We have *Shabbos* dinner at home on Friday night. Usually we have soup, chicken, gefilte fish, and sometimes we have rice or *falafel* (chick-pea patties). On Friday night I go to *B'nai Akiva*, and in the morning I go to the East Side Orthodox synagogue. I don't always go on Friday night. Sometimes I sit with my mom, but they have this little playroom with kids babysitting. Usually we're in there.

When I grow up I want to be an artist. I like doing that. Also sometimes I want to be a writer, like someone who writes books. I'm writing a story at the moment, but I can't find the book I'm writing it in.

The Student from the Pluralist Day School

MISS SHARON ACKERMAN

Sharon Ackerman was eleven years old, and she was about to enter the sixth grade of the Golda Meir Day School. A serious girl with beautiful long black hair, she looked older than her years.

I was born in 1982 in Metropolis in the Jewish Hospital. We moved to this house in 1985. I have a brother and he's eight. First I went to the Jewish Community Centre pre-school, then to *Beth Israel* pre-school, then to kindergarten at Golda Meir. I was five in kindergarten. In pre-school we learnt about holidays and Jewish foods – sometimes we made the food with the teachers. My family used to belong to *Beth Israel* synagogue – I had a baby-naming there. I haven't started training for my *Bat Mitzvah* yet. We've set a date; I'll be like twelve and a half; it'll be at *Beit Torah* Synagogue. We moved there. I won't read from the *Torah*. It'll be from the *Haftarah* (the prophets) and some other things. I'll sing it. I can pretty much read Hebrew now.

At school we have Hebrew and Judaic. In Hebrew we read stories and translate them. In Judaic last year we learnt about the rabbis – like Rabbi Akiva – and we learnt the *Book of Exodus* and we studied about Jews in America, like in the colonies and immigration. In the whole fifth grade there were forty-five kids – we were in two classes. Hebrew is forty-five minutes, and Judaic is forty-five minutes each day. I'm going into Mrs Kaye's (*The Teacher in the Pluralist Day School*) sixth grade next year. We have ten minutes at the beginning of the morning with the class; then one class has Judaic, and the other has language arts. Then we have the opposite.

Then we have *shaharit* (morning prayer) every morning for half an hour, and once a week we have a *Torah* service on Thursday. The boys have to wear *yarmulkes* (skull caps) for *shaharit*, for lunch because of the blessings, and during Hebrew. Then we have a ten-minute snack. You bring your own. I bake my own . . . like chocolate chip cookies. Then we have math; there are three different math groups. I'm in the best group. Uh Huh! Then one class has science and another has social studies. Then we have recess. We have twenty-five minutes for recess and twenty-five minutes for lunch. Then we have twenty minutes of free reading time. Then we have writer's workshop. Then we have Hebrew, and then for the last forty-five minutes of the day we either have gym, music or art. I play the piano, but it's not through school. In music last year we did a musical. I was the fairy!

I think all the kids are Jewish in my class. Some are more religious than others. Some kids don't go to synagogue at all or maybe just like on the holidays. Then there are others who go every week, like to the East Side Orthodox or to *B'nai Akiva.* There's a boy in my class who doesn't believe in God – he's very weird. This year we had a Reform Judaic teacher. She kind of went on about all the different movements in Judaism. We went around to different synagogues, and she kind of tried to force her views on us. We had to write a poem about what we thought was most important to Judaism – God, the *Torah*, Israel. So I wrote this poem: '*HaShem*' (God).

Creator of all,
We pray to Him at the Western Wall.
He is always very honest,
Gave to us the land He had promised.
He led us through the wilderness.
We built the *mishkan* (tabernacle) to show His holiness.
He gave us the commandments, carved in stone.
Finally we had eyes of our own.
HaShem. Father of the Jews.
Someone we can't bear to lose.

We had to bring the poem up to her, and she read it and said, 'You know, you refer to God as "He" three times. I really think it would be better if you referred to Him as "She" twice or more.' What did I do? I just kind of took it and walked away. I won't have this teacher next year . . .

We have homework every day. I drag it out . . . it takes two hours. I'm not allowed to watch television on school days in term time. I go to bed at 8:30; usually it's after that. Next year will be my last year, then I'll go to the Hebrew High School. Some kids left this year and are going into the public schools. I'll go to the Hebrew High School for seventh and eighth grade, and then we'll decide if I go into the public schools for the last four years. No one in my class is going to *Beis Rahel* or the *Yeshiva*. I don't know any kids from Maimonides Academy. I met some at camp, there may be a couple at synagogue. Most of my friends go to Golda Meir. I have one good friend from across the street; she goes to another private school. Her dad's Jewish; her mom isn't.

All the classes at Golda Meir are mixed, girls and boys all the way through. My friends are both really. I like to play sports with boys. The girls probably talk more in class. The boys do more bad stuff – some of them tend not to do their homework more. They get sent out more. One boy had to do the same work we were doing in the library by himself because he always got sent out. None of the boys in my class want to be rabbis. I want to be a lawyer when I'm older . . .

The Traditionalist Bat Mitzvah Student

MISS NICKY STINGLESTEIN

Bar Mitzvah is the Jewish coming-of-age ceremony. Thirteen-year-old boys read publicly from the Torah and so symbolically take on their adult responsibilities. In recent years, a similar ceremony (Bat Mitzvah) has been devised for girls. In Reform congregations the ceremony is egalitarian; the girls do exactly the same as their brothers. Traditional and Orthodox congregations, for ritual reasons, do not allow women to touch or read the Torah and so a different (and generally shorter) service has been devised for young girls.

We asked the secretary of Har HaShem synagogue for recommendations of a recent Bat Mitzvah candidate. We wanted someone who had not been educated at one of the Jewish day schools and who had conducted the service particularly well. Nicky Stinglestein was immediately mentioned.

The religious establishment of Metropolis, as in most American cities, is highly embarrassed by the extravagance of many Bar and Bat Mitzvah celebrations. The ceremonies are frequently the excuse for lavish entertainment; it has not been unknown for zoo animals to be hired to add a 'circus theme' to the party. Sit-down banquets for 300 people with decorations and several professional entertainers are commonplace. The Stinglesteins did not want to do that . . .

I went to pre-school at the South Metropolis Reform Temple, and I go to a public school. My parents are members of *Har HaShem* synagogue. I had my baby-blessing there, and my mom and dad were married there, and my dad was *Bar Mitzvah* there. I go to religion school. All the Traditional synagogues combine for their religion schools, and we meet in the Suburban High School. For the last seven years I've gone every Tuesday and Thursday after school. Now I'm just going on Wednesday. We learn like history. Last year we learnt all the history and turned it into the Simpsons (you know, the cartoon characters) – just to make it more fun. We learn about the *Torah* portions week by week, and we see film strips, cartoons and things. We also learn to read Hebrew. Reading only – we don't do understanding. A few words we know how to translate.

For a while, when I was eleven, we were thinking maybe of having my *Bat Mitzvah* in Israel. But it's very expensive to go there so it got out of the question. Some of my friends' parents don't want them to have *Bat Mitzvahs*. It was sort of my choice. My mom didn't have one. Girls didn't in those days. My dad did. My aunt tutored me; she's my mom's sister. She goes to Rabbi Berkovski's (*The Hasidic Rabbi*) synagogue. She's a regular tutor though most of my friends go to Danny Mizel (*The Bar Mitzvah Teacher*). I saw her once a week for an hour for about four months. I could already read Hebrew. Yeah, I could read real well.

I had to learn my *Haftarah* (prophetic reading) and my speech. I wasn't reading from the *Torah* scroll, no. Which prophetic book was my reading from? I think it was *Exodus* . . . (*Exodus is not a prophetic book. Miss Stinglestein's memory is defective here.*) We wrote the speech together. I said something, and we'd sort of make it sound more interesting. My speech was about what becoming a *Bat Mitzvah* is about, and about my family . . . things like that. It was about five minutes.

The service was on Saturday night. It wasn't in the synagogue, it was in the chapel. My grandparents' friends all came, and I was allowed to invite some friends. It was around 200 – maybe not even that many. There was a big *Bar Mitzvah* in the synagogue on Saturday morning. I didn't know the boy . . . I had a new dress. You can see it later if you want to. It was all over blue sequins with a white satin skirt and jacket. It sparkled. We were at the synagogue really early. We took out all the prepared decorations and put them in the bridal preparation room. My uncle's a caterer. He made popcorn buckets that had my colours which are teal, purple and pink. He made like streamers and balloons and confetti and stuff like that out of it. There were pots full of foam with flowers and ribbons. It was really pretty. Then I sat in the chapel and watched everyone come.

Then Rabbi Kornfeld (*The University Professor of Judaica*) presented me to the congregation and I just said, 'Thank you for coming to my *Bat Mitzvah*. I hope you enjoy it as much as me' . . . stuff like that. After that I said some prayers in Hebrew. I didn't really do any in English – it took too much time. Then I did my *Haftarah* and I said my speech. The rabbi was on the *bimah* (dais) just sitting in the back. Then I said a *Bat Mitzvah* prayer in front of the Ark. Then we had a *Havdalah* (the conclusion of the Sabbath ceremony). It was really nice. We kind of dimmed the lights. All my family came up and everyone had a part. My little sister did, yes! I've got a cousin aged four, she did! No, not the dog! He stayed at home. The service was like fifty minutes.

Then we had a little party and I welcomed everybody. Everybody kissed me! Yes! I didn't get to eat anything. We had ice-cream sundaes and cakes. It was 9:30 when it started. It was really late. I was nervous, but I was okay. Doing a *Torah* portion like the boys takes much longer. I don't think I'd have been allowed to do that. It didn't necessarily bother me. I enjoyed it. I'm glad I did it . . .

The Student at the Pluralist High School

MR JOHN HOROWITZ

*John Horowitz was the son of Howard Horowitz (*The Photographer*). He was fourteen years old and a student of the Hebrew High School.*

I'm fourteen and a half and I was born in Metropolis. First of all I went to the Jewish Community Centre pre-school. I don't remember that too much. Then I went to the Golda Meir Day School from first grade through sixth. Mrs Kaye (*The Teacher in the Pluralist Day School)* was my last teacher there. She was okay. Now I go to a place called the Hebrew High School.

I did have a *Bar Mitzvah* at *Adath Israel* synagogue. My mom is a member there. Rabbi Oppenheim (*The Traditional Rabbi*) is the rabbi. My portion was about laws or something. The name of my teacher was Danny Mizel (*The Bar Mitzvah Teacher*). I think I saw him once a week. I had to learn most of the portion, but it wasn't as hard because I knew how to read Hebrew and stuff. I had to sing it. I knew kind of what it meant, but I couldn't translate it. I could recognize some of the words. I was kind of frightened, but when I got up there it was fine. There was a little party afterwards, not a big one. I was relieved it was over with, and I'm glad I did it. Everyone wanted me to, and I got a lot of presents. I got money and stuff and some clothes; one of my grandmas took me to Africa for a *Bar Mitzvah* present, and my other grandma gave me two krugerrands. So I got a lot of stuff – books, wine cups and things.

I found the Hebrew High School more Jewish than Golda Meir. You had most of the same classes, but it seemed more Jewish. Strictly *kosher*. More prayers. At Golda Meir they said only *kosher* for lunch, but if you brought other stuff, they didn't really care. I knew almost all the kids when I arrived because they came on from Golda Meir. There were twenty in my class at Hebrew High School. The other kids from Golda Meir went on to Sussex Academy or other private schools. Those who went on were either the more religious or they went to the Hebrew High School because the other private schools were too expensive.

To begin with, it didn't bother me that it was more Jewish, but it really bothered me later on. Everyone seemed so narrow-minded and strict. They kind of assumed everyone was as religious as they were, and they wouldn't explain any questions. In Bible class they would just say, 'God did this'. If you asked, 'How do you know that?' they would just ignore you. I used to ask a lot of questions – stuff like miracles. I said, 'Couldn't this be something that happened in nature?' They just wouldn't even answer. Then you'd get talked to after class for being disruptive and stopping other people learning. So near the end of the year, I just sat there in the class and didn't do anything, because I'd get in trouble if I did. The stories in the Bible teach you lessons, but you don't have to think God did everything. The teachers didn't give you any opportunity to think. The religious kids didn't have a problem with it, but me and most of my friends were always in trouble. It was bad. They were really narrow-minded.

I was in the highest Hebrew group. I shouldn't have been there, but I got stuck there. I was lost the whole year as we had to do the Bible in Hebrew, not in English. They were concentrating on the Hebrew, not learning what the Bible had to say. The other subjects were fine. We did gym, but we didn't have any sports teams except a basketball team. That was kind of fun.

The kids go to all different synagogues. I go to *Adath Israel* because my mom goes there, but if I had a choice, I probably wouldn't go – maybe Temple *Shalom*. *Adath Israel* is too Orthodox. I'm leaving the Hebrew High School at the end of the year. Most of my friends who were having all these troubles are going. I'm planning on going to public high school. Probably about half the class will be leaving. I'm looking forward to public high school. I hope I won't have to go to the synagogue religion school, but my mom may make me. After the Hebrew High School, I hope I don't have to . . .

I don't know what I want to do when I grow up. I wouldn't want to be a rabbi. Most of my friends are Jewish, but I hope I'll make some non-Jewish friends at public high school. All sorts of different people go there. I want lots of different friends. I don't just want to be friends with Jewish people. I think that's kind of narrow-minded. Lots of people at the Hebrew High School didn't know anyone who was a Christian and probably didn't want to.

We talk about Jewish things at home. My brother's in a stage: he's an Orthodox Jew; he's growing *pais* (sidecurls). He's twelve. He walks to Rabbi Berkovski's (*The Hasidic Rabbi*) synagogue every week. He keeps *kosher*; he doesn't eat pork; he doesn't mix milk and meat; he tries not to work on the Sabbath. I think it's kind of strange, but he's gone through a lot of stages. Once he wanted to be an Indian; once he wanted to be an ambulance driver, and my parents got him all sorts of walkie-talkies and radios. I don't know. I think it's a stage, but he says it isn't. He thinks I'm wrong, and I think he's wrong. He's really into it. He says he wants to go to the *Yeshiva* High School!

I do think of myself as Jewish. It's important, but it's not the most important thing about me. My personality is more important, I guess. I'm John and American more than Jewish.

The Summer Camper

Camp Shalom, the children's summer camp attached to Temple Shalom, was situated thirty-five miles away from Metropolis. It was deep in the country in a thickly wooded area. We drove our car two miles along an unmade-up road before we came upon a banner declaring 'Welcome to Camp Shalom'. The camp itself was a small collection of log cabins all bearing a letter of the Hebrew alphabet. To the north, next to the stables, was an open-air synagogue and an activities room. By the side of the camp was a picturesque stream.

Camp Shalom accommodated eighty children between the ages of seven and fifteen. To supervise them were approximately forty camp counsellors – older teenagers – a rabbinic Director, and a Deputy Director. We arrived just in time for lunch, and everyone was gathered around a tall flag pole at the centre of the compound. Flying from the pole were both the American and Israeli flags. The Senior Camp Counsellor introduced us to the assembled company, who promptly broke into song:

We welcome you to Shalom Camp,
We're mighty glad you're here,
We'll send the air reverberating,
With a mighty cheer!
We'll sing you in,
We'll sing you out,
We'll raise a mighty shout.
Hail, hail the gang's all here,
And you're welcome to Shalom Camp!

No response to this was expected, and everyone dived into the dining hall. Grace was sung in Hebrew, and we all tucked into excellent pasta salad and French bread. The noise of chatter was deafening, but a slight diversion was caused by one of the female counsellors appearing dressed as a fairy with a mop for a wand. She announced amidst catcalls that Aleph cabin had won the daily prize for the tidiest cabin. Then a young man came forward clutching a guitar. He led a fairly half-hearted singing of the Birkhat ha-Mazon (grace after meals) before we got down to the real business of after-lunch camp songs. All the songs had a Jewish theme; many were in Hebrew; and they were uniformly accompanied by clapping and impromptu dancing. The din was overwhelming. We could have been heard in Metropolis. One of the more memorable ditties went as follows:

> *Wherever you go, there's always someone Jewish,*
> *You're never alone when you say you're a Jew.*
> *So when you're far from home,*
> *And you're feeling kind of newish,*
> *The odds are, don't look far,*
> *Cause they're Jewish too!*
>
> *And some Jews wear hats, and some Jews wear fine streimels,*
> *And some Jews wear sombreros to keep out the sun,*
> *Some Jews live on rice and some live on potatoes,*
> *Or waffles, falafels or hamburger buns.*
>
> *Wherever you go, there's always someone Jewish,*
> *You're never alone when you say you're a Jew...*

After about half an hour of this and similar, the campers were dismissed to their cabins for 'rest hour'.

MR DAVID LANDSMAN

We interviewed David Landsman sitting by the stream. He was a dark, serious lad of fourteen, and this was his seventh summer in the camp.

I was born here in Metropolis, and I've lived here all my life. I live in the south of Metropolis near the Suburban Country Club. From kindergarten to sixth grade, I went to Golda Meir Jewish

Day School, and then from seventh I've been going to Sussex Academy. In Golda Meir about half our classes were Judaic classes. Sure I know John Horowitz (*The Student at the Pluralist High School*) – we were in the same class. I had a *Bar Mitzvah* at Temple *Shalom*. Yeah, Danny Mizel (*The Bar Mitzvah Teacher*) was my teacher. He's everyone's teacher. We had a really large crowd to the service, about 350 people. I had a party after at Temple, and I got a lot of presents. I guess I wasn't really in it for the gifts and everything. I was more there for the experience. I wasn't too nervous until like five minutes before, and then I got up there and said my first words and wasn't nervous any more. I don't know what I want to do eventually. I've thought about becoming a rabbi. I think that would be really neat, helping the people and all.

I was seven when I started coming to camp. I really remember the first year. I was in a cabin with sixteen other kids. I used to get picked on a little there, but it was a very good experience. I've been back for every summer since, generally for four weeks. This summer I went to Australia for three weeks, so I could only come here for two weeks.

On a weekday you get up at 7:25. They play music to wake you up. At 7:50 we put up both flags. You sing 'This Land is Your Land' in English, and '*Hatikvah*' (the Israeli national anthem) in Hebrew. The Israeli flag shows it's a Jewish camp, I guess. I'm not too sure. I consider myself a Jew more than an American; I'm not sure about the Israeli part. After flag-raising we have breakfast at 8 o'clock. That's always pancakes, French toast, *blintzes* (crêpes). It's very good. The chef cooks the best meals. After breakfast we have cabin clean-up for half an hour. Every day, except *Shabbat* (the Sabbath), we have the cleanest cabin award. At 10:15 we go to services. They're in both Hebrew and English. Kids participate and different groups lead. Do the kids behave well in services? Not really . . . some do. Some really participate, and some don't. Then we have various activities. I chose sign language for the deaf. I could have done archery or arts and crafts or music or journalism or a whole bunch of stuff. Sign language was really great. Then we do whatever the counsellors plan – it could be horseback riding or a day-hike or 'capture the flag'. At 12:30 we have lunch. We do the *Birkhat ha-Mazon* after every meal. We sing, yeah.

Then we have rest hour in our cabin. You write letters, take a shower, whatever. Then we have a snack in the dining hall. It's generally a granola bar and juice. Then we have two more planned activities. They generally say, 'You can do this, or this', and we have a vote. We have a free period from 5–5:30, and then we have dinner. That's different every day. Normal food, macaroni and cheese, that kind of thing. After lunch and dinner we have a song session, and then we have an evening programme. Yesterday we had movie night. It varies when we go to bed. In my cabin this year there are nine campers and three counsellors.

Shabbat is the best time ever. You have an hour to get ready, taking showers and getting dressed up. I brought a pair of long pants and a nice coloured shirt and waistcoat to wear. The counsellors walk up to the synagogue from the rabbi's house singing songs and you join them. You have a service, and people are asked if they want to participate. Last *Shabbat* I wrote something for the service, and I read it out:

> Yesterday I went on a hike through the forest, and I slept under the stars. I got into my sleeping bag, and it was the coolest thing. I saw a shooting star. It went right over my head. The moon wasn't out yet so I set my watch for 3 a.m. When my alarm went off, the moon was so bright that I could see the whole valley. This is the reason that I came to camp.

Usually one of the rabbis comes up from the Temple and tells us a story. This week it was Rabbi Acker (*The Administrator of a Dating File*). Then we all go down to dinner. The tables are set up in a W shape, and are laid with tablecloths. We generally have *matzoh*-ball soup, salad and chicken. Sometimes ice cream and a cookie. Then we have a really long song session. They move all the tables away, and we dance around – it's the best time.

On Saturday we get up at 9 o'clock. Breakfast is at 9:30, and we have bagels and cream cheese. Then we have *Shabbat* morning services. Those are long services. We read the *Torah*. If you've had a *Bar Mitzvah* you can bless the *Torah*. Then after lunch you have a couple of hours of free time. You can play basketball or something like that. We don't have study sessions. Not really. In the evening we have *Havdalah* (end of Sabbath service) across the stream. We have camp fires there and sing songs.

I love it. It's a real Jewish experience, and it's a lot of fun. It's so hard to figure out what I like best. I love everything out here...

The Reform Confirmand

MR DAVID FINE

Reform, Conservative and Traditional synagogues have instituted confirmation at the age of sixteen. It is primarily an encouragement to young people to stay in religion school after their Bar/Bat Mitzvah.

David had just come off an eight-hour stint at McDonald's. His parents were away on vacation, but he had chosen to stay at home to earn money for his future college career. He was a junior in his local high school, and his family lived in a modern housing development in South-East Metropolis.

We moved to Metropolis from Illinois when I was thirteen, after my *Bar Mitzvah*. I have one older brother aged nineteen and a younger sister – she's seven. When I was younger I constantly thought of being a rabbi. I was not the rebellious type as a younger kid. When I moved out here I still thought about it, maybe here maybe there. But I was less interested in it.

I attended Temple *Shalom* religion school for three years, from seventh to tenth grade. I was a newcomer there, and I had not been to the Temple before. It is really rather a beautiful big congregation. I felt a bit of an outcast. They were kind of cliquey. People had their friends from kindergarten up. Those were their friends, and that's basically how it was.

What we learned was not exactly standard religious education – more of morals, values and situations – anything from teenage pregnancy to drug abuse. They told us the same old stuff, that it was wrong. Our teachers had experimented with all the drugs, say pot, in their high school years. They said basically that they didn't do it now because they didn't need to. I don't know. Classes went from drug abuse and social topics to visiting other congregations – not necessarily Reform, more Orthodox and Conservative. When they talked about social things, the teachers shared their opinions. It was more of sharing their opinions than saying, 'That is right; this is wrong.' They brought some examples from the *Torah* and *Talmud*. One of the teachers was an Orthodox Jew and very strict in her faith. Earlier in her life she was not. She was Reform or something and decided to change. Everything she said, she always had back-up.

Most of the kids were less than interested in the classes. They were there because their mommy and daddy made them go. Some were disruptive in class. One person was kicked out because of disruptive behaviour. He yelled at a teacher, and he just walked off. There were about thirty in the class. Not everyone had gone through *Bar Mitzvah*. We arrived at 9:15 and worked until about noon with a little break at 10:15. We had one class before the break and one after. I took classes in social issues, current events, and one in Jewish Law, and that was about it. The confirmation preparation lasted two years. The rabbi only taught us in the confirmation year. Rabbi Reinhardt (*The Reform Rabbi*) didn't necessarily teach a course. He did a little bit of history; he took over the odd subject. He's a fairly overpowering person, and the class paid attention usually.

As well as attending classes we had a certain requirement of attending Friday night service. In the ninth grade we had to go maybe six times over the year, and in the confirmation year it was about eight times. I went every Friday night up until I got my requirement. I went with my father. We had a sign-up sheet to check we went, and we had to greet the rabbi. Most people went through it. Either you attended the services or you didn't get confirmed. I don't think more than two dropped out. The guy who was thrown out of class came back the second year.

In the ninth-grade year – I didn't attend this – there was a trip to Washington DC as an educational thing, and also to get to know your fellow peers. In the confirmation year we went to New York. I went to this. I felt I got to know my fellow pupils a bit better, I suppose. Up to a certain point they were friendly, but they preferred their old friends. I guess that's human nature.

I was surprised we didn't have to make a declaration of our dedication to Judaism. I don't know. Personally I'm not that strong in my faith. I didn't want to be confirmed because I wasn't quite yet firm in my own thoughts. I've been interested in the Eastern philosophies and Shintoism. Just the ideas. I'm not completely rejecting Judaism. I figure if I reject Judaism then I'm rejecting my past, and I can't do that. But right now I'm unsure of my thoughts and I don't think there's anything wrong with that. There is a sense of home in Judaism, a comfortableness. But I feel there are so many religions out there that I just can't make a decision if I only know one thing. I'm rebelling in my own sort of way. At the moment I'm free-floating. I told my boss, 'I'm in between religions right now.' If I was asked, 'What are you? a Jew? an American? What?' I'd probably answer, 'I'm David: I'm my own person.'

My parents are aware of my thoughts. When I told my parents I didn't want to be confirmed, they were not pleased at all. I didn't want to fight my parents over this. It would have been worthless. If I didn't get confirmed, what would it have proved? So I went through it but not necessarily agreeing with every aspect. I went through the actions of it to keep my parents happy. I really did! We had heated discussions about it, and I decided to back down. They thought I should get confirmed for family sake, because one day I might regret it if I didn't. They didn't have very strong arguments.

At the service we dressed in robes. The first part of the service we all stood up together; we all sat down together. It was very structured. It's what every confirmation service is like. I read the Ten Commandments. I switched with someone else. I was initially supposed to do an interpretation of the Tenth Commandment. The other guy was very unsure about reading the *Torah*; he thought he'd screw up. So I said I'd do it. Actually my Hebrew's not that good at all. Last time I really practised Hebrew was my *Bar Mitzvah* a long time ago. I mean, I need a translation. Sure, I can read Hebrew, I just couldn't tell you what it said.

The second part of the service was called 'Cantata'. We said some poems, sang some songs. It was all planned up ahead of time. I wrote my own bit; I wrote about the *Bar Mitzvah*. The rabbi kind of changed it a bit. My basic gist was that this is where we begin thinking for ourselves what religion is. He changed it. I was a little more negative about *Bar Mitzvah*. I mean today, at thirteen, people are just kids. I see in myself, I've gained a lot of maturity from thirteen to sixteen.

I don't have to go to religion school any more. I could have gone on, but I chose not to. My parents didn't say anything about that. They'd probably like me to go . . .

The Yeshiva Dorm Counsellor

MR MOSHE WENNER

Moshe Wenner was a dark, muscular young man of twenty-three. We first saw him playing roller hockey with his ten-year-old nephew in the Yeshiva dormitory playground on the West Side. In spite of his jeans and trainers, he wore his black velvet skull cap and his ritual fringes.

I was born in Montreal, Canada, in 1970. I'm a sibling of five boys and one girl – the girl being the oldest. I'm second to last. I'm not the baby, but people call me the black sheep. We were all boys growing up, as wild as we could be. I seemed to be different from everybody else. We were a strictly Orthodox family and got along together pretty well. My father is European – he was born in Belgium just before the war – and he is a European father, very strict in his ways. A lot of his relatives were murdered in the war. My mother is a Canadian and she was a teacher. She's a pretty intelligent woman.

I went to a real strict, black-hat, black-jacket school from kindergarten. The range of tolerance was negligible. It was strictly, strictly *Torah*-based. All my brothers went through it. I was, I guess, more tolerant. I hung out with other people. I didn't have non-Jewish friends, but not all my friends went to that school. No, I wasn't more liberal. Let's be careful about that word. Not more liberal – more tolerant. I went through that school, and I didn't accomplish much in seventh, eighth, even ninth grade. I was wasting my time and gaining minimal. So my eldest brother, who was teaching in the *Yeshiva* High School here, encouraged me to come to Metropolis.

I didn't mind; it was another adventure. I had turned fifteen and I came here. I didn't know anybody here, and it was excellent. I didn't want to be the big goof, just the goon walking around. So I put my head to work, and if I had any problems my brother was always here. As far as I'm concerned, it was the start. I've been here seven years. I've lived in the dorm all along. I've finished high school, and now I'm in the *Beis ha-Midrash* (post-high school) programme. College isn't the same thing at all. They almost look down on college, though personally I am also working at the University of Metropolis. I'm studying Psychology. My schedule now is very hectic! Yes!

My whole life changed when I came here. At home I had my own room; I was able to come whenever I wanted; in the fridge there was always something to eat. Here in the dorm, it's not your room; it's not your space. The dorm consists of apartments. There's just room space and a bathroom. Each apartment has space for five. You have your own bed, closet and dresser. No desk. You study in the *Yeshiva*. You are allowed to put things on the wall. Obviously sports figures get up there, but they really discourage that. Lots of people stick up famous rabbis or scenery from Israel. They really don't have pictures of family – they may have them in their wallet. You have to have a dark *Shabbos* suit and a white *Shabbos* shirt. It's the dress code that every child wears a tie, and not casual stuff. Nothing overly loud, and a black velvet *yarmulke*. Casual clothes are for play. Yes, they do play. They have all Friday afternoon off, and they play tackle football in the snow and crack heads like everybody else.

Kids do get homesick. There is a telephone in the dorm. Since I was twenty, I've been the counsellor. It sounds so powerful! I have to make sure the kids are neat and behaving properly. If they have a problem, I should be there to discuss it with them. I should at least be able to realize if something is wrong so I can talk it over with the Principal or with their *rebbe* (class teacher). They don't necessarily have to open up to me. I have seventy to seventy-five high school kids to look after. I confiscate radios, yes! They are allowed tape recorders but they are only allowed to play Jewish music. I check 'em in at night.

Each grade has a curfew, and they should be in their pyjamas, brushing their teeth, reading books, and so on. It's natural to be homesick. Everyone wants a mom. They don't say, 'I'm lonely'. They stop talking to friends, they sulk a little bit; their grades start dropping.

The *Yeshiva* is very close-knit. This is a neighbourhood where you can sometimes hear gun shots go off, but we're very close. Kids come to me and say, 'Listen. Something's wrong with Avraham . . .' All the food is provided at the school. Yeah, they can bring in snacks. *Kashrut* isn't a problem. Usually we're not dealing with families that are so far out that they wouldn't know what's *kosher* and what's not *kosher*. You can get plenty *kosher* food from the supermarket. They don't need much money. When I first came I was living on $5 a week, and since I was such a great sports fanatic, I had to buy my magazine which was half my allowance! Ordinary novels aren't allowed. Jewish novels are generally all right. I wouldn't be so against a book like *Exodus* – I've dealt with worse, like Ken Follet books. They're adventures, but there's always a big sex scene.

Certainly there are kids who cannot cope with a *yeshiva*! What could cause you to be kicked out? Not going to a movie – there are kids who have gone to a movie, but they will definitely get into trouble. Having relationships with a girl – that's taboo! There are no proms, no discotheques. No, no, no. Contact with the community families really is minimal. They just don't want you to be out of the *Yeshiva*. We don't go to the synagogue, no. The *Beis Rahel* girls do, but we *daven* (pray) in the *Yeshiva*. The boys do read the newspaper, that's not forbidden.

I am paid for being dorm counsellor. I get up to *daven* with everybody else at 7:30. While the boys are having their breakfast, I check the dorm and then I go by bus downtown to college. Hopefully by the end of this year, I will have my Bachelors degree. Will I leave the *Yeshiva* at the end of this year? I guess only G-d knows that. I don't know where I'll do my Masters degree – maybe Montreal, maybe New York. I would like to be a clinical psychologist eventually, strictly observant and specializing in Jewish children. I found zero in my secular studies to question my faith in *halakhah* (Jewish

Law). Many rabbis don't agree with psychology. Personally, after studying Freud I can confidently say that I feel he was a little off the mark.

As a child I was sent to psychologists; I saw religious ones and non-religious ones. No one ever seemed to have hit home with me. No one ever reached me. My ultimate goal is to try to reach children who had a similar road as I had, and to try to make them be aware of what is expected of them. Not only what their parents expect, but what Judaism expects of each and every one. If I hadn't come here, I'd have been a total social misfit at best – I could have been a terrorist! This way of life in the *yeshiva* made me aware that people are people. Not everyone thinks as I do; not everyone acts as I do. People have feelings and things they want to do. You have to respect what they want. I've had friends who were rammed through the black-hat *yeshiva* and had it rammed down their throats; now they're non-observant and that's really sad. My dream is to help kids like that.

I'm unique in being part of the *Yeshiva* world and being interested in psychology, and seeing where the two can meet. My mother was thrilled that I wanted to do this. My *rebbe* at the *Yeshiva* is an unbelievable person. He doesn't condone college at all – normally he doesn't allow the boys to go – but for me he said, 'I think it will be right for you.'

I love kids. I want to get married and have lots of children. I suppose it is a pattern in the Orthodox community. I have one cousin who has twelve. Absolutely! I want a traditional domestic life. I owe my life to the *Yeshiva*. I'm serious. I was just crazy as a kid.

The Senior Camp Counsellor

MISS SIDNEY SCHWARTZBERG

A pretty young woman in her mid-twenties, she sat with us beside the stream at Camp Shalom.

My mother converted to Judaism when she married my father. Then my parents got divorced when I was maybe six or seven. My mom continued to raise us – my brother and I both – with very strong efforts to keep us Jewish. She was very interested in Judaism and fell in love with it. So we grew up learning Judaism on our own: reading books, doing every holiday out of a book, following the prayers as best we could. We did belong to the Temple. They didn't receive us real well once my parents were divorced because my mother had converted. They really alienated us and kept ties with my father. They sided with him. We went to services for High Holidays, and it was really a kind of uncomfortable thing. Before the divorce my mom was really active, and we were in the Temple all the time. And then there was this sort of weird separation from the synagogue. So we did it all at home out of books.

I didn't really have any Jewish friends. I went through the public schools. Then I went to camp, and that was my only real Jewish affiliation. I came to Camp *Shalom* first in 1980 – I was twelve maybe. I cried on the bus all the way from Metropolis. I arrived and there was this counsellor wearing these googly-eyed glasses and antennae on his head. He was telling me jokes till I laughed. Then at the end of the fortnight, I cried all the way home. I didn't want to leave the camp. My mom thought I'd cried the entire time! I loved it! I had the time of my life! Being with Jewish people up here, I attributed everything I did here as Jewish. The friendship circles, the campfire were all Judaism to me, and it was wonderful. The singing and dancing on Friday nights, that was Judaism to me and it made me want to be Jewish. Because of the situation with my parents, when I got to about camp age my mother proposed to us that it was up to us to choose our own religion. She sent us with friends to different churches, and tried to open things up a little. Coming to camp confirmed that I wanted to be Jewish.

I came back to Camp *Shalom* six straight years in a row. First I was a camper, and then a counsellor. Though things changed a little over the years, there were certain camp traditions that remained the same. When the kids came up in the bus, the staff held a huge paper roll across the road saying, 'Welcome to *Shalom* Camp', and the bus comes tearing through it and rips it to shreds. And as the kids get out of the bus they sing the welcome song. That happened back in 1980. It was great! It was a different experience every year, but every year it got better.

After high school, I went to the State University and I studied Communications. I was there for four years. I only really kept in touch with Jewish things through camp. I tried a little bit. I organized a Saturday morning bagel club with kids I'd known in camp. We'd get together once a month for cream cheese and bagels and talk about camp – that's really all we had in common. Then we had the occasional *Shabbat* dinner together. It's a tradition at camp always to wear white on the Sabbath, to welcome the Sabbath bride, and to this day I always wear white on *Shabbat*. It's my thing. I can't in the real world rest all day Saturday. I can't have a dinner party and dance and sing every Friday night, but I make a point of putting on my white shirt or sweater to do something to celebrate the Sabbath.

I took a year off after college and worked. I lived in a group home with the developmentally disabled. Then I went to graduate school in Washington DC to the All-Deaf University. I was really specializing in deafness so that was a culture shock. I'm teaching sign language up here. Yeah, we're signing prayers and things. That's the area I'm really interested in. How I ended coming back up here this year after being away for several years was I went to Temple. I hadn't done that in a long time, and was very separated from it. I was in interpreting school in Metropolis, and there was a thing which said, 'Temple *Shalom* needs a signer for Friday night services.' So I called the Temple and they said, 'Come down to services.' The whole drive down I was thinking, 'I'm not Jewish! I'm so non-Jewish! I haven't been connected to the community for such a long time!' All this was going on in my head, and I was really confused. And I walked into the Temple and was just so warmly received. People who I hadn't seen in years made me feel I'd walked into home or my college reunion or something. I was just kind of blown away! I was so moved! It was such an amazing experience.

It turned out to be an interfaith service. The Hispanic Catholic Church had been invited, and a black husband-and-wife Gospel team. The whole synagogue was packed with all these different people. There were sermons from all these different religions, and at the end everyone stood up and sang 'America the Beautiful'. And I'm like – I'm so Jewish; I'm so religious; this is so me! If this is religion, about bringing people together, it was such a beautiful thing. Anyway after the service, the rabbi said, 'Where've you been? Would you like to come to camp?' And I signed the contract to be Senior Counsellor there and then!

The first fortnight here I burnt myself out. I tried to get to know every single kid. Then I realized I couldn't do that. What I had to do was to let every single kid get to know me. I need to be in a very public eye so that they know who I am. The first session I goofed, and I exhausted myself. From the third session I started teaching sign language, and that really made camp for me. Teaching kids something I'm passionate about, and watching on *Shabbat* all their hands come up and signing, their arms just flying through the air! That meant something. That's what camp is all about: teaching and learning, and learning and teaching.

I vacillate in my Judaism. I go to services, and it makes so much sense to me and it's something I want to pursue. I'll be like that for a week. Then I go to services, and it doesn't make any sense. It's so much crock – it feels like a bunch of crud. Even at camp I get really confused about the religious part. I'm not confused about the camp traditions or the feelings I have about the people, but I'm confused about God and about reading words in a book that I wouldn't say every day. I really swing. Camp challenges you to question your Judaism, and to create your own religion and beliefs. I'm fortunate that I can use the rabbi as a resource. I'm so involved and camp is so much part of my life, and I have chosen that. I have also chosen not to be involved in the Temple, and not to participate in Judaism in the outside world. Synagogue to me is a really family thing, and because of my own family situation, I haven't been involved.

What is the purpose of the camp? I think the mission of the camp is to give the kids a Jewish experience, to live Jewish and to feel Jewish. The purpose is to find Judaism in everything you do. Hugging someone when they're crying, that's Jewish because Jewish values teach us to be kind to one another. When someone is struggling, you volunteer to help them out because Judaism teaches us to help people get over their stumbling blocks. We respect nature because Judaism teaches that nature is God's creation. We hearken to ourselves, we hearken to God and we hearken to nature. Everything we do up here is one of those three things. You live your Judaism. A lot of kids go to High Holiday services and camp, and that's it! So for a lot of them the Hebrew and the observances are overwhelming. It's got more observant over the years, and even I have felt that I wasn't going to like camp any more. It had got too Jewish. We've had to construct it very carefully to bring it in in a fun way. It's been progressive, it hasn't happened all at once. I have difficulty with the Hebrew myself because I don't know Hebrew, but the rabbi explained that sometimes when we sing Hebrew things up here, even if you don't know what it means, it elicits some emotion. That's the power in it.

The kids pay $700 to $800 for two weeks. It sounds a lot, and the counsellors are paid almost nothing, but camp loses money every year. It's maintenance. To close camp down, the windows have to be boarded because the snow gets as high as the roofs. The upkeep is horrendous. Right now it's being discussed to close the camp down completely. A lot of members of the Temple Board don't come up here, and don't have kids, and don't have any idea what goes on. What I think they should do is close down the Temple and keep the camp!

Eight

THE OLD

The Community Patriarch

We had heard about Mr Bernard Black from many people. He had been designated the 'Godfather of the West Side'! He was said to be enormously rich and to support single-handedly Maimonides Academy, the Yeshiva High School for boys, the Beis Rahel High School for girls and Etz Hayyim synagogue. Certainly Rabbi Marmorstein (The Orthodox Rabbi), *the Etz Hayyim rabbi, was his son-in-law. He had five sons, two daughters, at least thirty grandchildren, and he was described as a formidable figure. When we telephoned, he could not have been more helpful. We were invited to spend the Sabbath with the household, and it was made clear that this was a royal command.*

When we arrived on Friday evening the house was abuzz with activity. Hairdryers hummed; children shouted and stamped; there was the constant sound of running feet. An urgent message was conveyed down the intercom. A telephone call must be returned immediately because the telephone, according to Jewish Law, could not be used on the Sabbath. Our hostess emerged from her bedroom in her bathrobe; she was in the process of putting on her make-up and her head was completely covered by a scarf. Then the rabbi appeared, magnificent in black hat and shiny black kaftan, and the men went off to synagogue.

In the dining-room, dinner had been laid for twenty people. Two women – clearly not Jewish – were making extensive preparations in the kitchen. All the women suddenly appeared – Mrs Black, her two daughters (all exquisitely dressed), three little girls in long party frocks, three small boys (one only a baby), an elderly Russian lady with her daughter and granddaughter (none of whom could speak a word of English), and another

Russian woman who had been in Metropolis for a year. We all lit candles and said the traditional Sabbath blessing. There must have been thirty candles and the table was ablaze with light.

Then the front door opened and the men returned from synagogue. 'Good Shabbos, good Shabbos!' they said to the women. Besides all the husbands, there were various nephews and rabbinic students. They were all dressed in dark suits and big hats. An elegant young Hasid with a long red beard wore a magnificent streimel (fur hat) above his kaftan. Mr Black took his seat at one end of the table and Rabbi Marmorstein sat at the other. Blessings over the wine were said by every man present, one after the other. Then Sabbath songs were led by the younger son-in-law. The women did not sing – they listened. And then the food was served. There was gefilte fish, matzoh-ball soup, pickles, roasted chicken, breadcrumbed chicken, sweet chicken, apple kugel (pudding), potato kugel, onion kugel, tomato and cucumber salad, and ice cream with strawberry sauce. Mrs Black and her daughters served the men and scarcely sat down. Meanwhile the two gentile women in the kitchen toiled with the washing-up, and with taking yet more food out of the oven while the masculine singing continued.

It was a long, long meal. After no more could be eaten, we started on the Birkhat ha-Mazon (grace after meals). The elderly Russian man led it and his wife wept throughout. They had arrived in Metropolis from St Petersburg that very day. The prayer was lengthy and was said in a rapid mutter, with the leader pulling everyone together at intervals. Afterwards one of the small boys was invited to sing the child's version of the prayer to the assembled company. He was lifted up and sat on the hatch between the kitchen and dining-room. With very little prompting, he sang the whole grace in Hebrew. He was three and a half years old and was afterwards a little concerned that he had got his trousers damp from sitting in a puddle.

At long last everyone dispersed. We could not record Mr Black that evening – the use of tape recorders is forbidden on the Sabbath – but he spoke openly and freely to us a few days later. Despite his formidable reputation, he was charming.

MR BERNARD BLACK

I was born in a small town in the United States. In that town was a relatively small Jewish community. This was prior to the Second World War, and within the community many people were related. I was there through my high school years. We had a small *shul* (synagogue), and there was a *kosher* slaughterer who was also a teacher. We were all *Shomer Shabbos* (kept the Sabbath) even though we lived among *goyim* (gentiles). The *goyim* knew it. They knew that the Jewish people were this way and, because of that, there was very little anti-Semitism. There was a consistency among the Jewish people that the *goyim* recognized and respected. For example, in my grade school we had a Bible teacher who came in. I was the only Jewish child in the class, and when the Bible teacher walked in I stood up, walked out of the room, and sat in the Principal's office until the Bible teacher had left. There is no Jewish community in that town any more. The younger people moved to larger communities and the older people followed. I consider that pattern is part of the normal evolvement of the Jewish people in this country.

I went to Harvard and I majored in Chemistry. What was Jewish life like at Harvard? It depended on how much effort you wanted to put in it. I made a decision. I got off the train and I didn't know anyone. So I looked in the phone book and I found a rabbi, and I asked him if there was a place I could get *kosher* meals. He said that the *shammus* (beadle) in his *shul* served meals to some of the students, so I made arrangements to go there. And I want to tell you that of all the memories I have from Harvard, these are the best. There was a fellow from the law school; there was somebody writing a book; there was someone going to piano school – and we had lively discussions there. It was great!

The Second World War was going on, and after graduation and basic training in the infantry, I became involved in the Manhattan Project for three years, making the atomic bomb. I was in uniform the whole time. After that, life went on: I went to different places; I lived in different cities; I worked as a chemist, and then went on to other things. I became a trainee in a family enterprise, and finally I moved around and ended up here in Metropolis.

I arrived here thirty-three years ago at the time when there were a number of additional synagogues here besides *Etz Hayyim*. I had first visited the city in 1945, and at that time the entire West Side was Jewish. When I came here in 1960 to settle, the motivating factor of my moving here was so I could conduct my business and have a Jewish environment for my family, with particular emphasis on the Jewish day school, the Maimonides Academy. I became very involved with that. I had four sons, and now we have a fifth and two daughters – a total of seven children.

I have always maintained an interest in intensive Orthodox Jewish education. I always considered it was fundamental to the preservation of the Jewish people. I still do. I've said publicly that the elementary education of Maimonides Academy was similar to the outlook of the elementary education anyplace. It should be followed up by a high school education, so we established the *Beis Rahel* High School for girls, and the *Yeshiva* for boys. These did not exist before I came. Both buildings were turned over to us. We never had to pay a nickel, but we have rebuilt the *Beis Rahel*, which is now a beautiful building – very nicely done. I was instrumental in bringing in the individuals who were knowledgeable in these types of institutions. I'm interested in the fundamentals and in intense schools. I am aware that the environment of the United States is so powerful that unless the Jewish people created an intense atmosphere for themselves, it would be difficult to sustain themselves. A religious person can be involved in the secular world, but in order to sustain himself, he must have a strong anchor or background. I've always thought that. I can never remember thinking any differently. I know you have to make a choice: you either have to be intensely Jewish and be tough about it, or you disappear as a Jew. You weren't going to be able to ride the fence for too long.

I have seen cosmetic Jewish education, and I don't think it works. By cosmetic education I mean Jewish education given after the public school. A more exaggerated situation is the Sunday school. The Sunday school is totally bankrupt. It took the Jewish people of this country thirty or forty years to find out that cosmetic education does not work. It took a long time for them to find that out. The Maimonides Academy is an intense school. We founded the *Beis Rahel* for my elder daughter, who is living here – yes, Mrs Marmorstein (wife of *The Orthodox Rabbi*). My sons all went to a *yeshiva*, but I also gave them a secular background: one majored in Psychology; another has a Masters in Business Administration; another has a Law degree; and the fourth also has a pretty fair background.

I believe – and the literature bears me out – that the Jewish people have fallen away greatly. The one thing I would say: this Allied Federation here in Metropolis has as its motto, 'We are One'. That is the joke of the century. I have stood up at various dinners over many, many years and I have injected into my remarks the statement, 'Now you people out there, some of you are grandparents, some of you are parents. You have a chance. We have provided Maimonides Academy, the *Yeshiva* and *Beis Rahel* here in Metropolis. You can place your child in a proper environment until he graduates from high school. It's not too late.' I say it over and over again. Why? Because I wanted everyone to be totally guilty for not doing it. And they are! They are totally guilty of not doing it! You scratch them today, and with the possible exception of those people who are in the liberal wing and think they are the avant-garde for the American Civil Liberties Union, most people probably wonder today if they did the right thing. Even those who live in South-East Metropolis, who think they are somehow fancier (which of course they're not) and who think there is something wrong with those who live on the West Side, must have moments when they think they have done the wrong thing. Even so, the estrangement among Jews is growing. The Reform Jewish group, for example, is offering different kinds of definitions of who is Jewish. The contact between the Reform Jewish element and the rest is very limited. Instead of 'We are One' a correct motto would be, 'We are growing apart'.

The religious people are getting more educated. Their children are going through the intensive schools. What you see in Metropolis is a very small sample of what you are seeing in many cities. You should go to Boro Park in New York where

150,000 *frum* (observant) Jewish people live. That's almost five times the Jewish population in Metropolis, and they are all observant. New schools are opening; the birth rate is very high, and the schools are expanding enormously. In Monsey, New York, for example, there are a hundred synagogues. Can you imagine it? I hate to say this, but the people in Metropolis are so localized they don't even know about it. But these people are moving rapidly and with great force. There's a simultaneous thing going on – the general groups of the Jewish community are diminishing and falling away while the Orthodox groups are growing at a significant rate.

Why is there this efflorescence of Orthodox life? Maybe people have a similar concept to my own. The rules of behaviour of the Orthodox community are in contrast to the general promiscuity of the world about us. So if they have any doubts of the beneficial effects of living an intense Jewish life, why they don't have to go very far to see the alternative!

We do try to bridge the gap. The *Yeshiva* has a gentleman by the name of Avraham Klein (*The Yeshiva Official*). He is our reach-out person. He is a very knowledgeable person, and he schedules classes, seminars, all kinds of things for the general community. The programme of Rabbi Lubetkin (*The Russian Rabbi*) is an Outreach programme to the Russian Jews. In his own way, Rabbi Berkovski (*The Hasidic Rabbi*) tries to do Outreach things, whatever they might be. I myself try to be friendly to people, but I don't spend my time thinking about what someone living in South-East Metropolis is doing. My time is much occupied, and one must prioritize. I told you, I make my public announcement whenever I can: 'This is your chance. We have provided the schools. If you don't want to take advantage of them, I can't force you.' I don't know what to do beyond that . . .

The Older Member of a Temple

MISS BARBARA FRANKLYN

Her house was in an old section of Metropolis, near downtown. There were large shady trees and children riding bicycles up and down the sidewalk. Barbara Franklyn had been born in the house and had lived there all her life. She was a small woman in her late seventies with bright black eyes. She wore a pink shirt and a pink and white striped skirt with a crimson scarf around her waist. We sat in the music room drinking fresh home-made lemonade. There was a much-played grand piano and a cello lying on its side. Old sepia photographs of her grandparents were hanging on the walls, together with press cuttings about her father. He had been a well-known labour lawyer who had fought for workers' rights in the bitter labour confrontations of the 1930s.

My grandfather – my mother's father – came to Metropolis in 1870. He had come from Bavaria to the United States as a young boy. I'm not sure why he came here. I think simply to see what this part of the country had to offer. I have his diary from before he came to Metropolis. He records how terrible he felt when Abraham Lincoln was assassinated. The railroad had come to Metropolis in 1870, and I think it was sort of an adventure. In 1871 he went back to New York to marry my grandmother. This was a fixed marriage. They didn't know each other beforehand, which always strikes me as funny . . . They came out here on the railroad.

In 1872 he was one of the founders of Metropolis Hebrew Hospital. He was very thrilled with that. Then two years later came Temple *Shalom*. He was a founder and first President. Temple *Shalom* was the first synagogue in Metropolis. It was a small community, and it was mostly German Jews who were all Reform.

My father's family came to Metropolis in 1879. My father was born in New York City, and he was a year old when he came here. My parents met at a neighbourhood dance in 1902. My father was a lawyer. I've been asked if my mother's family objected to her marrying my father because he was not one of the German group. The community was polarized then – the Germans thought they were much better socially. Daddy's parents were Orthodox and were members of the *Adath Israel* synagogue on the West Side. They came from Poland or Romania. My parents were married by the Reform rabbi. I don't think there was any friction between the two families. My grandfather had died the year before, and Grandma was very easy-going.

My parents when they married were involved in Temple *Shalom*, but my father was one of the few people who had his foot in both camps – Reform and Orthodox, the East Side of town and the West Side of town. He remained a member of *Adath Israel* and he also belonged to Temple. As a child I went to Temple *Shalom* and was confirmed there. I went to religion school there. My brother studied Hebrew, but didn't get very far with it. The rabbi in those days, Rabbi Feinstein, has been described as an assimilationist, but that's not the case. I don't know why I'm so sensitive to it, but it makes me terribly angry when people say that. He believed in strong Jewish identity; he believed in symbols; he stressed the Friday night *kiddush* (blessing over wine) and holidays. We always had the *sukkah* (ritual tabernacle) at the Temple. He worked very early in the century to aid the new Russian immigrants. When I read about his work, it could be today. He always used to say: 'A Jew has to be a little finer. We have to be more careful in our behaviour.' I thought that was good.

The sanctuary of the old Temple was a sacred place. You wouldn't talk; you wouldn't even whisper in services. It had a sanctity that I loved when I was growing up, and I miss it now. Now it's sort of like a social – and that's true in all the synagogues. In the first place, no one ever read the service like Rabbi Feinstein. It was music, it was rhythm, it was beautiful. When I hear portions of it now, I remember how he read it. No rabbi has ever equalled his reading. He wasn't tall or particularly good-looking, but he had great dignity, great presence. They had a professional choir, but no cantor. Everyone got very dressed up for Temple in those days.

My Jewish education was very unsatisfactory. I'm ignorant in so many fields, and I think most people are. I did go to religion school, but we didn't have good teachers. Anyone who wanted to teach Sunday school among the women of the congregation, Rabbi Feinstein would say, 'Fine'. They weren't learned in Judaism or in teaching youngsters. None of us really liked Sunday school. It wasn't presented right. People always misbehaved in class.

Most of the Temple *Shalom* congregation came from the East Side. I hate to say they were upper-class – I don't like that term. But they were better-off and they thought they were superior. A lot of people from *Adath Israel* or *Har HaShem* wanted to join Temple *Shalom* before their kids were confirmed, because it was more socially correct to be confirmed at the Temple. That's not true any more. In those days there were many cliques in the community.

The Temple is far more democratic now. In Rabbi Feinstein's time, the Board would do whatever the rabbi wanted. The membership used to be all of one strata of society: Germanic, Reform. Now it's far more diverse. The change took place at the time of the Second World War. We had a new rabbi at that time. He had strong convictions and was an ardent Zionist. He begged the congregation to support the Zionist cause, but the Board responded by staying neutral. I thought that was terrible! My family was always Zionist. Anyway, one little group broke away from Temple *Shalom* and formed Temple *Beth Jacob.* It was based on anti-Zionism and not so much Hebrew, not so much ritual. Apparently the last straw for this faction was when our rabbi wanted to wear a prayer shawl for services. They now have a woman rabbi. (*The Woman Rabbi*)

My parents didn't want to move the building of Temple *Shalom.* I wanted to stay where we were. They wouldn't say it, but the main reason for the move was the new neighbourhood was better. The old Temple was not in a good neighbourhood any more, it was too near downtown. The old building was so beautiful, but there wasn't much opposition to the move. It took me a long time to get used to the new building. I think it's too large. The sanctuary's too far away. I still feel it's awfully impersonal. It intimidates people instead of drawing them. I liked the stained glass in the old building much better. It had more Judaic feeling.

I also haven't been crazy over the new rabbi (*The Reform Rabbi*) who came in the 1970s. I don't mind the changes in ritual in the Temple. I have a friend whose grandfather also founded the Temple. She doesn't like them at all. She says, 'That's not what my grandfather wanted', but I always say, 'Unfortunately, your grandfather is no longer on the Board.'

The Retired Educationalist

MR FRED TABBICK

Fred Tabbick was a familiar figure in Jewish Metropolis. Universally known as Uncle Fred, he had taught generations of children in Temple Shalom religion school. He had also been President of the Jewish Educational Council of Greater Metropolis for twenty-three years. Although long since retired, he still had a small office in the Temple. It was a tiny room dominated by a large flat-top desk. His in-tray was labelled 'Sacred'; his out-tray 'Top Sacred'. Balanced on the well-stocked bookshelves were many photographs of his family and his students. Hanging on the wall was a large sign saying 'Listen', and another asking 'Are We Having Fun Yet?' Uncle Fred himself sat behind his desk in a rocking office chair. He was in his late seventies, bespectacled, and looked a little like a benign turtle.

I was born in Scotland in 1914. My folks were on their way to America from Poland. World War One broke out and we had to stay for a bit. In 1916, when I was a year and a half old, we came to America. We came to Metropolis in 1918 where my father was an Orthodox rabbi. He had his rabbinic ordination from a famous talmudic academy in Poland. We were here for only a year. My father was with *Har HaShem* synagogue, and then we moved to Waterside Springs, still in this state. He was the rabbi, the cantor, the religion school teacher, the slaughterer, the teacher, everything. I really grew up in Waterside Springs. This was in the 1920s.

I graduated from high school in Waterside Springs and went off to the Hebrew Union College for a year. This was in 1931/32 – the time of the Depression. I had all the great German professors. I only spent a year there and then came back and I graduated from the State College in 1935. I was on the history/politics side, but I knew I was going to law school. I thought I wanted to be a lawyer. So I went to the University of Metropolis law school and graduated there in 1938, passed the bar exams in 1939, and practised for a few years before the war.

Then I went into the Army for about three and a half years. I served with distinction in the Army. I was awarded the Bronze Star; I was a company runner. I can show you the citation, but without modesty. When I was being honoured by the congregation a few years back, and one speaker after another was lauding me, I had to repeat what Henry Kissinger once said on a similar occasion. He said 'It's difficult to look humble for any length of time!' So I served in Belgium, France, Germany. I was with the troops that helped liberate Buchenwald. Buchenwald was fifteen kilometres from Weimar, the seat of the German Republic, and the people in Weimar learnt to say in many languages: 'We didn't know!' And yet the stench from Buchenwald you could smell in Weimar. I have a picture of me standing next to a sign on the outside of Buchenwald. People on their way to work passed this sign and the sign said in German, 'No one is allowed in the crematorium'. That helped influence my life. When the war was over, I spent some time as a credit manager for a furniture store in Metropolis. They used my stationery to frighten people into paying the bill!

Even when I was a lawyer I taught at Temple *Shalom* as a volunteer, and I continued until 1956. That was when Rabbi Green came – yeah, the rabbi before Rabbi Reinhardt (*The Reform Rabbi*) – and he wasn't interested in having an assistant. There'd been a lot of friction. He preferred to have an Education Director, and they didn't have much trouble convincing me to do this full-time. It was not a great financial move, but I never regretted it. The psychic income more than compensated. From 1956 to 1984 I was the Educational Director. I was also the Summer Camp Director, and the Youth Director. In the Temple, I was in charge of all the education – for adults as well as children – and our school during the baby boom had 900 students. It's levelled off now to about 600. There were about fifty teachers. I was fortunate; my greatest talent was to surround myself with talent. There are some people who want to surround themselves with incompetents to make them look good! But obviously you're not going to have all stars . . .

In 1984 I was aged seventy, and that was retirement age. I was ready. So from 1984 to the present I'm a volunteer again! Well, I do have my own office. Originally I was behind the kitchen until this part was built. With Social Security, and the rabbinical pension fund, and the Temple added some, I am able to live modestly, but I really enjoy the volunteering. The

Educational Director Emeritus is my title. I come in, I teach. One of the things I do on a regular basis is see kids six months before their *Bar* or *Bat Mitzvah.* They come into a class which I teach. They are supposedly able to read Hebrew, but that's not always the case. Danny Mizel (*The Bar Mitzvah Teacher*) does a wonderful job, but if they came in with proficiency in Hebrew his job would be easier. I work on what they're going to do in the Prayer Book. Danny works on what they're going to do in the *Torah,* and then he takes them and polishes them up for the last couple of weeks!

How have things changed? I don't know that kids love religion school any more than they ever did. You do have to do different things. There is a philosophy that the curriculum should be a *smorgasbord.* Kids'll pick up what they want. I said that was fine, but we also have to put a few things on their plate. I mean if a kid is going to go along and just pick ice-cream and potato chips, we've got to put a little piece of meat and a green vegetable or two. The curriculum may have changed but I hope the core is still the same. We want them to come out carrying their Judaism with a song in their heart rather than a burden on their back!

Divorce has made a difference. In my day the registration card showed a mother and a father and a home and an address. Now registration cards have to say 'lives with'. Let's see – I have a good cartoon here of a little girl giving a note to her teacher. She's saying, 'This is a note from my parents, my former parents, my step-grandmother and my dad's live-in.' There's a difference from the old days . . . it does cause problems . . . it makes it hard on the kid.

What do I look back on with the greatest satisfaction? Well four of my students have become rabbis. One of them did an exercise with his confirmation class: 'The People Who've Influenced Me the Most'. He did it with them and he gave me a copy of his list; and I'm number four. So I say, 'How come I'm number four?' And he says, 'It's alphabetical!' That's a pleasure. It's hard to see results. A shoemaker makes many shoes and he can see them, but a teacher can't see his results so directly. But you know what it says in the *Talmud*? 'Much have I learnt from my teachers; more from my colleagues, but most from my students . . .'

The Russian Physician

DR TANYA PETROV

In Metropolis, near 1st Avenue, was a large block of apartments. This was maintained by the Jewish community for elderly people who needed sheltered housing. Dr Tanya Petrov lived on the sixth floor. She was a lively woman in her seventies.

I was born in Russia in the city of Moscow after the Bolshevik Revolution. There was a civil war at the time, and my parents couldn't feed me so they bought a goat and because of that goat I survived the civil war. My father was a tailor and my mother was a seamstress. They were simple people. It was a difficult time in Russia. Before the civil war was Revolution – a bloody time – and before Revolution was World War One. A horrible time. My parents supported the Revolution very strong. They believed only the Revolution could help Russian Jews to be accepted. They were not religious.

I graduated from the Soviet high school in 1936. They wanted a new socialistic generation. We were never taught history except the French Revolution, some math, and a lot of workers' skills. Marxism/Leninism was our religion. How couldn't I believe it when all teachers, all propaganda tell us it is our future? I graduated when I was sixteen. In 1936 the time in Russia was very bad. It was the Stalinist regime and killing, killing, killing. Parents spied on children and children on parents. I was a good student and got a gold medal in Moscow. Because I got a gold medal, I could go to learn science in any university or institute in the Soviet Union. I decided to be a physician, and I graduated from the Medical Institute in Moscow.

This point of my life was very important. My mind began to change. First of all there was no one family in which someone had not been arrested. My uncle was arrested for nothing, and my father was exiled. I had negative thoughts about the political situation, but I could not tell anyone. It was very dangerous. I qualified in 1941 on the same day that the war between Russians and Nazis began. I went to the war immediately as a doctor, and I served in the Soviet army six years. After six years, they offered to make me a major, but I refused. I hated the war.

I was full of these pictures of blood and dying people. I can say that I encountered no anti-Semitism in Army. I met a lot of Jews in the war. Jews are good fighters.

The Nazi propaganda found good soil in Russia, and anti-Semitism was growing very fast. I returned to Moscow and I did a three-year residency, specializing in cardiology. You mustn't compare with American cardiology; the gap between Soviet and American medicine is very big. After that I got married. My husband was my friend in medical school. We found each other after the war. Yes, he survived the war and I survived the war. We lived for a time in the Far East of Soviet Union, and two children were born. Then we returned to Moscow after the death of Stalin. I practised medicine without interruption through all those years.

I must tell you about Russian anti-Semitism. I am very angry with my country because of that anti-Semitism. When I was in East, I heard terrible stories about how Jews kill children and take their blood for Passover bread. Anti-Semitism was like a fire in the Far East. When we returned to Moscow, my friends helped me to find a job pretty fast, but no one could help my husband. He was a physician, but he couldn't get a job for nine months only because he was a Jew. I was so angry and there was a big depression with him. I was very brave. I went to a special political office and said my husband was a member of the Communist Party and had served in Army twelve years. He could not find a job. Why? Because he's a Jew. It was a serious accusation, but the official took the telephone, called to someone, and said 'Tomorrow he'll work!'

He worked in a very big hospital, but I was a physician in Moscow University. I decided to leave Russia because I felt enough is enough. I cannot complain they persecute me, but I knew the University policies. It was so anti-Semitic you cannot imagine. It was a secret, but I knew through my long work there. I work at the University for nearly twenty-five years. I checked the health of future students. From 1960s, they stopped taking any Jew to learn law. Nothing, not one Jew. Only 1.5 per cent of all students could be Jews. Every day they checked how many Jewish young people were applying. They used to give me files of students and tell me, 'This student is a sick man – try to find something wrong with him.' It was criminal, terrible. Then I saw a special mark sometimes in the top right corner of files. What did it mean? I did not know. Then I found out it stand for 'False Russian'. They were students with Russian passport but with Jewish face or Jewish name. They used to interview these young people, and the conversation is like a torture. Perhaps the father was half-a-Jew, and when they found out, it was enough to make sure student was never accepted. Why did they do this? They did not want to have a Jewish intelligentsia any more. They did not want Jews. The economic life was getting more and more hard in Russia, and they wanted to have a scapegoat.

My husband died in 1970. All the time I saw what was going on at the University, I was getting sicker. I could not stand anti-Semitic action. So I decided to go. I wanted to go to Israel – I never thought about America, though I liked to listen to *Voice of America* on my radio. My children were very against Russia from the start. They both graduated from the University because I had many, many good friends. My daughter had a pretty good job as a chemist, but my son was a physicist and he couldn't get a job. They didn't need to see his passport once they had seen his face! This young boy could not get a professional job. It was enough!

We applied to go to Israel. I was smart. I applied just before Olympic Games in Russia, and at that time they were giving permit, permit, permit. In Vienna my daughter's husband, who is now a professor in Washington, wanted to go to United States not Israel. I could not insist any more on Israel. They sent us to Chicago, where my daughter has a very good job. She and my son-in-law got divorced and she has married again, to an American man. He is not Jewish. My son and I went to Metropolis where he studied at the University. For the first three years we were in Metropolis, from 1980 to 1983, that was a terrible time. We lived in an apartment in basement. We were poor, real poor. I was not poor in Russia, but here I was poor. I knew nothing in English, not a word. I got welfare support and my son got a small part-time teaching job while he studied. But I was sure that I did right. I could not stand the Russian social regime, and I could not stand the anti-Semitism. My children had no future there. Russia was like a deadlock for us.

After my son graduated, we separated. He now has a very good job with the NASA space organization. I came to this apartment. I went to English classes at Jewish Community Centre, and for six months I learnt six hours a day there and three hours at home. Then I studied history on Jewish people, and I delivered twenty lectures in Russian at the Jewish Community Centre. I am preparing a second course of eight lectures at the moment. Rabbi Lubetkin (*The Russian Rabbi*) helped me a lot with the books. I am deeply interested in Jewish history, but it is very painful for me to remember the history of the Jewish people and to understand my own life. A lot of new Russians have come over and their head is like an empty pot. They know nothing, nothing. They need to hear. I never have gone back to Moscow. For what would I go? To see their chaos, their flourishing anti-Semitism?

The Assimilationist

MR PETER ISAAC

We interviewed Peter Isaac in his beautiful, spacious apartment. There was a thick grey carpet on the floor and capacious grey and purple upholstery. The bookcases were full of books, and the pictures on the wall included a signed lithograph by Chagall. The house plants were large and glossy, and there were exquisite pieces of sculpture dotted around the room. Peter himself was in his eighties. His first wife had died five years ago. He sat upright on the sofa with his second wife beside him. He was wearing a check jacket and grey flannel trousers. His white hair was freshly brushed and his moustache neatly trimmed.

I was born in Chicago, Illinois, in 1907, and I grew up in one of the northern suburbs. I had two years of college at the University of Wisconsin and the final two years at Swathmore College, just out of Philadelphia. My family was not formally religious. I did go to Reform religion school and I was confirmed. I was never *Bar Mitzvah*. I had no formal connection with a synagogue after that.

Following graduation from Swathmore and Northwestern law

school I entered a firm of lawyers, of which my father and my uncle were senior partners. That lasted for four years. After my father died the firm broke up, and I went in with a couple of other people. In World War Two I was drafted into the Army and served for about a year and a half in this country and in Germany. Following that I was asked to join a chemical firm as in-house counsel and after a year a group of us broke away and came to Metropolis. Yeah, Paul Hetter (the husband of *The Unbeliever*) was among the group.

I was married back in 1932. Being employed by my father's firm at the time I was drawing a good salary. This was during the Depression. I was married to Beth Volger. Her family was Dutch originally and she had been a member of the Dutch Reform Church. I was taken into her family very, very easily. We met through a mutual friend. She was staying in Chicago with a friend and we met because I was lending the friend a copy of James Joyce's *Ulysses.* Her family accepted me very readily, and at one point her mother said that she was happy Beth had married me because I was a member of the Chosen People. My family loved Beth almost from the start. She was immediately accepted, there was no question about it.

In Metropolis we immediately had friends in the Jewish community because a college classmate gave us an introduction to a friend of his. Immediately on arrival we became part of the group. They were all Jewish. We were all involved in Democratic city politics at that date. Shortly afterwards, around 1951, I volunteered as a member of the Recording for the Blind, a group which had been started by some non-Jewish society women. As a result of that there was a certain amount of social interchange between that group and me because I was one of the early members. We would occasionally have dinner with some of them and some of them would come to our house – that sort of connection.

I've never belonged to a synagogue in Metropolis. As a matter of fact, it's fair to say I never really thought about the question. Beth and I were a unit. We lived in a world which had frequent contact with both the Jewish and the non-Jewish world. We didn't have children. How would I have brought them up? You're asking me a hypothetical question that I don't know that I can answer. I think probably as agnostics and with the moral virtues, and that's it!

I would say I am not religious. I was not particularly interested in Jewish religion, even in Jewish history. I don't even recall any religious discussions. Did I think of myself as a Jew? No . . . that was not my uppermost thought and reaction. I think the first time that I considered myself strongly as a Jew was after we had moved here to Metropolis. The representative of an insurance company also represented a real estate development which had a policy of barring Jews from their property. When he attempted to sell me insurance, somehow or other my back went up. I told him that when they changed the policy, we would think about discussing with him the question of insurance. That attitude towards Jews changed subsequently – partly with a nudging from the Supreme Court!

Five years after we came out here, a lawyer whom I knew supported me for the Metropolis University Club. This did have a reputation for not welcoming Jews. He came back to me and reported that he couldn't get me in. This indicated the somewhat social anti-Semitism that existed in those days. We remained friends – he subsequently became a United States Senator – up until the time of his death.

But things changed, the next important thing in connection with the community was the fact that Beth and I had been active with the Symphony and the Art Gallery. In 1962 I became a member of the Board of Trustees of the Metropolis Art Gallery. In 1963 I was approached by two of the non-Jewish members of the Board asking me to become the President of the Board. I was elected and was President until 1971, and of course had contacts all over the place. I had to make speeches, meet groups, and persuade people to make substantial donations. So at that point I was fairly well known in the community. In 1971 I was made an honorary member of the Board and I still attend Board meetings. Among the Board members I should think there were probably no more than about four or five Jewish members out of a total of about twenty-three. I was the first Jewish President of the Board, and I think that indicates a change in attitude. We all began to realize there was no longer an opposition or even a distinction between Jew and non-Jew.

I behaved myself as President of the Board and came out of it, I think, smelling very well. Yeah, the reception hall of the gallery was named after me the year after I retired.

I will say this – when somebody with a Jewish name or who is known to be a Jew does something wrong in this city, the rest of us cringe. We've had our problems here; we've got one or two big crooks. When something like that occurs I'm embarrassed. I don't like to see a Jew do something visibly wrong because it does reflect on all other Jews. Over the years, I may have become slightly more sensitive to being a Jew, but it is not my first consideration in meeting people or in doing things. In fact it's way down the list. We have friends who are ultrasensitive as to anything involving the Jews and I resent this terribly. This sensitivity I've never developed . . . and I don't want to.

The Grandmother

MRS DOROTHY SCHUMANN

Mrs Dorothy Schumann lived with her husband, Harry, in a modest house a couple of blocks away from Temple Shalom. We sat with her in her comfortable sitting room, surrounded by her books, ornaments and family photographs. She was in her seventies.

Both of my parents were born in Romania. They didn't know one another then. They met in New York and got married there. Then an aunt came out to Metropolis and little by little the whole family moved here. I think they were Orthodox at that time, but my mother was never terribly strict. We belonged to *Har HaShem* synagogue, and I had what I suppose you can describe as a Conservative Jewish education. My parents thought Temple *Shalom* was like a church, and both my brothers had *Bar Mitzvah* at *Har HaShem*. I was confirmed there, and I learnt Hebrew reading from a gentleman who lived under the viaduct. My dad kept a dry goods (haberdashery) store and money was scarce.

I had very few Jewish friends at high school, and I had to lie a little bit if I wanted to go out with a non-Jewish boy because that was absolutely something you couldn't do. I remember I went with a boy called Greenfield, and I passed him off as a Jew! Then I went to the University of Metropolis, and I belonged to a Jewish sorority there. It was called *Delta Phi Epsilon.* It was really kind of snobbish; it was the best Jewish sorority, and there was another one to which we sent our rejects. We were terrible. I remember rejecting two girls because we classified them as coming from the West Side. We thought they were too Jewish! We went out with boys from the Jewish fraternities. It just was not acceptable to go with anyone else. Because it was not acceptable, it just wasn't done. We've often talked about that as parents. It was a different time.

Harry did not go to the University of Metropolis. He came from a small town upstate, and went to the State University. We met at the Hebrew Hospital. My brother, who was a doctor, got me a job as a telephone operator there, and Harry's dad was a patient. We ran into each other and went out and that was it. He's two years older than I, and we got married when I graduated in 1938. He was still going to law school at that time, and he sold shoes at the shoe store to earn his tuition. We really didn't have very much money. We'd wait for my parents to invite us to dinner, but, you know, you didn't need much money.

Harry came from a little town and he only had non-Jewish friends there, but he always knew that he was going to marry a Jewish girl. We were married by Fred Tabbick's (*The Retired Educationalist*) brother. It was a very small wedding. I think there was a stigma if you didn't get married soon after leaving college. I wanted to have an engagement ring the next day after meeting Harry! It was important to have a man. It's completely different now, I know. I think I got my engagement ring real soon because we were engaged for two years before we got married. It was a different time, it really was.

When the war came, Harry was drafted into the Army. I was pregnant and had a miscarriage, but that made no difference. He was taken into the Army as a foot soldier in the infantry. Then later he got into the military police because he was a lawyer. He went to Hawaii and Japan, and he was gone for three years. That was hard. He wrote to me every day. I've still got lots and lots of letters – they're all downstairs. You waited and you planned until your husband came back.

On his return we talked about children immediately, but I had one miscarriage and then another. So we decided we'd try to adopt a baby. It wasn't easy, even then, but we did. We got Danny in 1948, when he was just one day into life, and we were thrilled with him. He was a darling little boy, a really good-looking little kid. We were still living at my parents' home at this stage, but Harry bought two building lots here and we built this house. We had to compromise a lot because money was still not very much, and Harry started to practise law. When we moved into this house, I immediately got pregnant and we had Sam in 1954. There was six years' difference between Danny and Sam. Yes, it was exciting. Sam was a cute kid, too, a really cute kid.

We heard Rabbi Feinstein speak, and Harry decided he'd really like to join Temple. My parents, as I say, thought it was like a church, with the organ and all, but they didn't press us to join *Har HaShem*. Temple was more modern and gave the best deal for young people money-wise. We really liked it, and immediately they asked me to teach in the religion school. They were pleased with me; I loved it. I taught there for thirty-eight years, right up till a year ago. Danny and Sam both went through the religion school – they were both *Bar Mitzvah* and confirmed.

They both went to the public schools. Danny went to the State University. He stayed maybe two years and found the competition more than he could handle so he graduated from the Community College here. I don't think he ever went out with non-Jewish girls. We had conversations about it, and it was expected of him to marry a Jewish girl. We knew the parents of the girl he eventually married. In fact Danny and Lynnie were in the same confirmation class at Temple. They were about twenty-three when they married, and it was a nice wedding. Sam was best man and lots of our friends were there. They had two children very quickly. Lynnie felt compelled immediately to have a child. I don't think Danny was ready – he told us he thought it was too soon. First they had Dan Junior and then a little girl, Sherry. I was really thrilled from a grandmother's point of view, but there were problems. They moved away for a while to Washington where Danny had a very good job. We saw them occasionally.

Then they moved back to Metropolis about ten years ago. They immediately joined Temple and both kids were confirmed there. Today Dan Junior is nineteen and has just graduated from high school; he's going to Israel for a year, and then will decide about college. Sherry is a senior (last year) in high school. She goes to regular classes in the morning and to a beauty school in the afternoon. After two years she will graduate with enough credits to be a beautician. She has no aspirations for college, but Dan Junior does. As far as I know they are committed Jewishly.

Sam went to Princeton and studied Chinese. He grew up in a Jewish neighbourhood and most of his friends were Jewish. I don't think they had dates then. He went out with a whole group. He also got a degree in Taiwan. He went to business college in Arizona and got an MBA, and then he went to law school in California. He had a lot of education! His Law thesis was on copyright law in China, and through that he got a great job offer in a law office in Hong Kong. Of course I was very distressed it was so far. I still am upset about it. It's far away. To be fair, I don't think I ever thought Sam would settle in Metropolis. He is an adventurer. Metropolis is too confining.

There's a funny story about how he met his wife. Solange went to a lecture that Sam was giving. She thought he was such an arrogant person; the way he talked that Chinese really annoyed her – it was as if he was Chinese. Afterwards she went up to him to tell him she thought he really was an arrogant cuss, but instead they went out for coffee! As far as I can tell, it was immediate. Then Tiananmen Square happened, and it grated against Sam's morality so he left that law firm. I guess by that time he and Solange were involved. He called us from San Francisco and he said, 'Are you sitting down?', and we said, 'Yeah'. And he said, 'I just got married!' Well, I stood up then! I said, 'Is she Jewish?', and he said, 'No'. And I said, 'Well, are we going to see her?' This was the first I'd ever heard of it. They got married without any family.

Well, they came to see us, and Solange is a darling girl. Really a charmer. I guess I was troubled she wasn't Jewish. Sam had been very involved in Jewish things and Israel, and was outstanding in Sunday school. It would never have occurred to me that he wouldn't marry a Jewish girl. I couldn't account for it, but Sam is really cosmopolitan. But she is a darling, darling girl, and a wonderful daughter-in-law. They've been here a few times.

I don't think she's ever suggested conversion, but she wanted to read about Judaism. I don't think their children will be brought up as Jews, but how can you know? Of all the kids in my family Sam was the most tuned in to Judaism, so who knows? Even though he's made compromises, he's strong in his belief. I do believe that. Their two babies are called Jeremy and Abigail. Here are their pictures. See how adorable they are – that's real grandma talk for you!

The Holocaust Survivor

MR THOMAS FRIED

The house stood in the most exclusive suburb of Metropolis. Forty years ago there had been a gentlemen's agreement that houses in the area would not be sold to Jews. It was situated among green hills and there was a wonderful view from the back. Downtown Metropolis seemed very far away.

Thomas Fried was a small man in his late sixties. He was wiry and strong. His speech still contained its native Hungarian cadence. While we sipped Coca-Cola in his elegant dining room, he spoke of the most terrible things.

I was born in a little town in the Carpathian mountains. I can show it to you on the map here. We were about thirty kilometres from the Polish border. In my time it was Czechoslovakia; before the First World War it was Hungary; during the Second World War it was Hungary again; then Czechoslovakia again; and in 1945 it became part of the Soviet Union. Today it is part of the Ukraine. I was number nine in my family. We were ten children. Here is a picture of my family. My sister sent it to me. I cherish this because I do not have any pictures from my youth. When you talk about the Holocaust that's a pain, a daily pain for a person not to have in our twentieth century a picture of himself as a youth. My father was a professional accountant with a big salary. I was born in 1924 and during the Depression his salary dropped to one-third of what it used to be. So we came from well-to-do to being very difficult economically . . .

My father and my grandfather were both *Rosh Yeshiva* (head of the talmudic academy). My father was very strict Orthodox. He was not a *Hasid,* no. My parents decided to let me go into the Hebrew gymnasium with its Zionist spirit. I spoke Hungarian till I was six years old, and still speak that with my wife. This is my mother tongue. When I was six I went to Hebrew school, what they call a *heder,* and immediately started learning Hebrew and Yiddish. Two months later I went to a Czech elementary school where I learnt everything in Czech. I remember I cried the first day because I didn't understand a word. Three years later I entered a Russian school. I did this because the Czech teachers had become anti-Semitic. Two hundred Jewish kids were taken out of the Czech schools and put into the Russian schools. I learnt for five years everything in Russian, Ukrainian or Romanian because there were fights between these ethnic groups, just like you see in the former Yugoslavia today. When I finished the Russian school, I was fourteen years old. After a year I went to this gymnasium, and I was the last graduating class before we went into the Holocaust in 1944, April.

As a matter of fact we were ten kids: six boys, four girls. What's unique about us is from the ten children, nine returned from the Holocaust. Passover 1944, the last day was the Sabbath; I studied the *Talmud* with my father. Next day the Hungarian gendarmes came and put the Jews into the ghetto. We were there maybe two or three weeks, I don't remember. Then we were put on the cattle trains the usual way to Auschwitz. We went for two days and two nights. It was my father, my mother, myself, and two of my sisters. One of my sisters was already married; another was away; and five brothers were with the Hungarian army. We went to Auschwitz separately. We arrived after a long, suffering trip, with no facilities in a cattle car. We came at night. With the lights, we couldn't do anything. A minute and I was here; my father was there; my mother was there; my sisters were someplace else. We got separated so fast.

No one could even say a word. So I suspect my parents were gassed the same night.

The rest of us, five brothers and I and four sisters, were all in Auschwitz, and we all went through the *Gehenna*, the Hell of the Holocaust. In the end we came home – nine of us – which was absolutely . . . I've never heard of it. I was in Auschwitz probably two weeks or so, and then I was taken to Mathausen. Two thousand of us, young people. We arrived on *Shavuot* (Festival of Weeks) day. The reason? They were building about twenty-eight tunnels into the mountains to hide airplane factories. They needed labour very badly. We were put to work there, but the reception committee, so to speak, made us stand to attention for almost four hours in the sun just to humiliate us. The assessor came afterwards with a – how do you call it? – a whip and a dog to look at us and yelled, '*Yuden* (Jews), look at that chimney over there. That's the only place you can get out of here.' That was the reception.

I worked in these tunnels. I was unlucky and lucky. I fell down and hurt my knee. My leg blew up so they took me to the camp hospital. When I got there, there was a doctor, a Jew, an inmate like myself. When he talked to me, he realized I was educated. He became friendly and he saved my life. I taught him to sing, 'Somewhere Over the Rainbow'. I'd learnt English in the gymnasium, and I'd seen the *Wizard of Oz*. Our whole class went to see it. This doctor took me, two people held me down; he took a nail scissor and held it over a candle fire and then he stuck it in my knee. I started yelling with pain and he hit my face two times, and he just cut it out. I lost brown pus; it looked to me like a quart at that time. Then he nursed me. He told me, 'You see what a song can do!'

I don't remember the day, but probably March of 1945. I was down and weighed so little I wasn't fit to work any more. They took about 600 of people like me – weak – that they wanted to dispense with. They gathered us to be killed. I had a friend from my home town; he went to school with me. He had a position in the camp administration. He was in good shape, and he had a little power with the people because the guys who ran the block, I think they were homosexuals. I didn't know then, obviously, I just think so. He knew what was happening and he came and took me out of the line. He lives in Long Island now.

After this the Germans knew they were losing the war, but the Mathausen administration was so anti-Semitic, as a last act, they still wanted to take revenge on the Jews. They took 17,000 Jews from the camps and marched us for three days without food and water. The whole thing was seventy-five kilometres, but they wouldn't let us go down the regular roads because they were hiding us from the regular population. This was Austria; this was not Poland or Auschwitz. And the American army came and liberated us. I remember it very well. On the last day I came out, I had to have some liquid and all of a sudden I heard shooting. I saw on the road trucks and in every window of the trucks was a black man. I'd never seen black men before. Today the black people are angered because they were segregated during the war, and they never got credit for what they had done. And that was the end of the war. One, two, three it was over.

Afterwards I went to a nearby city. We went to a warehouse. It was full of food. But so much food that we got crazy. Like they had hundreds of kilograms of sugar, and I just opened it and took sugar. There were cans of beef, and I opened that. There were dried noodles and we put them together. A lot of us made fires and cooked it and ate it, and a lot of us got diarrhoea and a lot of us got really sick . . . All the people with me at this railroad station got fever, typhoid fever, and the people of the city got really scared and took us to a military camp. That's where they weighed me. After I got clean clothes, a German SS uniform, all black and heavy shoes, and they put me on the scales and said 'Thirty kilograms!' I almost passed out there already, and that was the liberation.

After the war, well it's a long story because I got sick. I had to wait in a hospital. I spent over five years in hospitals. It was a tragedy; all my family went to Palestine, but I wasn't well enough. As a matter of fact, I have seven surviving families, brother and sister families in Israel today. When I got better, Israel wouldn't take us because we were called the hard-core sick. So I went to America instead of Palestine. By that time I was married. My wife and I were married in 1949. We got to New York, and the ship was four days late. My wife's cousins did not know to meet us so they put us on a train to Louisville,

Kentucky. I was there and I had a job with very nice people in a wholesale furniture store. But I got sick again with pneumonia. I got to the Jewish hospital – I didn't have money; I was on charity. I knew I need a sanatorium, and after three or four weeks they had to get rid of me so I got sent to the hospital in Metropolis. That's how I survived again. It was an odyssey.

After I got out I was desperate. I couldn't do anything. I bought a correspondence course in accounting, and it cost me $200 – $10 a month. So I went into the tradition of the family (my father and three of my brothers). I finished sixty of those lessons and I started looking for a job. For six weeks nobody would hire me because I was told by the doctors not to do overtime. The Jewish Family Service of Metropolis wouldn't co-operate with me. They told me I should go back to Louisville, I tell you. My wife is still mad and won't give the Family Service money. I've given over $1 million to the University Judaic Centre by now, and more money than I dreamed to make to charities, but this one organization she will not help – she's still so mad.

Eventually I was hired as a junior junior, and I stayed with that firm till 1971. But by then I was already starting to build apartments in my spare time. In 1971 I decided to leave accounting and become a builder. One gentleman, Henry Greenbaum (see *The Museum Curator*) who was already a millionaire at age twenty-eight/twenty-nine, invited me to join him. In 1972 we became public; we were on the New York Stock Exchange. Then in 1974 we started a chain of banks. I was Vice-Chairman; he was Chairman. Then Rabbi Kornfeld (*The University Professor of Judaica*) got involved with me and tried to solicit me for $15,000. I liked what he said, and I liked the idea of the Judaic Centre. My field was education – nothing else counts. He talked me into a programme, and I pledged $250,000 as a permanent endowment for the University Centre. Then I came up with the money in two or three years and created a Chair; that is called now the Anna and Thomas Fried Chair of Judaic Studies. And Rabbi Kornfeld is the Professor!

There is an irony. I'm not a religious person after being in Auschwitz, but in Judaism you get your rewards right here – and your punishments. I gave away stock enough to come up with $800,000, and I gave it away at $6/$7 a share. Then it goes up to $22 . . . Now wait! Then bad times come in 1987, and the stock went down at one time to 12.5 cents! So I would have lost a lot of the money . . . So I created something that makes me feel good. It ties in with my studies, and I get rewarded even monetarily! On this I always laugh!

We've had such a tough life. We've had to start life again and again from scratch. It was a very tough life here to be a refugee. They were unfriendly. I told you, the Family Service was terrible. It was very tough. We worked so hard. No one ever paid me for my looks or family, only for my brainpower. How have I survived? Well . . . I'm like the Jewish people – enduring.

The Resident of the Old Age Home

MRS LENA SAMUELSON

We first came across Mrs Samuelson when we were invited by Mr Trope (The President of the Hebrew Old Age Home) *to the new Hebrew Old Age Home. Before the birthday cake was cut at the party, Mrs Samuelson had stood up and made a speech. She was ninety-nine years old, and clearly in full possession of her faculties. After the party we made an appointment to go and see her.*

I was born, I think, in 1894 in Lithuania in a very small province. We were a big, large family. There were ten children. We were Orthodox, but not as Orthodox as the extremes. We weren't anything like that! There were nine girls and one boy; I had two older sisters and one older brother. I was a reader and I wanted to get out of this little town. My people were not wealthy; my father was a grain merchant. I wanted to go to work, but this was unknown for a Jewish girl. My mother had some brothers and sisters in America. One of these uncles had a department store in Lebanon, Ohio, and in 1913 he was willing to sponsor one of us to go to America. Everyone wanted to go except the five-year-old! It was decided that I was the proper age, and maybe they thought I was more emotionally and psychologically fit to manage. This is how I came to this country.

My brother went with me to Germany to the ship. The

journey was a week. We set off on a Saturday and we arrived on the Saturday before Thanksgiving. The ship was the *George Washington*. I couldn't speak a word of English; Yiddish was my mother tongue. My uncle had written a letter, 'To Whom It May Concern', to put me on a train to Ohio, and they came to meet me at Dayton. Lebanon was twenty-five miles from Dayton. I went to night school to learn English. After I was there about a year, I gave out green stamps in the department store!

After about two or three years, they were worried about me getting married because there were no Jewish people for me to associate with. My uncle was very free and broadminded, but he did not take intermarriage very easily. I had another aunt in Chicago and went to live with her. By then I had already learnt English, and I worked in one of the stores. After a few years, I felt the lack of a home. I met a girl who worked for the National Hebrew Hospital here in Metropolis, and she liked it. I thought it would be a good thing. I would get my food and could work for a – what do you call it? – a qualification. So I wrote a letter. It was during the horrible period of the flu in 1919. There was a terrible lack of girls working in hospitals all over. They were very happy to have me.

My husband was a medical student. He was born and raised in Poland. He went to school in Odessa which had a very fine Jewish university there. America accepted credits from there so he could register in medical school. We were married by a rabbi on the West Side. We went to his home. We had nobody to make a wedding for us, and we only had enough money to live on. We rented a room on the West Side. I wasn't very well – I was sickly and wasn't used to working. We were there until he graduated, and he did an extra year's internship. They felt he needed that. He graduated in 1922, and he went into practice in 1923. Then we bought a little house in South-East Metropolis – about ten blocks away from here. It cost $2,750. I did my own cooking, and I did keep *kosher*. Then I became Reform. How can you believe in all that other stuff? We were not ready from the money point of view to join a synagogue though later I joined Temple *Shalom*. My husband was a very nice person. He practised from the house so we didn't have to pay a high office rent.

Then in 1942 he took sick with pneumonia and died. I never

remarried. We didn't have children. I didn't think our genes would be good! You know, the longer I live, the more I cannot see how an intelligent thinking person can bring children into the world. I see a world that's not civilized.

Did I ever see my family again in Lithuania? That's my big heartache. I lived very frugally after my husband died, and went to Europe several times on a freight ship, but I never got to see them. I don't know what happened to my brothers and sisters. I think they were all annihilated. My brother was a very fine boy. I have a great satisfaction. When I was in Chicago, I saved up $135, and he was going to school after the First World War. I knew that he needed money, and I sent him $125. He didn't ask me, but he was very grateful. He sent me something, and he had a feeling in his heart that I had done something for him. He was a very fine boy.

My marriage was a very fortunate match. I needed him, and he needed me. He gave me a home, and he needed me badly. I used to go to see the relatives in the East, and I went to California. I was very much impressed by Santa Monica. It's right at the backdoor of Los Angeles. When my husband passed away, I had no ties so I went to California. I took a little apartment; food was very cheap; and I lived on $50 a month. So I sold the house in Metropolis. It was a beautiful place, and I sold it for $4,800 in 1942. I lived in California until 1980. I didn't go to work, because I could live so cheaply. Then I had a little sick spell, and felt I needed more security.

My husband used to give time to the Hebrew Old Age Home in Metropolis. I decided my place was in a home, and I knew this home had very good food. So I wrote to them that I wanted to come. I had accumulated some money and was willing to give them that money. All the doctors knew me, and they gave me a very nice room. This was the old Hebrew Old Age Home on the West Side. We've been in this building just a year. Did you hear my paper for the birthday party?

How have I lived so long? Firstly, life is a mystery, the whole thing – but I did take care of myself. I try not to worry about things I can't help. I think it was Voltaire who said, 'Accept what you must, correct what you can, and the rest leave alone.' No, it wasn't Voltaire. It was Aristotle!

Nine

BUSINESS AND PROFESSIONAL PEOPLE

The Paediatrician

DR ROBERT KRANZ

We found Dr Kranz at the end of a long maze of corridors at the Jewish Hospital. His office overlooked lush green trees and was lined with books. In one corner there was a large set of filing cabinets, and boxes containing medical records were scattered on the floor. One wall was full of framed degrees, and on a bookshelf there was a teddy bear wearing a green surgeon's outfit and a mask. A tall, balding, bespectacled figure, Dr Kranz spoke slowly.

I grew up in New York City and we moved to Great Neck, a Long Island suburb, when I was twelve. I was one of three children – an older brother and a younger sister – I was in the middle. My grandparents had been Orthodox Jews; they were first-generation from Russia. I grew up in a family environment that was very devoted to intellectual excellence. I was *Bar Mitzvah* in a Conservative synagogue. We did not keep *kosher* at home. I also grew up in a family that was dedicated to causes. My father was very much involved in the trade union movement. He viewed the importance of workers' rights as paramount to the future of the United States. He was a very liberal Democrat. By professional training he was an economist, and my mother was a social worker. So I came from a background of community service. From an early age I saw medicine as a way to give back to the community someone's own skills, time and energy. I also saw it as an intellectual challenge.

I went to school at Brandeis. I started out in Sociology, but quickly found it was not concrete enough for me. So I focused on Biology. Then I went to Harvard Medical School, which turned out to be a wonderful experience. It was at that point I learnt how much I enjoyed the patient one-on-one relationship, and I particularly enjoyed kids. I also found the one-on-one relationship had certain limits: you could only fix that one kid. For a number of years I pursued Public Health interests – I spent three months in East Africa and three months in India, which were real rewarding in some respects but real frustrating in others.

After medical school I came out on an internship in Paediatrics to Metropolis. I really enjoyed the more people-orientated atmosphere here. In the East there was a lot more pressure. Then I did two years in Public Health in Houston, and came back and finished my residency here. I still saw myself moving into International Health, but towards the end I realized that what I really enjoyed was one-on-one teaching and one-on-one patient care. I could combine both of those in Paediatrics. At that time I also met my wife, who is a remarkable lady with a remarkably similar family to mine. Her dad had been an economist with my dad back in the thirties.

At the present time, I'm Chairman of Paediatrics at the Jewish Hospital. I teach medical students as well as residents, and I'm involved actively in continuing medical education with practising physicians. I do a lot of direct patient care, and I do a lot of writing still. The Hospital deals with a fairly broad diversity of patients – ethnically, culturally, socially and economically. One of the nice things about Paediatrics is that kids don't discriminate among themselves.

There's a fairly close-knit Jewish community in this town. The Hospital does have a disproportionately large share of that community, and I am impressed with the ability of the community to mobilize itself to assist a family that is in need. The stress may come from needing someone to take care of a child, to car-pool, or to feed someone. There is a real sense of genuine warmth and caring that is rapidly mobilized. I see that as a very consistent finding within the community – it's really very nice! I think this is a reflection of Metropolis which you don't often see in other urban areas.

Do I deal with circumcision? In this hospital, the majority of circumcisions are done by obstetricians. A fair number are done by a rabbi – Rabbi Feigelbaum (*The Mohel*) is the only one I've ever seen here. He's great! Did he show you his card? Yes, we see him a lot. The Hospital has been very responsive, and we have receptions here for the circumcisions in the chapel or one of the other rooms. Opinion on circumcision has evolved markedly. Ten years ago, if you read the literature, there was a fairly large body of data which said that circumcision exposed a child to risk. The more recent data is that circumcision probably reduced the incidence of urinary tract infections. So the pendulum has swung the other way. I think the vast majority of Jews who are born here are circumcised. When a parent asks my opinion, there really are a number of issues. There are both medical advantages and disadvantages. My usual recommendation, if they're really wavering, is to enquire if the father and the boys this child is going to grow up with are circumcised. If so, I recommend circumcision. I don't think being different in the shower at age five has particular advantages.

Medicine and particularly Paediatrics allow me to feel good about a career that I can find intellectually challenging. It has a level of position and respect, and simultaneously, at the end of the day, you can feel you helped someone. There are very few professions where you can say, 'I'm not sure what this day is going to be like.' Each day has different experiences. You can enjoy the process of your profession. In other words, you can enjoy kids growing up, and kids getting better while at the same time you are pursuing the necessary evil of earning your living. Concurrent with making money and being successful, you're giving something back to the system. I see that as what makes medicine a unique profession.

The Psychotherapist

MRS NATALIE BLUESTONE

We arrived at the address to be confronted by a sign 'N. T. Bluestone, Certified Public Accountant'. It turned out that Mrs Bluestone had an office in her husband's suite. She was a kindly, humorous woman in her fifties, wearing a pink pyjama suit with a red AIDS awareness ribbon.

My father was born in Europe, in Russia that was Poland that was Russia that was Poland. He was the youngest of twelve children, and he came over to this country by himself at the age of fourteen. He settled in northern Texas, near Amarillo, where he met my mother. My mother's family had lived in Chicago. They were very poor and lived on the wrong side of the tracks so to speak. She played with black children and didn't know from discrimination. She was a fabulous woman. Together they kept a ready-to-wear store in Borger, Texas.

I was the younger of two sisters. It was a little town and there were very few Jews. We belonged to a synagogue in Amarillo and the rabbi came over to Borger to teach us every other Wednesday, if the weather was good and when there was a rabbi. My religious education was very lacking. We did celebrate the holidays at home, and our house was open to any Jews who were passing through.

We moved out to California in 1944 because my sister was getting to be of marriageable age, and there were no Jewish boys in Borger. My parents opened another business in Los Angeles, and my sister did get married – to a boy from Metropolis. I graduated from the Los Angeles public schools and the University of California in Los Angeles. My parents were very anxious that I get my Masters degree. Their philosophy was a woman must prepare herself to be a widow. They wanted me to have a career, just in case . . . I was an old maid of twenty-two before I got married! I married a boy whom I had met at my sister's in Metropolis. We were married in 1953. I started on a Masters programme at the University of Metropolis and I hated it. It was very psychoanalytic. I had worked in the Los Angeles Welfare Department, and I knew that psychoanalytic theory didn't work. I wasn't going to buy into it. So I didn't finish and got pregnant. I had two girls and stayed home, because I felt that was important. My husband is a CPA (Certified Public Accountant) and this is his office.

Then my husband had a heart attack. It scared me to death. My father and mother had said, 'You have to prepare to be a widow', and I thought, 'I really need to get this Masters degree. If the writing is on the wall, a BA is not going to do it in this day and age.' So I finished my degree at the age of forty-seven.

I told my husband I wanted to go back to work and he said, 'As long as it doesn't interfere with the children or our life.' He didn't mind if we ate out, but it couldn't interfere with our life. While I was doing the degree, I was also working part-time as a school social worker. I was looking at kids who didn't go to school. It may have been economic problems, family problems, behaviour problems . . . I made home visits and talked to the parents. If a child was having a problem in school the teacher would say, 'Fix him!' So I tried to fix him!

After I got my degree I continued in schools. Then a friend of mine called me and said, 'Are you in private practice or aren't you?' And I said, 'But, but, but . . .' And she said 'I'm referring you to a client. You'd better make a decision.' This was in 1981. When I started up, I said there were two sections of the population I'd rather not work with: one was the aged and the second group was alcoholics. That was a dumb thing to say. Ageing and alcoholism is so prevalent in today's families. A lot of battering and child abuse takes place with alcohol. I consider myself a family therapist, right!

Some problems are universal among my clients and some problems have a Jewish feel to them. It feels good to some people to come to me because I'm Jewish. What are the universal problems? Absent parents, absent fathers, divorce, sexual abuse . . . Yes – there's sexual abuse in Jewish families. One of the books I refer my Jewish clients to is Laura Davies' book *The Courage to Heal*. A Jewish girl talks about her grandfather sexually abusing her by the Sabbath candle. It was the only light that was on. I did a group for survivors of sexual abuse. There were about thirty people and I was aware of three Jewish people who were there. The wife of a well-known Jewish doctor in town was one; this doctor had sexually abused his children. The mother had actually gone to jail because she had refused her husband visiting rights to the children.

There's also alcoholism and drug abuse. Rabbi Berkovski (*The Hasidic Rabbi*) runs an alcohol programme. I remember years ago hearing the Metropolis Welfare Department saying, 'We don't have Jewish or Oriental kids here. Their parents don't have alcohol problems.' Well, obviously the problems were there, but they were hidden. I don't think Jews go to their rabbi about these problems in the way Christians go to their minister. Jews are also reluctant to go to the Jewish Family Service, though it's a fabulous agency. It's an excellent clinical place to go, for people with problems. The Director is fabulous, but the Jewish people don't use it. They think they'll be seen. It's funny the response I get being in a CPA office. People feel a whole lot more comfortable coming in here. There's still a stigma attached to psychotherapy.

In my experience, the issue that is most preoccupying the community is loss and bereavement. Not just death; divorce, separation, and absent parents, those sort of things. You go through the same process of grieving in each case. That is a biggie. Then there are relationships. Men are marrying younger women. The women in their late thirties and forties have a terrible problem, a terrible problem. Also, Jewish men are just not dating Jewish women. That's an issue. Professional women are not necessarily interested in marriage. I have two daughters: one directs and produces films and is not married; the other directs and produces children. She's married to Bob Friedman – yes, Ruth Friedman's (*The Owner of a Jewish Gift Shop*) son. Yes, I know! Metropolis is a village. When I came here I learned very quickly not to speak badly of anyone, because someone is related to them! These women really do want a 'Significant Other', but it really is like pulling teeth to get them to do something about their singlehood. I see one woman; she comes to see me with depression. That's the big one – depression. Is she getting everything she wants out of life? She wants a partner to go places with, but I can't get her involved with anything. I keep sending her stuff. Finally, she's joined Rabbi Acker's (*The Administrator of a Dating File*) dating agency, but I've been seeing her for over a year now. I don't see so many men; there are far more women in therapy in my experience.

What about dysfunctional Jewish families? We've got them too! The child is generally the identified patient, but I try to insist on the whole family coming. Sometimes the fathers and mothers don't like this, but I prefer to see them all. The resistance usually is that they only want to bring in the kid who is having the problem. I'm thinking about one I saw last year. There was this Jewish doctor, and his wife who was highly educated. I asked to see all four of them. The good kid as well as the bad. I only really got to see the family that one time, and I still have mixed emotions about it. Perhaps I did instant therapy and fixed them! The father was really removed. Maybe if I had allowed the kid to be the identified patient and treated him as a sick kid, then I might have been able to work with them. The father didn't see why he needed to come in, and I think that was the trouble.

Is my profession connected with my Jewish values? Absolutely, absolutely! I see it, I feel it. I saw a woman this morning who said, 'I don't know how you *do* the work you do. It's God's work!' And I said, 'Well . . . well! I wouldn't say that, but thanks a lot!' But you know, it really is God's work!

The Lawyer

MRS ROBYN GRAFF

We interviewed Robyn Graff in a massive boardroom in a downtown office block. We were on the 23rd floor and far below us the city shimmered in the heat. She was wearing a smart black and white dress with no jewellery except a watch and a long rope of pearls. She had curly hair, prominent brown eyes, and was in her late forties.

I was brought up in Metropolis. My father had come here for an interesting reason. He believed that because there were Jewish quotas for entrance to medical school on the East Coast in those days, he would be better trying to apply to schools in the South and Mid-West. So he did that and eventually got a job at the Jewish Hospital here. My mother came here to visit her sister, who was a patient of my father's. We lived here the entire time of my growing up, and I went through the Metropolis public schools.

We belonged to Temple *Shalom*. I think at that stage it was the only Reform Jewish Temple in the city and was still primarily made up of German Jews. Like many Jews, my family came from all kinds of different countries, but in general we had greater affiliation with the German Jewish community. On my mother's side, there are five generations of Reform Jewish connections. My father's family was Orthodox, but he very warmly adapted to the Reform perspective. I went to Sunday school from kindergarten to confirmation. I had two older brothers and a younger brother, so I was in the middle in the lower half, and I was the only girl. Yes, my religious upbringing had an impact. It seems to me we had very good teachers in religion school, and Fred Tabbick (*The Retired Educationalist*) is one of the most accepting people I have ever met. Jewish topics were also discussed at home, but there wasn't much in the way of Jewish celebration. For example, my mother did not light Friday night candles when I was growing up. She did not; I do. I did go to *Shalom* summer camp at least twice. It was a very warm, non-competitive experience and that was important for me. There was a lot of competition in my life. At the camp I learnt about consistent Jewish celebration and its value.

After high school, I went to Wellesley College on the East Coast. I don't think anyone from Metropolis is prepared for what they find in the East. It was difficult academically. It was fine after the first semester, but the first semester was very hard. When I was at college, I absolutely refused to have anything to do with Jewish activities on campus. I wanted to explore. The non-Jewish world was kind of exotic to me. Also, the Jewish girls at college tended to be more Orthodox. I felt that brand of Judaism tended to be exclusive. They tended to want me to join that group as a way of being exclusive in my relationships on campus. That's not the way I ever felt about the world; it's my one problem with more Orthodox Judaism. So for three years, except for perhaps at home, I wasn't involved in Jewish activities at all.

I had had a pivotal experience the summer before entering college. It was a real learning experience for me, but it took a few years in college for me to assimilate it. I had gone to Europe, but most of the kids I was with were older than me. I didn't feel very comfortable with this age group, and I spent much of my time by myself. We were in Lyons, and I felt very alone. A young man came up to me and he said, 'Are you okay?' I guess I looked a little despondent. Then he said, 'There's a rabbi here who's very sympathetic, and if you need to talk to somebody you're certainly welcome to do that.' I was very surprised, but I walked into a courtyard, and it was Friday night. The family had set a table out in this courtyard. I could see from looking at the table that this was a very Orthodox family. I felt embarrassed because I didn't realize I was walking into the middle of a Friday night celebration. But behind was the synagogue, and I walked in. While I was inside the family started singing songs and they were songs that I knew. And I realized very stunningly that there was a connection between them and me which I didn't understand, but which was very strong. I still didn't feel comfortable just walking over there, partly because my French wasn't that good. They didn't say anything to me, and I didn't say anything to them, and I walked on. But when I was in the synagogue I started to cry. I realized there was something clearly familial about this experience, but they weren't exactly my family either.

After college I felt a very strong need to seek out Jewish interests. That experience clarified my thinking of who I was, and what I wanted to do. It became important to me to ally myself with the Jewish community. By the time I graduated, I knew I wanted to be a lawyer. All my brothers are doctors, and I thought, surely that was the course for me. My father had wanted us all to set up a clinic together! That was his hope for us, and he wanted us all to be self-supporting. He had come from a family of great poverty, and this was important for him. The expectations for me as a girl were exactly the same as for my brothers. But I had this chemistry class . . . I didn't do very well, and I felt I wouldn't be accepted at medical school. I had a high school friend who suggested I go to law school. Yes, William Murray (*The Gentile Spouse*) – do you know him? I had nightmares, absolutely chilling experiences about telling my family. My family's reaction was, 'Well, gee, that's a really good idea!' Kids don't always know their parents' expectations for them.

I knew I wanted to live in this area. I went to law school at the State University fifty miles away, and I lived on campus. In my law school class there were only four women and I was the only one who finished. It was really nice coming back. It was clear to me I didn't belong on the East Coast, and it's enabled me to know lawyers throughout the state. I got married during this period, and immediately I graduated we moved to southern California. We lived there for five years, and there weren't any Jewish families within miles. As I said, it was becoming very important to me to be part of a Jewish community, and as soon as we returned to Metropolis we joined Temple *Shalom*.

That was okay, but it was not the only thing we joined. We also became involved with Don Samuelson's (*Havurah Leaders*) *havurah*. Yes, Ecclesiastes. If you want to get anything done in the city of Metropolis, you go to Saturday morning services at Ecclesiastes: it gets done. I became very much more interested in *Torah* study. It satisfied me in a way that perhaps Temple *Shalom* didn't. It was more intellectually stimulating, but Temple *Shalom* was also interesting because of what it was trying to do. I give it more credit than many of my Orthodox friends do, but it's hard; it's like moving an elephant. Ecclesiastes can be lighter on its feet. By the same token Ecclesiastes has become very Orthodox. I'm not personally comfortable practising that way, so I still find myself treading my own line.

Professionally, my first job was with a Jewish commercial firm – Goldstein, Goldberg, Schwartz and Mandelbaum. How about that! You should ask me about that firm! It was the most intense working experience I ever had. Everyone was frantic all the time – constantly frantic. They practised a very good brand of law but it was a very noisy, frenetic experience. There was no way I was going to be a partner in that establishment. Firstly, at that age, I had no ability to bring in the kind of client base that would make me a partner. Secondly, everyone worked fifteen hours a day. I was told, for example, it wasn't necessary to come in at weekends. The first weekend I got there, I arrived at about 9 o'clock on a Saturday, and everyone had been there since 6:00! It's awful to say so, but there was a kind of Jewish frenzy. These people saw each other all the time on all sorts of different occasions. They all belonged to the same synagogue. They all belonged to Windy Oak Country Club. There was no respite.

There was no earthly way I could live with this so I started out on my own. I got a lot of construction clients, and then a lot of clients wanted advice on family relations. So gradually half my practice was construction, and half family relations. It's an interesting fact that all my working life I've had difficulty attracting Jewish clients. A lot of women lawyers find that. I think, traditionally, Jewish families deal with the same person, and a lot of Jewish women, until recently, have been protected from the working world. They are used to going to a man for advice. Among the more Orthodox groups, this feeling is even stronger. There's a barrier for a man to come and see a woman attorney because there's such separation between the sexes. Yes, I have dealt with Jewish divorces. I've mainly dealt with Rabbi Berkovski (*The Hasidic Rabbi*) and Rabbi Oppenheim (*The Traditional Rabbi*). Fortunately the community has these two wise and benign men at the helm of those congregations, which has been helpful. Rabbi Berkovski is really a prince of a guy! They insist you have to get the civil stuff finished before you get your Jewish divorce, and that takes the pressure off the thing entirely.

Do I see a connection between my Jewishness and my work as a lawyer? Oh absolutely . . .

The Businessman

MR HARRY BAKER

Baker's Dairy provides milk and cream for the whole Metropolis region. In the foyer of the plant were numerous photographs of Harry Baker shaking hands with United States Presidents, past Presidents and miscellaneous presidential candidates. On another wall was a regiment of plaques from a grateful community commending his philanthropy. There was also a notice thanking one for not smoking and another announcing a vacancy for drivers. Inside the Company President's office there were yet more trophies: medals won in the Korean War, including two for gallantry; a Silver Beaver Award from the Boy Scouts of America; and personal citations for charity and community work. The office was lavishly furnished with black leather upholstery and a massive desk. Easy-listening music played softly in the background.

The business had been founded by Harry's father and remained a family concern. Harry, a robust man in his early sixties, had already played golf that morning. He was dressed in

a white sports shirt and navy blue trousers. There was a gold Rolex watch on his wrist, and he looked tanned and relaxed. Outside the factory buzzed. The telephone rang continuously, and during the interview both Harry's brother and his son put their heads round the door to greet us.

I was born in Metropolis – a fourth-generation Metropolitan. My great-grandfather came here in 1885. I went to public schools all the way through, and the State University. Actually I ended up President of the University Board. I served eight years on the Board and was President for three. I was raised in a Conservative Jewish family at *Har HaShem*. I was *Bar Mitzvah* and confirmed there, but we did not keep a *kosher* home. We didn't eat ham or bacon or pork in those days – I love it now!

Then I was married in Temple *Shalom* because my wife belonged. We were married in the old Temple, and we joined after that. Eventually I became the President. I didn't feel comfortable at Temple at first, but then I enjoyed it and got very active. Rabbi Green – the rabbi before Rabbi Reinhardt (*The Reform Rabbi*) – was a cousin of my mother's. I spent a good time on the Board, and was President from 1979 to 1981. I had to take care of the retirement of Rabbi Green. The transition wasn't an easy time.

The first dairy was established by my great-grandfather. Then my grandfather started another one until they sold it in 1929. My dad started a third with some other people and my brother and I bought into that in 1963. We sold it to another company in 1967, but bought it back in 1975, and that's what you see today. We've lived in various parts of the city. We used to be in East Metropolis, in the Jewish area, but we now have a house just south of the Metropolis Country Club. We have no farms any more. We buy the milk from a co-operative every day. The dairy does distribution and processing. We break the milk down and put it back together. We make ice-cream, sour cream, yoghurt – that sort of thing. When I was growing up, I was sure I'd go into the business. After I graduated from college, I spent two years in the Army – including a spell in Korea. Yes, those are my medals. I commanded an artillery unit, and was there till the war ended. My brother and I have worked together since he got out of the service and I got out of the service. When we were first in it, my father ran the dairy and I was basically in sales. I didn't worry too much about production. My son is the Sales Manager now.

What have I done in the Jewish community? I've been on the Board of the Anti-Defamation League and the Board of Temple; I spent some time with the Allied Federation; then I spent some time with the American Jewish Committee and the Hospital. I don't do the same things as my brother. I also got involved in the general community. I was Chairman of the Metropolis Chamber of Commerce; I was Chairman of the Employers' Council; and I was President of the Boy Scouts. Dad was always involved in community affairs. He felt that you had to give back, not always take; he was very strong on that. It's probably a Jewish heritage. Charity is one of the things Jews do very well. Most of them are pretty generous people. If they have it, they'll give it away, as evidenced by the amount of money the Allied Jewish Federation raises. They raise $6-8 million every year in this town. That's good!

There is a difference between Jewish and gentile organizations. In Jewish organizations the people get more involved and they run it as a charity, not as a business. Gentile organizations are basically structured as businesses. I mean that. Some people have been on the Board of the Jewish Hospital since they built the building. It's too long. These other places – you're on the Board for three years, then you're out. I think the gentile way is better. Absolutely! You get new ideas. I think the Jewish organizations block younger people from coming in. People get very proprietorial as far as their position on the Board is concerned. They begin to think of that organization as theirs, not the community's, and that's wrong! If someone suggests they go, they get mad. What happens is you have people sitting on Boards who shouldn't be there.

What is happening more today is if you take a Board membership, you're expected to give. That didn't happen for a long time. Obviously, people give at different levels. I go to a lot of fundraising dinners. I'm tired of them; I think there are too many. I've been honoured at two or three or four. I think it's gotten out of hand. I call it diseased dinners – what disease is going to have a dinner this week? When you're honoured, you're used. You're a piece of meat which they want to use to get somebody else to give. People come down to see me. If somebody says, 'I want to talk with you. I'm not going to ask you for any money,' I know right away what it is. They want my body! Jewish people like to honour people. Then my friends are solicited. It's kind of embarrassing. If I give them a list of friends they ask them for $5,000 for a table, or they go to friends and say, 'Will you co-chair it?' I don't like speeches. After dinner there's an entertainment. They then give you a plaque and say goodbye. Recently I've been saying 'No' an awful lot.

We give a lot of money, a lot of money away here. We have a foundation that gives up to $500,000 away a year to both Jewish and non-Jewish causes. The biggest one is the Allied Jewish Federation. I've always wanted to be involved with Jewish organizations. I was on my first Board when I was twenty-nine years old. The community is totally different now. The people who were the leaders years ago are gone and a lot of their children didn't get involved. They went in different directions. A lot of them didn't marry Jewish girls or Jewish boys. It makes a difference. But you've got to have new faces, and that's why the people who sit on these Boards, the old ones, are wrong. I'm too old to be on Boards any more. We're going to wither and die if we don't have young people. The Jewish Community Centre is in trouble; the Allied Federation didn't raise what they were trying to raise; the Anti-Defamation League is having its problems; and so on . . . There's more assimilation.

I don't see anti-Semitism as heavy as it used to be. I've never had a problem except once when I was in college. I was asked to join a fraternity and I said, 'I'm not sure you want me because I'm Jewish', and they said, 'Yeah – you're right! We don't!' That was forty-six years ago. I belong to the Metropolis Country Club – everyone told me they'd never take Jews, and there's eight or twelve or fifteen or twenty of us in there! I also belong to Windy Oak. I also belong to the Metropolis Club, and the Metropolis Athletic Club. I'm on the Board of the Metropolis Club, which is the oldest club in town. I don't see any problem. Some of my best friends are not Jewish – probably my closest friend isn't. My daughter was in the Junior League. My niece was a débutante. My son's fiancée's in the Junior League. I was a member of the Young President's League. They say they're anti-Semetic; it's not true. The gentile clubs I belong to also take blacks, but Windy Oak doesn't have black members. We always used to say that the average age of Windy Oaks was deceased! We'd like to bring younger members in. The new Manager's a good man (*Employee of the Jewish Country Club*). Did you meet Janey? She knows everybody! They're all getting older, and it can't go on.

Yeah – I'm integrated into the community. Don't forget, 90 per cent of our customers are not Jewish. We're dominant. Sure – we still do the Passover milk for the Orthodox. I figure someone's got to. The Orthodox *kashrut* guy (*The Kashrut Supervisor*) is very tough: 'You can't put that in! You must have this!' It's only 500 gallons, but for that week the plant's turned upside down. As I say – somebody's got to do it and I suppose it had better be us!

The Inventor

MR YOSEPH SNYDER

Mr Yoseph Snyder lived in a small house on the West Side. Despite his four children, it was impeccably neat and tidy. A brown-haired man in his early forties, he wore his black skull cap over his bald patch. He spoke slowly, but was quick to see a joke.

I'm from Metropolis; I grew up here. My parents were born in Poland. My father was eighteen years old when the war broke out, and he was among the first to be drafted for the youth work camps. He spent from late 1939 in one camp or another until they were freed by the Americans in 1945. I think he was in Treblinka; I think he was in Buchenwald. He was in a work detail more than he was in a concentration camp. Just prior to the war breaking out, my father was in a *yeshiva* (talmudic academy). When things were getting really bad, at the insistence of one of his elder sisters he was sent to trade school, and he learnt the electrical trade. When he was drafted, he worked as an electrician within the factories, hooking up the equipment. He had a pair of *tefillin* (phylacteries) with him for two and a half years in these camps, and he would hide them in the electrical panels. Every day he'd have some excuse to go down to check something. He'd run down, he'd put on the *tefillin* and hide them back again. So he had a strong religious background.

My mother was also in the camps. My parents met and married in Belgium after the war and came to the United States. They first lived in New York, where I was born, and soon after they moved to Metropolis. I'm the eldest. Yes, I have two younger brothers and a sister: four of us in all. In Metropolis, my father worked as an electrical contractor – he remained equally religious. Both my parents are still living, thank G–d. I went to Maimonides Academy. The *Yeshiva* High School in Metropolis was not yet in existence so after eighth grade I went to a *yeshiva* in Chicago for five years. I was fourteen. It was very strict and run on a schedule. It was very good for me, because I'm not the most disciplined person in the world. Getting up in the morning was never a problem for me, as it was for many guys. I'd been getting up and attending the synagogue every morning since I was eight or nine. After Chicago I had planned to go to study in Israel, but my father wasn't well at the time. He'd just started this business with laundry equipment, and since I was good at fixing things, he asked me to stay here. I learned in the *Yeshiva* here for a short time. I was very uncomfortable. The philosophy of the Chicago *yeshiva* was very different from the philosophy here. In Chicago things were very clear-cut – black and white, clearly based on Jewish Law. In Metropolis twenty years ago, people were less committed. There were more compromises. For example, in those days many people belonged to both *Adath Israel* and *Etz Hayyim* synagogues. That made me uncomfortable.

So I started going to college. I went to the University of Metropolis to study Engineering. Most of my classes were in the evening. I would study at the *Yeshiva* with a study partner until 11 or 12 o'clock. Then I would go to the office to take care of business things, and then I went to college in the evening. I did that for nearly three years. I actually never finished for my degree. It didn't seem to stop me too much. I felt I got a lot out of it. I was one of the few students who learnt something in the morning and put it to work in the afternoon. I know what I don't know.

When I was twenty-three I got married. Obviously, I needed more money, so I was spending more time at the office. We started having children pretty much straight away. I have four: three boys and a girl. I started the laundry equipment business with my father and worked with him for a number of years. I've been very dissatisfied with it. During that time I've been working on some patent stuff. I filed for one patent – I got it. I didn't go very far with it, but it led me to the next one. I filed for a second patent last March, and I am in the process of applying for a third one. This has nothing to do with washing machines. I've designed and got the financing for a new parking meter.

It's a kerbside parking meter, the kind you put a quarter in. I designed mine from the ground up, redesigned it, and taught myself micro-electronics. I've been working on this for a number of years. When I started I was told, 'You'd better build one before we'll believe you can do what you say you can do.' I built a prototype and found some problems with it. Then I built a second and a third. Eventually I built a fourth. After I made a business plan and that sort of stuff, I got someone to back me financially. The first prototype will be on the streets just after *Rosh Ha-Shannah* (Jewish New Year). It has the advantage that as soon as the car drives away from the spot, the meter automatically switches to zero for the next person. There's no free five or ten minutes for someone!

I don't know if being rich will change my lifestyle. I don't think I'll leave the West Side, though I have considered moving to other cities in the past. If everything works out, I'd like to support my brother who is studying in a *kollel* (higher talmudic academy). One of the failings in this community is we have not hired other Orthodox Jews. There's very little helping other people out. Other communities have grown significantly because people have worked on partnerships to create jobs. The key to growth is jobs; everything else is secondary. If the young people had jobs, they would stay.

I'm certainly not going to retire. I can't sit still, and anyway I have more ideas to work on. I'd like to restore the West Side to what it was – a big Jewish neighbourhood. It's not easy to see how to do it. The biggest fear every Jew has is that his key employee is going to become a competitor! So you have to walk a fine line. If I can succeed in what I want to do, I think there's plenty of opportunity for a lot of people. I'd like to bring people into partnership in new enterprises – that I'm sure is the key to growth.

Yes, I still go to synagogue every day . . .

The Photographer

MR HOWARD HOROWITZ

We interviewed Howard Horowitz together with his son John (The Student at the Pluralist High School) *in a large house in an older neighbourhood of Metropolis. We sat at a butcher-block table in a homely kitchen. He was a large man in his mid-forties. He wore a check shirt, and he smoked a pipe and drank tea as we talked.*

I grew up in a small town in the north-east part of the State. My father was a small-town doctor, and I have an older brother and a younger sister. When I was thirteen years old we moved to Metropolis. In the small town there was only one other Jewish family, and I really had no Jewish education. My father came to the United States from Germany in 1937, and he came from a very assimilated family. We had Christmas, his parents had Christmas, and his grandparents had Christmas. It was not a religious but a national holiday. We had a tree and presents. It's ironic. My second wife was raised Catholic, and she has a lot of unpleasant memories connected with Christmas. But some of my most joyful childhood memories are connected with the festival. The family would come on Christmas Eve, and it was a very festive occasion. One of my aunts played the piano, and we sang Christmas songs and carols. You bet we did! It was terrific!

We did have Passover *seder*. We had it with the only other Jewish family in the town. They were Russian, and they did the service in an extremely Orthodox way. No English. We had these exotic foods and it was about as foreign and as alien as it could be. Christmas was a lot more fun! But I never had any doubts that I was Jewish.

When we moved to Metropolis we belonged to Temple *Shalom*. My father was a little bit antagonistic towards formal religion. My parents gave me the option of either preparing for a *Bar Mitzvah* or using the same time and money to learn modern Hebrew. I chose to learn modern Hebrew so I never got *Bar Mitzvahed*. The Christmases still continued! It went on really until it became a source of conflict with my first wife. She is Jewish and she thought it was just terrible. I graduated from high school, and I thought I would be a doctor like my dad. I decided I didn't want to be a doctor when my brother went to medical school. I didn't want to do the same thing as him. Then I thought I would be a historian because I really loved history.

I've always had a competitive thing with my brother, and he's easier to compete with if you don't do what he does! He went to Harvard. My high school girlfriend was going to college in Boston so I also wanted to go to college in Boston. I went to Brandeis. I didn't like it. It was full of people who I had no connection with at all. It was very Jewish in a way that was very foreign to me. I couldn't tolerate it. My relationship with my girlfriend had disappeared even before I arrived in Boston, so I returned to the State University. I loved it and studied English History.

I also got involved in photography, and I thought I would support my interest in photography by being a History professor. After I got my BA and MA at the State University, I went to Cambridge University where I was working on a Ph.D. in Tudor Constitutional History. The experience at Cambridge was very different. I realized what was expected of you if you were going to be a scholar. You had to do it all the time. My supervisor told me that graduate students don't have breaks! I decided through a lot of anguish that if I was going to teach something to support my interest in photography, I ought to teach photography not history. So I took a leave of absence from Cambridge and got a graduate degree in Photography from the University of Oregon. By this stage I was married. Barbie, my wife, was doing some batik work. I look back nostalgically on the times of being a graduate student; there's never a time like that again in your life. It was wonderful. There's a certain romantic quality to it. You have very little responsibility, and you never get that luxury again. I had very good teachers and I made some important contacts with other photographers in California. I primarily am known as a landscape photographer, and that's mainly what I've done over the years. I knew what I wanted to do was to be connected with the making of beautiful pictures.

By the time I graduated I was sick of school. I came back to Metropolis, and I decided I didn't want to teach. I tried to support myself doing commercial photography, portrait work and advertising. I did that for a number of years and started teaching part-time. I decided it was fun, and I ended up full-time teaching at the Metropolis Community College. I've been doing that since 1975. If I could afford it, I would like to teach part-time, but I've been told I would miss it terribly if I gave it up altogether, and I think that's probably true.

I have three children: John, David and Katie. Interesting you should ask about their religious upbringing. They started at the pre-school of the Jewish Community Centre. At that time Metropolis public schools were having a lot of trouble with bussing, and kids being sent way across town. There were reasons not to send them to public schools. They ended up going to the Golda Meir Jewish Day School. I call it the Golden Calf! It's a good school, but it costs a lot of money. In my divorce settlement, there was a court order that the kids would continue to go there. It's okay, but I grew up in a secular world. It really grates on me to go into a school to see not only the American flag but also the Israeli flag. I don't think growing up Jewish has to mean one is a member of that group too. I believe that the strength of the American way of life lies in public schools and in people mixing from all different backgrounds. My experience with formal Judaism is that it tends to be very isolating. It's meant to be. Assimilated is the worst thing to be. Barbie got more involved in Jewish things, and she wanted her children to have an intense Jewish education. We have very different views about this, and it's galling that I'm caught up in it.

Has my photography anything to do with my Jewishness? In spite of all that I've said, I feel like I'm Jewish. It must affect my work because it affects who I am. Without being able to define what a religious experience is, it happens sometimes when I am photographing. I am really focused on that particular moment and Nature (with a capital N) has a really awesome quality to it. Didn't some writer in Judaism talk about radical amazement? I think so. I'm not consciously trying to encapsulate something that is spiritual, but I think it happens. One way to describe it is that in a very wonderful way I feel very small. For me I feel part of the whole picture so to speak.

My second wife was raised a Catholic, but neither one of us practises our religion. We have Christmas and Passover, both of which are very nice. Sometimes I take off *Yom Kippur* (Day of Atonement), but I feel dishonest doing so. My eldest son John (*The Student at the Pluralist High School*) is pretty turned off by formal Judaism, but my second son David is going to *Hasidic* summer camp and is growing sidecurls and wears fringes! He collects *Hasidic* rabbi cards like I used to collect baseball cards!

My main problem is I think formal religions of any kind tend to separate people into us and them. I really don't like that! As a result of their school, my children don't know any kids who aren't Jewish. These kids in private school are so well-off and so homogenous. Their fathers are lawyers and doctors and very upwardly mobile professional people. There's no balance. I believe in the melting pot theory of American society. I think it's good to have Passover and to be Jewish and to learn Hebrew, but you should also know that there are a lot of other ways of doing things . . .

The Accountant

MR RAYMOND GOTTSCHALK

Raymond Gottschalk achieved fame in the Jewish community of Metropolis by writing an article entitled 'The Trouble with Jewish Girls' for the Metropolis Jewish News. *We talked to him in his high-rise office downtown. He was a rotund man of thirty-eight, and he spoke with wit and intensity.*

I'm a native of Metropolis. I grew up on the West Side and went through the public schools. My parents were members of *Adath Israel* synagogue, and I had a very nice *Bar Mitzvah*. The stuff

I learnt for my *Bar Mitzvah*, I still *daven* (pray) today. I can read Hebrew fluently, but I can only translate the odd word. We were rowdy in religion school, but overall we got a good Jewish education. My friends were primarily Jewish. Even in those days there was a large Hispanic population in the neighbourhood, and the Jewish kids kind of stuck together. There was a very big dichotomy between East Side and West Side. Ultimately everyone moved to the East Side.

I didn't date too much in high school. When I graduated I knew I wanted to stay in Metropolis because my father had passed away in 1972. I was fortunate in being granted a full scholarship to the University. I went there for four years, and it didn't cost me a nickel. I went to the College of Business and I took every accounting class they had to offer, so that's what I majored in. By that time we had moved to South-East Metropolis, but if you hadn't grown up on the East Side, you were never considered an East Sider. There is definitely stigma even today in coming from the West Side – yeah.

One thing you have to understand about me is that people talk about 'friends'. Well, you have very few friends in this world. You have acquaintances. You can count the friends who will be there when you need them on the fingers of one hand. Most of the people I met at the University were acquaintances. I lived at home so I didn't develop many relationships. I didn't belong to a fraternity or anything. I didn't do much dating in college because I thought my primary objective was my education.

On graduation, they want you to work in public accounting firms. That's the big thing. I was interviewed by all the big Metropolis firms, and I got all these rejection letters. I thought perhaps I wasn't good enough for these people. I don't know what they were looking for, but it wasn't me. My father had worked for the government. I knew you didn't get rich like that, but there was always food on the table and great benefits. I realized that's what I wanted to do. I went to interview with the State University and they said, 'We like you and we want to hire you.' I started, and I've been here ever since.

I took the CPA (Certified Public Accountant) exam in 1977, but they wouldn't give me my certificate. I was in a Catch-22 situation. I didn't want to quit my job at the State University to go into involuntary servitude with a CPA firm, but I wanted to get my certificate. I went to the State Board and they said there was one other way, namely to get a Masters degree in Business Administration. So I said, 'That should be easy to do. I'm working in a University.' So I worked all day from 8–5:00, and then went to class from 5–8:00. I got my whole MBA in about two and a half years. I took two courses per semester. It was wonderful. I was right here, and I just went downstairs to class. So I got my MBA in 1983, and I mailed that away with $25 and got my certificate. No problem whatsoever.

I've had three different jobs with the University. First I was in Data Control and General Accounting. Then in 1984 the administration of this University was very interested in me – I'm a good worker. So they said they had a real challenge for me. They wanted me to go into the Bursar's office. I took the offer, and it was in a state of upheaval. The auditors were in, the students were yelling at us because we couldn't get their bills straight, and so forth. I instituted a number of wonderful projects, but there was one problem: there was a lot of stress. Then they started having problems in this area, which is Sponsored Programme Accounting. Auditors were marching in and out, people weren't receiving statements in a timely manner, and so forth. My boss says, 'How would you like to move to Sponsored Programme as a lateral transfer?' So I moved over here five years ago.

What led me to write the article for the *Metropolis Jewish News*? I'm frustrated. I'm frustrated with the whole dating scene. When I got my education out of the way, I felt ready for dating. When you get into the dating mode you form certain impressions, and I wanted to write these impressions down. I'm in a conflict right now. What do you do about intermarriage? You look at Jewish women and you think, 'I'm a good guy. I've led a good life. I've never gotten into trouble. I'm a respectable member of this community, but I'm thirty-eight years old. Maybe I have to expand my horizons and consider women who are not Jewish.' So I asked myself what was wrong with the women who are Jewish. So I sat down at my computer one day and I wrote this article, and the next thing I knew they published it.

What is wrong with Jewish women? I knew you were going to ask me that! Let me begin by telling you the efforts the Jewish community is making to match people up – the efforts are fragmented. You get the Rendez-Vous Group (see *The Administrator of a Singles' Agency*), and there's this great dating agency at Temple *Shalom* (see *The Administrator of a Dating File*). I joined that. Let me quantify it for you. I went through these books, and none of these women had ever met me. I sent twenty-six women cards and I got twenty-one reject cards back. Once in a while I got a positive response, and I have gone out a couple of times. In a couple of these positive ones, I left messages on their answering machines. I did it about six times, and both this Jamie person and this Joanne person never called me back. So I said, 'Forget these two. Put them over there.' Now I dated this one called Pauline. She's an obstetrician, and you can understand why she never had any relationships working all night in a hospital. I went out with her three or four times, and one day I called her up and she says, 'Raymond, I really don't want to date you any more. I don't think we'd be compatible.' That was on 30 November so I put her in my reject file!

There's one girl I've been dating four or five times, but she's not Jewish. My aunt introduced us. She's about thirty-two and she's Italian. She's very nice, but there's this conflict. Do I go out with someone who's not Jewish or do I still play around some more with these Jewish women? I don't know . . . The dating file has had fifteen marriages out of 720. Let me see, that's exactly 2.1 per cent. Well if you're a mathematician, you would say random selection would get more than 2.1 per cent!

I blame the characteristics of Jewish women. Firstly, they are so career-oriented, marriage and the family is not a priority. I mean look at the careers these women have! I wrote them down: this one's a bi-lingual educator; this one's a management consultant; this one's a psychologist – you know how many years it takes to be a psychologist with a Ph.D.? No wonder they have no time for relationships! Secondly, there's a desire to be a perpetual student. They're going to school for ever and ever! They go into sociology, and then they go into business, and then they go into education! Thirdly, they're not interested in Judaism. I can document that. Go into the synagogue on a

Saturday and see how many single women are there! I go into *Adath Israel*, and I'm the youngest person there! I'd like my wife to have knowledge of the Jewish holidays and to celebrate Friday night at home. Fourthly, they've got this fixation on exercise. Doctors say exercise is a good thing, but what I'm talking about is what I see outside my window. I see them running and running fourteen miles a day. They can't go out till they've finished their morning work-out! Fifthly, they have no interest in dating, and that's demonstrated by all my rejection cards. Sixthly, they think it's okay to be single. Judaism teaches it's not good to be single; but they seem to have no interest in children or parenthood. Seventhly, they don't want the house with the white picket fence, the two-car garage and the dog. They aren't worried about working for their retirement. I mean, I have a good job and I make a good living, but it doesn't impress these women. I think the era of the Jewish American Princess has ended. Finally, they tend to own multiple dogs or cats. These women would rather do loving things with their pets than with another human being! It's a psychological substitute!

What was the reaction to my article? Some of my friends said, 'You know Raymond, you wrote a really good article. We're proud of you.' Too many of the women said, 'That guy has a problem!' Talk about problems! You read of all the problems that women have with abusing husbands and with other affairs, and God forbid, with AIDS, and with this and that. All I want is to get married and to have a Jewish life. I don't think I would be a bad husband. I just want someone who likes me . . .

The Air Force Officer

MAJOR RON BRICHTO

We spoke to Major Ron Brichto in his comfortable family-room in his house in South Metropolis. There were two cockatiels in a cage, and a friendly black and white dog of uncertain ancestry. Indian pottery and baskets hung on the walls, and two swords were propped up in the corner. Major Brichto was a tall man in his late forties; he was dark, bearded and bespectacled, and he leaned back in his chair as he talked.

I'm from the Boston area and I grew up in a town called Chelsea. We had a Traditional home – I don't know if we would say it was Orthodox, but we had a *kosher* home certainly. I most certainly had a *Bar Mitzvah*. I had had a fair amount of Hebrew education. In fact I started off in a Jewish day school, but I was the kind of child my mother didn't want me to play with, and after two years they invited her not to bring me back! So I went to public school. I have an elder brother and a younger brother, and I am the proverbial middle child. My older brother was always old enough to know better, so obviously he couldn't do anything wrong. My younger brother was too little to know anything better, so he wasn't wrong. I grew up to be a very responsible child – every time something went wrong, I was responsible!

My formal Hebrew education stopped with my *Bar Mitzvah*. I ended up going to a *melamed* (teacher) for my *Bar Mitzvah* who got all the problem children in the city. I graduated from high school and, at the time, thought I wanted to be a scientist. That was the summer of 1961, with the Berlin crisis. I went to Tufts University in Boston, and I didn't want to be drafted out of college. So I joined the Reserve Officer Training Corps which guaranteed deferment for four years. During those college years I decided that I really liked the value system that I was getting in the ROTC, and I probably got better grades in that than in anything else. I liked the rules and the standards to live up to – things were pretty much cut and dried, they were right or they were wrong. I prefer a black and white world – I don't like all the shades of grey. As mischievous as I was as a youngster, I think I had a pretty decent sense of right and wrong. The structure and the discipline were what attracted me.

In Boston in the mid-1960s, with the Vietnam War going on, we weren't all that popular with the other students. We had to take a senior-level course in International Relations. The professor who taught that was a flaming liberal who had absolutely no use for the military. It made no difference that two-thirds of her class were senior ROTC students. She took every opportunity to bad-mouth the military, and of course I took every opportunity I could to kind of tweak her a little bit! The obligation of the ROTC was to go on active duty after you graduated. We had a four-year active duty commitment after college. It meant you went in as an officer and could give orders to idiots rather than taking orders from morons! If the truth be known, I looked forward to going on active service, and it was the ROTC subjects that kept my grades at a level that prevented me from being in more academic trouble than I was.

I still kept *kosher* at home, and out I would eat no pork or shellfish, and I wouldn't mix milk and meat – so I wouldn't eat something like a cheeseburger. I did this all through college, and as much as I could when I was on active duty. There's plenty of times I said to the cook, 'Just make me a peanut butter sandwich.'

So, I graduated. Everybody said, 'Whoopee!', including the Professor of Air Science! I was Commander of the Cadet Honours Society but I was not Cadet Corps Commander because, as the Professor told my dad at the commissioning ceremony, up until a week before no one was sure I was going to graduate on time! I was called to active service in the Air Force. In the spring of my senior year my paperwork showed my first choice was Strike Command, which was basically the Air Commandos: the Air Force equivalent of the Green Berets. Mom had a heart attack, literally, and I knew that was preying on her mind. So I changed the paperwork and I asked for Strategic Air Command and Missile Duty, which would keep me here – not overseas or in the jungles jumping out of airplanes.

I got picked for Strategic Air Command and Missiles and went to Grand Forks, North Dakota, as a Second Lieutenant. I did have to go to technical school to learn about the missile system, and I was one of the guys with the finger on the button. Were they nuclear missiles? Well, the Air Force taught us never to confirm or deny the presence of nuclear missiles. I had my finger on the button of an inter-continental missile, and you can figure out whatever was on the front end of it. It was not leaflets!

After eighteen months I became a First Lieutenant, and that's when I got married. When we went to see the rabbi to get our pre-marital counselling, or whatever you call it, and he gave us the standard lecture, he asked us if we had any questions. And I said, 'Just one. I'm concerned about how we raise our kids to be Jewish while staying in the military, never knowing where I'd be and what access I'd have to the Jewish community.' The rabbi came up with a profoundly insightful answer. He said, 'It won't be a problem.' I said, 'What do you mean?' He said, 'If you're concerned about it now, you'll find a way.' Well here it is twenty-six years later. My son is a *kashrut* supervisor working under Rabbi Berkovski (*The Hasidic Rabbi*) and my daughter is a second-year med. student. They're both *Shomer Shabbos* (Sabbath observant), so we must have found a way somehow.

I was in North Dakota for five years; four years on a missile crew where I did very well, and one year on missile maintenance. For my part, I believed in strategic deterrence. The whole idea of nuclear war was so terrible that nobody who was sane and rational would engage in it. Those in charge would be sane and rational, both on our side and on the other side. If something was going to happen, it would probably be a weirdo or a kook. I had to assume that on the other side they used the same safeguards that we had. From our point of view, the system did not permit one person to go crazy and do it all by himself. No one person ever had all the accesses. We all understood that if one guy on our crew started getting a little flakey, we would shoot him and then call into the Command Post reporting an Officer Policy Violation!

There weren't many Jews anywhere in the Air Force. It's not a job for a nice Jewish boy! Did I encounter anti-Semitism? I encountered a little bit early on, as a Second Lieutenant that first year. The guys from my squadron were mostly from the South. There was one guy in particular: I don't know how we got on the subject of concentration camps and all that, but he made a crack to the effect that when I take a shower, do I make sure it's really soap and not stone. I came unglued. I went airborne and I was on him, and he was on the floor. It took two guys to pull me off him. I said, 'I don't have to put up with that horseshit. The Constitution guarantees me the right to believe the way I want!' That guy later became a very good friend of mine. I guess I just had to teach him where the boundaries were.

I guess that's one of the things that motivated me towards the military. Growing up in Chelsea, I can't count the number of times I was beat up after school by Irish and Polish kids because

I was Jewish. My father taught me to be proud of the fact that I was Jewish; that a lot of people resisted persecution and resisted forced conversion so I could be a Jew. My grandparents came to this country to find opportunity and religious freedom. The only thing that guaranteed that was the Constitution. So part of my motivation for going on active duty was to do my fair share to defend the Constitution. I had read *Exodus* in high school, and my own perspective was that at least wherever I was living was not going to be the Warsaw Ghetto.

If they wanted me, they were going to be dead coming to get me. I'm a strong believer in the Second Amendment – the right of the people to keep and bear arms. That is what really guarantees religious freedom and other freedoms in this country. I think I could be martyred for the faith, but I'd want to take a few of them with me. If I'm going to die for God, that's fine, but there are some sorry son-of-a-guns out there who are going to come along and keep me company!

Ten

THE NON-CONFORMISTS

The Unbeliever

MRS MARGOT HETTER

Mrs Margot Hetter lived in an exquisite modern house which had just been declared an urban landmark of Metropolis. It was full of beautiful sculpture and paintings including pieces by Henry Moore, Jacob Epstein and Rodin. She herself was in her seventies; she was not more than 4 feet 10 inches tall, and she wore a chic silk dress and a large sculpted diamond ring.

I come from a German household in Berlin where we only went to Temple on High Holy Days. It was a very musical household, with my father listening to the Bach concertos and telling us wonderful stories about William Tell, which we would repeat back to him. It was an intellectual household and a well-to-do household. My father had a very successful welding company with about a hundred employees. In contrast to many families who turned over the children to nannies, my parents did not do that. We were very closely-knit, and since we always had servants who were not Jewish, we would have a little tiny Christmas tree and presents. I did go to religion school at the Temple, but I did not have a *Bat Mitzvah*. My parents did not even light candles on a Friday night, but when it came to the New Year or the Day of Atonement, we went to Temple. *Sukkot* (Festival of the Tabernacles), in particular, is a very happy memory because there was a lot of candy at Temple.

I cannot tell you that I particularly believed in a God. I believed so strongly in my parents that they took on the role of the authority. In my reliance on them, I did not ever have the desire to believe in something besides us. The authority and the meaningfulness was really taking place within our household. Belief or non-belief in a God never came up. We did not take much notice even of religious holidays except that we were taken out of school, which was very nice!

I was born in 1921 and the Nazis came to power when I was eleven years old. Interestingly enough, whatever the Nazis did, they did it in the smaller communities rather than in a big metropolis like Berlin. I only really knew what the Nazis were up to when we had to turn in all our silver and gold. That was sometime in 1937. Then came *Kristallnacht.* As a matter of fact, we did not live in the area where all the Jewish stores were and where the famous synagogue was, but my mother took me by Underground to actually see it. So I have a very vivid picture of all the broken glass, the smoke of burning buildings and total destruction. That was the first time my parents really said, 'Our child has to get out of Germany.'

I had cousins in America, but my immigration quota number hadn't been called so I left Germany for England on a domestic permit. My piano teacher arranged for me to work domestically with a family, and that's how I got out with $10 in my pocket. You couldn't take out more than that, but you could take more out in goods. I use to this day linens for the bedroom and linens for the kitchen which I took out. My mother also smuggled out little silver pieces, and what I did later in my married life was to collect all the silver and have it made into one silver bowl. So I went to England as a domestic servant. I did not know the family; it was a non-Jewish family with one child. The child is now a circuit judge in England. I was with that family for a year. Then I moved into a *pension* in London, and the bombs were falling all around. I was still in contact with my parents until 1941. Then all stopped, and I knew that they had been taken away. They were taken away separately to different camps, and I lost both of them. I didn't find that out until 1945.

My roots were not religious roots; they were the music with which I had grown up. The young man who is now a judge visited me two years ago, and he remembers going with me to hear Dame Myra Hess at the wartime concerts in the National Gallery. This was when I was no longer working for his family. I had the good fortune at that point to be taken on by Anna Freud, Sigmund Freud's daughter. We were twenty-five students who became substitute mothers for children who had experienced loss. I lived near Hampstead Heath, and I really founded with Anna Freud the first day-care centre nursery for tiny little children. It was an all-new project. I was in charge of that nursery under Anna Freud's supervision.

Finally I received my visa for America. I left England, partly because it was my original intention to go to the United States and partly because I had been, to say it in the English way, 'a bloody alien' too long. The English were not good to their refugees. They made us feel real aliens. Also, with the end of the war, the nursery project was over. I must just say, that while I was in England I never went into any religious house of any kind, but I was thirsting for music. That was my link to my past. Every year I went to the Matthew Passion with Beecham in the Albert Hall. Music replaced my religion, and it has to this day.

When I came to America, I settled right away in Metropolis where I had first cousins. Immediately I had to have a job because my cousins were struggling themselves. So I worked with asthmatic children, and I became very interested in psychosomatic illness. I met my husband through a friend. Most of my friends at that time were Jewish, but this was coincidental. What we had in common was music. My husband said he didn't believe in quick marriages, but he proposed to me after six months. At first I didn't think I had heard right! Then six months after that, in 1948, we got married. He is as much a non-believer as I am. We were married by a district court judge, not by a rabbi.

You must understand, I feel very strongly that I am a Jew. I feel that very deeply in my heart. In those days, the chemical company for which my husband worked was known for not hiring Jews in important positions. I said to my husband, 'Please do not deny you are a Jew because I am very proud to be a Jew.' 'Proud' to me meant I had a heritage which goes back thousands of years. My husband did not deny it and he became the manager of his plant, which was almost unheard of. Would I have married him if he hadn't been Jewish? Probably yes, but with difficulty. If I had loved him and he had not been Jewish, I still would have married him. He didn't want children. He has a brother and sister; I knew both of them and didn't like either. I can understand what kind of experience he had that made him not want to bring siblings into the world. Also, I had been a substitute mother for so many years, and I had given my all to children. It wasn't very difficult for me to say, 'That's fine!'

Beauty has been my passion. Music was what connected me with my parents, and my experience is that when it is beautiful, it is uplifting. I travel a lot for opera, and it is uplifting to me as an experience. I love Wagner and that's because my father loved Wagner. Regardless of his anti-Semitism, the beauty of Wagner's music is insurmountable. But I have branched out. We had this house created. We interviewed three architects. It is special. Living in beautiful surroundings, surrounding myself with beautiful things – music, art, all these took the place of religion.

We know that we want to be cremated. We don't want a tombstone, but we commissioned this piece of sculpture carved by a husband and wife team. It's a large book made of Florentine marble. It's warped and it represents age. When one of us dies, the other one will pay for a quartet to play in the house. There will be good food, good drink and good music. People can talk about the departed one. The ashes will be put in pots which I've already commissioned and these will be buried in the cemetery. And the book will go on top. Yes, I have it all sorted out . . .

The Astrologer

MS SHIRA SIMON

Before we started the interview, Shira Simon asked us the days and hours of our births and, with the aid of her computer, cast our horoscopes. They were uncannily accurate. She was a large lady in her early fifties.

I was born and raised in Metropolis and my family are third-generation Temple *Shalom* on both sides. I was given a good Reform Temple upbringing, and I was confirmed there.

You really want me to tell you what I learnt at Temple *Shalom*? I learnt that there was something morally wrong with chewing gum . . . and that's about it. By the way, I was valedictorian of my class! What I got from Temple *Shalom* was roughly the equivalent of spiritual bankruptcy. It was definitely not a positive experience. It was serving a jail sentence. There was nothing taught about the belief system. What I learnt at religion school was about Jewish baseball players. They were trying to secularize the religion. Don't you remember the old *Haggadahs* (Passover prayerbooks) that ended not with 'Next Year in Jerusalem', but with 'God Bless America'? No, I'm not kidding! Many years later, when I was in Korea and I was faced with trying to deal with death, I realized I had absolutely no spiritual underpinnings at all. Judaism was for me at that time bereft of anything. I went to talk to the Catholic priest, not because I wanted to become a Catholic, but because what I found in Judaism was *matzoh*-ball soup and *lox* and bagels and 'God Bless America' at the end of Passover. That was Temple *Shalom*.

After high school, I went to Vassar. Actually, I wanted to go to the University of Mexico and I knew I didn't have a hope in hell of getting permission to go there. The high school counsellor told me that my grades were not good enough to get into an Eastern college. Consequently I applied to Smith, Wellesley and Vassar. I thought they would all turn me down and then I could go to the University of Mexico. It would have worked out except Vassar accepted me! So off I went to Vassar. I studied theatre, and actually it turned out to be a very good thing.

After Vassar I went out to California and worked in San Francisco. Then I came back to Metropolis and started on a Masters programme. Halfway through I got a job for a year as the Entertainment Director with the Seventh Infantry Division in Korea. The Korean War was well over by then. I was directing rock-and-roll bands and country-and-western singers, and I had a late-night radio show. It was a lot of fun! This was when I began to realize the degree of spiritual bankruptcy I had gotten from Judaism.

Then I came back to the United States, and I felt like an alien here. This was the 1960s now. So I decided I was going to move to Israel. I changed my name from Suzi to Shira. I learnt Hebrew and I worked in Israeli theatre. I would probably still be there if I could have found somewhere to live. I moved from one apartment to another. When you're not married, you get no support from the Jewish Agency. So after about two and a half years, I finally left. I travelled through Europe, and then I went to England. I ended up staying in Wymondham, England, for two and a half years. It's just a few miles outside of Norwich. It was beautiful. I was starting to write a novel about Korea, and it was nearly finished when *M.A.S.H.* came out. Someone else got the idea first! I decided I did not want to become an expatriate so I returned to the United States.

I came back to Metropolis, and I didn't know exactly what I wanted to do. I'd only been back a short time, and I took this course in belly dancing. That was just fun, once a week. One of the girls in the class said her mother had just had her zodiacal chart done. Then I saw in the Jewish Community Centre Bulletin that they were teaching a class in astrology. I went into this class, and within three or four weeks I was fascinated. I began studying practically full-time. The teacher had taught us how to set up a chart, and I was gathering birth data from practically everyone I knew. I set up two charts. One was my hairdresser, and the other was a psychologist friend who had been widowed twice and had lost both her parents. All I had were the two wheels and the teacher looked at the first chart and said, 'Is this by any chance a homosexual?' And I said, 'Yes.' She looked at the second chart and said, 'Is this someone who had to deal with death a lot?' And I said, 'How the hell do you know that?' And from that moment I was hooked! It all came very, very fast and I became an astrologer.

Most of my best friends are in the astrological world. One of the things that happened is I found myself at a Jewish function. I looked around and I said to myself, 'These are my people?' I identify very, very strongly as a Jew, but I do not identify myself as a member of the Jewish community. I find them for the most part Philistines! I'm appalled at how spiritually bankrupt these extremely wealthy people are, and I could go on and on about that . . .

I have studied with the best astrology teachers in the world. What astrology taught me is that we have a universe which is orderly and structured. Science is based on predictability as well. As you know, in the Middle Ages Jews were the best astrologers. I also found that a lot of traditional Jewish superstitions are solidly grounded in metaphysical and astrological principles. For example, Orthodox Judaism teaches that pregnant women are not meant to go to funerals. Astrology says there is a dead soul which may want to enter that unborn child. So suddenly, a great many of those superstitions made sense – when they made no sense at all in terms of enlightened reason.

I'm now a member of Ecclesiastes *havurah* (see *Havurah Leaders*). There, for the first time, I have had some sort of spiritual experience from a Jewish service. It isn't the Orthodox practice. If it were, I'd be going to *Har HaShem* synagogue or *Adath Israel.* It is not the form; it is the intent. The difference between Ecclesiastes and Temple *Shalom* is Temple is a beautiful, beautiful performance, while Ecclesiastes is a religious service.

Astrology is very much part of the Jewish tradition. Not many people know that, but it is an ancient part of the tradition. The more I study, the more I realize that it is part of my birthright . . .

The Restaurateur

MR JOE LEVY

Wolfie's Kosher-Style Deli was in South Metropolis. It was a modern, prefabricated block on the highway. Inside there was frenetic activity. The Deli could feed an army with no prior notice. People were packing away quantities of food – half chickens in cauldrons of soup; sandwiches eighteen inches long; salads served in glass washing-up bowls; mounds of coleslaw and pickled cucumbers; potato pancakes the size of dinner plates.

Joe Levy was a small man in his fifties. He was bobbing and weaving among the customers: offering a word here, sorting out a table reservation there, and speeding up an erring waitress yonder. It was a real family place with children and grandchildren, parents and grandparents. Everyone was enjoying themselves vociferously.

I was born in Metropolis and went through the public schools. Then I went to the University of Metropolis and trained to be an accountant. I did that for about ten years. Then I went into the food business, but we went broke in 1965. Then I went into the restaurant business and owned a place downtown. It was pretty successful, but it was a zoo down there. Then I went into the advertising business. I fooled around in advertising for five years, and sold it. Then I went back to accounting. I joined a landscaping venture and put a merger together. The merger went through and I went out! Then I knew the fella who owned Wolfie's Deli, and he says, 'Why don't you come to work as a manager or something?' So I says, 'Okay.' And that's how I wound up at the Deli!

I came from an Orthodox family. I went to Hebrew school at *Adath Israel* synagogue on the West Side. That's the biggest bunch of crap they ever invented. After my *Bar Mitzvah*, that was the last time I ever went to synagogue – other than somebody's wedding or *Bar Mitzvah*. I have totally given up on religion. I did marry a Jewish girl. I did have a synagogue wedding – yeah, I had to have that.

I could not reconcile anything these people were talking about with anything that made any sense: miracles, prohibitions – keep the whole thing! There was one thing that set the seeds in motion very early on. I used to go to the Metropolis Science Museum. The folks took me; I went there all the time. I loved it. You see these prehistoric things, and all that stuff. When I learnt how to read, I see these things are sixty million years old. They got dates on 'em. How come then, in religion school, the calendar is 5,000 and some years old? So I start thinking about it. This was when I was probably seven or eight. And I say, 'There's something wrong here. These people are telling me the world started 5,000 years ago and these things are sixty million years old.' So I go into the rabbi and I say, 'How come?' He says, 'That's the way it is.' And I say, 'How can you say that's the way it is? I'm reading the Bible already, and I don't see anything about dinosaurs in there. Somewhere, somebody's got something wrong. I don't know who, but somebody's got something wrong.' And all he keeps telling me is, 'That is what we believe in. Believe in it.' I say, 'Thank you,' and out I go. 'Screw you and your whole deal!'

Even though I got fairly good grades in religion school, by then it was like forced labour. I went because the folks say, 'You go till your *Bar Mitzvah* or else . . .' And in those days 'or else' meant you went! So I went. Amazingly enough, I can remember tons of stuff that I learnt, but it had no relevance. The first chance I get, like a convict, as soon as they open the gate, man I'm gone! So I had a *Bar Mitzvah* and that's the end of it.

You wanna talk about the restaurant? The restaurant buys some *kosher* meats, but the other stuff is *kosher*-style. It's prepared the same way as if it were *kosher*, but the meat is not ritually killed. They just go out and buy brisket somewhere. *Kosher*-style is just another ethnic style. We mix milk and meat? Sure. We have ham too, and shrimp. This is not a restaurant that's designed for Jews only. This is a restaurant for the general public. If you keep *kosher*, whether at home or out, you don't eat here. You don't go here even if you can rationalize -- which most of 'em do: 'I'll eat a tuna fish sandwich.' Because the fork has been everywhere, so has the spoon. That's another of those rationalizations these Orthodox Jews make: 'We'll go to this restaurant. We'll eat fish; fish is safe. We know fish is *kosher*.' Yeah, fish is *kosher*, but technically the minute it hits the door, forget the *kosher*. There's nothing *kosher* in this restaurant!

The clientele are a mixed bag. A lot of Jewish people obviously, but it's a lot of non-Jews too because that style of food has always been very well accepted. It has become more popular. We get the Orthodox, sure. They keep *kosher* at home, but I guess they've finally figured that God isn't going to strike 'em dead if they have a corned beef sandwich out. They'll go to weddings: If the wedding's in a synagogue, they feel very safe. The synagogues are *kosher*. If they go to a wedding in a hotel, they'll eat it anyway!

Can I tell the difference between Jews and gentiles? Yes siree! I can tell! That's the most obvious thing in the world. The Jews walk in, you give 'em a table. They say. 'I don't want to sit here! It's by the door! I gotta sit by the corner! I can't sit by the wall! It's too hot! This is too much! I don't want to see the kitchen! Not over there! I don't want to see the bathroom! This lady I don't like! I can't sit here! I might see him! I'm not going to see her! I don't want this! It's too hot! Gimme gravy! I don't want gravy! Maybe a little gravy! Maybe it's kind of lukewarm! Put it on the side! I want a dressing! It should be on the side!'

Now this goes on all day, all night, all the time. Whereas if you're not Jewish you just say, 'Let me have the corned beef sandwich.' Done! Whatever you give 'em, that's it!

The people who go to delis are by and large much heavier. These people like to eat. This is not the teeny-weeny petite crowd! These are the people that when they say they want a sandwich, the bigger the better. They'll bitch and moan, 'This is too much! We can't eat it! We gotta take it home!' But God help you if you give 'em any less. We give big portions. It's a lot of food. A lot of these people pack it away and then they have a dessert. Give 'em a black and white cookie; give 'em the killer chocolate cake, or whatever. It's all chocolate, chocolate.

It's generally older people who come, people who grew up in the Depression. They're strictly meat-and-potatoes people, that's what they're used to. You don't see many younger people. They come in with their folks sometimes. The older folks could eat in here five days a week. The kids you may see once a month. They know already that that's the kind of food you don't make a career out of because health-wise it doesn't fit the current standard.

They're generous with their tips. In general Jews are generous, they're very generous people. Look at the evidence of Jewish charities . . . Of course, they all know each other; they're all very friendly! When they come in, it takes ten minutes to seat somebody because they've got to say hello to everybody in the joint. So by the time they sit down I say, 'Hey, this is just like being in synagogue, isn't it?'

The Magician

MR MIKE GOLDBERG

The magician was a jolly man in his early forties, wearing blue jeans and a Hawaiian shirt.

I grew up in New Jersey. When my grandfather was still alive we belonged to the Orthodox synagogue, but then we moved to the Conservatives. I would say my upbringing was Conservative. I grew up in a *kosher* house. Yes, there was a lot of Jewish feeling all over – most of my friends were Jewish and most of my parents' friends were Jewish. I was not allowed to go out with girls who were not Jewish in high school. Once I got to college, things were different . . .

I have a younger brother – my brother, the doctor! We're very close; we talk all the time on the phone. He's an orthopaedic surgeon and also plays saxophone on the side. I always was interested in math and science, and when I was a little kid I was also interested in magic. I got my start as a magician because my mother used to take us to Macy's in New York and used to drop us off in front of Dan the Magician in the toy department. For the price of a $3 magic trick, she got several hours of babysitting! Then I outgrew those tricks and I forgot about it.

I went to college at Columbia University. I studied Math and Engineering. After I graduated I didn't know what I wanted to do. My mother was a schoolteacher and education was always a big influence on me. After Columbia I went to the University of Colorado. I wanted to go to Berkeley; I thought Berkeley was cool. My parents had supported me throughout college. When I was accepted by Berkeley I was also accepted by Colorado, but with a teaching assistantship. I felt I needed to be self-sufficient.

I did graduate work in math for a year and that's when I started to be a magician. I was on a trip to San Francisco and I saw a magician working the streets. I talked to him afterwards, and he told me of a certain magic shop. I invested in $200 worth of tricks. I came back to this state, built some tables, put my ad in the newspaper, and three weeks later I was a magician! I was a professional magician, but I was not a full-time magician. The pattern of my life has been a double career which has occasionally synthesized. I decided to become a schoolteacher, and for a number of years taught maths in junior high school in Metropolis. At the same time I was performing regularly in pedestrian malls. I did a comedy magic act. My goal was to make the show funny, but as with any performer, the key is to present yourself – your likeable personality. Seriously! People don't really remember the specifics, but if they had a good time, that's what they remember.

When I was a schoolteacher I would fly to Aspen, Colorado, for the weekend, and I would work a dinner theatre in Aspen with two other guys. I was the relief performer so I knew both parts. It was a lot of fun. More fun than you should be allowed to have! That show was a magic/comedy cabaret show and we did a couple of different tricks. Fire-eating was in that show. Anyway, they moved to Washington DC, and a year later I quit teaching school to work with them in a dinner theatre as a full-time career. I knew that I didn't want to go into show business as my career for ever, but I also knew that I needed to get it out of my system. Here was a salaried performing job, and there aren't too many of those in this country. It was a stage show, and it also involved bar magic. You'd walk up and down the bar doing card tricks and coin tricks. It has its own special flavour – it has a lot of innuendo and that kind of thing.

Because of my math interest I wanted to do something more. I wanted to create a field trip for math classes to come to, and that was this magical maths show. The point of the show was to explain a lot of different types of math-typology, matrices, network theory, probability – just to introduce things. After I do the tricks, I explain how many of them work so they can learn the math behind the trick. I was doing the mathematical show in the daytime and working the dinner theatre at night-time. I then decided I needed to get into the day life. So I started looking round and I ended up working at the Capital Children's Museum in Washington, developing some exhibits. But I continued to do magic shows and the magical maths show. I've done the magical maths show at science museums all over the country, and also in Australia and India. The ordinary magic show I do in night clubs, corporate events, parties – almost always adult shows, not kiddie parties.

I came to Metropolis about a year and a half ago. My job is called 'Creative Interpretation Manager' for the Metropolis Science Museum. Isn't that great? My philosophy is always try to negotiate for a job title that doesn't mean anything because it gives you that much more latitude. It's true! If your job title is 'Light-bulb Changer', everyone knows when you're not doing it! 'Creative Interpretation' is more flexible. I work on gallery presentations. What I like about this job is you're always learning new things. At the moment I am working on a quiz game on camouflage in the natural world. I also devise lots of educational programmes.

I'll tell you an interesting Jewish thing. I always go as Mike Goldberg, my proper name. I remember in Hebrew school learning about how Jews had to change their names to hide the fact they were Jewish. Something clicked in my mind, and I decided I was never going to change my name because I was proud I was Jewish. Anyway, when I was in Washington this Jewish guy wanted me to work at his dinner party. It turned out to be mainly Jewish people, upper-middle-class bourgeois. He says, 'Is your name really Mike Goldberg?' I thought that was such a ridiculous question, I said, 'No, no. My name is Goldini. I'm really Italian, but I use a Jewish name because I figure, in this neighbourhood, I'll get a lot more business!' Well what happened was, I could see him telling this story round the room, and people's warmth disappeared. All at once I was not a Jewish person, and I was treated very icily. It was a very interesting thing.

There are a lot of Jewish people in show business. Harry Houdini was Jewish – did you know his father was a rabbi? There are a lot of Jewish performers, a lot of Jewish comedians. I don't know what the correlation is. I don't think my decision to be a magician was anything to do with the fact that in the Renaissance Jews had a handle on conjuring. Maybe they did, and maybe they didn't! Is being a magician a job for a nice Jewish boy? I think my parents wanted a doctor, but they got one doctor. It always used to bother me. When I was growing up, I always thought the choice was a lawyer, a doctor or a bum. I wasn't a doctor or a lawyer, so I must be a bum. My parents always supported me though. Whenever she takes out the pictures of her sons, and people ask what they both do, my mother says, 'This one's a doctor and this one's a magician.' And people always say, 'A magician!' That makes me feel good!

The Sultan of Striptease

MR PHIL BLOCH

We found Mr Phil Bloch in a tiny drive-in booth in the middle of a shopping centre. He had retired from his former career and had become a shoe repairer and a key cutter. Traces of the old showman remained. Above the booth was a sign declaring, 'Phil

Bloch saves soles'. By the side of the booth was a large bin for donations of shoes for the homeless. He was a small man in jeans and a leather waistcoat, who described himself as ageless.

I'm Jewish, as you can see. I was born here in Metropolis. My parents came over from Russia and they settled here. My dad was in the plumbing business, and then he was in the building business. He built a lot of homes in the West Side by the lake. Yeah! Where Bernard Black (*The Community Patriarch*) now lives. That's a rambling ranch home! I belonged to *Adath Israel* synagogue. We had, let me see, three brothers and a sister in my family. I went to the public schools and graduated from West High School. Sure, I know Harry Trope (*The President of the Hebrew Old Age Home*). A very nice guy! Everyone knew just about everyone at that time on the West Side.

After school I did different things. I worked for a guy on a fruit stand downtown. I was there for quite a while. Then I saw my opportunity to go into a liquor store; I went into it with my cousin. Then I went into a place on East 15th Street. It was called the Cowboy Inn. It was a little bar, and it had a room at the back. I was there with an associate for a long time, and we done pretty good there. Then I had an idea to put dancing girls in the back room. They never had exotica or strippers then. So I hired a girl to do plain dancing in a bikini – not quite a bikini, a little heavier than a bikini. She done dancing there, and it was very good.

Then I thought of expanding. Already they were talking of hiring topless and bottomless in Metropolis. So I got into that. I hired very, very good-looking girls, and we filled it up doing the right promotion. So I expanded the whole place. First they had topless, and then they went bottomless. The bottomless were also topless? Absolutely! I put on shows. I'm a showman. I've always been that way – all my life. My shows were the greatest in the country. Celebrities would come to the place. I didn't just put on striptease; I put on burlesque. They called me the Sultan of Striptease! I was in the paper!

I gave these girls names. I'll give you an example. I had one girl and she was called Kyla Klapsaddle. I thought of that name! I said, 'I give you Kyla Klapsaddle from Russia, with Love!' Then

I had another girl: she was a 52-inch girl with a small waistline, and I called her Toughshitski Sonovitch. People came to see the show from all over the world. Elvis Presley came in. Clint Eastwood made a movie in my place, and he put me in the movie. We became very good friends. You see me in the movie with a big orang-utan on one side and Clint Eastwood on the other! We were drinking with the orang-utan monkey! It was real funny!

Then I had a very sensational Jewish girl. I named her Lena Hotlips Balenski from Tel Aviv, Jerusalem. I called her Lena Hotlips from the Circumcision Ward at Mount Sinai Hospital. She was a pecker checker! That's the way I done it. I made the shows funny, and that's how I did business. I named another Ming-Toy Epstein – half Jewish and half Japanese – a Jewpanese I called her! Here's another: I called her Twolips the Tassel Twirler. I put tassels on her, and she made them go in opposite directions. Yeah! Then I had a snake act with a real boa constrictor. I called her Cleopatra and Her Exotic Asps. I trained these snakes to go around her body. I was the Master of Ceremonies. I told jokes all the time!

One good thing about my place. I'm Jewish, and I dealt with gentiles all the time. The Jews came in too. They enjoyed it; they brought their friends and relatives. You see, most strip places right now cater to men, but I didn't. I said, 'Bring your wife, girlfriend, or out-of-town guests.' The Jewish community liked my show; they liked my place; and they liked the way I conveyed myself to the gentile population. In fact, even the Mayor came in my place. I didn't ask the rabbis, but I think they came in. They never said nothing. I won't say for sure they came in, but I'm sure they did. Yeah! Every Jew came in! They still talk about me!

It was called Phil Bloch's Sitting Bull Bar. I had a mannequin twirling around outside. It had a bra on, and some college kids took the bra! I didn't know about it, and it kept twirling around! Anyhow I thought of an idea which would help me have a good image with people. Every two months I would put on a charity drive for the Metropolis Children's Hospital. Let me tell you, on Friday, every two months, I would give all my proceeds to the Hospital.

In the end I had to give the bar up. They sold the building from under me, and the bank didn't want a strip place next door. I moved out and now they are sorry, because things dropped off around there. I used to bring in a lot of people – a lot of people. I used to hold 300 people in my place. It was a good thing; I was benefiting people. Have you ever heard before of a striptease that does charity?

The Prison Visitor

MR MANNY SHAPIRO

We arranged to meet Manny Shapiro in a very smart hotel near downtown. He arrived a little late and rolled into the lobby. With his tanned masculine face, he looked like a Jewish cowboy. He was well known to the waitress in the dining room.

I grew up on the West Side of Metropolis in what I would consider to be the Jewish ghetto. Those are the best memories I have. I knew everybody that lived within a mile of my house: at school, at the community centre, and at the steam baths. My house was back-to-back with what is now the *Yeshiva* High School. It was a synagogue then. In those days there were several synagogues on the West Side. It started off with the Orthodox, and then they got more Orthodox! I had my *Bar Mitzvah* at the old *Adath Israel*. That was in 1952. When you grew up on the West Side 99 per cent of your friends were Jewish.

I went through the public schools, and believe it or not, I wanted to be a lawyer. At school my grades were really good. I breezed through high school without doing a lot of homework. I entered Metropolis University, which was more expensive than the State University. I figured I could keep a job in the city and pay my way through somewhere along the way. In the first year the Dean called me in and said, 'You know you're not attending enough classes.' What I was doing was I had a job on the weekend, and I was doing pretty well at it. It wasn't only Saturday and Sunday – it became Thursday, Friday, Saturday and Sunday. So the Dean told me I had to start attending more classes. Somehow, as we talked, I got to find out he was making

$175 a week, and I was making more than $400! So I thought, 'What the hell can this guy teach me?' So I said goodbye to the University and never looked back! I always liked to spend money – a lotta money – sometimes more than I made. I was always fascinated by cars. Today I've got four Jaguars and an Austin Healey.

In 1961 I got married. I was twenty-one. Everyone got married at about twenty-one in those days; they don't now. At that time my mother was Rabbi Oppenheim's (*The Traditional Rabbi*) secretary at *Beit Torah* synagogue so that's where we got married. First we moved to an apartment near downtown. I made a deal with the apartment-house owner that I would get free rent if I could keep the apartment-house full, because I didn't have the money for rent. After about three years, we bought our first house. We had to pay $150 a month and put $900 down. We moved in and we had no furniture. Nothing. Yes, we did have a baby by then – and maybe a second one on the way. How did we pay the $150 a month? I got together with my uncle and we bought a shirt laundry. It was like a dog and a cat getting together! It lasted sixty days. We just didn't get along very well, and that was kind of unique. I was doing the truck driving and he was inside doing the laundry. We never saw each other, but still we didn't get along. Anyway, my mother-in-law loaned me the money to buy him out. So Bingo! I had a laundry right away! I was the owner, and that's how we paid the $150 a month.

About ten years ago I was at a function. Fred Tabbick (*The Retired Educationalist*), who's been dealing with prisoners at the State Penitentiary, happened to be at this function and asked me to come along with him. I knew Fred from a long time ago. He's a pretty neat guy. He's a little bit like me only highly educated. He's from England. He was born in Scotland, as a matter of fact. He had ulterior motives when he asked me to go. He asked me if I'd drive and he really wanted me to take the whole deal over. I'm not the right person for that; Fred is the right person for that. You really have to have a little bit of compassion for these people; you have to listen to them and half of it goes in one ear and out the other, because half of them are lying 90 per cent of the time.

The Penitentiary's about 150 miles from Metropolis and Fred goes twice a year at *Rosh Ha-Shannah* (the Jewish New Year) and at *Pesah* (Passover). We've been doing that now for the last ten years. Fred's been doing it for more than forty-five years. We always try to get people from the community to come. They go there one time, and they see the jail and these people down there, and they don't want to have nothing to do with it any more. I would say there were six to ten Jewish prisoners in the jail, but twenty or thirty show up to these services. The word goes round that you get food with the services, and you can take food away.

They call the prison a correctional facility, but it's a jail. Inside they call it 'the slammer' because when those doors slam, they really slam. Most Jews are in the minimum security part though one or two are in the maximum security for their own protection – they're the child-molesters. One particular fellow who I know quite well, and I know his family, is a little *meshuggah* (crazy), and he's in for child-molesting. He opens his mouth a lot, and I can see why anybody would want to pound him around a little bit, just to get him to shut up. There are some real psychos down there, people who have flipped out. When I grew up, I was always able to cope. I guess I've been as nutty as you or anybody else, but you have to kind of stay by the centre line. If you get too far off one way or the other, you wind up in jail or you wind up dead, or who the hell knows where you will wind up! Even if you have a chance in your life to gain illegally this, that or the other, you can't do that; you've gotta stay by that centre line.

One Jewish fella down there has a brother who's a professor at the State University. I thought he was in there for drugs or something. It turns out he was involved in two armed robberies. I guess he's about thirty-two years old, a pretty sharp-looking guy. He's pretty intelligent, and he's doing two twenty-five years consecutively. It's one of the longest terms in the jail. These guys are pretty good jail-house lawyers. There's one guy; he's a pretty sharp kid, and he's got a big mouth. He's got a long-term sentence too. He sued the State Prison because he claimed they were giving him soggy bagels! And he won the suit! It cost the State millions to remodel and change the kitchens around. He's not exactly the most popular guy around there!

Do these guys tell me about their crimes? Who wants to hear? I'm not tooting my own horn, but I've learnt the hard way. You've really got to have compassion. People are really fragile, no matter how tough and strong they think they are. These guys are off the street. They're criminals by any legality. They're not too sophisticated. They like Fred. He's an old guy and pretty corny, and he doesn't go over their heads. Some of 'em can read in Hebrew. They all want *yarmulkes* (skull caps). Not that they get real religious, but it's a symbol.

Here's what I think is really rotten: There's a service every week for the Catholics in the prison. Fred can only go twice a year. He's tired and he's worn out, but I've told him, while he's still breathing he goes down there! The rabbis are not interested because it doesn't bring them any money. There's a couple of prisoners down there who come from the West Side. There's a fella whose cousin is a past President of the Jewish Community Centre. He probably wouldn't admit this guy is a relative! There's another kid who's as goofy as hell. His dad was well known in the city, but when this whole deal came up and the kid went to jail, he quit town and moved to California. There's another fella who's not too sophisticated. This guy's dad has a big packing-house in Metropolis. The father won't see the kid, won't even help him. When he got out, I tried to help him get a job so he could get out on parole. His dad should give him a goddamn job. His father would never come and see him. Why do I visit these guys? I feel that someone's got to do it and if I don't do it, it probably won't get done.

The Feminist

MS MAXINE DREYFUS

She lived in an upmarket singles' condominium building, which stood less than two blocks from the best shopping area of the city. The apartment had a long, narrow living room, an open-plan kitchenette, a dressing area, a glossy bathroom and small bedroom. There was good modern art on the walls, a large business-like desk, comfortable white upholstery, and new-looking oriental rugs. Maxine Dreyfus was a large, dark, breathless woman in her forties. Her curly hair was beginning to show grey roots, and her nails were bitten down to the quick. As she talked, she sipped coffee from a mug which had on it the logo of the Metropolis State Suffrage Centennial.

I was born in Brooklyn, New York. I went to school in Manhattan. Then I went to Smith College, and immediately after college I lived in Europe for twelve years. I lived in Paris, and then I lived in London where I went to graduate school. I started working as a teacher in art schools and a polytechnic, and then in 1981 I came back to the United States and settled in Metropolis. For some time I taught at Metropolis University, and now I'm on the staff of the Greenbaum Museum. Yes, Marion Schwartz (*The Museum Curator*) is the Curator.

I had the archetypal experience, age four or five, in Coney Island of being taken to the corner Orthodox synagogue and being pointed at: 'Get her out, get rid of her. She's a woman!' It really happened! I went and, as a little girl, I was allowed in the men's section with my dad. I looked three years older than I was anyway, so the day came when I had all these fingers pointed at me and my dad had to get me out of there. When I was in Europe I had certain experiences. I was always a Zionist – I still am, and it is very important to me. I always thought of myself as Jewish in identity. I was in France during the 1967 War and I saw the turnabout of my friends in the French Left, coming up with these very strange analyses of the founding of the State of Israel. I lived at the Cité Université for a while. I literally had to walk the gauntlet to the restaurant pavilion. It had a big sign saying: 'The PLO Will Conquer', and then to the left and right these poster boards declaring how many Israelis had been killed that year by the PLO, and blow-ups of Egyptian cartoons which had iconography straight out of the Nazi period. You live with it. You negotiate your way through it, but it had an effect . . .

I do wonder if the phrase 'a Jewish feminist' is not a contradiction in terms. I often do wonder why I don't just leave Judaism behind. If you insist on being Jewish and a feminist you're kind of locked into this argument. Many people just step outside and forget about Judaism entirely. I haven't. I'm not interested in the old complaints. Obviously Judaism is a patriarchal religion; obviously it's institutionalized sexism. It's role-based; it's gender-based. As far as feminists go, I have so much experience of women starting off exploring their Judaism and ending up being goddess worshippers. I've seen this trend a lot. I went to this fascinating lecture by someone called Starhawk, who's written several books. She was born Jewish, and she said in her talk that she's a little bit of everything. And you can see why. She's having a great time; she's banging a drum; she's the centre of her life. So I ask myself, 'Why this attachment to Judaism?' I don't particularly want to beat a drum, but figuratively maybe I do want to beat a drum!

Feminism has always been a very natural progression for me. In the early days I went to one of the Women's National Conventions with Betty Friedan, who of course was from Smith. In fact, I think Gloria Steinhem went to Smith too. I'm not sure. She of course is half-Jewish. I would go on marches and stick my neck out in those days.

Now the reason I consider myself a Jewish feminist is finding anti-Semitic tendencies in the women's movement and being very, very sure I wanted to participate in women's issues from a Jewish base. For example, I am State Treasurer of the Coalition for Choice which is a State-wide umbrella for forty-five major organizations. It was formed when the initiative to use public funds for abortions failed in this state. I've been active in it for the last three years. Its purpose is to show a broad base of women's reproductive rights. I am the member through Hadassah! Everyone laughs, but Hadassah is the largest women's volunteer organization in the world and it has a very pro-choice stance . . . Oh? You've met Anne Ginsberg (*The Hadassah Leader*)? She's a past President, a lovely person. I know her daughter who's also very involved.

I specifically chose Hadassah. I sought it out and investigated it. I made sure it was pro-choice. I wouldn't have joined otherwise. It's not just abortion – I regard reproductive rights as the cornerstone of feminism. If you're not entrusted with your own body, you're not likely to be entrusted with multi-million dollar corporate decisions. If the State feels it can prevent women having the final say over their own bodies, it is not likely to let them have the final say over anything else!

Although I'm resolutely heterosexual and liked the variety of dating when I was younger, I don't regret not getting married. My life is not couple-based, but I don't object to marriage as an institution. I am a little tired of the glorification of the family. Families can be fine; they can also be very constricting. Families come in all shapes and sizes. I don't think they're either good or bad; they just are.

I know that Orthodox Judaism suits the traditional family. It attracts those who want to live in that manner, and it is a growing area of Judaism. I certainly see its attractions for men. Perhaps if I were a man, I would be an Orthodox Jew. I think it's the only boys' club left. I mean, today you can't even segregate Elks' meetings! And these guys in *Etz Hayyim* synagogue are having a great time! I think it's a racket! You have your wife waiting on you hand and foot. You're the king of the roost, and you have all these wonderful rituals. Honestly! For me it's deplorable. I will not support that kind of organization with one cent of my money. I'm not going to give my paltry little contribution from my paltry little salary to any organization that does not conform with my beliefs.

Still, I'm not going to waste my time being actively opposed to any Jewish institution. I'm much more interested in the positive side. Reinforcing and listening to Jewish women who have done something significant, resurrecting Jewish heroines, encouraging Jewish women's accomplishments. Everything is a compromise. Unless you want to form a religion of one, there are a lot of contradictions. There is so much to do that you can't only dwell on the difficulties. You have to make allowances; you have to join in; you have to be a social person . . .

The Radicals

DR GEOFF POULTER

We met Geoff Poulter and Adrea Pitkin in an office downtown. He was the Editor of the International Metropolis Film Festival Catalogue *and she was his assistant. It turned out that they were both leading members of the* New Jewish Agenda, *a politically radical organization.*

I was born and raised in the New York area. My family were Conservative Jews, and my religious education ended more or less after my *Bar Mitzvah*. We did go to Temple every week – like I said, we were Conservatives. I wanted to be a professional actor. My parents said, 'That's very nice, but you must find something to fall back on.' I studied theatre at college in New York for my first two years. Then to cut a long story very short, I got politicized and decided drama was a frivolous thing. I ended up majoring in Political Science and I graduated in 1967. It was an exciting time. The anti-Vietnam movement was hotting up and I got involved with that, and theatre seemed kind of peripheral. In those days I was more or less a liberal – I've become somewhat more radical since then. Like many people at that time I was captivated by the Kennedy mystique.

The draft affected every male of that age at that time. Sure I was constantly preoccupied by it. After college I went into the Peace Corps for two years before going to graduate school. Somehow there was a little loophole, and I got deferment until the draft was no longer a threat. I worked in the Ivory Coast with the Peace Corps, with a team of male nurses doing basic health education. I'll tell you the same thing as 90 per cent of all Peace Corps volunteers say – I got far more out of it than I contributed. It was a great experience: seeing firsthand the effects of US policy on the Third World probably radicalized me a little more.

Then in 1969 I came out to the School of International Studies at the University of Metropolis with the idea of getting a Masters degree and going into international service work. I continued to be involved with the anti-war movement. I guess I must have enjoyed it because I got talked into staying on to do a Ph.D. I was studying Ethnic Politics and my dissertation was on two Caribbean societies. I tried to get an academic job, but the colleges and universities I applied to did not have the same idea. It happened to a lot of us. One of my best friends from graduate school is running a bakery now and another is driving a cab. It was a bad time to be getting into universities.

I got married as a graduate student. It just happened that my wife is Jewish; the woman I was dating before was a black Catholic. My parents would have had a heart attack – a double whammy, yes! I stayed in Metropolis out of inertia and took jobs working in bookstores and suchlike. Eventually I started writing fiction – I've sold a few short stories, but it is still very tentative. This job – I'm Editor of the *Programme of the Metropolis International Film Festival* – it's an ongoing thing; I've been doing it for the last five years.

I'm now Co-Chair with my wife of the New Jewish Agenda. The motto of the organization is rather cute – a Progressive Voice in the Jewish Community and a Jewish Voice in the Progressive Community! Jews traditionally have had a liberal voice in American politics, but in the 1970s and 1980s that began to change. Everything became more conservative. It's a national organization, though they're in severe financial trouble at the moment. In the 1960s I never felt a need to be identified as a Jew in any political activity – in those days, you couldn't put your arm out without hitting a Jew. Now that's no longer the case. The usual explanation is that in the 1980s Jews, like everyone else, became preoccupied with making money. The class interest took precedence over ethical norms. In Metropolis we have a mailing list of about a hundred, with about fifteen active members. The oldest members are in their seventies, and Adrea here is about the youngest – she's thirty-three. Yes, it's a tiny group. The amazing thing is that whenever we do anything, so much notice is taken of us!

Basically, we have adopted the two-state position in the Middle East, and we have consistently supported Palestinian rights. As you can imagine, that puts us very much on the fringe of the organized Jewish community. The mainstream Jewish community tries to perpetuate the myth that there really was no Palestinian community, that the Jewish settlers entered an empty land. It's not true. I know here in Metropolis a man who keeps a restaurant, whose family lived in Jerusalem for five generations; his grandfather was Mayor of Jerusalem. We're trying to cut through the illusions and make the point that if Jews have a right to their own homeland and self-determination, Palestinians necessarily have the same rights. I don't know how to put it more clearly.

How have we been received? With anger, with derision, with hostility. I think there's been a conscious attempt by the mainstream organizations to marginalize us, to present us as fringe elements, wackos. Oddly enough I have been able to get some pieces in the *Metropolis Jewish News*, despite the fact that the Editor (*Editor of the Jewish Newspaper*) is about as far right-wing as anyone in this community gets. Despite that, he makes an effort to cover all aspects of the community. Not the gays, that is true!

We've had several run-ins with the Anti-Defamation League. There was a small Ku Klux Klan rally in Metropolis for Hitler's birthday. That's their occasion I suppose! A number of organizations, including Agenda, got together to plan a counter demonstration. Well, the Mayor's Office and the ADL got on television and said, 'Just ignore them. Don't give them publicity.' We thought that was an absurd position to take and at one point I asked Philip Rosenbaum (*The Director of the Anti-Defamation League*), 'Is this what you would have said in 1933 in Germany? Just ignore the Nazis and they'll go away? . . .' So we had a basic disagreement. To my mind the ADL was trying to stop grassroots people from becoming involved in a response to a clear threat to the Jewish community.

On our agenda is the Middle East, racism, anti-Semitism, women's issues, gay and lesbian issues, and social justice. I think among the general Jewish community, regarding Israel, there is more agreement with our position than would appear from the established organizations. These organizations' stand of unconditional support of Israel undermines credibility. Yes it does! Why they do it is a mixture probably of insecurity and racism: the fear that another holocaust could happen and a very real racism against Arabs and Palestinians. I don't think you can minimize that . . .

MS ADREA PITKIN

I was born in Metropolis and my family were members of *Har HaShem*. Rabbi Kornfeld (*The University Professor of Judaica*) conducted my *Bat Mitzvah*. I am the youngest child, and my mother was in her forties and my father fifty when I was born. My parents were always liberal in their views. They deliberately chose not to live in the Jewish area in South-East Metropolis. We lived farther north in a much more ethnically integrated part of the city. They thought Martin Luther King was a wonderful man. I went through the public schools and in fact was bussed into the ghetto for high school. My graduating class was 50 per cent white and 50 per cent black as the result of bussing. Most Jewish people were either fleeing to the suburbs or sending their kids to private school.

I went away to Boston to university, to an all-girls' college. Initially I was going to major in Journalism but within a week I knew that I had to be a History major. I loved it. I never particularly thought of myself as a feminist – in a women's college you didn't have to. Women's opinions and women's learning was what the college was all about. I decided that I didn't want to be a lawyer. My father was a very well-known lawyer in Metropolis and both my brothers are lawyers, but the family was very good about it. I've decided I want to try to be a professor.

I did my Masters degree at the University of Metropolis. I was very homesick in Boston, and I really wanted to come back here. I encountered sexism for the first time at the University of Metropolis. It was horrendous. I was actually thrown out of class for challenging the Professor – he would never have done that if I had been a man. I was frightened that I wouldn't get the degree, and I set up an alternative at the University of California but it turned out to be all right.

In 1984, while I was still at the University of Metropolis, I attended the first few meetings of the New Jewish Agenda. I had been troubled about some Israeli policies, and I had tried to explain my reactions in various left-wing groups. I had been made very uncomfortable there, feeling that their anti-Zionism very quickly turned into anti-Semitism. They didn't always see the distinction. So I wanted to discuss Israeli policy in a Jewish group and that was what attracted me to the New Agenda. I remember everyone at the first meetings being very frightened. They felt if they made their belief in justice for the Palestinians public, they would be ostracized by the Jewish community. Initially it was run like an underground cell, surrounded with secrecy, and I remember saying, 'Look, we're not doing anything wrong!'

At about the same time I went into the religion school at *Har*

HaShem to give a talk on the Palestinians. The rabbi didn't seem too upset by what I had to say, nor did the teacher. It was the kids. They became hysterical, really hysterical. They were about twelve years old, and some of them were screaming. They must have got that from home. Another occasion I remember talking about the possibility of a Palestinian homeland with some of my mother's friends. They were arguing that the Arabs wanted to destroy us and push us into the sea. I realized then that a lot of re-education was going to be needed.

I started on my Ph.D. at the University of California in Los Angeles, and I'm still working at it. I'm studying sixties' radicalism. I have been very struck by the number of Jewish women radicals there were. Obviously Judaism is a highly patriarchal religion, there's no denying that. But Marx and Lenin confronted the women question early on and certainly Jewish women brought up in communist households tended to achieve real equality. I was drawn to these women, and I do understand my own radicalism in the light of my Jewish background.

I came back to Metropolis to finish my thesis. I'm doing some teaching in the Community College, and I know that teaching is what I want to do. I'm also helping Geoff with the film catalogue. I know the Metropolis Jewish community very well. I am part of it; I was born into it. I'd like to see the New Agenda have more impact, become more mainstream. I do believe that there has been a change of attitude among many people since the invasion of Lebanon. People are not quite so uncritical of the hardline Israeli policy and they're ready for the New Agenda message. Most of our members don't really see this; I suspect many of them are really more comfortable as outsiders. When you're a radical, you define yourself by what you are not and who you disagree with. It's hard to become part of the majority.

I'd like to stay in Metropolis. I'm very committed to the community here – there are some very good people.

Eleven

AMBASSADORS TO THE GENTILE WORLD

The Director of the Anti-Defamation League (ADL)

DR PHILIP ROSENBAUM

The Anti-Defamation League is a national Jewish organization that combats anti-Semitism and prejudice. The Metropolis office of the Anti-Defamation League was situated in the Allied Jewish Federation building, overlooking the Jewish Community Centre. It was a modern room with a video television and a word processor. Jewish lithographs were on the wall, and the bookshelves contained such titles as To be a Jew, The Real Anti-Semitism in America, Enlightened Leadership, *and* Computer Shopping.

Dr Philip Rosenbaum was a tall, dark, handsome man in his mid-forties. He had a beautiful speaking voice.

I was born in Philadelphia, Pennsylvania, and was raised in a Conservative synagogue there. We moved to Skokie, Illinois, and I attended after-school Hebrew school. My mother was extremely committed to Jewish education. We had a *kosher* home, and were Conservatively Sabbath-observant. I must have demonstrated some vocal talent early on because my mother pushed me up, at the age of about six, to begin leading services! Thirty-seven years later I serve as a cantor at *Beth Israel*, the Conservative synagogue here in town.

I went to the public schools in Skokie, which were predominantly Jewish. There were lots of advantages; the primary disability was we never won an athletic event of any consequence – which is probably a discriminatory stereotype on my part. We had a terrible football team: we just weren't big enough and our mothers didn't really want us getting hurt on the field! I met my wife at synagogue youth group, and it became a serious romance in high school. We married each other when I was just finishing undergraduate work.

I went to the University of Illinois in Chicago, and I stayed for eight years. I got a Bachelors, Masters and Ph.D., all in Sociology. I finished in 1975. I'm still a sociologist, and I'm a people-watcher. I never thought of being a rabbi; in my family that was a job that was perceived as being inappropriate for a nice Jewish boy! I was focused on becoming a professor and writing books, and that sort of thing. The first job I was offered was in Louisiana. I was being walked to the plane by the Department Chairman, who said to me that he hoped I would take the position because I would be the first Jew-boy on the faculty. That was perhaps my first encounter with Semitic ignorance. I don't think he thought he was saying anything bad, but I decided before my second foot hit the plane steps that I would drive cabs before I took that job!

I spent a year as a visiting professor in Florida, and then I spent six and a half years teaching Medical Sociology at the Catholic University in Omaha, Nebraska. After seven and half years as a professor I made the decision to look for a position in the non-profit-making arena. I wanted to bring about social change instead of being a chronicler of social interaction. I got to the point in my life when I wanted to be doing something to affect the world in which I lived. I seriously considered a position as the first male Director of a Planned Parenthood clinic in the United States, but instead I came to Metropolis as the Assistant Director of the Anti-Defamation League. This was in 1983.

My responsibilities were primarily in the area of Middle East and international affairs, leadership development, and a certain amount of media work. At that stage I was more impressed with the distress of a Jewish community with enormous intermarriage rates, and one which lacked the appropriate resources. There was very fledgling Jewish education in terms of day schools; youth groups were relatively sparse; the lay leadership didn't seem to be particularly committed to their professional staff; there were no *kosher* restaurants, and I was struck by the divisiveness between the West Side and the East Side.

In general, the ADL's mission is to end the defamation of the Jewish people and to secure justice and fair treatment for all citizens alike. That's the motto. In practical terms, we're first and foremost in the anti-Semitism industry. It's our job to identify, catalogue and to teach about anti-Semitism. Linked to this, we are in the business of building relationships between the Jewish community and its non-Jewish neighbours to reduce the risk of anti-Semitism. We also serve as the Community Relations arm of the Allied Jewish Federation. We deal with Black-Jewish relations, educating about the Middle East, Catholic-Jewish dialogues – those kinds of activities.

There is sometimes a conflict between our role as an Anti-Defamation agency and as Community Relations agency. For example, there's conflict over gay rights at the moment. Nationally we have a policy supporting gay rights legislation, but this does not enamour us with the Orthodox community who have a very different view on the subject. We have had several public debates, and some fairly vocal exchanges took place. Some were in the pages of *Metropolis Jewish News*, between the Editor who is Orthodox (*Editor of the Jewish Newspaper*) and the ADL. The gay issue is a civil rights issue, and part of our brief is to be concerned about discrimination. But there are people in the Jewish community who have a much narrower view of what we should be doing. They believe that if the issue is not about Jews and anti-Semitism, we ought to stay out of it. This is something we constantly struggle with.

We do not make decisions on which issues to support on the basis of Jewish Law. We're a secular agency functioning in the twentieth century. But as representatives of the Allied Federation, we have to find a way to create a comfort zone for most people in the community. If we look at probably the most important issue the community has had to deal with in the 1990s – the *kashrut* war: we had to find a *kashrut* certification that was acceptable. This has been very problematic for the Jewish communal agencies. Over the years there has been this steady elevation of the level of *kashrut* demanded, to the point that there are now two choices, both of which can be perceived as extreme. Yes, Rabbi Vardin's and Rabbi Berkovski's (*The Kashrut Supervisor* and *The Hasidic Rabbi*) certifications. We made the decision that all public programmes of our agencies should be *kosher* at the highest reasonable level. However, the sad reality is whatever level my agency practises, some parts of the community will not participate. It's a fact that some people from the West Side feel they cannot support ADL because of our ideological position on such things as gay rights and abortion choice.

What kind of programmes do we sponsor? We have dozens. There's the Governor's Holocaust Programme. Yes, Sam Holbein (*The Head of the Governor's Holocaust Programme*) is its Chairman. We do a very successful educational programme called 'A World of Difference'; we started 'Project Pride' which is designed to teach people how to respond to anti-Semitism. It begins with the premise that Jews will never be effective in dealing with anti-Semitism until they stop behaving like victims. We've been talking with Rabbi Lubetkin (*The Russian Rabbi*) about extending this project to help the Russian Jews. The Conference of Christians and Jews do similar, but not identical things. We've worked with Debbie Murphy (*The Director of the Conference of Christians and Jews*), for many years. Her activity tends to be a little more ecumenical – it's less biased towards the Jewish community. We work with the state Civil Rights Commission and several other agencies in town such as the Civil Liberties Union and People for the American Way. We're in the process of putting together coalitions with a number of these groups to deal with the extreme Religious Right in the Christian community. They're apocalyptic. The ones who are patient don't worry me. It's the impatient ones, who want to bring about the Second Coming a little more quickly than the rest of us are ready for it, that are troubling. We have a task force on missionaries and cults, and they do public education on deceptive missionary activity – particularly among the Messianic Jews. Oh, you've talked to Jake Stern (*The Pastor of the Messianic Jews*) . . . It's a major problem in the state.

We also do a lot of work on international affairs. We are the interpreter of Israel to the outside world, and we have a fairly active programme of outreach to the media. If they have a Jewish question, they know to come to us for a comment.

It's very hard to be in a public position like mine without getting an overinflated sense of your own importance. Luckily I've got a wife and two teenaged daughters who work very hard at keeping me humble . . .

The Graduate of a Prestigious American College

DR GLORIA LEAVIS

The house was in a southern suburb of Metropolis. We sat in the family-room surrounded by an extensive collection of modern art and sculpture. There was Indian pottery on the marble coffee-table, and inherited Russian silver in the glass-fronted cabinet. Gloria Leavis herself was small and dark-eyed. She was wearing a white pyjama suit with Indian turquoise and silver jewellery. There was a large solitaire diamond on her left hand above a wide silver wedding ring. She was in her late fifties, and she sat restlessly on the olive-green sofa.

I was born in Brooklyn, New York, and I lived there until just before World War Two began. Then we moved to a two-family house, then our own single-family house, and then a rather nice house. I went to the same high school as Philip Roth. If you know Philip Roth's books – which I'm sure you do – the description of the community is the community I grew up in: it's Newark, New Jersey, in the 1940s. My experience of growing up was one of relative means – middle-class – as my dad became more successful. We were not outrageously wealthy, but happily 'comfortable', as people would say then. My family was, in my eyes, a kind of ideal middle-class American Jewish family. We were on the edge of the real beginnings of the mainstreaming of Jewish life in America. My parents had enormously high expectations of me. I was the first child – we were two girls – and I was very successful as a student.

Even from my freshman year in high school, we began looking at colleges. I was all of thirteen years old! Looking at colleges meant looking at the finest women's colleges in the country. So, after I had seen Bryn Mawr and Radcliffe and Smith and all of those, my aim became to go to Mount Holyoke. Mount Holyoke, as you may know, is the earliest women's college in the country: it was established in 1836. There was one young woman who was very pretty, and very bright, and very classy who was at the Jewish country club that we belonged to. I met this woman and she became what you would call today a role model – though we didn't have that language then. She went to Mount Holyoke. As a child, therefore, I had a very, very rich life – rich in both my social life and my intellectual life, with all the accoutrements of the middle-class. I felt we had a perfect family, and I was given every opportunity. My parents encouraged me to be a special type of person and to reach for whatever I wanted to do or be. I thought I could do the most that any girl could do. I graduated from high school in 1949 and I was very proud of myself.

So I went to Mount Holyoke. I was the first girl in my family to go to college, and I was going to go to one of the finest colleges for women in this country. It was absolutely wonderful! I went from a Jewish high school and I found out what Christianity was. I was introduced to America in a very different way. I adored it! I learnt there what being taken seriously as a woman was all about! It was the opportunity to have everything in the world that is first-rate come to you! I've just been to my fortieth reunion, and I'm a very loyal alumna. I sang in the chapel choir; I was part of the fellowship of faiths; I danced a lot; I did debate: I was part of the Jewish group. I also dated many people – both Jews and non-Jews. I spent a lot of time at West Point Academy, at Williams, and at Yale during those years.

Then, I must tell you one thing that was critical. Just before exam week in my freshman year, my parents came up to Mount Holyoke to tell me they were going to be divorced. After my perfect childhood I couldn't really believe what I was hearing. That began a period in my life that was very different – becoming a professional woman. Being able to support myself became very important. I saw my mother left with relatively little compared with how much she had had and which she helped my father to accumulate. It was a hell of a lesson! The whole family was beside themselves. It was 1950 and not a usual thing to encounter, particularly in the Jewish community.

My father married again, but my mother was alone. She got advice from Judge X and smart-guy Y, and all the advice was lousy. She had done all the right things: she had been a good wife; she had had dinner on the table every night; she had household help; she went to the country club; she kept herself lovely; and so forth. The model of that kind of woman said to me, 'That is not safe. If you walk down that path, you are walking down a stupid path.'

After graduation I was conscious of wanting to go to law school, but I didn't go to law school! I should have gone to law school! I guess I didn't feel feminist enough at that time. I saw that as a little *too* much of a career. So I got a scholarship to the University of Wisconsin, and I spent a year getting my Masters degree in Speech Pathology. And after that I didn't want to go back to New Jersey. My mother had moved; there was nothing there for me. So I got a job in Metropolis and came here all by myself. I knew nobody. All of my girlfriends were married, and at that point I felt I was ready to get married. I met my husband on a blind date within a few months of coming to the city. Jerry was Jewish and he also was alone in Metropolis. I wanted to marry a Jewish guy. I knew that if I met a Jewish guy whom I really loved that would be best. I had dated non-Jewish men, but when I got close to the possibility of an engagement I had backed off. But even with Jerry I wasn't doing the traditional Jewish New Jersey thing of marrying a doctor and staying in New Jersey.

Anyway, I met Jerry on a blind date. The two of us had a very good time, and had a wonderful year together. By then I decided if we were going to get married, we'd better get married. I was twenty-three. I married him in 1955, and I was a speech pathologist working with children with cerebral palsy. Then I had a baby – a girl – nine months later and left my job. Within three months I was writing letters to Mount Holyoke saying, 'You didn't tell me how awful this would be!' I felt very constrained so I went back to my job part-time. Then I had two more children very quickly. My friends thought I was terrible because I was still running around pursuing my profession while I had three children under five.

At that point I got very involved with the civil rights movement. I organized a Community Council for Human Relations, and we got up to here with integration of blacks into housing. What happened was the civil rights and organization stuff I was doing became a full-time job. I was always on the see-saw between my profession and my love for organizations. When my kids started school, we joined Temple *Beth Jacob*. We felt Temple *Shalom* was too posh-y, and the rabbi of *Beth Jacob* in those days was very involved in social action. The kids went to

Sunday school there and had their religious education there. I became involved with the local Community College in the 1960s, and I became known professionally as a sociologist. They wanted me to teach a sociology course on minorities in America. Then in 1969 I was asked to be Chairman of the South Metropolis Institute for Community Development, which concentrated on building low-cost housing and other projects. At the end of the 1960s the Community College got involved in the alternative education movement. They asked me to come and design the University Without Walls. So I did. I became the Director of University Without Walls in 1979.

Then I left there and went to get my Doctorate. I thought it was time to do that. If I was going to stay in higher education, I had better have a Doctorate. So I wrote these books. I did journalism for the newspaper, and I went to Harvard one summer. I did things I never had done before. I finished my Doctoral programme in 1981, and the Community College invited me back to be the Dean of Adult Education and Public Service. I stayed there until they changed their President, and they weren't going to go in the direction I thought was important. In 1986 I won a contract for $7.5 million with the telephone company to design their training and retraining programme, and I won another one for $15 million to extend it to fourteen states. I did this until 1991.

In the meantime, my kids were growing up. What happened to them all? They all went through public high school. The eldest went to the School of Engineering, which was so inhospitable to women that she left Engineering and transferred to Economics. She now works for the Governor's Office, and she is not married. My second daughter went to Wesleyan – she got into Mount Holyoke, but it was the era of women going to men's schools. She then got her Masters from Yale and went to work for General Motors. She is also not married. My son, who went to Cornell, is the first one to be getting married. He is thirty-three and is being married in August to a non-Jewish girl. It's okay, I suppose . . . I really do like Sally, our daughter-in-law-to-be. When I look at my close Jewish friends, there's a whole mass of intermarriage. There is only one family among them whose three children all married Jewish.

I've just come back from my Mount Holyoke fortieth reunion. It was an incredible experience, not only because I loved this college. It was also that the women – even those who were the May Queen type – were genuinely decent, wonderful people. They had worked for social justice all the way; they had spent their lives working on housing, integration, those kind of causes; they had done it professionally as well as voluntarily; they were all extremely impressive in terms of the values we held in common. In truth, the College produced some terrific women . . .

The Jewish Partner in a Mixed Marriage

MRS BECKY MACLAY

Becky Maclay and her husband lived in a small house in an established Metropolis neighbourhood. She was a psychiatric social worker, and he was a corporation lawyer. They had an adopted Vietnamese daughter, a large labrador dog, and a fluffy white cat. The house was comfortable and decorated with objects collected from around the world.

I was born here in Metropolis, and I am actually third-generation living in the city. My grandmother was born in this state, and they must have been some of the first Jewish people here. They were clearly culturally identified as being Jewish but were very much Reform. My grandmother used to have Friday night dinners; my grandfather was rather an irreverent person, but God help the person who made an anti-Semitic remark! My parents were always members of Temple *Shalom*. I went to religion school and was joint valedictorian of the confirmation class. The other valedictorian became a doctor and is now a member of a Hindu *ashram*! I'm the youngest of three children: my sister has never married, and my brother is married to an Egyptian Jewish woman and lives in New York City.

I liked the Temple religion school, but many of the kids there didn't give a damn. I loved the history and the music. I went to *Shalom* summer camp and I still remember the camp songs. I'm now teaching them to my daughter. I went to public school, and then I went to university in Baltimore for a year, on the East

Coast. I already knew Patrick by then. I've known him since I was eleven – we were high school sweethearts and we've been married for twenty-five years. When I went away we weren't engaged. We had a sort of tumultuous relationship. Patrick went to Harvard, and I returned to Metropolis and went to university here. We got married at the end of his third year at Harvard, and I went with him to Cambridge [Massachusetts] for his senior year.

Was there any difficulty about Patrick not being Jewish? I remember my parents saying, 'Gosh, you're awfully young for being this serious!' And a piece of that was, 'You're going to get real serious and fall in love with a boy that's not Jewish, and there are implications about that . . .' It mainly came from my father. Patrick's family were fine. There was a to-do before we got engaged, and there were a couple of times when there were some strong words. Nothing ever about, 'We'll disown you.' Nothing on that plane at all; but simply fears that I might abandon my people and my religion and my background. As I look back on it as an adult, I realize they were expressing the fear that they might lose me somehow. Then when they saw they were not losing me, and I continued to identify as being Jewish, they accepted it. Our wedding was a very happy occasion, and we were married by a Jewish judge.

Patrick has no religious background in his immediate family. His mother was raised as a Mormon in a small town in Utah. She has very strong, negative feelings about the Mormon Church. Patrick's father had no religion at all, so he grew up as nothing. There was no religious discussion of any nature in his household, though they are people of very high morals and values. Patrick describes himself as a humanist, I suppose. He has said that he is sometimes very envious, not that I have a religion, but that I have a strong inter-generational identity and rootedness. Although he has no desire to convert – and converting would not give him that rootedness anyway – he does feel that I have something that he does not. It never occurred to me to ask Patrick to convert to Judaism. There was nothing to convert from, if you understand what I mean. Our values and beliefs are so consistent anyway. When all's said and done, we're both secular humanists.

In our relationship, we have several times changed gear. One of the shifts was when he was in law school and he wasn't absolutely sure he wanted to be a lawyer. So we moved to England and he studied Economic History at the London School of Economics. His thesis topic was about how economic necessity influenced the early Mormon settlers in Utah. I've always thought that writing that paper was a way for him to capture a piece of his family history. His great-great-grandmother had been one of those who pushed push-carts over the mountains to Utah.

When we were just married we moved away from Metropolis. We went to New Hampshire, and then to New York City – I finished my degree at Columbia University. Then we went to England for a year and afterwards returned to New York, where I did my Masters degree. Yes, I'm a psychiatric social worker. Then we lived in Atlanta for ten years and returned to Metropolis eight and a half years ago. We came back because this city always felt like home, and both our parents were ageing and we wanted to be nearer to them. Down through the years – probably in part associated with Patrick's success and partly due to sharing many interests with my dad and being very much parallel in terms of his values and concerns – my father and Patrick became very, very close. My father truly considered Patrick his son and fully approved of him.

We went through many years of intensely wanting to have children and not being able to biologically, so we had a lot of time to think about the impact of children on our lives, including teaching them values. When we decided to adopt we had some very interesting experiences. We were both forty years old, and many adoption agencies are religiously affiliated. Most of the state agencies would not deal with us because we were too old in their books. The religious agencies require you to promise to raise your child in whatever religion they happened to be. In fact, we ran into a couple in New York: the woman is Jewish and the man is not. They adopted a child through a Christian agency, and I said, 'Didn't they make you promise you'd raise the child as a Christian?' and she said, 'Oh I just lied.' I wouldn't do that. We talked about it: I could not have lied to buy a kid, so to speak.

After travelling in Asia we seriously considered adopting a Vietnamese child, and that is how we got May. We sent her to Temple *Shalom* pre-school, partly because it's one of the best pre-schools in town and partly because for me it seemed to be a comfortable place to be. No, we're not members of any Temple. I go with my mom on the High Holy Days, and we both go with my mom on my dad's *yahrzeit* (death anniversary). So she went to the Temple pre-school for three years. She was not the only child from a mixed marriage, and in fact they have many Christian children because it is a great pre-school. She dressed up as Queen Esther and everything . . .

I want her to grow up as a secular American humanist. I want her to care about other people, to have a sense of responsibility for her community, and to take pride in herself and her varied background. I don't particularly want her to have a Jewish education. I don't think I will send her to religion school. We talk a lot about Vietnam and that background. She's a Vietnamese American, and we encourage her also to think about being an American – Thanksgiving and pumpkin pie, and all that. She may, as an adolescent, join some other religion. I don't know. I certainly talk to her very freely about my being Jewish. I certainly would not want her to be a fanatic of any ilk!

She did run into some racism and insensitivity at Temple *Shalom*. After loving going to pre-school for two and a half years, she suddenly didn't want to go. They were insensitive both about her being adopted and being Asian. At the very beginning of the year, the kids were asked to bring in photographs of their parents and grandparents to make 'A Book About Me'. She didn't want to do it. This was a brand new class with teachers she did not know. It did not occur to them that this child would have to bring a photograph of her family when she was the only member who looks the way she does. She had also suddenly realized that she had had another mother and was asking me questions like, 'Did I come from your tummy?' So she was dealing with her adoption at that time. Luckily the Principal was very receptive to my coming in, and did some sensitivity training with the teachers. It's very good to teach that not all families look the same, but you have to wait until the child knows and trusts her teachers and peers.

Then there were other problems. Other kids would say, when I came to pick her up, 'That is not your mommy! She doesn't look like you!' It became increasingly clear that keeping her in a system that was primarily Jewish and Caucasian was not really a good idea at all. We prefer to live in an integrated area. We want her to be in a school where there's a racial mix. I want her to see people from India, and African-Americans and blacks and brunettes and people with green spots . . .

The Society Lady

MRS MARILYN SCHONFELD

The house was enormous. It was hidden behind electronic gates and surrounded by lawns and flower-beds. The entrance hall had a marble floor and was lined with supra-realistic paintings. There was a life-size waxwork of an armed guard, and two enormous motor-cycles. It was not entirely clear whether they were there as art or as modes of transport. We were led into one of many sitting-rooms. The carpet was inky-blue, the furniture was ice-white, and there was a massive marble fireplace. Again, it might have been an art gallery. There was supra-realism everywhere. The television was encased in a chrome container, and there were several chrome abstract sculptures. The temperature was chilly; the house was silent except for the hum of air conditioning; and everything was clinically clean.

Our hostess was a petite woman in her late forties. She wore short, white denim shorts which were decorated with gold stars. Her jewellery was gold, and her short, white ankle socks had rhinestones attached. Her make-up was expertly applied, her blonde hair was bouffant and her long fingernails were painted shocking pink.

I was born in Metropolis about ten blocks from where I am right now, and I grew up in a very observant home. We kept *kosher*. My grandfather was one of the founders of the *Har HaShem* synagogue, and my dad got up and prayed every morning. I went to *Har HaShem* and was confirmed there. My brother had a *Bar Mitzvah*, but in those days there were no *Bat Mitzvahs*. My parents did eat non-*kosher* food out, and they were members of Windy Oak Country Club. They were very much part of that scene. My father was also the President of the United Jewish Federation. My parents had two children, me and my brother. My brother was steeped in the tradition, but today he is not at all religious. It just doesn't do a thing for him at all.

I went through the Metropolis public schools. Yes, I was head girl of my high school. Like my brother, I went to the University of Michigan. I studied English and Art History. But I was going with Ray, my husband, by that time, so after two years I moved back and finished my degree at the University of Metropolis. I graduated in June and married by the following December. Then I became a high school English teacher before my eldest son was born. He is now twenty-two and has just graduated from Harvard. I loved teaching and was really sad when I left. In fact I thought about going back, but I've gotten so involved with volunteer work that I just haven't.

After I got married we lived in an apartment. Then we built a duplex near the shopping centre and lived there for seven years. Then in 1973 we bought this house, and we moved in 1974. We joined a synagogue when my boys were ready to go to religion school. *Har HaShem* was going through a bad time at that point, so we joined Temple *Shalom.* So my boys grew up in Temple, though we've kept membership in *Har HaShem.* We still belong to both. We have all the holidays at this house, but we no longer have Friday night dinner. Everyone always seems to be going in twelve different directions, and it became quite impossible. We don't keep *kosher*, no.

I've always been involved in the Jewish community. I have this thing about people who are involved in the secular community and forget they are Jewish. That's never appealed to me. I've worked for the United Jewish Federation; since 1975 I've had jobs in the Women's Campaign, and I've been Chairman of that campaign. Two years ago we raised $1 million. At the moment I am Secretary of the Board of the Federation. Are you going to meet with Laurie Paine (*The President of the Allied Jewish Federation*)? She's very capable. Ray's cousin was married to her husband for thirty years. Then we're very big supporters of the Temple and *Har HaShem*, and the new Hebrew Old Age Home. We support everything. I've been active in the Anti-Defamation League. I just don't go on the Board because I can't do another thing, but eventually I will. I've supported them a lot.

I've also been very active in women's things. I'm on the State Economic Development Council where we help women start businesses. We've a Women's Foundation here where we help women get out of the cycle of poverty and become economically self-sufficient. I've been President of the Junior League, which is an organization of 2,000 women. I'm not a screaming women's libber or anything like that, but women are different from when we grew up. I was unusual in that I didn't have a child immediately I got married. The fact I taught for four years after I got married was quite unusual. That's not the way people think today. In the 1970s there was a friction between those women who were staying at home and the ones who were working. They battled this thing out, and the Junior League moved ahead to become an organization where working women could have a place. Seventy per cent of our members are working – maybe it's part-time; maybe it's full-time. Our parents used to play cards, go shopping and play golf. It's different now. I don't work for paid employment, but I need some substance in my life or I would feel there was no worth to it at all.

The Junior League used not to include Jews. It changed in Metropolis in about 1970 because the organization was meeting at Temple *Shalom*. The Anti-Defamation League said to the President, 'You're meeting at the Temple and you don't have a single Jewish member. We don't think that's right.' So they looked around for a Jewish member. The reason, in all fairness (though I'm sure there were plenty of bigots in there), was you had to have six letters of recommendation from people who knew you. In those days, things were very separate and Jewish women wouldn't have known six members of the Junior League. Anyway, I was maybe the second or third member. Now there are a lot of Jewish members, and now we're concerned about black and Hispanic members. But you do have to reach out and make a concerted effort. Social change doesn't happen easily. I did hear that when the first Jewish member got in, some people were pretty shook-up. Personally, I always felt very welcome there, though at a committee meeting once a gal from the South used the expression, 'to Jew them down'. She called me next day to apologize; she knew it wasn't right.

I felt it was very important for non-Jewish people to know Jewish people. So I wanted to be part of the League. Some cities have been slower to have Jewish members. On a national level there's been a reach-out, but there are little ways to get round having minority members. Some of the Southern Leaguers get around it by saying there's a cap on the number of people they can take, and you have to enter a suburban League. We passed a resolution nationally not to hold a League meeting at any club or institution that discriminates against minorities. That's major. When I was President I made a big speech at the National Convention about being Jewish in the Junior League. It was quite exciting. They published the speech and circulated it among all the Leagues nationally. But one girl who spoke against what we were trying to do was a Jewish girl from Florida. I called her in her room. She was one of those who thought it was very classy being Junior League, and she didn't want other Jewish women being as hoity-toity as she was. Isn't that something?

It's very hard for the clubs to keep out minorities, though there are very few Jews in Metropolis Country Club. I go there often for parties, but I wouldn't want to sit around the pool, no. There are Jewish débutantes. I was invited when I was eighteen, and I didn't want to be. Now I'm on the débutante committee. Sherry Cohen and I are the two Jewish members. She's a darling, and her daughter (*The Débutante*) was a débutante. It's a way to raise money, but it's very stuffy. Still they feel they need to look for Jewish girls, and bring out one or two each year. It's expensive: it's at least $1,000 or so to bring out a daughter. This year it was a very small group.

There's still anti-Semitism in Metropolis. No question about it! Some of the very old Metropolis families are anti-Semitic. You know it's there! I think the minute Jews forget and think that the world has changed so much that there is no anti-Semitism, that's when you have problems like a Hitler. You look through history. The Germans forgot they were Jews. My relatives in Hungary were in with the government. They thought they were different.

They weren't. They were carted off like everybody else. I just think you have to remember who you are . . .

The Director of the Conference of Christians and Jews

MRS DEBBIE MURPHY

The Conference of Christians and Jews is a national ecumenical organization that combats all forms of prejudice. Debbie Murphy had just spoken at a meeting at the University of Metropolis, and we met her at a nearby branch of Dunkin' Donuts. She was a small, dark-eyed woman in her early forties. She wore a navy short-sleeved shirt and a white skirt with a faint navy stripe. She had no jewellery except a modern diamond ring and a watch on a gold bracelet.

I was born in Metropolis on the West Side. Both sets of grandparents lived nearby and my religious upbringing was Orthodox. We belonged to *Adath Israel* synagogue, and we kept *kosher* until I was sixteen. When I was seven we moved out to an outer suburb, and then we were the only Jewish family in the neighbourhood. We did continue to go to Sunday school at *Adath Israel*, but it was a different atmosphere. So I didn't grow up in the Jewish community. Nearly all my friends were non-Jewish. I didn't think it a big deal to go to a non-Jewish home or talk about Christmas. I mean, we didn't celebrate Christmas because we knew who we were, but if I was invited to a Christmas party, I could go. All my non-Jewish friends enjoyed coming to our home for the Sabbath, and for Passover in particular. They loved the Passover cakes! Apart from my sister, I was the only Jewish girl in my high school, and I went out with non-Jewish boys. It wasn't serious – I was in high school.

After high school I went to the State University and I studied Biology. I got involved a little bit in the anti-war movement in 1970. I was very conscious of civil rights, but I wasn't actually marching out then. I did that later! After I graduated I felt I should go to medical school, but I didn't pursue it. Instead, I fell into working for the Zionist Federation here in Metropolis. That's when I got very involved in the Jewish community. I was working for Israel and studying about it; I was out there marching for Russian Jewry, for Sharanski, and against the Moscow Olympics. I also started teaching current events one night a week at the Community High School. It was fun! I was at the Zionist Federation for a year and then went to the Jewish National Fund – you know, supporting development in Israel. Neither agency still exists in Metropolis.

I was only there for a couple of months, but I was volunteering at that time as a speaker for the Conference of Christians and Jews. I used to speak about growing up Jewish in a non-Jewish neighbourhood. After two months I was taken on full-time as Programme Director of the Conference. We did programmes in schools; we organized a State Governor's Interfaith Breakfast; and there was an annual fundraising dinner. The Conference is a national organization based in New York, and Metropolis is one of its regions. It has very good support, equal between Jews and Christians. In fact Don Samuelson's *(Havurah Leader)* grandfather was one of the founders of the Metropolis branch, together with some very prominent Christians. Rabbis were involved, like Rabbi Kornfeld (*The University Professor of Judaica*). They had an interfaith forum at which both rabbis and Christian clergy spoke, and the speakers at the fundraising dinners were very distinguished. Past-President Ford came to one. It was a very strong organization. I became Executive Director in 1979. I was young, but I felt I had the necessary experience. Yes, I was the first Jewish and the first woman Director.

Then I got married in 1980. I had a lot going on in my life at that time! I got married to a Catholic man. I met him through Jewish friends. At the time that we seriously got involved, I told him that I would never think of marrying a non-Jewish man unless my home was Jewish and my children were raised as Jews. That is what happened. We have a Jewish home, and we have five sons. The children had Orthodox circumcisions with Rabbi Amos Feigelbaum (*The Mohel*) and Rabbi Oppenheim (*The Traditional Rabbi*). My parents had no negative response to my marriage, but I think that was because they knew the grandchildren would be raised Jewish. On the opposite side of the spectrum, we had a very negative reaction from his parents who are very devout Catholics. They accept it now, and they love their grandchildren, but I am sure it is still a sore point.

My husband had mixed feelings. He does believe that if you teach children to be good and trustworthy and honest and responsible, it doesn't matter so much if they are Catholic or Jewish or whatever. As long as they had the foundation of being really good people. He received a dispensation from the Bishop to marry outside the faith. We brought a rabbi in from outside the state, and the Catholic bishop was very wonderful and very supportive and said a blessing at the wedding. Rabbi Oppenheim also counselled us and was wonderful, but I knew he would not do the marriage. No rabbi in Metropolis will do a mixed wedding. Our children now go to his religion school in *Adath Israel*.

Since the early 1980s the focus of the Conference of Christians and Jews has changed. We still do interfaith programming, but we now concentrate on young people. Our mission statement is that we fight bias, bigotry and racism through educational programmes. By the way, we are now just called 'The National Conference' because we want to be inclusive rather than exclusive. We still do the Governor's Interfaith Breakfast, which is very well attended. We now have Muslims, Hindus, B'hai, Buddhists – but not the cults. We have about 200 corporations supporting us in Metropolis, and 500 individuals. We work with the Anti-Defamation League – we're both involved in prejudice reduction, but we go one step further. They work with educationalists; we actually work with high school students! We have a budget of $100,000, and the staff is myself and a part-time secretary. It's a lot of work, but we have quite a volunteer core with a very extensive speakers' bureau. The Board of Directors is very diverse. We have the Chairman of the Bank of Metropolis; we have Rabbi Robert Reinhardt (*The Reform Rabbi*); we have the Catholic Archbishop; and we have a Mormon attorney.

There's definitely a breakdown today in the relationship between the black and the Jewish communities, but so many of the black youth are unaware of Jewish activism in the civil rights movement. They are more conscious of Israel and their feelings about the Palestinians. They don't know the history. They hear Louis Ferrakhan, and they listen to that type of information.

Even Jewish youth are very unaware of the Holocaust, and we do do Holocaust programming. In the Conference we emphasize that we want each group – whether it is Protestant, Catholic, Jewish, African-American, Latino, Native American, Buddhist, whatever – to maintain its own identity and still be able to have respect for others. Yes, the image of America as a melting-pot is long gone!

The Head of the Governor's Holocaust Programme

MR SAM HOLBEIN

The Governor's Holocaust Programme takes place for a week every year. It is sponsored by the state government and it consists of a series of events to try to raise consciousness about the Holocaust.

A large man in his sixties, Sam Holbein sat at his dining table in his elegant modern house. It was situated in one of the best residential developments in Metropolis. The room was cool with air conditioning, and the house was spacious and comfortable.

I was born in a small town in Germany called Landau in 1930. My dad was a cattle dealer, and we were able – through my mother's wisdom – to escape Hitler. She had made arrangements and got the papers. By the time we got them, my dad was also ready to leave. When I was six years old, I remember, I was beaten up by an SS trooper. This kid across the street had just turned seventeen. His folks had been friends of my folks prior to the SS movement. This kid, to show how brave he was, decided to beat up on a Jewish kid. When he heard my screaming, my dog came out of the yard and literally bit his arm off.

It was quite an experience coming over. We went through Berlin. We came to France, and came over on the *SS Washington* in 1936. My mother had a brother in northern Louisiana, and my dad was able to get a job as a janitor working for $10 a week. He was glad to have a job. We came to this little town in northern Louisiana, and the first thing we saw when we drove in were three black guys being hanged in the square. Not knowing anything about it, they may have deserved to die. They had raped a white woman. Nevertheless seeing something like this, we were very unsure if we'd done the right thing leaving Germany!

My dad was working as a janitor. I finally got a job as a janitor's helper. I was seven years old. We all worked together. We saved money: we were able to save $1,500 and bought a house that had three bedrooms. In order to make the payments on the house, we had to rent out two of the bedrooms to roomies (lodgers). There was only one bathroom, and God forbid if you wanted to go to the bathroom because you couldn't infringe on the roomies' rights!

There were a lot of anti-Semitic things that happened in Louisiana. We're thinking of the late 1930s and 1940s. The Ku Klux Klan was in evidence. I was a football player in high school. After I got tackled, I was down on the ground and a guy rubbed his football shoe into my hand and said, 'How d'you like that, you dirty Jew?' I exploded, and if it hadn't been for the coach, I might not be here today because he was in the sandpit choking when they pulled me off.

After high school, I was able to go to college on a partial scholarship, but I worked my way through. Any job was fine as long as I could make some money to pay my way through school. I usually held two to three jobs. I studied Marketing, Business and Accounting. Then my younger brother contracted asthma in Louisiana, and the doctors suggested we move to Metropolis. We started a men's clothing store here in the city. We plugged along and we were able to expand, until 1951 when I had the chance to sell the business.

Soon after, I got married and opened a larger store out in the suburbs. There have been anti-Semitic cases laced throughout my business life. For instance, one of the largest shirt companies in the early days did not want the Jewish business. Since that time, when they did decide they wanted the Jewish business, I still haven't given it to them. Those things carry over in my mind. There were still gentile cliques in the country clubs and downtown clubs in those days. But you've got to cope with the situation. I always felt I could mingle with the *goyim* (gentiles), if you like, and I never felt I had a huge problem.

One of my friends told me I ought to be part of the Anti-

Defamation League, and I thought I'd like to be part of that. The Director (*The Director of the Anti-Defamation League*) is one of the people I really respect. I was very worried about the Ku Klux Klan, which I knew in Louisiana. I'm willing to work against the skinheads and so on and give money to fight them. I joined and I was asked to be Co-Chair of the Holocaust Memorial Week. I was very interested in it. Through the auspices of the Anti-Defamation League we were able to get United Airlines to fly one of our helpers to get this woman over from Holland. During the war she had saved ten or twelve Jewish people, and she had three people actually living in her home. We brought this woman over and had a big event in the theatre downtown with the Governor and the Mayor.

The Programme's been going on for seven years. It's an awareness week with speakers. Most of the Jewish business community is involved, and a lot of the non-Jewish community and political people come too. People co-mingle. It lasts an hour or so, and we were able to put out literature and recruit people and remind them what happened.

The older people are easier to bring back into the fold. It's going to take a little more education to get our younger people. I think there's a lot of young Jewish people who don't even care, or think there are other things more important than the Holocaust. They think it's something in the past. That's the thinking that got Hitler in. They think, 'It'll never happen to me. It'll never happen again.' Until we can dispel that sort of thinking, there's work to be done. And non-Jewish people need to be aware of what we've gone through, and how we've been able to do so well in business and how to get along with people. It's a rewarding experience.

Six years ago my mother and I were invited by the German government to come back to Germany. They paid our way to go back to Landau, where I was born, with 101 other people. They had a big shindig and we stayed for a week at their expense. I'd never been back before. I'd always resisted the urge to go back and see the family roots. As it happened, on the corner of the street where I lived was a little butcher's shop. A little boy of my age lived there and we used to play together. When I walked in, this kid and I, we knew each other. He showed me the house where I was born and I saw where the guy had attacked me. It's hard to describe what I felt – it didn't have the impact I thought it might have. It instilled in me the necessity of keeping alive the Holocaust memory, and of trying to explain to people how easy it is for these things to happen. Yeah, I think it could happen in America if we're not careful . . .

The Débutante

MISS AMANDA COHEN

She was a very pretty girl with brown, straight hair and a golden tan. She was nineteen.

I was born in Metropolis in 1974. After Temple *Shalom* pre-school, I went first to a Metropolis public school and then to a suburban public school. My school was out of the Metropolis school system - and so there was no bussing. My four best friends in high school were all Jewish, but I have lots of non-Jewish friends. This is a fairly Jewish neighbourhood. My parents thought about private school, but my high school was a very good school. There were no minorities. There were no black kids in my class and no Spanish kids at all. It was extremely Jewish and WASP. It's very highly regarded: when I was looking at colleges, everyone had heard of it.

I went through the Temple *Shalom* religion school until I was confirmed. I had a *Bat Mitzvah*. I loved that. Danny Mizel was my teacher (*The Bar Mitzvah Teacher*) – he was wonderful. I went to Temple *Shalom* summer camp and I loved that, and I went to Israel with the youth group – that was the most incredible trip. I always had good Jewish experiences except for religion school. In fact I dreaded it. I begged my mom to let me leave after *Bat Mitzvah*. I felt like it was nothing. I find the history of Judaism very interesting, but religion school was really boring. I liked learning Hebrew, and I liked learning my *Bat Mitzvah Torah* portion – even though it was kind of a bad *Torah* piece about the killing of animals. I didn't like that! My mother's never been religious. When she was a little girl, she had Christmas trees! Her father, my grandfather, was very religious. He was Reform and went to Temple all the time, but my grandmother never went to anything; she didn't like it at all.

My dad always says I should find a nice Jewish boy. It's kind of a joke, but I think they mean it seriously. My parents have always said if I found someone I fell in love with and wanted to marry who wasn't Jewish, that would be all right. They would like him and would like me. But it just makes things easier if he's Jewish. I'd like to meet a nice Jewish person. I want my children to experience Judaism. I would want them to grow up Jewish, and I'd want them to go to Israel and know everything I know. I don't like Christmas. I've never felt comfortable going into a church. They put Jesus up on a cross, and he looks at you. I hate him staring at me. It makes me squirmy. So if my husband were Christian, I'm afraid I'd never be able to go to a church with him, and I would not want my children raised Christian. If I found the right person and he wasn't Jewish, he'd have to make serious sacrifices. How many Jewish boys have I dated? I only dated one Jewish boy in high school, and my parents didn't like him at all. The rest were all non-Jewish. Now I'm in college, almost all the boys I know are non-Jewish. There aren't many Jewish students at my school.

There are two different débutante balls here in Metropolis. One is the Suburban Ball. My father didn't want me to be a débutante there because they used not to allow Jews in the Suburban Country Club. The other is the Winter Ball. My mother had been a débutante at that – her mother had been a great friend of the Ball's founder. My mom said I might, just might, be invited to be part of that. The Winter Ball is the old ball at the Kensington Hotel downtown. The Suburban one is a new one. Some girls do both, but the Suburban one is no good. I wouldn't have wanted to do it. They do it round the swimming pool at the Suburban Country Club and the girls waltz round the swimming pool with their fathers, and they wear fake diamond tiaras! I think it's sort of vulgar. It's very tacky – that's the right word, tacky.

For the Suburban Ball, you put in an application form. For the Winter Ball, you get asked and no one knows who does the asking. You're asked to be a débutante in January, and then you go to a tea with all the mothers in May. Starting from then on, girls have parties all summer long. Four other girls and myself had a croquet party for all the débutantes and their dates. The committee give a curtsey party. It's the funniest party! You learn to curtsey. There's this one lady who does it every year and she lives and dies for the curtsey! You practise walking down the stairs and curtseying at the bottom. The season then ends with the Winter Ball.

It's very pretty. The hotel is done up with flowers and with lights. I had so much fun. There were about thirty-five girls, and I knew almost all of them. A lot came from this neighbourhood. I was Jewish, and there was one other girl who was half-Jewish. Then, everyone else was Protestant or Catholic. There were no blacks; we haven't had a black débutante yet. My dress was big and white with pearls all over it; it was very pretty. Actually it was very difficult to find a dress. You have two escorts at the Ball. One was my brother; he is sixteen. I don't think he had much fun. The other was my boyfriend of the time.

At the Ball we were presented to a line of ladies and their husbands. They were the Co-Chairmen of the Ball and two ladies who have been around for a very long time. One of them was my grandmother's best friend. Each débutante has to come down the staircase and curtsey. They announce your name, and then you waltz with your father; then you waltz with your escort; and then you sit down and have dinner. All the adults have quiet little sit-down dinners, and all the kids go over to the West Ballroom and a more modern band plays. After dinner everyone dances. It was so much fun. We really did dance all night. Everyone looked beautiful because they were all dressed up. At about 2 a.m. there's a big breakfast.

The Ball raises money for the Metropolis Opera. I think the purpose of it all is to raise lots of money. You have to pay to do it, and your parents invite all their friends and they pay to come. It makes a ton of money. Last year it was over $100,000.

I know my mom was one of the first Jewish débutantes. For a long time, they didn't have Jewish girls. It was nice that my mother did it, and I was continuing the tradition. I really think, unlike other cities, Metropolis is very open. In the South I believe they still don't have Jewish débutantes. My mother's not part of the Junior League, and we don't belong to a country club. I was only asked because my mother had done it. I did have one friend whose mother desperately wanted her to be a débutante. She once said something to me like, 'You can only do that because your mother was a deb,' something like that. It was a very rude comment. She was the only one of my friends who seemed to resent it. She was a débutante at the Suburban Ball. Maybe a few more Jewish girls were Suburban débutantes, perhaps three or four. Some of the girls did both, and it was a lot. I was glad I just did the one. You can overdo it, and it gets boring.

Was it fun? It really was. At first I wasn't sure I wanted to do it. It sounds kind of strange, and I didn't know if I'd like all the girls. But they were all very nice girls, and we all had a very good time. Did the experience change me? Not really. People are always saying débutantes are so horrible and it's such a snooty thing. None of the girls were like that. I really liked everyone. There were no bad feelings and everyone had a good time. I just realized that everyone is really all the same . . .

The City Treasurer

MR ALEX ACKERMAN

Alex Ackerman is the father of Sharon (The Student from the Pluralist Day School). *We interviewed him in his office in Metropolis City Hall. It was an attractive, lofty room overlooking the city park. Alex himself was in his late thirties; he sat behind a large desk covered with files.*

I was born in Chicago, and my folks moved here when I was about nine months old. I grew up in *Beit Torah* synagogue and went to religion school there. After the *Bar Mitzvah* I sort of dropped out, and my parents moved to the Conservative synagogue in South Metropolis. Rabbi Oppenheim (*The Traditional Rabbi*) was what had kept them at *Beit Torah*, and when he left they were very attracted to the Conservative rabbi. They've now rejoined Rabbi Oppenheim at *Adath Israel*.

After I graduated high school in Metropolis, I then went to Harvard. I majored in Government and Political Science. My elder brother had also been at Harvard and encouraged me. He's now a doctor, as is my sister. My younger brother is an attorney. My father was also a doctor; he taught at the medical school. I never had any interest in science; basically I was always very squeamish about blood and hospitals! When I went to college, I was basically rebellious and went very infrequently to synagogue. I was not at that time part of a circle of Jewish friends. It was really my being away from home that made me realize that Judaism really meant something to me. From the end of freshman year I became part of an every-Friday-night *Shabbos* (Sabbath) dinner and get-together, which was sponsored by the Jewish chaplaincy. It became a very important part of my weekly routine.

After Harvard I came back to Metropolis and I worked for the state Governor. I was in the Citizens' Advocate Office, which handles all the questions, problems and complaints about state government. I ended up specializing in prison problems because that was the largest caseload at the time. One thing led to another: I loved it and became Assistant Director of the office and stayed four and a half years. It was a political appointment, and I was there basically during the Governor's second term. After that I went back to school full-time, to the University of Metropolis, to get an MBA. That took me a year and a half. I didn't know then I would come back to government, and I thought an MBA would give me more options.

When I came to be looking for a job after getting the MBA, having gone to Harvard made a big difference. I got an internship with the City Treasurer's Office. It was at the beginning of a brand-new administration in the city. Fernandez was Mayor, and he replaced the Macmillan administration which had been in existence for twenty years. There was a lot of work to be done, and they were looking for new people. From the very beginning I worked side by side with the Treasurer. One thing led to another, and I went into a civil service position for two years. Then the Treasurer left, and I was appointed into his position by Mayor Fernandez. In the other counties of the state, the Treasurers are elected, but not in the city because of our special status. So I don't have to run for office. I love this job, and with the blessing of the Mayor my position was converted from an appointed, political post to a career, civil service position. The pay and duties remained the same. I'm not one of the Mayor's Cabinet. I report to the Director of Revenue, which is the political post.

I'm responsible for tax collection, property tax, sales tax, and all the other taxes the city collects. I look after the city's bank account and investment portfolio, and then we do all the bond issues for the city. I have a staff of about 180 people, and we handle everything that has to do with the city's money.

Does my Judaism and my work for the city intersect? Yes I think so. The Jewish teachings about responsibility for the community and one's fellow man, and the widow and the orphan, tie in with trying to get a higher rate of return on the city's investments. If we get more money, we can translate it into neighbourhood health centres, social service payments, and public libraries. I like to think of myself as being pretty responsible for augmenting the public services of the city by managing the city's money. In the Fernandez administration, ironically, there were more Jews in senior positions than Hispanics. I am Jewish, the Manager of Revenue was Jewish, the City Attorney was Jewish, as were the Budget Director and the Chief of Staff. There was a large representation. Jews are certainly electable in this city. The state may be different because it includes the suburbs and the rural communities. Metropolis itself returns a number of Jewish legislators to the State Legislature even from Republican areas.

I am not a member of any clubs. The other Treasurers from around the state meet every two months, and the first time after I was appointed in 1987 their meeting was to be held at the Suburban Country Club. You probably know that that club didn't accept Jewish or black members. I said that I would not go. One of the members of my staff who was also entitled to go was black. So I wrote a letter to the Treasurers saying that as people of my religion and of the race of one of my staff members were not welcome at the club, I would not attend. I was very pleased that my staff stood behind me, and none of the people of my office attended. They did not change the venue; they said it was too late and they tried – and I think they really did try.

People know I'm committed Jewishly. I do feel a real distance between me and the other members of the Treasurers' organization. This is for a number of reasons: they are all gentile, and they know that I'm Jewish because I made a big splash about it at the outset by boycotting this meeting. They are also mostly from small counties; they're all elected; they're mostly older women; a lot of them don't have a degree; all they handle is property tax. So it's a very different job from mine. Laying those things aside, whenever we're together, I'm very conscious of my Jewishness. The environment, the conversation and the food is very gentile. It always makes me feel conspicuously different. It's not just being Jewish, but it's a different world. They are always very cordial, but I'm sure a number of them, if the truth were told, have all kinds of antagonisms towards Jews. A lot of them are rural people, and not particularly well-educated. But I don't have any hard evidence of that. They do interact with the member of my staff who is black in a patronizing way. She was very pleased at the stand I took about not going to the Suburban Country Club. At the very outset of my tenure that cemented my relationship with her.

It has happened twice in my hearing that people in the office have used the expression 'to Jew someone down'. On both occasions I took the person aside and told them how inappropriate and offensive it was. The reaction was shock – they didn't mean me; it's just an expression, and so on. I have become more Jewishly observant in recent years. Partly it is because of having two children in Jewish schools. Nowadays I like to be home in time for the Sabbath, and so in winter I leave early on Friday afternoon. I have to say my staff have been very supportive about this. They don't make late appointments and they protect me from getting tied up with a final telephone call – that sort of thing. I feel real admiration among my staff for this, even though they're all gentile. Am I the first Jewish Treasurer? Yes I am, now I come to think of it . . .

Twelve

CONVERTS

The Director of an Outreach Programme

MRS NAOMI MARKS

Temple Shalom has recently instituted an Outreach programme called 'Every Day the Jewish Way' for the children of intermarried couples. It has been very successful and is widely imitated in other communities. Mrs Naomi Marks devised the programme. She was an articulate woman in her fifties.

I was born in Metropolis and I grew up on the West Side. I attended *Adath Israel* synagogue and was confirmed there. In high school when I started dating, I dated boys from the East Side as well as the West Side. Only Jewish boys, of course. The whole community did not question that. On one occasion in junior high school I was invited to a church Thanksgiving dance with a young man I was enamoured with. His father happened to be the clergy of the church, but his father had a fit and my parents had a fit. It was just not what was happening in those days.

I met my husband in kindergarten. We are the same age and we were very good friends in Sunday school. Then we began dating halfway through university and we married after we graduated. I studied Education at university. He was in medical school, and I supported him by teaching in elementary school. He eventually became an orthopaedic surgeon. We have three children, all girls, and a female dog. He is outnumbered! I worked on and off but primarily I was a mother.

In the late 1970s I decided to take some courses at the university School of Theology. The first one I took was with James Holland (*The Teacher of Interfaith Relations*). The classes were just fascinating. It was all very serendipitous, but I ended up with a Masters degree. Then I was taken on by the Centre for Judaic Studies and worked for Sam Kornfeld (*The University Professor of Judaica*). My title was 'Director of Culture' – it was one of Rabbi Kornfeld's projects. The Family Service wanted somebody to facilitate an interfaith support group, and I thought, 'That's what I should be doing!' I used to meet with interfaith couples to discuss the issues, and to talk about their feelings and to learn a little more about Judaism. What was the aim of the programme? When you are talking about programmes that the Jewish community is supporting, the interest is the maintenance of Judaism. I hope there is also concern about people as human beings. I only worked there for a year and they didn't have enough funding to continue.

At that time Robert Reinhardt (*The Reform Rabbi*) asked me to come and work at Temple to do support groups for interfaith couples. It's been eleven years now, and I'm still doing it. I see a great number of what I call 'ambivalent Jewish males', but sometimes people come because of parental pressure or the non-Jewish spouse wants to know more. They come for all sorts of reasons. The cost is minimal. Very often I hear from interfaith couples that all the Jewish community cares about is money, not about them. So I charge $36 for a ten-week course. Obviously it would be nice if these couples would eventually join the Temple, but there's never any kind of pressure. The aim is communication, and to learn a little bit about Judaism. I do communicate to them that I feel unequivocally that it is better for a child and for a whole family if there is a decision to raise a child in one religion. Whether one partner maintains her own religion but is supportive of the decision, or whether there is a conversion, there should be one religion for the child. Research shows that adults who are brought up between two worlds are caught in the middle and spend much of their adult lives trying to find out who they are.

After I'd been working here about a year, the Allied Jewish Federation (in response to a demographic study they had done showing intermarriage was way over 50 per cent) invited the community to set up programmes for the children of these marriages. Robert Reinhardt suggested a two-year, tuition-free course. I wrote the programme and it's called 'Every Day, the Jewish Way'. There was a lot of hassle from the Federation. The

Orthodox were not very pleased by it as you can imagine, but they did accept it, and it is a community programme. The more I think about it, the more amazing it is that we were able to do it. But we did.

I involved the teachers, the parents and the children, and everybody was invested in this programme. The first year we had about sixty children, and this number has been maintained. We do it Sunday afternoons in the Temple. We have five classes from kindergarten through high school. The smallest class is the high school, but it's the most amazing because these children have found us. They choose to spend Sunday afternoons here for a school year to find out who they are. I think that tells us a great deal. We have five teachers and a music teacher. The teachers meet every week after class to discuss what's happening, what worked, and what didn't work. Wonderful things developed. The parents do not necessarily feel positive about Judaism. I deal with a lot of angry people. They may be furious at Judaism; they may be furious at what has happened in their relationship; they may be furious at their in-laws; they may be furious at being told they can't have a Christmas tree – any number of things. They may be frightened, they may be angry, they may be fascinated – the whole gamut. The only expectation we have of parents is that they support their children. They must come to the parents' programmes, and they may not send their children to a Christian school at the same time they're in 'Every Day'.

What proportion of the children or their families do decide they want a Jewish identity? We are seeing approximately 60 per cent, but it doesn't always happen immediately after leaving the programme. Maybe three years later we run into them in the supermarket and hear about the *Bat Mitzvah* of the child. We didn't even know the family had joined a congregation. We've had families go into every mainstream congregation including *Adath Israel* and *Har HaShem*. In the parents' meetings, I encourage the rabbis from every branch of Judaism to come and talk about their kind of Judaism. And I encourage them to synagogue-hop and visit all the different services. We have done some follow-up and most become Reform.

In any of the liberal congregations these days there are many,

many interfaith families. I'm sure there's still some stigma – a feeling that converts aren't really Jewish, and there are certainly some insensitive teachers. They sometimes forget that even if the mother has converted, these children still have a whole bunch of the family that aren't Jewish and there has to be recognition and respect. When you see a conversion to Judaism, someone coming from a Christian background sees religion as God and church. I remember someone said, 'How can you convert to an ethnicity?' The convert's success depends on various factors. Are the in-laws accepting or rejecting? Is the congregation welcoming? There are a lot of ambivalent Jewish males both in Jewish-Jewish marriages and interfaith marriages.

Converts are often tremendously zealous about Judaism and put Jewish people to shame. I see all the time Jewish men who are fairly indifferent about their Judaism married to women who, at their husband's insistence, have converted and are spiritual persons. They want to find in Judaism what they found in Christianity. Why, therefore, is it the woman who converts rather than the man? I think there is such a deep-seated, ingrained feeling about Judaism and about the loss of ethnicity. The Jewish man will say he doesn't like organized religion, but he feels Jewish. The non-Jewish woman says, 'He doesn't go to synagogue, he doesn't go to Temple, but he says I have to be Jewish!' Very often the Jewish man comes from a more affluent family than the gentile woman and so the grandparents can put on the pressure. Then you are going to ask why Jewish women are not insisting on the conversion of their Christian husbands? In some cases, again, the economic circumstances play a part. The man has the money in a family and therefore also the power. Very often I hear Jewish women in mixed marriages say, 'I can't ask my husband for the money to join a synagogue.' The issues are so many and every family is different. It's so complicated . . .

What have I learnt from 'Every Day, the Jewish Way'? That people need tender, loving care. People need to be welcomed.

The Convinced Convert

MRS SOPHIE GINSBERG

She lived with her husband and two sons in a leafy

neighbourhood and, when we rang the doorbell, a friendly cocker spaniel could be seen bounding about on the other side of the glass. We were led to a spotless living room. There was a white rug on the parquet floor, mauve upholstery, and polished mahogany furniture. She was a petite, dark-haired woman in her late thirties. She sat upright on the sofa and spoke with animation and humour.

I am from Minneapolis, Minnesota, and I come from a big family. There were five of us in nine years so we were pretty close in age. I was raised Greek Orthodox, and growing up I was very involved in the church. We went to Greek school every Saturday and religion school every Sunday. There was only one Greek church in the city, and the youth group would meet there every Saturday evening. Through my childhood I went to Greek Orthodox camp in the summer, and all my good friends were from the Greek community. I was raised as an observant and religious person. I took all the sacraments. I guess it was more than a religion. It wasn't just 'you go to church on Sunday' – it was really part of your whole life. There was Greek food, Greek customs, and extended family . . .

After high school I went to college in Minneapolis. Through college I continued to be really close to the kids I had grown up with. I studied Physical Education. I met my husband when we were both interviewing a bunch of students who wanted to go abroad on exchange. A few months later we started dating. I was twenty at the time and he was twenty-five. So we dated for a year. He was raised a Reform Jew, very Reform: his mother had a Christmas tree at Christmas! Then he moved out to Metropolis. I came to visit a couple of times, and then we decided that I should move out here. We probably got married a year and a half after that.

What was the family reaction to our involvement? His parents were outwardly very happy we were dating. From what I hear, this was because of who he had dated previously! I come from a pretty demonstrative, caring family, and that appealed to them. It definitely appealed to him! My parents are very understanding, and they were very accepting. It was all very okay.

After we moved here and decided to get married, we decided together that I would convert to Judaism. I felt real strongly that whatever we did, it was important that we were both the same thing so that we had a value system we both agreed on. I knew that he wasn't going to be able to convert. I come from a much stronger religious background, but I had a much easier time taking what I believed and not having to change that a whole bit. If you're raised Greek Orthodox, you either believe in God or you don't believe in God. In our Church the Trinity wasn't all that important because there was so much else going on. It's the relationship with the Spiritual Being that makes everything okay. The Trinity isn't so much stressed, I guess. I was very spiritual and very observant, but if I chose to put that in another box that was all right.

My husband sees himself as a Jew, but he never would have converted. He's not a real spiritual person, and for him to convert to some other religion when he wasn't clear on his own beliefs . . . well, he'd never have done it. That's not to say he's not observant. He's very observant, but like a lot of Jews he's observant kind of by rote – not because of spiritual belief.

I went to like every synagogue in town before I made the decision. It was a really big deal for me, and I wanted to be sure wherever I converted I felt comfortable. The people at Temple *Shalom* were the most warm and open and caring – that always makes you feel good. The classes lasted for almost a year. I got to know the other converts, and that was interesting because everyone was there for a different reason. I don't know how many of them stayed in Judaism. I don't see any of them now . . . We learnt about the differences between the types of Judaism; we had a lot of books to read; we didn't have to do any Hebrew; we met with people who showed us how to do the blessings; and we learnt about the holidays. At the end, I met with Rabbi Reinhardt (*The Reform Rabbi*) one-to-one to talk about all my concerns.

When I was done, I went in there and said, 'Okay, I'm ready to convert. Let's set a date.' And he said, 'What makes you think you're ready?' And I started crying. I said, 'Why are you saying this? I went through this class. I gave up a year of my life making this decision.' And he said, 'I want to make sure you're ready to do this.' I was totally appalled, but he was very concerned. He knew what kind of family I had been raised in. He knew I was a spiritual person. And he wanted to make sure I had thought about it. Once I had convinced him, the fact that I had convinced him, convinced me. That, I think, was his tactic. I knew that I could be the person I was, but with, I guess, a different coat on.

A lot of people in my class were converting because they were marrying men who were Jewish only in the sense that they had a Jewish mother and went to a Jewish dentist. To me, that was the typical conversion couple. At that time there were very few men converting, and I don't think things have changed much. In fact, I only know two men who have converted. The women invariably came from a lower socio-economic stratum than the men. Yes, it does seem that way. It is a social advancement for the women. I think the key to whether the conversion 'works' is the attitude of the Jewish spouse, whether he wants it to work. A very common complaint I hear from the women is they can't get their husbands to celebrate the Sabbath at home, or take the day off on the High Holy Days. For them it's a real struggle!

I found the ritual bath very interesting. Growing up as a Greek Orthodox, there are so many things that are really bizarre that the Greeks do. I grew up in a religion where things were strange. So the ritual was real interesting to me. I went in and was instructed to wash my hair, cut my nails, all those sorts of things. The woman who was there was an older woman, and she basically threw you in there and scrubbed you down and kept telling you to go back in and scrub down some more. Then I went into the ritual bath and heard the three rabbis up there saying the blessings. Greek Orthodoxy was really a very good preparation. I said to Rabbi Reinhardt that I didn't know how people who are, say, Lutheran, convert to this religion because it must be so bizarre to them. For me that part of it was very easy. I could convert much more easily to Judaism than Methodism.

What has been my most difficult thing – especially recently – is I'd like to belong to a more Traditional synagogue. I don't think Reform Judaism offers much spirituality. I would love to go to Rabbi Berkovski (*The Hasidic Rabbi*). He is wonderful. I do find Temple *Shalom* very non-spiritual, and I do have a difficult time with that. All the sermons are social action or political. We don't talk about God. There are a million places in this city where I could hear about social action, but there aren't many places where I can get spirituality. The prayers are very rote. I want more about God. But we stayed with Temple because I wanted the kids to have a strong religious education.

The Temple became our family. We became involved with the Mr and Mrs Club, and we became the Presidents. That's probably where we met most of our friends. I've served on the Temple Board. I taught religion school one year. I was Head of the pre-school one year. My husband was Treasurer of the Board. We were real involved in Temple over the years. Then we sent our boys to the Golda Meir Day School. I was on the Board of that for six years and President for the last two. I've loved it.

There's a better effort to work converts into the congregation now. I converted eighteen years ago, and I really can honestly say I never felt alienated. Some people, because they're not educated, say things they don't mean. About three years ago, a woman whose kids go to school with my kids came up to me and said, 'I cannot believe you're not a Jew!' She just went on and on, not ever thinking it was insulting or offensive. It's just out of ignorance that people say things like that. I've never thought about it, but it probably helps that I look Jewish; I'm not blonde and blue-eyed . . . Off the top of my head I would say that about 40 per cent of Temple *Shalom* families today are either mixed marriages or conversion marriages . . .

The Lapsed Convert

MRS CHRISTINE JACOBS

Tall and fair, she sat in an armchair in the corner of her living room. The room was comfortable, furnished with old rugs, shelves of books and antique prints on the wall. Her husband was a successful ophthalmologist and the house showed evidence of both money and taste. She spoke bitterly.

Well, what can I say? I was never interested in Judaism in the first place. I converted because his parents made it a condition of our marriage. They said they'd disinherit him if I didn't. Joe and I met at college. He was older than me, but we liked each other and got involved as people do. I was vaguely aware that he was Jewish, but so what? I was raised a Presbyterian.

But when we announced we were going to get married, the balloon went up. Things were different then. It was twenty years ago. Intermarriage wasn't so common. His family insisted, absolutely insisted on a Jewish wedding. And if we were to have a Jewish wedding, then I had to convert. There was no option. To be fair, Joe found it as bewildering as I did. He knew nothing about Judaism. He'd had a *Bar Mitzvah* in Temple, but he'd simply learnt the reading from a tape recorder. But even if he knew nothing, I – as a convert – had to know everything!

To begin with, I went along with it. I wanted to please his folks. But it was a bummer from the start. I had an awful interview with the rabbi. Without exactly saying so, he made it quite clear he couldn't understand why a boy like Joe would want to get involved with a little tramp like me. My parents aren't rich and Joe was going to be a doctor; he deserved a Jewish girl. I mean, if I could have produced a Jewish mother out of the woodwork, then I'd have been welcomed with open arms, but as it was . . . Well, I'm afraid, the Jewish community wants its children to marry its own. There's a real racist edge to it.

Anyway, I went along to the weekly conversion class. I had to. The teacher – I'm sure she was a very nice lady – but she wasn't very bright. I was very wicked. I spent the whole time asking her questions which I knew she couldn't answer. But, of course, to some extent I had to toe the line. If I went too far she wouldn't give the word, and I wouldn't get the necessary certificate and then no marriage.

Every week we had to go to Temple. Poor Joe! It was a bit much. I felt so sorry for him. He'd never been before and if he'd found a nice Jewish girl, he wouldn't ever have had to sit through all those boring services . . . It was all so silly . . . and so different from what I was used to. I'm an agnostic, but my family's Presbyterian. And there, if any stranger comes to church, they're thrilled to have them: 'Come right in – have a cup of coffee!' But because of the accident of my birth, the Jews just didn't want me.

Anyway, at the end of the year, I had this real embarrassing conversion ceremony. Mercifully it was in private, and I insisted that Joe didn't come. I just felt so compromised. My conversion class teacher acted as a witness . . . poor old thing . . . beaming all over her face. I mean the difficulty was I didn't believe in God; still don't. Nor as far as I can see do many Jews. But, in order to get the certificate of approval, I was bullied into this hypocrisy. It was just so embarrassing. I had to stand in front of an open Ark and recite the *Shema*. Then, apparently, abracadabra I was *kosher*.

Actually it didn't work out quite like that. We may have had a Jewish wedding, but Joe's mother never accepted me. I don't exactly look Jewish, and apparently a convert is never the real McCoy. Whenever we visited, I always had to hear about the rich and beautiful girls he should have married. It was very tricky . . . She's dead now, but I saw her as little as I decently could when she was alive. I just couldn't understand her priorities; the whole thing was a mystery. She didn't know a thing about Judaism and, after all those classes, I did, but she was Jewish and I was a *shiksa* (non-Jewish girl) and that was the end of the matter. And it's been a difficulty in our marriage. Joe has always felt guilty at pushing me into something that was so against my integrity. It's something we never talk about, something we prefer to forget.

After we were married, that was the end of that . . . Well, actually, it wasn't. Another condition of marriage in Temple is that you have to take out a year's membership. We didn't have much money at the beginning, and that was one thing I did rebel about. I said that I really thought his parents should pay the $500. They were loaded and we weren't going to get any benefit from membership. But in the end, we paid up: anything for peace.

Our kids? Yes, we have two boys. We're not bringing them up in any religion. They can decide for themselves when they're old enough. Actually, yes, this is a problem. I didn't want them circumcised. I thought about it a lot. I thought maybe it was because I was prejudiced, because of my unhappy experience with the Temple. But I talked to the paediatrician and he said it wasn't good for babies to be circumcised. It was traumatic for them. But in the end, we had it done. My parents-in-law would have had a heart attack if we hadn't. I did refuse to have a ceremony. It was just done in hospital by a surgeon like a normal operation. As Joe says, at least it'll give them the option to be Jewish if that's what they want, though neither show any sign of it yet.

I'm sorry. I don't think I've been much help to you. It was all a long time ago now. I wish I had something more positive to tell you. It was a miserable experience from first to last . . .

The Marrano

DR MANASSEH GARCIA

After the Inquisition many Spanish Jews pretended to be Roman Catholic while secretly retaining their Jewish faith. Dr Garcia maintained his office in a Hispanic area of Metropolis. He was of medium height with dark olive skin. Underneath his trousers he wore cowboy boots and on his finger was a college ring engraved with a Star of David.

My mother's mother's last name was Relles, which is a Hebrew name. In 1492 in the great expulsion, when the Jews were expelled from Spain, her family went to Turkey. For some reason that my mother didn't know, they didn't last in Turkey. They stayed a few years and then they went to the New World, to Mexico City. They did well for a time in Mexico City, for fifty or so years. Then the Inquisition came and I have a record of one of my ancestors being burnt at the stake in 1574. He was accused of blasphemy, and the other charge was of 'Judaizing'. He was a pharmacist. There was a lot of chaos at that time, and my family fled to a northern region of Mexico. They changed their name to de los Reyas to make it more Spanish-sounding, but they never became Catholics. They never did.

My grandparents had a liquor business. My grandfather was doing business from Mexico City right up to Wyoming. He was a very shrewd businessman, and as Jews they kept out of politics. Then there was this revolution in Mexico, and my grandparents ended up living in this country for a few years. They were Jews, but they didn't know anything about religion. My grandmother had learnt the Sabbath blessing from her mother, and she said it every Friday night. My mother could remember her mother reciting these strange words. They also never ate pork. After the revolution my grandfather went back to Mexico, and he died in an accident. We don't know what happened to my grandmother.

My mother's brothers and sisters grew up in orphanages in the States while my mother was raised with her aunt in Mexico. My mother married my father in Mexico. My father was a Mexican Catholic. They came to Metropolis in 1954 when she got back together with her brothers and sisters. By that time they had three children – all boys; I was the eldest. All the family had Hebrew names. I was called Manasseh, and when I was a kid I used to wonder why I had such a strange name. My mother always used to say, 'In Hebrew there's a saying about Ephraim and Manasseh. I remember learning that from your grandmother.'

Growing up as a child I would see my mother on the Sabbath lighting the candles and saying this strange prayer. I would say, 'Mom, why are you doing this?' And she would say, 'I don't know, but your grandmother told me to do it every Friday at sunset.' She did know it was Hebrew. There were other things. In every Mexican home they eat green chilli, and in 99.9 per cent of Mexican homes the green chilli is with pork; in our home it was with beef. She made tamales with beef. She used to say, 'You kids, don't eat pork.'

I grew up in North-East Metropolis and every Hispanic family was Catholic – except us. When I was a child, my father did try to get us to the Sacred Heart Church. I remember my mother telling him, 'My children will never go to your hypocritical Catholic Church. You can go but my children will never go!' She had a deep hatred for Catholicism. All I ever knew was I was a Jew. I remember, as a kid, she wouldn't let me go to church with my friends – she would say, 'You children are Jews!' I didn't even know what being a Jew was. She had a small business downtown. She sold a lot of religious icons, the Virgin of this and that. I asked her, 'Mom, if you don't like the Church, how come you sell all these Virgins and crosses?' And she would say, 'Because they buy 'em and it's business!'

Some of the negatives I remember. As a little kid, whenever I had a fight or a disagreement, it came down to 'Goddamn Jew . . . My mother says your mother prays to the Devil . . . Jews killed Jesus . . . You guys have horns.' I'd be very hurt, because I didn't have horns! I'd go to my mother and ask why they said that about us, and she would say, 'Because they're crazy!' Another difference between my home and those of other Hispanic kids was we had books. My mother taught me that her family were either merchants or doctors. She told me that she wanted me to be either a lawyer or a doctor. She'd bring in books on law and on science. I remember, as a young kid in the seventh grade, all my Hispanic classmates would tease me and call me 'Scientist'. They wanted to work for the Post Office, or the city, or the rubber factory. I would say, 'I'm going to be a doctor!' and they would laugh.

I got married young and was already starting to raise a family when I graduated high school. So I went to the State Community College. I believe my wife's family is also Jewish in origin. She doesn't know, but her family also didn't like Catholics. We were married by a judge. I was working forty hours a week, and at the same time took a degree in Psychology. Then I went to the University of Iowa to get my pre-med requirement. I was still working full-time and so was my wife. I wanted to be a dentist. It took me six years to get an undergraduate degree. Then I took a year off. The pre-med took two and a half years, and the dentistry and the residency took another five years. Then I came back to Metropolis and started my practice here.

My mother and I were very close, we had a special bond. She would pull me aside and tell me little folklore things which I now know are Jewish. I didn't know it then. I'll give you an example: She told me about the *ojo*, which is when an adult and baby are really attracted to one another and kind of hypnotize each other with the evil eye. That's folklore from the Jewish mystical tradition.

Then there was another thing. When I was at dental school, my mother got ill and was found to have a trichinosis worm within her body. You get that from eating pork and I couldn't understand it. She didn't eat pork. She said, 'When I was young there were things we had to do which we didn't like, but we had to do them to survive. As Jews in Mexico, the government and the Catholic Church were one and the same. At times we had to act like we were Catholics,' and she started crying. And I thought, 'No wonder she hates the Catholic Church!' I asked why we weren't brought up as Jews. She said that all she knew about was what she had learnt from her mother and that wasn't much. I pointed out there were Jews in Metropolis and she said, 'They won't accept you because you're a Mexican.'

About three years after I qualified, she died. By that time my father had taken over pretty much, and my younger siblings were going to the Catholic church. All of a sudden we had Christmas trees, and I resented that. It was not what Mother wanted. After her death, I went into a period of deep depression – I even contemplated suicide. My mother and I had an extraordinary bond and when she died, I died. I always remembered her saying, 'Don't ever forget you are a Jew! Promise me that!'

Then one day I called up one of my Jewish dental colleagues and I told him I was a Jew. I told him I wanted to learn more about it and he suggested I go to Temple *Shalom*. There was a class there for Jews who had intermarried with non-Jews. So I enrolled in this course. It was a phenomenal class! It opened my eyes. A lot of things I was learning I remembered from my mother. It was something I knew, but I didn't know. Rabbi Reinhardt (*The Reform Rabbi*) was there, and Rabbi Acker (*The Administrator of a Dating File*) and Rabbi Fox (*The Woman Rabbi*). Phenomenal people! Beautiful people! I loved it! I turned into a super-Jew! I would have converted, but I didn't have to. I was a Jew!

I belong to *Har HaShem* synagogue now with Rabbi Kornfeld (*The University Professor of Judaica*). I liked the Traditional. I liked wearing a *yarmulke* (skull cap) and *tallis* (prayer shawl). I think it's beautiful. I liked Temple *Shalom* too, but it was street-clothes! That's okay, but I prefer the other. My mother was wrong – I was accepted completely, but my mother had always tried to protect me. You see we were very poor – it might have been different if we had been rich Jews like in Mexico City.

I've been studying some background. My own children didn't have any religious training because, when they were young, I didn't know about it. My daughter's husband is a Rodriguez; their family comes from the same area as mine, and I believe they were Jews too. Both my daughter and her husband were anxious to know more. Yeah, I want to raise my grandchildren as Jews . . .

The Roman Catholic

DR JESSICA AMENDOLA

We found Dr Amendola in her small house behind State Street, where she lived with her cat. She was a small, dark, bespectacled woman in her late thirties. She wore a gold cross around her neck. In the bookcase was a Catholic Study Bible *as well as a copy of The* World of Our Fathers. *There was a statue of the Madonna on the windowsill, and a framed calligraphy of the Creed on the wall.*

I grew up in Philadelphia. My parents were first-generation born in this country. My mother's family were Orthodox Jews from Austria/Poland – some of her family were lost in the ghetto uprising and in the concentration camps. My mother could not talk about that. My father was an Italian Catholic. My mother claimed that she didn't know he wasn't Jewish until they were engaged – which doesn't make much sense to me. I don't buy that story! Anyway my father converted to Judaism and was circumcised at the age of thirty. He was hospitalized. Her family was very upset. Even though my father studied for a year and everything was totally *kosher*, none of them would go to the wedding. Having said that, even though we had the smallest quarters it was my father who opened up his home to his mother-in-law when she grew too old to live on her own. At that point, my mother's family started accepting him. My father's family were accepting of the marriage from the start. My Catholic grandmother said, 'There's only one God', and she accepted my mother right away.

Why was it my father who converted? I asked that question.

In Italian families the father is out working. So my father figured he wanted unity of the family and Judaism would be passed along by the mother. The problem was Judaism is a patriarchal religion, and in my mother's day girls had very little religious education. So there was a little misunderstanding there. But my father continued to study Judaism, and he was a very committed Jew. he studied Hebrew, and when they had me, as I knew more, he wanted to know more. I was an only child.

I was educated through the public schools, but I went to religion school from the age of four or five. I was brought to the synagogue every Friday night by my parents and every Saturday morning by my grandmother. It was a Conservative synagogue, but more Orthodox than the Conservative is now. We kept *kosher* at home. They would eat out, and I can remember my mother ordering *tref* (non-*kosher* food). I was more religious than that and would challenge her. She thought I was a fanatic, but at home the rabbi could have eaten at our house. I didn't have a *Bat Mitzvah* because, according to my mother's Orthodox beliefs, girls didn't have *Bat Mitzvahs.* I was confirmed.

I should tell you that as a child with an Italian last name, there were Jews who felt I wasn't Jewish. Even rabbis used to ask me, 'Do you feel you're not completely Jewish?' It was an extremely ignorant question, because even if my father hadn't converted (which he did), you're Jewish if your mother is Jewish. It was absolutely ridiculous. And sometimes I did feel not Jewish because they as a community made me feel that way. Certainly I was more drawn to my Catholic cousins than my Jewish ones, and when my mother noticed this I wasn't allowed to be with them so much. My father believed in keeping peace, and to keep peace he would just do whatever she asked.

I went to the Conservative Jewish summer camp. Yes, I can read Hebrew. I studied the Bible and Rashi's commentary. I went for two hours every day after school and every Sunday morning. While I was in high school I was also going to Graetz Jewish High School, and I had scholarships along the way. I went for one year to college in Philadelphia to study pharmacy, but then I left for Israel. I went for six months and ended up staying five years. I went really to get away from pharmacy. I didn't think it was for me, but I had gotten a scholarship and you didn't refuse that. It was an honour. But I couldn't imagine being a pharmacist so I went to Israel and stayed. At that point my parents disowned me. They didn't want me to stay in Israel. They wrote me a letter saying I'd never make anything of myself; America is the country to be in. This was a Jewish family who was Zionistic! My mother was a member of Hadassah (the women's Zionist organization)! I tried to be reconciled. I went back and visited them, but I wasn't welcome. My mother's reaction was, 'Didn't I ever teach you not to go where you are not invited . . .' I lived on an Orthodox *kibbutz*, and I wound up going to Bar Ilan University to study Education. Then, when I was twenty-two, I came back to the States to get a Doctorate at Columbia University in New York. Luckily I went with teaching credentials because I had to teach full-time to support myself.

While I was in New York I got involved with the Overeaters Anonymous programme. As a child I was chubby but my overeating was largely due to a dysfunctional mom. She preached one thing and did another. I had to sit by myself in the school lunchroom and put a napkin on the table in case other people's crumbs got mixed in with my *kosher* food. Yet she would eat *tref* (non-*kosher* food) out. Food was always a problem. I wasn't allowed to go to friends' birthday parties because the food wasn't *kosher*, but I knew what she did. We couldn't engage in any conversation which had to do with her personally. Yes, I had quarrels with her – some typical mother/daughter stuff and some about her hypocrisy, saying one thing and doing another, which really got to me.

When years later I went to California, after I got my Doctorate, I realized how Christian the Overeaters Anonymous programme was. It was based on unconditional love, unconditional acceptance of the members of the group, and a personal relationship with a Higher Power. The Higher Power can be anything, even a plant; they don't define it. I realized suddenly that as an Orthodox Jew, even though I prayed every day, I had never had a relationship with God. I only developed that relationship through the programme. At the group sessions people can tell their stories without the fear of rejection. It's a very warm, caring group of people. In Judaism, God seemed to be the God of wrath, the God of punishment. He looked down on you; He saw everything you did – according to my mother, He saw every morsel you ate! He was not a loving God at all; He was a judgemental God – and you'd better do what He wanted . . .

My spiritual awakening came over time, it happened in stages. Early on my mother noticed that I preferred my Catholic family to my Jewish family. Then when I first stepped on Israeli soil, my first thought was, 'Jesus walked here.' I'd never learnt anything about Jesus, but that was my first thought. Then in the Overeaters Anonymous programme it was my relationship with God – with the 'Higher Power' – that stopped me from taking that first bite and helped me gain control of my weight. I realized I could never find what I had in the programme in a synagogue. So in the late 1970s, early 1980s, I stopped keeping *kosher* and going to synagogue. I was totally involved in the programme, and my values were no longer Jewish values. I was single, and Judaism was a family religion. I wasn't married; I wasn't giving my parents grandchildren. The whole thing had become a guilt trip. In fact, I feel like a completed Jew. I don't hate Judaism. The Catholic laws on sex and marriage, abortion and birth control, are very similar to the Jewish laws. It wasn't like closing a door. It was a gradual realization that my relationship with God through the programme was like my Catholic cousins' relationship with God.

I taught Special Education in California for several years. Then, when I was reading the educational journals and I realized I liked what was going on in education in this state, I moved to Metropolis. People said, 'You'll never get a job!' I got a job in two weeks, and that was four years ago.

The second Christmas I was here I went to Mass with some friends, and that night I decided it was time to become a Christian. I was living Christianity anyway. I started going to classes immediately in January, and I continued for over a year. And I was baptized two Easters after. They were mostly Protestants in the class who wanted to marry Catholics. I was the only Jew. I'm much happier. I finally feel I belong. I always prayed to be part of a larger family, and I've got very involved with the church in all sorts of projects. Catholics want to get back to their roots. I always thought I had better hide my Judaism, but it's very special to the Church that I was a Jew – very precious. I'm asked to speak; I've conducted Passover *seders*; I've read the Old Testament in Hebrew. When I was baptized I thought no one would be there because I had no family. After the service there were seventy gifts waiting for me there at the reception. You see, the Church was there waiting for me.

I did tell my parents I converted. My parish priest insisted I wrote so they'd know. He wrote a covering letter. Basically I told my parents that I learnt a lot from them. They were very active in the synagogue, just as I was very active in the parish. I was very much who they were. My father was on a spiritual journey all his life, and I was on a spiritual journey all my life. I mentioned all the good I have received from them, and I gave them the blessing. The priest was so sure we would hear from them, but no . . . they never wrote back.

The Krishna Devotee

MRS RUTMINI DASI

Krishna Consciousness, commonly known as the Hare Krishna movement, is an ancient monotheistic devotional tradition within Hinduism. Rutmini Dasi was a beautiful woman of forty with a long plait of dark hair, olive skin, and an aquiline nose. She wore a grey and maroon sari and had a gold bracelet on her wrist. We interviewed her in her house just across the street from the Krishna Consciousness Temple. The bookcase was full of Hindu books, and on the coffee-table were copies of the Atlantic Magazine *and an illustrated volume entitled* Light of the Bhagavata. *Next to her, sitting in a rocking chair, was her husband. He was a blond American, but was also wearing Eastern clothing.*

I was born in Chicago and was raised in Highland Park, a suburb of Chicago. My name used to be Wendy Weiser. I think I was always more religious than anyone in my family. They were very Reform, to the point of being almost secular Jews. I think my mother was just never really very religious. She enjoyed the religion school because of the arts and crafts – making *dreidels* (Purim spinning tops) and all that kind of thing! I was the one who wanted to go to Hebrew school. I was the one who wanted to go to a very religious Jewish camp, and my parents couldn't understand why. I think I was always on the search from the time I was very young. I didn't want to become a doctor or a lawyer or a housewife. I wanted to find God. I recall sitting in the window of my house and watching people go to work and thinking, 'Why are they working so hard? What's the meaning of just living and working and dying?' I was always looking for meaning.

I went to high school in Highland Park and actually joined Krishna Consciousness when I was sixteen. As time went on, I was becoming more and more the rebel and was becoming interested in Eastern thought. I was always reading. I'm really following the path of *Bhakti,* which means to link with God in devotion. I think my first experience of *Bhakti* was at the religious camp I mentioned. There was a rabbi there – a wonderful man – who really had the *Bhakti* spirit. There was something in this man very different from anything I'd ever met. He was full of joy and was obviously experiencing something. But apart from him, I found people's expression of religion to be superficial. It was based on social life, and the answers given were very savvy, cute little answers. For example, I've recently come across a book by a rabbi called *I'd Like to Call God But I Don't Know the Number.* That's just a trendy, socially correct way of saying, 'I don't know the answer; let's all be cute about it!' But I was looking for very genuine answers.

I don't mean to be so arrogant as to say these answers aren't in Judaism, because I believe they are. It's just very difficult for many Jewish people to find those answers. Just speaking from my experience, I think that the knowledge is there, but it is being kept very cloistered and esoteric. Yet people long for that knowledge. I know I did. People's lives are prosaic, but we are spiritual beings. People long for spiritual satisfaction. A very close friend was telling me that when she was a little girl she went to her synagogue religion school. She had a teacher who said in one of the classes, 'There is a God, but we will never know Him; we will never see Him; we will never experience

Him,' and she thought, 'What am I doing here? I'd rather watch cartoons on a Saturday morning!' She really checked out of Judaism at that point. She was eight or nine years old, and she checked out. She is one of my God-sisters; she is also a Krishna devotee.

When did I check out of Judaism? I don't know. I don't think in that way. My mind and body will probably always be Jewish. There will always be a Jewish part of me. But I am a spirit-soul, and the knowledge of *Bhakti* has been very fulfilling. I feel my identity with this tradition predates my identity with Judaism. I feel it very strongly. It all clicked when I first went to India. Everything made sense to me, whereas Highland Park didn't make sense to me.

What I did was to check out of suburbia; I left home. I was reading all these books, and I felt I had to get out of the superficial world of suburbia and see what the real world was like. I more or less ran away from home. I was fifteen. I guess I was part of the hippy experience. This was in 1967. I had friends in Chicago, and I was living with them. My parents were looking all over for me, and after a couple of weeks I came home and said, 'Look, I've left.' They were the Dr Spock generation and they thought, 'Well, let her go through it.' I have a younger sister and a younger brother, and I think my brother still doesn't really forgive me for breaking the family traditions. He's a doctor; he went to Harvard.

Anyway I wanted to see what the real nitty-gritty scene was. I like to sing, and one teacher had told me that my voice would improve once I had suffered. So I really wanted to suffer. I was reading a lot of existential authors so I delved into that world. I went with some friends to Los Angeles, and I stayed behind there while these friends went to San Francisco to a Hare Krishna festival. There were loads of books in the house and I was reading everything, but nothing was right. I was beginning to feel frustrated. On the coffee-table was a magazine, and I was avoiding this magazine all weekend because I thought the art work was really trite on the front. I was purposely avoiding it, but finally picked it up. It was published by the Hare Krishna society. There was a real experience of *Bhakti* which I could see from reading this magazine. The spirit was there. I looked at the address on the magazine and I thought, 'I've got to go and find these people.'

When my friends came back from their trip they said, 'These people are just awful: they're down on drugs; they're down on sex; they're down on everything!' In spite of this I went to find the Temple in San Francisco. I could see it was right for me; it was like coming home; everything clicked. All the questions I had that no one had ever been able to answer were answered. Questions about the soul, about the nature of consciousness, about death, about *karma*, about evil in the world. The philosophy of *karma* answers the question of evil in a profound way – accepting responsibilities for one's actions instead of condemning God as cruel. Or maybe He's basically good but just a little bit inept, as Rabbi Kushner suggests in his book (*Why Do Bad Things Happen to Good People?*).

So I went with some other devotees to Montreal and I was initiated there. Then I went to live in the Temple in Boston. As a matter of fact, my father came to my initiation. I've always been in touch with my parents. They thought it was a phase. I played the violin, I played the clarinet; I was into this, I was into that. They didn't know that this wasn't just another phase. They're really very open-minded people. I think it probably would have been a mistake if they had tried to stop me. I was going to do what I was going to do. My parents would have preferred me to be selling real estate, or be the President of General Motors, but they can see that we have a very full life and we are doing something to make the world a better place. I think my mother has a little bit of pride that we're not materialistic, and we're not in the grind.

I have to say that my parents were approached by 'friends' offering the services of deprogrammers. It never went far with me. There is one woman here in the community whose parents spent thousands and thousands of dollars to get her out of this religion that they didn't understand. It was very sad. Twenty years later the woman is still a Hare Krishna devotee, but her relationship with her family is irreparably damaged. I think my relationship with my parents is stronger than that. Even though they are not religious themselves, they respect my right to do what I believe in. I'm in touch with them all the time.

Every year they come here, and we go there.

The religious quest probably becomes perfect when you realize yourself fully as an eternal soul and servant of God. I'm just a neophyte, but I'm definitely walking on the path. We had an interesting experience recently. We went to a meeting to hear a rabbi who was advertised as a 'famous cult-buster'. We thought they were probably talking about us so we thought we should go. It was being held at *Har HaShem* synagogue. We went in Western dress and we sat in the back; we didn't want to cause any trouble. The rabbi began to speak, and he actually had a very beautiful and profound religious understanding. We were quite inspired by hearing him speak. In a nutshell he said that if you want your children to remain Jews, then you have to teach them Judaism and be a Jew. In my terminology, he had a real *Bhakti* spirit. Maybe if he had known we were Hare Krishna, he would have been less hospitable!

He told a story. Right after World War Two there were these missing persons' camps in Europe. A group of rabbis felt some of the children in these camps were Jewish, and they had the right to raise them as Jews. The Catholic Church was going to allow these rabbis to take these children if they could establish they were Jewish. So they had to come up real quick with something that would distinguish these kids. So what they did was they started to recite the *Shema* prayer in Hebrew: *'Shema Israel, Adonai Eloheynu, Adonai Ehad'* (Hear O Israel, the Lord our God, the Lord is One). Those kids who picked up on it and began to recite it with them were Jews. That was an interesting story. I think I would have been one of the kids to say it also. It is there in me. Personally I don't really feel that God is going to mind if you worship Him by bowing down, or standing up, or calling Him one name or another. The point is to call God. I think that is the main purpose of life. To call Him, not just to say something cute like, 'I'd like to call, but I don't know the number.'

The Pastor of the Messianic Jews

PASTOR JAKE STERN

The Messianic Jews are Jews who have accepted Yeshua (Jesus) as

their saviour. Congregation Ruah HaMashiah was in South Metropolis in an industrial area. It was a converted warehouse and consisted of offices, classrooms, storage, and a large sanctuary. The sanctuary had an Ark in the eastern wall which, as in a synagogue, contained a Torah *scroll. There was a purple curtain with an embroidered Star of David hanging in front of the Ark. In the storage area of the building a group of congregants were packing food parcels for the Metropolis Russian Jews, and several of the men wore yarmulkes and fringes.*

We spoke to Pastor Stern in a small office. The bookcases were full with Old Testament theology, a Talmud, *Hebrew prayerbooks, and a dictionary of Yiddish slang. On the wall was a large photograph of the Wailing Wall. Pastor Jake Stern himself was a large, curly-haired man in his forties. His hair and beard were light brown, and he wore a yellow sports shirt.*

I was born in Metropolis and I grew up in Summertown, fifty miles from here. I was adopted and grew up in a Conservative home and was very active in the Jewish community. At the age of twelve I wanted to be a rabbi, and my parents sent me to the Jewish academy in Chicago for a while. That's sort of a modern Orthodox school. I found I didn't have a good enough background in terms of Jewish studies, growing up in a small town, and I didn't have the proficiency in Hebrew that most of the students had. Many had already studied *Talmud*, and it was very difficult. I stood it for about a month or two and then I came back to carry on with my formal education in Summertown.

I was still very involved with the synagogue. We didn't have a rabbi, and I was pretty much responsible for running services and being the Sabbath school administrator. I always had a love of Judaism, but when I came back from Chicago one of my teachers took an interest in me. She was a Christian and she asked me what the Jewish people believed about the Messiah. I told her it was something we really didn't talk about much. It was something that was sort of put on the side. I talked to her, and we maintained contact for many years. She sent me literature, that kind of thing, but I was still very, very tied to Judaism. As I say, she maintained the friendship and, as we say in Christian circles, she prayed for my salvation for twenty-five years or more.

I went on to graduate school – I have a Masters in Social Work, and I worked for Summertown county in the Division of Child Welfare for many years. All these years I was active in the synagogue, but after a lot of reading, a lot of study, in 1983 I professed my belief in Yeshua. I just prayed that if it was true, God should show me the truth of it. Even today – I believe the same things as Christians, but I don't want to be called a Christian. I'm still Jewish. All our Jewish believers here believe we are fully Jewish, even though the rabbinic community may disagree with that. It's unfortunate the rabbinic community is so negative towards the Messianic community at this point, but I can understand that. In the name of Christianity, our people have been persecuted – Holocaust, pogroms, all the things through history, Inquisition: all in the name of Christ. But I don't believe the people who did that fully understood the teachings of Yeshua or of Rav Shaul (the apostle Paul). That's why our congregation prefers to be called Messianic Jews. The gentiles of the congregation – and we do have gentiles – are not Messianic Jews, they're Messianic gentiles; but we're all considered one group of believers.

It isn't just an intellectual thing. You know you can call on God through Yeshua. It is a personal relationship to know that He works in your life. But it was a real struggle. There I was: I was President of Temple Micah, Summertown; I was reading the religious services; I was really observant – not like a *Hasidic* Jew – but to the extent that I could. But I needed some more, and I prayed. And afterwards I felt I must surrender my will to Yeshua; He was my *kippur*, my atonement. About six months before I made my profession of faith they asked me to serve another term as President of the Temple, and I said, 'No, there are some other things in my life . . .' But I was still advisor to the Board.

Anyway, I was introduced to one of the elders of this congregation. He was a Holocaust survivor from Poland. He was in Israel in the War of Independence. He has a very interesting history, and was one of the founding elders here about fifteen years ago. And this elder said I didn't have to give up being Jewish. I could keep the Sabbath; if I wanted to keep *kosher*, there was nothing wrong with keeping *kosher*. He asked me to come up and visit the congregation, so I came to a Sabbath service. Here were people who were praising Yeshua, and they were reading from the *Torah* as in any other *shul* (synagogue). I realized I could accept Yeshua without giving up my Jewish identity. In fact, that's one thing the rabbinic community fails to understand. I've heard this accusation: Hitler tried to kill our people physically; what you Messianic Jews are doing is trying to kill our people spiritually. It's not true. I'd never tell a Jewish person to give up their Jewish identity. That's the last thing I'd want to do!

About six months after I came to make a public profession of my faith, I lost my job – I got an unsatisfactory rating. It was a personality clash with my supervisor. I would no longer party with my staff, drink a little booze, smoke a little marijuana. I was told I'd become a religious fanatic; I couldn't let my hair down. The upshot of it was, I was terminated from this job. As I look back on it, I think God didn't want me in that position any longer. For two years the Lord put me through some real tough times to test my faith. The Jewish community said, 'The reason he left Judaism was because when he lost his job, the churches were helping him financially.' I don't deny we were getting some help – food baskets and things – and that wasn't easy. But over two years, the Lord was preparing me. At the end of that time I was asked to become a pastor of a small congregation in a small town upstate, and then three and a half years later I was asked to be an assistant here in Metropolis – I've been here two years now.

About 400 people come here every week. They're not all members; we get a lot of visitors. I have a Masters in Social Work, so I do all the counselling. I prepare our young people for *Bar* and *Bat Mitzvah*. We keep all the festivals – *Rosh Ha-Shannah, Yom Kippur, Sukkot, Hanukkah, Purim* . . . The Jewish community won't provide a rabbi for circumcision, but we get it done as a surgical operation. That's only for the Jewish believers. There's no need for gentile believers to be circumcised. We have our own *mikveh* (ritual bath) here – that's what we call baptism. It's just a hot tub; I wish it was better. We believe in the deity of Yeshua. Yes, we believe in the virgin birth. We keep biblical prohibitions on food – no pork, for example – but we don't separate *fleshig* and *milchig* (meat and milk). We only keep to rabbinical practices if they conform with Scripture. We do keep the festival *Hanukkah*, which is rabbinic. We don't keep Christmas or Easter: they're pagan festivals. We celebrate Yeshua's resurrection as the First Fruits. Paul says that the Messiah is the first fruit of resurrection. The gentile believers may celebrate Christmas or Easter in their own homes – that depends on their background. Certainly as a congregation we discourage them from having Christmas trees; we think that's a pagan tradition.

Yes, we do want to draw other Jews into Messianic Judaism. We're often told we're deceptive – we're kind of Jewish as a front, but really we're Christians. Okay, I can understand that. There has been this schism between the Church and the Synagogue for the last 2,000 years. But Yeshua is very clear: 'Go into the world and preach the Gospel.' So if we're to follow the New Covenant, it's imperative that we do preach the Gospel, the good news. It's a controversial issue what we call our leaders. I have no *semihah* (rabbinic ordination) from a rabbinical *yeshiva* (talmudic academy). I don't pretend I do. I might call myself a Messianic rabbi, but because there's such opposition to us in the Jewish community, I don't really like to do it. My business card calls me a Messianic rabbi. That's how they printed it up, but usually I go by 'Messianic pastor'. But then the Jews say, 'You call yourself a pastor! You can't be Jewish! You must be a *goy* (gentile)!'

I am not a member of the Metropolis Rabbinical Association. The Metropolis Rabbinical Association would just as soon that we weren't even here. I know Rabbi Kornfeld (*The University Professor of Judaica*). I've worshipped in his synagogue before I became a believer; he knows me. A friend of mine went to him for *Shabbos* services and he said, 'Rabbi, you've got a great congregation, but there's something you don't have.' And Rabbi Kornfeld was stringing him along and said, 'What do you mean? We have a youth ministry, a senior ministry, whatever you want.' And my friend said, 'You don't have Yeshua!' You know what Kornfeld did? He referred him to that elder I was telling you about. But generally the Rabbinical Association doesn't like us, and to be honest, nor do some of the established Churches. We get as much opposition to our faith from the mainline Churches as from the rabbinic community. They've taken the position we're neither Jews nor Christians: if we were Jews we wouldn't pretend to be Christians, and if we were Christians, then we wouldn't pretend to be Jews. It's amazing. We seem to be caught between a rock and a hard place . . .

The Director of an Anti-Cult Organization

DR PAUL KARLIN

The new religions are making a significant number of converts among young Jewish people. When we met him, Paul Karlin was wearing denim shorts and a T-shirt with the logo 'Know Yourself' in Hebrew. He was a tall, attractive man in his forties. We sat on the porch of his house in South Metropolis drinking mandarin tea while a squirrel overhead pelted us with small bits of bark. He was anxious to conduct the interview before the Sabbath began. Behind us the front door of his small house was open. There was a woodburning stove, and a wonderful patchwork quilt given to him by a grateful patient.

I was brought up in a Conservative home in Boston, but we were not very observant. I was brought up in the 1950s, which was a period of rapid assimilation. That was the goal: there was more assimilation than Judaism. My particular experience of Judaism was in a synagogue where I was uncomfortable; it was very much a social thing, there was very little spirituality – women would come and show their fashions, that sort of thing. I left after my *Bar Mitzvah*, never to return to a synagogue for eighteen years.

In college in the late 1960s I involved myself very heavily in the Left movement. I was an activist; a leader of marches, demonstrations, organizations. Someplace there's an FBI file on me that is 400 pages long! But the answers the Left offered were not satisfying, and as I got older I asked more and different questions. I played around with Eastern philosophies, transcendental meditation – that type of thing. It wasn't very practical; the answers were too ethereal. In my political days, when I was asked my religion I used to say, 'I was born Jewish, but I didn't like the programme, and I wouldn't vote for it!'

When I came to Metropolis, just on a fluke one day I ended up on an urge going to Temple *Shalom*. I walked in, hoping to find something, and what I found was absolutely first-cousin to what I had left behind in Boston. It was another two years before I went anywhere else again. But gradually I worked my way back in. I went to Israel several years ago, and that was a very peak experience for me. I had a tremendous feeling of having come home. I joined the Reconstructionists, but actually I worship in Rabbi Berkovski's (*The Hasidic Rabbi*) synagogue.

When I came back to Judaism, I wanted to give something back because I had got, and am getting, a great deal from my involvement in Judaism. I applied my past political thinking to the whole question of cults, and especially the Hebrew Christians and the Jews for Jesus. I analysed it from a political perspective and saw that it had many similarities to the way the Left groups and sub-groups would operate. Since I had experienced that, I figured out I could work out a way to combat it. A few people in the community said, 'Go ahead! Why don't you organize something! We'll back you up!' Most of the support really has come from the Orthodox. Rabbi Berkovski's group has been the single most helpful group. He's wonderful at understanding situations. But all the Jewish leadership were concerned.

No one close to me had ever joined a cult, but I had been approached by some of them. *Ruah HaMashiah* – the so-called 'Messianic Temple' here in Metropolis – was one. Yes, I do know Jake Stern (*The Pastor of the Messianic Jews*). The Moonies are not particularly big around here; the Hare Krishnas are more significant. The so-called 'Messianic' movement is the one that specifically targets the Jewish community. The Hare Krishnas are meant to have 30 per cent Jewish members, but they do that without concentrating on the Jews.

The thing that is even worse about the 'Messianic Jews' – not only do they target the Jews, they are extremely deceptive. At the core of their theology is their belief that Jesus was God, but they won't tell you that straightaway. They only say He is the

Messiah. I have to say that at one point, I myself was as open to Christianity as I was to Judaism. It is in our background as Jews to argue and question. The *Talmud* itself is a debating forum. For Christianity, the ultimate virtue is faith; but for a Jew, reason, logic, knowledge are all much more important. So Jews are always questioning and looking for things, and that's why they're open to the cults.

So first of all, our programme is based on that of the other counter-cult organizations. Sometimes people are referred to us by a rabbi; sometimes the 'Messianic Jews' themselves want to study Judaism from an authentic source; sometimes people see our advertisements and come to us. We are not deprogrammers; we do not kidnap people, or do those dramatic things you may see on television. We just counsel and work with people. As the psychologists say, if a person doesn't want to change, there is no way to change them – it's all very voluntary. I also speak to groups such as the Synagogue Council, and last year we had a very successful public forum. We got radio and newspaper coverage. We got a well-known anti-cult rabbi; he spoke to several groups and he spoke at *Har HaShem* on *Shabbos*. It was very successful.

We have a staff of four rabbinic counsellors including Rabbi Berkovski, all wonderful people, and some ex-'Messianic Jews' whom we can call on. Most of the work is just counselling. We really answer their questions and try to introduce them to authentic Judaism. By 'authentic' I don't necessarily mean Orthodox. Usually these people do gravitate towards Orthodoxy because they're coming from a fundamentalist point. We give them books to read; we take them to Sabbath services; we make sure they have a Sabbath experience at someone's house; and we'll see they have a place to go on Jewish holidays. We find that if a person comes to us and has a real curiosity, that person will come back to Judaism. If on the other hand they have some emotional tie to the 'Messianic' congregation, it's more difficult. People do need to know why they should be Jewish and what there is of value in Judaism. That's what we try to show them. Yes, it's an Outreach programme.

We really see our mission as part of the larger, important problem of assimilation that is facing Judaism nationally. We're not going to solve it, but we do certainly reach one segment of that problem. We are quite successful in bringing people back. For example, we helped to bring out the former 'rabbi' of the 'Messianic' congregation of Northville, to the west of Metropolis. He found them via the Moonies. He was their leader, and I've used him to speak to various groups. In fact, I like being round these people. They're seekers; they're thinkers; they're questioning; and I find them very interesting, very interesting. And most of them are very nice so it sort of makes it very pleasant. I've had one or two unpleasant experiences: one of them cursed me and said God should take away my ability to speak, and another called me an Antichrist – which I'm quite proud of actually!

It would be a big mistake to characterize the 'Messianic' movement as being weird or strange or unimportant. Unfortunately the movement is growing. They will tell people they are the most rapidly growing group in Judaism. They claim they're larger than the Reconstructionists – that's probably true. We think there are approximately 200,000 Jews who are caught up in it at the moment, and several times that number who have joined and left. So to take it as a passing, unimportant phenomenon would be a very large mistake. They are so dedicated, and are getting more and more bold. There is no question that this is a movement that is out to destroy Judaism and put in its place a bastardized form of Christianity. It is something the Jewish community up till now has not been willing to talk about. It is like intermarriage twenty years ago, or maybe AIDS ten years ago. People don't want to talk about it, but they know it's there. As I go around, I am amazed by the number of people in the Jewish community who have been touched by it: it may be a cousin; or people go to a circumcision, and it turns out to be in a 'Messianic' synagogue; or someone's sister's child is being married in a 'Messianic' ceremony. We work very hard to save these people and we are happy with any success. As the *Talmud* says, 'If you save one Jew, it is as if you have saved the whole world.'

Thirteen

OUTSIDERS LOOKING IN

Employees of the Jewish Country Club

The Windy Oak Country Club House stood among ninety acres of rolling lawns. There was a golf course around which the members drive in electric carts. The course was dotted with magnificent trees, and the putting greens were perfectly circular, smooth and manicured. There was a large lake for boating and water skiing, a swimming pool in which toddlers in water-wings were learning to swim, and a large pool-side area for perfecting one's tan. The parking lot was full of Cadillacs, and the Stars and Stripes flew valiantly in the circle at the top of the drive.

The Club House itself looked like a cross between a minor French château and a grandiose cricket pavilion. Inside the carpets were thick, soothing music was playing constantly, and in niches up the large staircase were life-size reproductions of ancient Greek statues. The dining room was pink; there were flowers on every table. At lunchtime the room was full. Young college-age waiters and waitresses pulled out the wicker chairs for the guests and presented them with the menu. There was no attempt at keeping the Jewish food laws. The first item on the menu was avocado with shrimp, and this was followed by Cobb salad with fresh turkey, bacon, avocado, blue cheese, diced tomatoes, eggs, and a choice of dressing.

The elderly ladies who sat in groups of four or six stared intently at the menus. Their hair was fluffy and gold; they were beautifully made-up; and they were dressed in expensive sportswear. Most of them would not see seventy again. As more groups of ladies walked across the dining-room to their tables, they stopped to have little chats: 'Well, hello there girls'; 'You're looking so pretty, as always'; 'How're your grandchildren?' They patted and hugged each other before proceeding on their way.

The men in their golfing clothes sat at different tables. They were all well known to the waitresses who bustled about them saying: 'I've saved the latkes (potato pancakes) for you Mr Freedman'; 'And how are you today Mr Milstein?' The ladies waved across the room to the men, but in general there was segregation of the sexes.

MR JOSEPH BERG

Despite his name, Mr Berg the General Manager was not Jewish. He wandered round the tables saying a jolly word to everyone. Upstairs in his office he was surrounded by files. There was a photograph of his wife and three pretty children on his desk, and an admonitory plaque saying, 'You are what you do, not what you intend to do.'

I started in the hotel business in Dallas, Texas. For a little less than fifteen years, I guess, I was with hotels. I ran from Dallas, to Atlanta, to Palm Beach, and then finally to Manhattan. It was a great time, very time-consuming. When I finally did get married and had children I thought it was time to settle down a little bit, and with country club management – although very hectic during the summer – you have an off season that you can spend some time with your kids. That's why I moved over to country clubs.

The difference between hotels and country clubs is you have a fixed clientele as opposed to a transient clientele. That's the only difference. I worked in two country clubs before I came to Windy Oak. One was in Greenwich, Connecticut. That was a mixed club. Different backgrounds, different religions, that sort of thing. The other was in Larchmont, New York. That was also mixed but it was predominantly Jewish, about 70 per cent. Windy Oak does have some non-Jews. The total membership is in the range of 475 families, and I guess that better than 90 per cent are Jewish.

I think people join for the facilities. That's the bottom line . . . and business connections. But we try to hold that down because it runs into a tax problem, and we certainly don't encourage any business transactions being done here. However, playing golf with somebody alone – if you mutually have something in common, it's going to open up a business avenue. It's just a fact of life. The reason to join a country club is for social contacts, not business contacts. That's the only reason to join a country club of any type. It is for those social contacts, because they are people that you want to be associated with and enjoy your free time with. Any other purpose, it's not worth the money you have to pay. There are a lot easier business contacts you can make for a lot less money.

Membership is $25,000 initiation fee, spread out over a payment plan. Then the dues alone are approximately $300 a month. And that doesn't include your food minimum: you have to pay a number of dollars in the dining room or we'll bill you anyway, whether you use it or not. That's cheaper than the clubs I worked in out East, much cheaper. Definitely country club living is a luxury, and there's no two ways about that. At the Connecticut club it was $25,000 to join, but that was up front. At Windy Oak we spread it over a number of years.

Members have to be sponsored by two members here at the Club before we could even accept your application to join. Presently there is not a waiting list here. There is an information form to fill out; that's forwarded to an Admissions Committee. They'll sit down and talk with you concerning why you want to join Windy Oak, and whether socially you will blend in with the membership. Assuming that goes okay, you are posted to make sure that no one in the entire membership has a problem with your joining the Club. The point is it's a social club. What we're here for is for members to associate with people that they want to; like a family.

I would venture to say that the average age of members is up around sixty. We certainly would like more young members, but that's a country-wide average too, pretty much. Getting up to a financial level where you can afford it, that's the main reason. We would encourage any younger person to join because that's going to be the future of the Club. The members have a wide mix of professions which kind of surprised me because I didn't see that kind of mix on the East Coast. We've got everything from cattlemen right on through. There are, of course, a lot of doctors and lawyers; a lot of private businessmen, including a couple of people who own banks; a lot of stockbrokers. The rabbis can use the Club. At least six rabbis are on the membership list. They're not paying full dues of course . . .

Members seem to come from most of the religious groups, though I haven't seen many Orthodox. Most are probably Reform, but that's a guess on my part. We have in the past cleared the kitchen (to make it *kosher*) for a party – we got in Rabbi Vardin's (*The Kashrut Supervisor*) people – and we do try to separate meats and dairy products in separate boxes to informally try to satisfy that requirement. We don't have a *kosher* (ritually clean) kitchen. It would take eight to ten hours to get it cleaned for a rabbi to pass on it. We serve bacon and shrimps. Our members don't have a problem with that.

I would get into arguments about the difference between a Jewish and a Christian club. I find that the demands of a Christian club are more than a Jewish club, and the reason for this is that you have a more diverse background. Dietary demands, different agendas. What they wanted to do in a mixed, predominantly Christian club was so diverse. It was impossible to even satisfy 75 per cent of the membership. I think that if you streamline the background it's easier.

What the Windy Oak membership want is top-grade food. That's number one. And that has changed over the twenty years – then it was the golf facility, that was number one. Top. The reason to join the Club was the golf, but that's changed. Now the food and the Club House facilities have become more important. The pool is way down, and tennis too. We serve a wide variety of food. The entire industry here in America is leaning towards the health-conscious so we all have a spa cuisine and pasta entrées, and red meats are going down the tubes.

There are quite a few Jewish events here. As a matter of fact we do a Passover, and during the winter months a Friday night service. Weddings of course. You see, the members see this as a kind of an extension to their homes. This is where they feel relaxed. If the Christian country clubs started to take Jews, I don't think this would hurt Windy Oak for two reasons: 1, history; and 2, the fact that we are predominantly Jewish would keep us right in there. If you join a club for the right reasons, I can't imagine too many Jews wanting to join the Metropolis

Country Club even if it was open. They'd always feel uncomfortable, I think . . .

MRS JANEY DEXTER

A small woman in her sixties, Janey Dexter had worked in various capacities at Windy Oak for twenty-six years.

I came to work at Windy Oak to earn college money for my kids. When the first one went off to college he said, 'Momma's got to have a job so she won't worry about us.' So I came for four days a week, and now it's about seven days. To start with I took care of the ladies' card games. Then I was a hostess for one year and I hated it, because they don't like you to work when you're a hostess. You just tell people what to do, you know. Then I came out here to the golf snack-bar. I also took care of the tennis people for a couple of years.

It's changed so much. The members are older and I'm older. There aren't any young people as there was. I don't know why. Maybe the cost has something to do with it. Young people want to be doing things, not just playing cards and golf. Many of them live where there are swimming pools and tennis courts, you know, and let's face it: the economy isn't all that good for young people to pay the fees.

Right now most of them are grandmothers. There are a lot of widows. The ladies particularly come in on Wednesdays and Saturdays, full force. There are big card games then: four or five tables, and ten at a table. This is really their home. They come at 11:00 and stay to 4–4:30. I know 'em all. My husband died and I'm alone. What would I do if I didn't come here? There are some widowers here as well as widows. I've watched so many die. And a few died right here in the Club.

They all know each other. They greet each other with hugs and kisses. I've cooked in many of their homes. I've served dinner and cleaned up afterwards as a favour to them, you know. They pay very well, very well; they won't let you do anything for nothing. The women talk about their families, and what's going on in the community. And they're all readers. Yes, they read everything. I have a lot of good books they've given me. They talk about the books. Once in a while they have a little group who get together and have a book review, but that hasn't happened for quite a while.

There are a few non-Jewish members. One year we had about maybe six gentiles. We had a Metropolis Moose (the local football team), a black man, as a member. Then we had a young man who used to caddy, a Spanish guy. All the time he caddied he used to say, 'Some day I'm going to be a member here.' And he is, he is.

I've watched the kids grow up. I've helped with the *bris* (circumcision) in the home, and then I've watched that little boy grow up and get married. You know, that's the most interesting thing. The little girls growing up, the naming of the child: I've been to at least twenty or thirty of those. I've served at the house when they were named. Then with deaths, I've been to *shivas* (mourning gatherings), you know, and helped with that. It's sad, watching a member die. Watching them eat and go home, go out to dinner, and next day they're dead. It's sad. Even though we know there's another place to go, it's sad. I'm absolutely amazed at the members. They don't mourn as we do. I don't know why. They talk about the member who has passed away, but it's not like us. I mean when my husband died, I thought I'd die. I'd like to have learnt to be like them, to get on with life. It's the way to do it.

When I came most of the women were in their fifties. Now they're in their eighties, and they're still gorgeous. We've got a lady, she's eighty-two years old. She plays cards twice a week; she can dance up a storm; and is as kind as anyone. Amazing . . . I've seen a few angry people too. They can be demanding. They don't want a glass of water. They want the glass, the ice, the lemon, the straw, and a smile too. And crackers. They like good food: *lox* (smoked salmon) and bagels, cottage cheese and fruit. Real good food.

But I've loved it here. It's my home too . . .

The Child Minder

MRS JANE MOYLAN

There were toys outside on the porch, and a small boy came in and looked at us as we talked. Mrs Jane Moylan lived in a small

house a few blocks away from the shopping centre. Besides a husband and three sons, the household also contained a labrador dog and four large cats. Jane Moylan was red-haired and vivacious. She was dressed in jeans and a shirt, and she spoke with lively enthusiasm.

I was born in Massachusetts, just outside Boston, and I was raised a Baptist. We were part of what you'd now call 'White Flight'. When blacks moved into our housing project in Boston, we moved out to the suburbs. I always remember there was only one Jewish boy at school. He was kind of picked on and ridiculed. He was beat up, and the only reason for it was because he was Jewish. It was a big stigma to be a Jew. Everyone knew he was the Jewish boy. Yeah, I was raised prejudiced. Jews were always said to be cheap and stingy.

My family was a religious Baptist family. We went to church every Sunday. It was a nice Baptist church. People think of Baptists as 'Aa-men, Dunk'em in the river, Hallelujah!' But it was a nice church. It taught you to be kind and nice. I went through the public schools; I'm a high school graduate. Uh huh! When I was in high school I wanted to be either a farmer or a racing car driver. I didn't do either! As a matter of fact I didn't get my driving licence until I was in my twenties.

After I graduated I did lots of jobs. I worked in a discount fashion shop; I was a short-order cook; I was a secretary. It was hard work, but I had to do it to support myself. When I was twenty-five I moved to Metropolis. It was sort of an adventure. I flew out my cats, two of them, and I came here. That was fifteen years ago. That's when I moved into daycare. I love kids! They're fun! I got married after three years, and I've got three kids of my own: one and then twins. It was very exciting! I'd do it all again!

My first job in Metropolis was working for a Jewish family. I didn't live in, but I was there full-time. They had two kids – real good kids. I was there for a year, then I had a few quick jobs, and then I worked for the Samuelsons (*Havurah Leaders*) for five years. I went every morning; I got there at 6:30 in the morning. I made the whole family breakfast and helped get the kids ready for school. When I was there, one of the boys was at the Jewish Community Centre pre-school so I drove the car there, and the little one was still at home. We'd play – my job was strictly taking care of the children. I did some of the shopping and I'd get everyone's dinner. I'd have to pick up one from the pre-school at 11:30, and the girls from their school at 3:30. Then maybe I'd drive one to ballet, another to the dentist; a lot of driving time. I left once everyone started dinner. They were a nice family to work for. I've worked for lots of families and they were the best.

Now I do daycare in my house. I pick up four or five kids from the private school opposite my house. They come over here; they finish their lunch. Then sometimes they want to watch TV; sometimes they are really tired and need to nap. We go to the park a lot. They love the animals. A lot of the kids, particularly the Jewish ones, don't have animals at home.

Are there any special characteristics of Jewish families? Well, I'll tell you: When my first son was little I put him in the Jewish Community pre-school. I liked the whole feel of it. The first year was great. Then one of my twins was diagnosed with a brain tumour. Of course I'd made a lot of Jewish friends by that time. We were in a car-pool, and I said that I wouldn't be coming back to the pre-school because financially we couldn't afford it with my son being ill. An anonymous donor then paid my son's full tuition! I know it was a Jewish person. That following summer when we were in turmoil with brain surgery, the Director of the pre-school knew what was going on. He let my son go to the full summer programme at no charge.

It was strange. I was raised a Christian, and I was raised with different innuendos about the different races. I was raised that Jews were cheap. It's the total opposite. Since then I always swore that I'd never stand and listen to a crack like that about Jews, because it's not true. We white Christians were raised to think we were on top, that we were better than Jews and blacks. We were supposedly superior. It's just not so! I don't find any difference in Jewish and gentile kids. They're the same; they like the same things. The only difference is in holidays: Jewish kids don't celebrate Santa Claus. That's a difference! Otherwise they're similar. If anything, Jews are kinder. I'm not just saying that. The Jews that I've dealt with are nothing like what I was taught!

The Samuelsons were the opposite of cheap. Their children meant the world to them, and they were willing to pay top dollar. They got the best – not to pat me on the back, you know! They both have a career, but they made sure their kids came first. They paid top dollar and made sure whoever was taking care of their kids was qualified. They are different about animals. I mean, my cats and dogs are just like my kids. Since my son had his brain tumour, I resolved not to be so emotional every time one of my animals dies. But I tell you, every time it happens, it's just as bad. Don Samuelson wasn't like that. Maybe he hid it. When their dog was real old, it was just time to have it put down and I thought, 'Jeez . . . I'm more sad than he is!'

Like I said, I was raised prejudiced. Everything has been eye-opening: living in an integrated society; having a handicapped son and being put in a different category. It all made a difference. I'm not prejudiced any more . . . and my kids won't be either.

The Principal of the Pluralist High School

MR PETER COPE

Despite his skull cap, Peter Cope was not Jewish. A good-looking, bearded man in his late thirties, we interviewed him in the Principal's office of the Hebrew High School. The High School was located on the second floor of Beit Torah synagogue.

I was born on a military base in Utah. I was in a military family: from the ages of two until six I lived in Germany, then we were in Nebraska, and when I was twelve we moved to this state. My parents are Protestant. They attended a rather liberal Protestant church, and I went to Sunday school before church every Sunday. I would describe my parents' religion as being tolerant Protestantism: not much emphasis on fire and brimstone, and a great deal of emphasis on personal interpretation and working for the social betterment of society. When I was young, I was very enthusiastic about it – I was going to be a missionary in India. I went to public schools, through high school, in Metropolis. I probably quit being a churchgoer in my senior year of high school. It just became less relevant.

I started at a small, West State College for two years, and then I transferred to the major State College. I basically did the whole Liberal Arts thing, and then I majored in History. I didn't really know what I was going to do. I entertained notions of teaching, but at college level. Mostly I was just studying and not knowing what I was going to do. After graduation I worked for a year in an adult high school programme here in Metropolis, and during that time I made application to the London School of Economics to study the History of Political Thought, which I did for a year. It was a great experience – very challenging. I was very successful in college here, but I really struggled there in the academic programme. It was very different, but it was wonderful. When subsequently I became an educator, it was good for me to have faced these difficulties – I can sympathize with students. I was there with some marvellous students. Interestingly, there were a few students who were on a higher level than everyone else. I had had very little contact with the Jewish world at that stage. It became clear that these three students had attended Jewish schools, and they credited their talmudic study as real important to the way that they thought.

I came back and tried to figure out what I was going to do. I started teaching here at the Hebrew High School just one period a day. I was tutoring some 'English as a Second Language' students. I got State Certification after I started teaching. Then I started teaching history, and it was a matter of three years before I became a full-time teacher. I was also a security guard and was taking classes. So I have been here for my career. Then when the Principal left I interviewed and was invited to take over – that was a year ago.

The school is seventh grade through twelfth. All the children are Jewish, and the majority now come up through the Golda Meir Day School. We also have a few from Maimonides Academy and elsewhere. We have classes of about twenty coming in at the seventh grade. The boys and girls come in together, and ideally we would like them to stay all the way through. At present, in the numbers that we would like, they don't. We face attrition at the end of the eighth, ninth and tenth grades. One factor is the perception that public junior high schools are not satisfactory, but the public high schools have better programmes. Then there's the approaching expense of college. Then there's the desire, at about that age, to be in a bigger pond – we have about seventy in the whole school. Then there are the various activities the public high schools offer – we have some sports, but nothing like the big schools. I should perhaps say that a few years ago our chess team beat the chess club of the largest, most élite suburban public high school! We have about nineteen teachers, most are part-time.

When parents come to see me, I tell them the things they should be interested in if this school is to be a good choice for their child. The two thrusts of our school are a college-preparatory programme with a genuine challenge for the child, and the Jewish education. There are lots of good private schools. The reason this school exists is for Judaism. As it happens, we're considerably cheaper than the other private schools – I don't mention that, but it is an important consideration. The Jewish studies are a required part of our programme: they are the atmosphere of the school; it is the way we set up our calendar. If either of the two thrusts are not important to the parents then we probably won't meet their needs, and we probably won't be a good match.

We're housed in the premises of *Beit Torah* synagogue. We have to share our rooms with their religion school on Monday and Wednesday nights. There are certain rooms that are ours exclusively – our science lab, our computer, our library, our offices. It would be a real problem financially if we couldn't share, but we are looking at other alternatives. As a matter of fact, there's an agreement in principle to make a move to the Jewish Community Centre. It would give us a lot of sports facilities, and this is something we would like to see happen. It's all a matter of lining everything up. Joanna Miller (*The Director of the Jewish Community Centre*) is organizing a lot of very ambitious things there.

The kids arrive in the morning at 7:55 and they go straight to classes. One of the things about the school right now is that there's no *davening* (praying) in the school, which was the way the school traditionally started the day. There are a number of reasons for that. One of the reasons has been the difficulty in making it work well. It hasn't often been the experience we wanted it to be. It's very tough to do. At present, it's on the shelf how we're going to deal with this. Do they salute the flag? It's not a tradition. In fact we don't have a flag in the school. It's never come up in all the years I've been here. So they all go straight to their classes in the morning. Lunch is at about 11:40 or 12:20. They bring their own and we basically follow the synagogue's *kashrut* policy. There's a lunch-room downstairs. School finishes 3:20 Monday through Thursday, and 2:15 on Friday. Homework is visualized as being two to four hours a night.

You want to know about the Judaic teaching? Some of the teachers are Orthodox, but we don't have a definite school policy. Some of the teachers will say, 'This is my perspective on that', but I cannot imagine any of them shutting off discussion. I haven't ever heard of that happening. Others will take great pains to point out all the different points of view. We are a Pluralist school, but we hold to the traditional tenets of Judaism. I have found that as long as a certain attitude is maintained, I have never had a furore on the religious teaching. You probably know that Rabbi Max Goldstein (*The Conservative Rabbi*) is President of our Board.

I'm not the first non-Jewish Principal of the School, I'm the second. When the first one was chosen, the feeling was they needed a competent administrator. I'm sure they wished the competent administrator was Jewish, but that's what they had to have! For me, I think the fact I had been here for twelve years, that I had grown with the school, that I had become very well aware of the Jewish world, and that I had an attitude which was respectful meant that I never had a problem. Over the years I have got to know kids and to know families, and my not being Jewish just doesn't seem to be an issue. That understanding has passed from family to family. I think it would be ideal if I were Jewish too! But there are certain significant advantages. On any kind of religious issue, I can sit back and say, 'Well, I can tell you the practical implications of this choice', and no one can question my motives. I don't have an axe to grind and no one would ever think I do. A lot of kids, particularly Traditional kids, just love it that I know things about Judaism that even other Jews don't know.

I suppose I look sort of Jewish so, when I meet people for the first time, I always make a point of telling them I'm not. I don't want to mislead anyone. I get called Rabbi Cope quite a bit . . . Being at this school, I understand the Jewish desire for self-preservation whole-heartedly. As a student of history, I respect it. What we're hoping to accomplish here is to maintain a sense of Jewish identity, and I make no apologies for that. In American society as a whole, I am a strong supporter of public education. Most people in America are not under threat – Jews are.

The Gentile Spouse

MR WILLIAM MURRAY

His office was on the twenty-fourth floor of a downtown skyscraper. It had reproduction mahogany furniture and pictures of flying ducks.

I'm a third-generation Metropolis lawyer. My grandfather was born a mile away. He and my father lived here all their lives. I live in the house where I grew up. I went through the Metropolis public schools. I was raised as a Presbyterian; my mother had us go to Sunday school. I was confirmed as a Presbyterian at thirteen or fourteen, though I would say the confirmation process made me less religious! They tried to teach the basic tenets of Presbyterian belief, and what I remember was my difficulties in believing the Apostles' Creed. Most of it gave me trouble! Jesus died – that I accepted. But I was interested in science: the vertical take-off of the Resurrection and the Ascension gets to the root of the trouble! I did sign on the dotted line, but it was with substantial reservations! I probably still feel a bit guilty about it!

I knew some schoolfriends were Jewish. I knew Don Samuelson (*Havurah Leader*) and Robyn Graff (*The Lawyer*), yes. It didn't bother me much. My father belonged to the Metropolis Country Club, and I was aware they excluded Jews in those days. My mother was a member of the Junior League. Yes, I suppose I was part of the gentile establishment, though one of my first jobs was picking up tennis balls at Windy Oak, the Jewish Country Club. I was probably sixteen. When I was in high school, I went out with a lot of girls. Were any of them Jewish? I didn't worry about it.

At college I was looking for a Jewish girl to marry. I went to Stanford. For a long time I was interested in genetics. Basically I concluded that through 2,000 years of repression Jews had had natural selection forced on them, to the point that Jews were smarter than other people. I wanted the smartest girl I could find. Why? I wanted the best genes I could get for my children. I met Lisa on a blind date in my junior year. She was from Los Angeles. Lisa was one of the top sixteen students at Stanford freshman year, and she was great. I don't think she's more academically able than me. She worked harder the first year. By the fourth year, I was doing a little better than she was. We married at the end of my first year in law school.

How did the families react? The Jewish factor didn't bother my family at all. I was very careful about who I picked to marry so I thought about all the problems. They worried about some other things. In particular, her parents had had a very bitter divorce and that was a serious problem. Ideally I would have liked to have married someone from a happy family. We were married by a rabbi in California. I didn't think of converting to Judaism. At that stage, in 1968, the Vietnam War was very much a factor. I was thinking about being a conscientious objector, and I joined the Quakers at law school at Yale. By being a member of the Society of Friends (Quakers) I persuaded the Draft Board and did qualify as a conscientious objector.

Instead of going to Vietnam I had to work for a non-profit organization. I had to do something that was public service, and I had to receive a private's pay. I could have driven an ambulance, but I could also stay in this country. I ended up with a wonderful option: I worked for the Metropolis College of Law. I wrote articles and taught a class with the State Governor. How did I get the position? I arranged it. I knew the criteria, and I satisfied the Draft Board. I was married by that time. Lisa worked for the Metropolis city administration; she did not go to graduate school.

The children came after thirteen years of marriage. That was deliberate. My wife, for a time, was a Democratic legislator in the State Senate. We had some thoughts that maybe she would like to make a career of politics. She was good, but she was in a small minority of Democrats. We had our son in 1981, and our daughter in 1983. For Tom, we had Don Samuelson (*Havurah Leader*) come over to give him his Jewish name. I think the doctor did the circumcision in the hospital. Then a few years ago, when the kids were six or so, we were thinking about how to give them a proper sense of values. So we sent them to the Temple *Shalom* 'Every Day, the Jewish Way' programme. Tom went for one year. He had a religious scepticism which I share, so he dropped out. Barbara, my daughter, went for two years. She enjoyed it, but they both thought it too slow; they were a bit bored. They're bright kids!

We go to the Presbyterian church about once a year to listen to the hymns. I have great affection for the Quakers, but at this point my politics and theirs differ. We made one other stab at religious training besides the Temple *Shalom* programme. They learnt Hebrew for a year with a tutor. The last two or three years they have not got much religious training. In the home, for a number of years, we lit Friday night candles. We have a Christmas tree and presents – they get both *Hanukkah* and Christmas presents! In past years, we've been through short forms of the Passover service. Easter eggs? Sometimes, yeah.

Both children are in the public schools. They're in a programme designed for the highly gifted. One of the extraordinary things about it is how many children are products of mixed marriages. We did think of private schools, but we believe they're with a brighter group of kids where they are. I'd prefer to have my son in business than in medicine or law at this point. I think we'll end up with socialized medicine, which will be bad for the doctors, and there are too many lawyers in America. I'd like him to go to Stanford or Harvard or Princeton or Yale, and then Oxford maybe. I want basically the same for my daughter; I think she is so instinctively maternal that my ambition for her is maybe a few years of career and then that she'll raise children.

Would I want them to marry someone Jewish? The quality of person is more important to me than the religion. I don't think the Jews are the only genetically superior group in the world! The Chinese probably qualify in some respects. I don't discount any group's ability to have someone who is good enough for me to be happy if my children married them.

Most people read Aldous Huxley's *Brave New World* as an anti-Utopia, but I saw a potential in it for great human success and happiness – not in its class system, but in its eugenics aspect. I suppose I have always valued intelligence, success, ambition, hard work, and a variety of other attributes that I associate with Jews and with other successful people. I wanted to be successful myself, and I wanted my wife and children to be as well.

The Teacher of Interfaith Relations

DR JAMES HOLLAND

Dr James Holland had recently retired from teaching Theology at the University of Metropolis. A mild, bearded man in his sixties, he talked to us in one of the University library's seminar rooms.

I grew up in Sterling, Colorado, in a protected provincial environment, and so when I went to college and encountered anti-Semitism I was quite shocked. I was exceedingly fortunate: not only my home environment, but the neighbours I associated with were simply not prejudiced. It was extraordinary, because that part of Colorado was a hotbed of prejudice. I can remember as a very small child seeing a long parade of the Ku Klux Klan at night. Very scary. That was about the last gasp of the Klan, but to a child it was a very impressive sight: these men in sheets and on horseback; like something in a bad movie! But my family was very tolerant. They wouldn't allow prejudice. If I brought home the wrong vocabulary from school, I got punished immediately. What I learnt was you had two vocabularies. One for the playground, and one for home! My home won? You bet! Not by lectures, but my mother got across the point: 'We don't do that. That's poor white trash who do that.' You got the message! When I found there were clubs Jews could not join, I found this difficult to believe on a college campus. When I was out of college, as a result of my upbringing, I reacted pretty strongly against prejudice – racial, religious, ethnic or whatever.

After college I went to seminary and had a closer association with churches. My upbringing was Presbyterian, and I was very shocked to discover the strength of anti-Semitism in churches. I had been taught otherwise. To find it in college, and to find it virulent among church people was just too much. This was during World War Two, when there was a good bit of strong anti-Semitism in the country. I was a crusader and against all that, and some of my fellow seminarians joined me. Then I became good friends with a Reform rabbi. He sent me materials – a lot of things I didn't know about, and that had a real impact. From then on I have always been involved in interfaith things. First I taught in the East and then I moved to Metropolis. I have taught classes on and off on interfaith dialogue here in Metropolis for the last thirty years. I have been involved in dialogue and so on, and I used to have people like Rabbi Oppenheim (*The Traditional Rabbi*) in to dialogue with.

This past spring I taught a course on the Holocaust, theological responses to the Holocaust. It was open to both Christians and Jews – that was the whole idea – but no Jews enrolled. It was advertised in the *Metropolis Jewish News*, so I was disappointed because I had hoped for some interesting dialogue. One of the students who did come had some very unfortunate impressions that he had picked up that blamed the victim. He thought if Jews would just be inconspicuous, there wouldn't be any problem. Jews are too conspicuous – they should just crawl back into the woodwork. I'm not exactly quoting him, obviously, but that is what he meant. But he was a nice person so the challenge was to come at it in such a way that he would come round and see things differently. Why were there no Jewish students? One reason would be – 'I'm sure not going to take a course like that from a Christian! We've got many people who know more than he does!' – which is true. I think that would be the main reason.

I've had Jews in classes before, though not in great numbers. Mostly they've been excellent students. I think Jews tend to respond in a different way. Number 1, Jews are much more comfortable with argument and enjoy arguing. Number 2, Jews are comfortable with something left incomplete or unsettled. This is generalizing and allowing for many exceptions. Christians often don't like argument. They are more inclined to try to convert, to try to reach agreement; and they are often uncomfortable with things left incomplete. A Jewish man – I don't know why I say 'man', but they are the ones who come to mind – will say, 'Well, it's like you say, "Who knows?"' And he's comfortable with 'Who knows?' He's comfortable with plaster not on the walls, while the Calvinist wants to get that plaster on there!

About interfaith dialogue and so on, it has become increasingly difficult to have interfaith dialogue and interracial dialogue in our society. There's a great deal of touchiness and antagonism going on. And that's difficult! People bristle. There's a lack of understanding there. I don't want to exaggerate that too much, but in terms of dialogue with Jews it's very difficult not to talk about the Middle East. I have found American Jews to be much more conservative and toeing-the-line for Israel than Israelis are. I've been able to talk with Israelis about problems such as the Arabs in the Occupied Territories and negotiations and so on without any problem. But American Jews, the minute you get into that area they hear you as being anti-Israel, and anti-Semitic is the next step. That's unfortunate and it's a change. I think it started with the invasion of Lebanon, post-1982. It's just difficult to talk. I do a lot more keeping my mouth shut than I used to . . .

The Catholic Ecumenist

MR ANDREW WILKINS

The house was enormous – an old Spanish-style mansion overlooking a public park. Inside it was comfortably shabby with much-used antique furniture and clutters of books and papers. Dr Philip Rosenbaum (The Director of the Anti-Defamation League) *had given us Andrew Wilkins' name. We had said we wanted a gentile who was known to be critical of the Jewish community. He turned out to be a large, grey-haired man in his sixties, well-read and erudite.*

I'm sixty-three years old and I'm from Chicago. I was raised in what we call an Irish-Catholic ghetto, which meant we didn't know any Jews and if we knew any blacks, it was because they delivered the coal or something. My parents were comfortably off, and I was educated in all-Catholic parochial schools. After law school I practised in Chicago, and then after five years I moved out here. I'm from a very large family: my mother has fifty-eight grandchildren. We have eight living children – that's a good number. I'll brag a little: Our kids somehow went in for spelling and five of them won the State Spelling Bee. Then one was ninth in the country; another was seventh; and Katy was first! We're active Catholics. I wish I could say we had loads of grandchildren; we have four. Families don't have the number of children they had in the 1950s.

I've always been interested in history. I became aware that the persecution of the Jews was not invented by the Nazis. Many, many people don't understand the history of that. In fact the Catholics have been perpetrators of terrible things against the Jewish people for many, many years. So I got interested in joining the Metropolis Catholic-Jewish dialogue back in about 1981. We used to go about once every two months to meetings and that's how I met Philip Rosenbaum. I don't know how you're going to characterize me in this book. I don't want to be characterized as anti-Semitic, though Philip has said that.

I originally crossed swords with Philip Rosenbaum because Philip would occasionally arrange speeches for the meetings of the Catholic-Jewish dialogue. He got some extremely wild-eyed pro-Zionist people who could see no other side of the coin. We would sit through about three hours of this, and pretty soon it began to occur to the Catholic members of the group – who were all pretty competent people – that we weren't hearing all sides of it. So we asked – and I persisted in asking – that he get someone from the other point of view. Eventually Geoff Poulter (*The Radical*) was given about ten minutes, and somebody else was there to contradict him for another half hour. I told Philip that this wasn't altogether right. I finally came to realize, after about six years, that we weren't engaging in interfaith discussion such as we've tried to have with Baptists, Presbyterians and Lutherans. With the Jews it was a political discussion. In my mind, the Anti-Defamation League was trying to place Catholics in a position where they would pressure their Church to recognize Jerusalem as the capital of Israel.

It finally came to a point when they decided they were going to excuse all the rabbis, and I really thought that was dumb. We Catholics needed to know the rabbis to learn more about the Jewish religion. What was the rationale? You'll have to ask Philip. It didn't make any sense to me. What we were told was that the purely clerical people would have their own discussions. Anyway, I'm a lawyer by training and combative by nature, I guess. So I began talking with Philip about it. We really had some hot words.

Then it was suddenly announced that the Catholic-Jewish dialogue had come to an end – it had served its purpose and the Anti-Defamation League was no longer going to sponsor it. When that happened I said, 'Oh, that's fine. We'll go ahead and get the Catholic-Jewish dialogue going under some other heading.' I visited with Professor Kornfeld (*The University Professor of Judaica*) and we were on our way to continuing everything. Then Philip resurrected again and said in effect – I don't want to put words in his mouth, but this is the effect of it – 'The Anti-Defamation League owns the Catholic-Jewish dialogue and nobody but the ADL can conduct it.' I thought that was interesting!

The Jewish-Catholic dialogue was never really of a theological nature. There were efforts made to take it in that direction, particularly from the Catholic side. Rabbi Oppenheim (*The Traditional Rabbi*) from the West Side was willing to talk some theology in the early days. He's a nice man. Rabbi Saul Bleefeld (*The Former Rabbi*) also made the open-minded suggestion to invite some Arabs. There was a very gentle man around Metropolis named Habib Aziz, and through my activities with other organizations I had got to know him. I was so impressed with him I thought, 'What harm can it do?' But no way was the Anti-Defamation League going to permit this! So this fine idea of that young rabbi went down the drain! I didn't like that. I'd like to see much more discussion of theological matters.

I ought to say that, although I'm combative, I knew the purpose of the dialogue was not to fight with the Jews, but to have better relationships with them. So biting my tongue, I decided not to go public with this. You're the first people I've ever talked to about it. But I do believe, and I believe it very strongly, that the Anti-Defamation League had a different agenda for the dialogue than the Catholics had.

My relationship with the Jews and the Jewish community is not combative with anyone except Philip. Without exception, I considered all the people at those meetings to be very good friends. I know the American Jewish community has some moral commitment to stand in a unified, solid phalanx about Israel, no matter what is done there. The feeling is they cannot afford to appear to be divided publicly. I've had that confirmed on a number of occasions. It's a terribly complicated situation and obviously those of us living in the middle of the United States can't have all that clear a picture of what is true in Israel. None the less I think the attitude of the Jewish community is unfortunate because it undermines credibility.

Philip may want to call me anti-Semitic, but I don't consider that's fair. His attitude to Israel is a defensiveness on every level. When I see a Jewish talk show host get killed, when I see the activities of the New Aryans and the skinheads, I get very worried too. I'm a lawyer, and in my profession the most able, the most educated tend to be Jews. There's a great Jewish tradition of education and learning and integrity. I'm a great believer that the Holocaust memory should be kept alive. I am appalled at the lack of awareness of some Catholics of the history of Jewish-Catholic relations and what happened. I'll give you an example: With the 1492/1992 celebrations (500 years since the discovery of America), there was this idea we should make Queen Isabella of Spain a Catholic saint! Queen Isabella! She and her ilk threw the Moors and Jews out of Spain! I've read about it. Why anybody should think she should be made a saint . . . well, people just don't know anything about it!

I think there are two important things: firstly is the continuation of good relations between Catholics and Jews; secondly, we should not give any openings for pot-shots by the true anti-Semites – and there are some. So whatever I say, I don't go public about the Anti-Defamation League and I don't write letters to the newspapers on these matters. You see, I'm talking like the Jews now!

The Policeman

OFFICER DENNIS GRACE

A tanned man of medium height, Officer Dennis Grace's uniform was impeccable. In addition to his police badge, he wore a Purple Heart and a Medal of Honour for being wounded on active duty. We had coffee together in a motel near to the police station.

Sure I'm on duty right now! The taxpayer's money's hard at work . . . But you don't see this place getting stuck up, everything's calm in here. So we're doing our job in here too!

I was born and raised in Metropolis. I joined the Navy in 1963. I got out of the Navy, came home, and was working up north in the mines as an electrician's helper. I was doing terribly hard, dirty, physical labour. At that time they were hiring police. I went down and took the test. This was in 1968 – and here I am! I've been in South-West Metropolis for two years; East Metropolis for seventeen and a half years; and the rest of it right here in District One, on the West Side. I got my Purple Heart medal in this war, in the Metropolis war. I got shot in 1978. There was a stick-up in progress. I stumbled into it and got shot at; nothing heroic. I was off work about a month. It's something that happens. I was fortunate in that I was shot in the leg – I imagine it's a bit different if you get shot in the head!

The only real dealings I've had with the Jewish community was when I came out here six years ago. I'm assigned to work in an area that's predominantly Jewish, down by the lake. These are very Orthodox Jews. I see 'em wearing their whatever-you-call-it every Saturday. I tell you, I have a high regard for those people. You know, they don't drive cars; they don't do anything mechanical on their Saturdays. I got a call of an alarm going off on a Saturday in this guy's house. This alarm is very loud and very annoying. I get to the house and the wife and the daughters are leaving to go next door, and he's walking around with ear muffs on 'cause it's so loud in there. He wouldn't turn it off. I said, 'D'you want me to turn it off for you?' and he says, 'No. I'll stick around here till sunset, and then I'll turn it off.' It wasn't the rabbi, it was just an everyday Jewish guy.

Now I'll tell you a cute story: You know the *Yeshiva* High

School? There's a lot of kids there, and they have to live in this dormitory. Although we don't hear about it I imagine they take a lot of verbal abuse from the surrounding community, just by their caps and their attitudes and their dress. You've got to picture these kids putting up with about a year of verbal torture, and all their counsellors and teachers probably telling them, 'Don't do nothing. Turn the other cheek.' Whatever they tell 'em, I don't know! So one day there's about twenty-five Jewish kids playing basketball one Sunday. Well two or three of 'em leave early, and as they're walking out they encounter five or six Hispanic kids. These five or six Hispanics think they're bullying these two or three Jewish kids, and a little scuffle ensues. Then who happens to be coming round the corner but twenty-three other Jewish kids? Needless to say the Jewish kids won that skirmish! Not only did they win, but I found the Hispanic kids three or four blocks away licking their wounds 'cause they got their butts beat. So I jail them for hate crimes. Those Jewish kids walked around all pumped up. They finally got their shot in! It was kinda neat!

I'm very seldom called to Jewish houses for domestic violence. I went to one once, and it was an old, old couple. Metropolis has a law that if you scream at your spouse or if you throw things, you go to jail; there's no passing Go. There's no bond – you go before the judge the next day. So we get called in. It was an older couple, I'm talking seventy years old. And it took several phone calls to get this straightened out. The whole Jewish community came around. I mean it ain't like anyone else. They just don't stay away if the police come around. Before I even get to the house, the neighbours are right there. It's not so much nosiness; they want to help if they can. In this neighbourhood, it's predominantly Hispanic. There's domestic violence; there's an awful lot of drugs; there's car theft. Maybe it goes on in the Jewish community too, but I certainly don't get to know about it!

They've got their own synagogue right there, and once in a while they'll be some clown that wanders over there and paints a swastika on their door. But otherwise, I see very little anti-Semitism. I'm around there a lot. I try to prevent it, but you've got to be right there.

When I was on the East Side I was often downtown in the black area, and I did know the pawnshop owners. That was a different breed of Jewish person from that out here. Some were really nice, caring, honest people, but that was a minority in my opinion. Others were just . . . well, every joke you've ever heard about Jewish people applied. They were a different breed of cat down there in those pawnshops, as opposed to those Orthodox Jewish people. I'm talking twenty years ago now, though a few still exist. It's skid row down there! They were constantly calling me in, constantly. I remember one of 'em got beat senseless one day by a couple of idiots. For the most part they were honest with the police department. They had to be, they were vulnerable. If a guy comes into this motel here with a gun, I get a little suspicious. If a guy goes into a pawnship with a gun, the chances are he wants to pawn it. But, just once in a while, he's sticking the whole joint up. I used to walk the street all the time and I'd go in and say, 'How's business?' And they'd say, 'Miserable!' There's customers everywhere, but every one of 'em say, 'Oh we're not making no money. It's miserable!'

Oh yeah, I can tell you one story! We are called to a house and there was this guy. He was a Jewish guy and he was crazy – he had loads of knives everywhere. A big strong guy, and he was wild and hollering. So in the end his landlord couldn't stand it no more and he called us. Well this is 1993, you can't just hit him over the head! So four of us had to wrestle him down to the ground. Well when we finished with him, he wasn't wearing many clothes, but he still had his hat on!

Have I ever come across a Jewish policeman? I don't know. There must be some, but I ain't come across any. They don't come to mind. That's strange. There's 1,375 cops on this job . . . but, no, I can't call any to mind . . .

The State Senator

SENATOR PATRICK O'SHAUGHNESSY

Senator Patrick O'Shaughnessy represented that part of Metropolis which included the West Side Jewish community. He was stout, jolly and bespectacled – a natural politician.

I was born in Metropolis in 1939. I went to a Catholic parochial school, and then the Metropolis Jesuit University. I got a scholarship there, and I worked my way through by being a janitor. My father was a fireman; we were blue-collar people. I majored in Classics (Latin and Greek) and English. Then I went to the Catholic University in Washington DC on a scholarship. I taught for a couple of years in a high school in Washington, and I thought that every discipline problem in the city landed in my Latin class! Then there was an opening at the Jesuit University here, and in 1969 there was an opening in the State Legislature. My district included the West Side, and that's how I got to meet so many people of the community.

The first Jewish person that I ever met was when I was in high school. It was a man named Isaac Joseph, who owned a little apartment house, and he told me his whole life story. He had gone to *yeshiva* (talmudic academy) in Russia, but on one occasion he argued with the rabbi and the rabbi just cuffed him behind the ear. He got very discouraged with that. He escaped from Russia, getting out through Poland, and he came to Metropolis. He loved Schopenhauer and Aristotle and Thomas Aquinas, and he was very topical on current affairs. We'd talk for hours on end. I really took a shine to him, and he to me, and we became great friends. That was my first experience with Jews.

After I was elected, I made a point of going to the book reviews held at *Adath Israel* synagogue. The rabbi would review the book, and he would even defer to me. I think I was the only non-Jewish person present, and he used to say, 'Now, Patrick, this means . . . or this was when . . .' He'd put it into context for me. I'd never been to a synagogue before and I didn't know much. But he and the congregation made me feel so welcome. Now I go to the events and they say, 'We forgot to introduce you', and I say, 'You don't need to – I'm family!' So that's how I got to know that community.

I do know there are differences between *Adath Israel* and *Etz Hayyim* synagogue, but I try to be open to all. It's sort of like Presbyterians and Catholics, you know. Of course, my former spouse taught at *Beis Rahel* High School for a couple of years. She was the journalism teacher. She had a wonderful time, and that's when we got to know all the *yeshiva* officials and the other rabbis. Wonderful people. I still speak every now and then at that little girls' school and one or two of the *Yeshiva* boys have come down here to learn about politics. I'll tell you a funny thing: I went to one of the *Beis Rahel* dinners. I didn't know where I was sitting, so I sat down with the women. Well, I was told pretty quick, 'O'Shaughnessy, get out of there!' Anyway my wife thought the school was very special. I mean, in a television age, it's very special that people can hang on to a tradition. I know to some of us on the outside the *Beis Rahel* may look inhibiting, but how can I judge? They're beautiful; they're the cream of the crop of the community, intellectually and spiritually. I admire it, I really do. I don't understand it all, I must confess. I have seen young women who are happy; young women who are not involved in any illicit activity; young women who are not burdens of the court; young women who are not out on the streets; who are not on drugs; who are going to raise a family and hopefully have a happy marriage. Even with the custom of arranged marriages – well, maybe *I* might have done better with an arranged marriage . . . (*Senator O'Shaughnessy had recently separated from his wife.*)

Every now and again I get a call or a petition from the *Yeshiva* that there's trouble round there with some of the gang members trying to beat the kids up, that kind of thing. Safety issues, security issues. So I get onto the police. They always call me as their Senator. They're troubled about increased crime in the neighbourhood. They worry that on the night of *Yom Kippur* (Day of Atonement) homes will be broken into because the criminal element in the neighbourhood know they're not there. I suggested some of us could come and watch – stand on the block and watch. I've always alerted the police about the dates. Those are the kind of issues they're concerned about. The security of the *Yeshiva* dorm is a real worry. The kids are by themselves, and they're a target for criminal mischief. There have been some assaults.

Sure they call me up. I heard from Bernard Black (*The Community Patriarch*) just yesterday about a Russian family who have just come to Metropolis. He's been helping them, and I'm looking into whether I can get them into subsidized housing in the area. This was a family who, despite all the prejudice in Russia, managed to learn about their religion and want to keep it. It would be nice if they could walk right there to the synagogue. I think Mr Black is very special. He and his family are very interested in preserving the religious institutions. I just think it's great.

I am very entranced with the community, I really am. I take considerable umbrage when I hear any anti-Semitic comment. Even with my Arabic students at the Jesuit University, I tell them up front, 'I'm very drawn to the Jewish community in this city.' Knowing the community has certainly made me look at the roots of Catholicism. I taught a course on the Holocaust once. It troubles me that the Church over the centuries has allowed a spirit of anti-Semitism to prevail, which eventually led to the Holocaust. That has given me cause for concern in my own faith. What is there about my own faith that allowed that to happen? I get very upset that so many documents belonging to the Jewish people are now in the Vatican library. If ever I get a chance to speak with the Pope I want to talk to him about birth control, married clergy, women clergy, and the documents taken in the Middle Ages during the Inquisition! Knowing the community has made me realize that my faith has some feet of clay that we need to work on.

I'm sort of an honorary member of *Adath Israel*. They've always made me feel welcome. I've never had anything but positive vibes. I always joke with them that if ever I switch religions, I'll be right over there . . .

EPILOGUE

Wherever you go, there's always someone Jewish,
You're never alone when you say you're a Jew.
So when you're far from home,
And you're feeling kind of newish,
The odds are, don't look far,
Cause they're Jewish too!

And some Jews wear hats, and some Jews wear fine streimels,
And some Jews wear sombreros to keep out the sun,
Some Jews live on rice and some live on potatoes,
Or waffles, falafels or hamburger buns.

Wherever you go, there's always someone Jewish,
You're never alone when you say you're a Jew ...

Camp Song

GLOSSARY

Adath Israel: The congregation of Israel. A Traditional synagogue
Akiva: First-century Jewish scholar
Aliyah: Emigration to Israel
Bagel: Circular bread roll
Bar Mitzvah: Coming-of-age ceremony for thirteen-year-old boys
Bat Mitzvah: Coming-of-age ceremony for twelve-year-old girls
Beis Ha-Midrash: House of study, post-high school academy
Beis Rahel: House of Rachel. Orthodox girls' high school
Beit Torah: House of Jewish Law. A Traditional synagogue
Bensh: To say grace
Beth Israel: House of Israel. A Conservative synagogue
Beth Jacob: House of Jacob. A Reform synagogue
Bimah: Dais in the synagogue
Birkhat ha-Mazon: Grace after meals
Blintz: Crêpe or pancake
B'nai Akiva: House of Akiva. A Hasidic synagogue
Bris: Circumcision
Cantor: Official who sings the synagogue service
Confirmation: Ceremony for sixteen-year-old boys and girls
Conservative: A progressive denomination within Judaism
Daven: To pray
Dreidels: Spinning toys used on the Feast of Esther
Etz Hayyim: Tree of Life. An Orthodox synagogue
Falafel: Chick-pea patties
Fleshig: Meat foods
Frum: Observant
G–d: God (Orthodox)
Gefilte fish: Fish dumpling
Gehenna: Hell
Gentile: Non-Jew
Get: A certificate of divorce
Glatt: Ultra (used of kosher food)
Goyim: The non-Jews
Goyish: Un-Jewish
Hadassah: Women's Zionist organization

Haftarah: Reading from the prophets
Haggadah: Passover prayerbook
Halakhah: Jewish Law
Hallah: Plaited loaf
Hanukkah: Festival of Lights
Har HaShem: Mountain of the Lord. A Traditional synagogue
HaShem: God
Hasid: Member of an ultra-Orthodox Jewish sect
Hasidism: The philosophy of the Hasidim
Hatikvah: Israeli national anthem
Havdalah: Close of Sabbath ceremony
Havurah: Jewish prayer group
Hazzan: Cantor
Heder: Jewish elementary school
High Holy Days: New Year and Day of Atonement
Humash: The Bible
Intermarriage: Marriage between Jew and gentile
Kashrut: Jewish food laws
Kiddush: Blessing over wine
Kippot: Skull caps
Kippur: Atonement
Kollel: Advanced academy
Kosher: In accordance with Jewish food laws
Kristallnacht: Nazi pogrom against the Jews in 1938
Kugel: German pudding
Latke: Potato pancake
Lox: Smoked salmon
Macher: Important person
Maimonides: Twelfth-century Jewish scholar
Mashiah: The Messiah
Matzoh Ball: Dumpling
Melamed: Teacher
Menorah: Multi-branched candlestick
Mensch: Good person
Meshuggah: Crazy
Messianic Jew: Jew who believes Jesus is the Messiah
Mikveh: Ritual bath
Milchig: Milk foods
Minyan: A quorum of ten men for prayer
Mishkan: Tabernacle
Mishneh: Oral Law
Mishneh Torah: Maimonides' *Code of Jewish Law*

Mitzvah: Commandment or good deed
Mohel: Ritual circumciser
Orthodox: Observant of Jewish Law
Pais: Sidecurls
Passover: Spring festival of unleavened bread
Pesah: Passover
Pluralism: The belief that there is more than one legitimate interpretation of Judaism
Purim: Feast of Esther
Rabbi: Teacher or minister of Judaism
Rav Shaul: The apostle Paul
Rebbe: Teacher. Hasidic leader
Reconstructionism: A non-theistic denomination within Judaism
Reform: A liberal denomination within Judaism
Rosh Ha-Shannah: Jewish New Year
Ruah Ha-Mashiah: Spirit of the Messiah. A Messianic synagogue
Sabbath: The day of rest – Friday sunset until Saturday sunset
Seder: Passover meal
Semihah: Rabbinic ordination
Shabbat: Sabbath
Shabbos: Sabbath
Shaharis/t: Morning service
Shalom: Peace
Shammus: Synagogue beadle
Shavuot: Festival of Weeks
Shema: Hear! The Jewish Creed
Shiksa: Gentile girl (insulting)
Shiva: Mourning
Shlep: Ordinary guy, or to trail around
Shoket: Kosher slaughterer
Shomer Shabbos: Observant of the Sabbath
Shtetl: European Jewish village
Shul: Synagogue
Siddur: The Jewish Prayer Book
Streimel: Fur hat
Sukkah: Ritual tabernacle
Sukkot: Festival of the Tabernacles
Synagogue: Place of worship
Tallit/s: Prayer shawl
Talmud: Oral Law, books of Oral Law
Tefillin: Phylacteries
Torah: Jewish Law, Scroll of the Pentateuch

Traditional: Orthodox, but compromising in certain matters
Tref: Non-kosher
Yahrzeit: Death anniversary
Yarmulke: Skull cap
Yeshiva: Talmudic academy. Orthodox boys' high school
Yeshua: Jesus
Yiddish: Language of Eastern European Jews
Yom Kippur: Day of Atonement